ROBERT MILLS

Rob.t Mills
arch.t Public Buildings

AMERICA'S FIRST ARCHITECT

ROBERT MILLS

John M. Bryan

Princeton Architectural Press *New York*

2001

PRINCETON ARCHITECTURAL PRESS
37 East 7th Street
New York, NY 10003

For a free catalog of books published by Princeton Architectural Press,
call 1.800.722.6657 or visit www.papress.com

EDITOR: Jan Cigliano
COPY EDITOR: Heather Ewing
DESIGNER: Sara E. Stemen

Special thanks to Nettie Aljian, Ann Alter, Amanda Atkins, Nicola Bednarek, Janet Behning,
Penny Chu, Jane Garvie, Tom Hutten, Clare Jacobson, Mark Lamster, Nancy Eklund Later,
Linda Lee, Anne Nitschke, Evan Schoninger, Lottchen Shivers, Jennifer Thompson, and Deb Wood
of Princeton Architectural Press   —Kevin C. Lippert, publisher

ISBN 1-56898-296-8

CATALOGING-IN-PUBLICATION DATA AVAILABLE FROM THE PUBLISHER

PRINTED IN CHINA

Contents

Dedication

THIS VIVID STUDY of the life and work of Robert Mills is the product of Dr. John Bryan's career and long devotion to the rediscovery of the Mills legacy. It also symbolizes the long friendship between the author and my father, Herbert Wellington Hoefer, in whose memory this work is dedicated.

As I read John's manuscript, I am struck by the many parallels between Mills' and my father's life. Robert Mills was deeply interested in history generally and South Carolina history particularly. He may have been the first American to articulate the "historic preservationist" point of view. My father was one of the few men in Columbia to help get preservation off the ground in the state capital. One early result was to save Ainsley Hall, still the most fully documented residence designed by Mills.

Robert Mills envisioned the great economic potential of South Carolina's natural resources. My father and his family were pioneers in South Carolina silica mining and created the company, Columbia Silica Mining. The mines operate today as a part of the state's vibrant mining industry.

Mills was a visionary in the unprecedented scale of his plans. Papa believed deeply that thoughtful planning was the engine of personal accomplishment. John and I share many memories of Papa's descriptions of the practical power of "previsualizing," or imagining a desired outcome, as a way of making things happen.

Mills had the tinkering instinct of born engineers. His architectural and engineering training were a combination of the practical pedagogy of the times and experience acquired by working with America's earliest master designers and builders. My father was the son of a self-educated mechanical engineer. Early in his life, he became fascinated with electricity. He created a small hydroelectric generating facility for his father's Lexington County farm in the 1920s while a student at Clemson, long before rural electrification came to that part of the country. Papa earned bachelor of science degrees in electrical and in mechanical engineering from Clemson College and Cornell University. He earned his masters in these subjects while on the faculty of Cornell. He used his engineering knowledge to build and operate his mining business.

Robert Mills was sincerely religious and devoted to his family. Papa was a devout Roman Catholic whose life was centered on his wife and children. He and Mills each had five children. Robert Mills was a Jacksonian Democrat who believed in the dignity of democracy. Papa was a life-long Democrat who believed part of his civic responsibility was to encourage and support candidates for public office.

In Papa's memory, my family is privileged to sponsor this definitive and beautiful work on Robert Mills by the preeminent historian, our neighbor, John Morrill Bryan.

Jean Hoefer Toal
Chief Justice, Supreme Court of South Carolina
April 2001

Foreword and Acknowledgments

ROBERT MILLS (1781–1855) helped establish the architectural image of American government. His career (circa 1802–1855) coincided with a formative period in American history, and he created federal buildings from Newburyport, Massachusetts, to Key West and New Orleans. His surviving work evokes a sense of permanence, utility, and the dignity of democratic ideals. Mills' buildings and monuments offer no hint of the compromises and constraints that altered most of his major proposals; however, his papers often show why things turned out as they did.

Mills left more than a dozen publications—books, pamphlets, reports and memorials—totaling approximately 2000 pages. In addition to the printed material, there are some 3300 manuscripts, including domestic and professional correspondence, contracts, journals, and unfinished essays. Several refrains echo through his writing: he had an abiding interest in history balanced by a fascination with new technologies; he returns often to the need for new modes of transportation in an expanding Republic. Whenever architectural work was slack, his ideas for useful non-fiction—guides, textbooks, manuals, and histories—cropped up like mushrooms after summer rain. In domestic correspondence we encounter an indefatigable search for work and an unwavering forbearance in the face of adversity. Taken together, his works and writings emphasize the collaborative, social aspect of architecture. Influenced by Thomas Jefferson and Benjamin Henry Latrobe, Mills viewed public projects as an architect's highest

calling, and the most evocative surviving documents were often prompted by his dealings with committees, commissions, and congressional inquiries. Viewing the records along with the results, we better understand how Mills balanced compromise with a pertinacious advocacy of his own ideals.

Mills always claimed to be the first native born American to study specifically to become an architect. Architectural practice was in its infancy in America during his early career, and he said he "acted as a pioneer" and struggled to obtain compensation as a professional.[1] Despite the successes we remember today, he found it difficult to make a living and constantly sought work as a civil engineer and engaged in writing projects intended to supplement his income or lead to employment beyond architecture. Serious and religious by nature, he was also innately diplomatic and, with few exceptions, enjoyed constructive relationships with clients and craftsmen. He was especially successful in introducing building techniques that were not part of local traditions—the two principal examples are the seventeenth-century French Delorme dome and fireproof groin-vaulted masonry. He was committed to functional plans and permanent structural systems, and on all but the most important monuments and buildings he tended to minimize ornament. He was justly accused of being visionary, for he designed on a grand scale—a scale he felt appropriate for the America he imagined. Mills deserves credit for establishing permanent, fireproof construction as a standard for public buildings. His Washington National Monument, although much altered from his published proposal, remains the most widely recognized and revered American monument, and he led in developing standardized building types—specialized hospitals, customs houses, court houses and jails—to promote the efficiency of a variety of government services.

Several of his publications were also innovative—the *Atlas of South Carolina* was the first systematic mapping of any state. The lesser known *American Pharos, or Lighthouse Guide* was among the earliest, perhaps the first, directory of American lighthouses, buoys, and aids to navigation written for mariners. His *Guide to the Capitol* was among the earliest American publications focusing on a single site. Many of the other writings contain innovative proposals—an elevated monorail, an intercity network of paved highways and a rotary piston engine—which were realized only after his death.

Mills' accomplishments, the diversity of his interests, and the historical context of his work make him a fascinating figure. He has been the subject of two biographies, an anthology of essays, numerous published articles and

1 Robert Mills [hereafter abbreviated RM], "The Architectural Works of Robt. Mills," manuscript transcribed by H.M. Pierce Gallagher, *Robert Mills, Architect of the Washington Monument, 1781–1855* (New York: Columbia University Press, 1935), 167–171. Also see Pamela Scott, ed., *The Papers of Robert Mills, 1781–1855* (Wilmington: Scholarly Resources, 1990) [hereafter PRM], PRM 4004.

unpublished Master's theses and Ph.D. dissertations. His papers (and those of his mentor, Latrobe) are available on microfilm and microfiche. With all this material available, Mills offers anyone interested in American history and culture a broad and fertile field in which to graze.

It is a joy to recall and acknowledge people who have sustained my study of Mills. At the outset, in the early 1970s, the late Dr. Robert Patterson, then president of the University of South Carolina, and the late Dr. John R. Craft, director of the Columbia Museum of Art, enabled me to participate in the restoration of the South Carolina College (the creation of which prompted Mills' earliest known design proposal) and to organize a regional exhibition of Mills' drawings. In the 1980s, Dr. Douglas E. Evelyn, then deputy director of the National Museum of American History of the Smithsonian, initiated and directed the Papers of Robert Mills, an historical editing project. I worked on that project with Professor Robert Alexander and Pamela Scott and learned a great deal from them. Scott edited the microfilm edition, the principal product of the Mills Papers, which, with her *Guide to the Papers of Robert Mills* is the indispensable resource for anyone interested in Mills' career. Following the Mills Papers, Judith Stein, then director of the Octagon Museum of the American Architectural Foundation, enabled me to curate a national exhibition of Mills' drawings. After that, I turned to other things, but Mills was always in the background.

For this book, Mana Hewitt once again helped with computing problems. The reader benefits from photography by Robert C. Lautman, Robert M. Smith, Jr., Judy Steinhauser, and Thomas Hahn. Carissa B. Cuny helped with computer scanning, and Steven Tuttle facilitated the photography of Mills' drawings at the South Carolina Archives and History Center. Most of the tedious microfilm work was done at the South Carolina State Library where the courteous professionalism of Deborah Hotchkiss, Karen D. McMullen, Mary L. Morgan, Dawn Mullin, Brenda J. Boyd, Anne Schneider, and Felicia Vereen made it pleasurable. Michael R. Macan, reference librarian, and Bill Sudduth, Head of Documents and Microforms, at U.S.C.'s Thomas Cooper Library, enriched the text by making arcane resources accessible.

It has been a pleasure to work with institutions holding relevant materials, and I am grateful to Barbara A. Wolanin, Curator at the Office of the Architect of the Capitol, to archivists at the Alderman Library, University of Virginia, the American Baptist Historical Society, the Office of the Architect of the U.S.

Capitol, the Athenaeum of Philadelphia, the Burlington County, New Jersey, Parks Department, the Charleston Library Society, the Franklin Institute, Georgetown University Library, the Historical Society of Pennsylvania, the Massachusetts Historical Society, the Mount Holly Library, the Museum and Library of the Maryland Historical Society, the National Archives, the Newburyport Maritime Society, the New London Maritime Museum, the New-York Historical Society, the Pennsylvania Historical and Museum Commission, the South Carolina Archives and History Center, the South Carolina Historical Society, the South Carolina State Library, the Thomas Jefferson Memorial Foundation, and the Thomas Cooper and the South Caroliniana Libraries at the University of South Carolina. I am grateful to Jan Cigliano, my editor at the Princeton Architectural Press, for smoothing the rough spots and shaping everything into a coherent whole.

Along the way, I have enjoyed memorable conversations with friends in the Loblolly Society, with Douglas E. Evelyn, now deputy director of the Smithsonian's National Museum of the American Indian, James M. Goode, then curator of the Smithsonian's castle, the late Richard X. Evans, Mills' great great grandson, Tony Wrenn, archivist for the American Institute of Architects, Lee H. Nelson, architect for the National Park Service, John Alviti and Mrs. Irene Coffee of the Franklin Institute. Several years ago, a conversation with Christina Hoefer Myers rekindled my interest in Mills, and this book is the result. I am especially grateful to her and to her family for their support.

Finally, to students, who have kept things interesting, and Martha, who has seen me through it all, I am especially grateful.

John M. Bryan
Columbia, South Carolina

"A View of Charles-Town, the Capital of South Carolina," by Thomas Leitch, circa 1774.

Youth in Charleston

ON JUNE 20, 1841, in Washington, D.C., August Edouart prepared to cut a portrait. He had created silhouettes in France and England, and his subjects during his stay in Washington included Senators Henry Clay and Daniel Webster, Joel R. Poinsett, Secretary of War and the future presidents, Franklin Pierce, John Tyler, and Millard Fillmore. Now the most prominent architect in the capital sat for his portrait.

The sitter, Robert Mills, was the creator of buildings from New Orleans to Newburyport, Massachusetts. He had a modest reputation as a writer, cartographer, and dabbler in technology—steam engines, railroads and the telegraph, and he knew President Andrew Jackson (they were both South Carolinians). Since Jackson's inauguration in 1829 Mills had been involved in a series of projects—the new U.S. Treasury building, the Patent Office and the Post Office—which were establishing a new scale for federal office buildings.[1]

Mills' success seemed secure when he posed for Edouart; taut, erect and self-assured, his posture portrayed no hint of the tensions and controversies that would destroy his career in the coming decade. The silhouette appealed to Mills' descendants. His great-great-grandson kept a photograph of it (the original is apparently lost) in a folder with family correspondence, newspaper clippings and a lock of Mills' hair.[2]

Like shadows, silhouettes are suggestive rather than descriptive; lacking interior details, they don't convey nuances of personality. Our knowledge about

1 Biographers typically do not define Andrew Jackson's place of birth. For example, he was born "on the border between North and South Carolina" (*National Cylopaedia of American Biography* (New York: James T. White, 1894), vol. 5, 289), or "in the Waxhaw settlement on the border between North and South Carolina" (*Appleton's Cyclopedia of American Biography* (New York: D. Appleton, 1900), vol. 3, 373), and "near the border of North and South Carolina—the exact spot is in dispute" (*Encyclopedia of Southern Culture* (Chapel Hill: University of North Carolina Press, 1989), 1189. Robert Mills considered Jackson a South Carolinian, and Jackson did too in thanking Mills for his map of the Lancaster District. Andrew Jackson

I

to Robert Mills, July 8, 1827; PRM 1080.

2 Mrs. F. Nevill Jackson, *Catalogue of 3,800 Named and Dated American Silhouette Portraits by August Edouart* (London: privately printed, n.d. [circa 1911]), 2; PRM 2211B. Interview with Richard X. Evans, June 1976.

3 RM to Eliza Barnwell Smith Mills, n.d. [circa 1817]; PRM 0906.

4 H. M. Pierce Gallagher, *Robert Mills, Architect* (New York: Columbia University Press, 1935), 158; PRM, 1233.

5 Rhodri W. Liscombe, *Altogether American, Robert Mills, Architect and Engineer* (New York: Oxford University Press, 1994), 3, says William Mills, father of Robert Mills, joined the Loyalist Militia and was a traitor. Liscombe has confused William Mills with William Henry Mills. Loyalist Colonel William Henry Mills, a physician, planter and owner of some 2000 acres in the Cheraw District, led slaves pillaging the back country; he was defeated by patriots at the battle of Hunt's Bluff, escaped and fled to the Bahamas where he re-established himself as a planter. The two men are listed next to each other in B.G. Moss, *Roster of South Carolina Patriots in the American Revolution* (Baltimore: Genealogical Publishing Co., 1983), 684.

Mills resembles the silhouette, for we have clear outlines, but lack the subtle shadings needed for an wholly empathetic understanding.

Mills published several books and left hundreds of letters, but rarely wrote anything introspective. His fragmentary autobiographies are little more than lists of projects. This reticence, or lack of interest in his own history, is captured in a passage to his wife about genealogy: "I took very little trouble in learning the genealogy of either branch of our family—conceiving that merit was or ought to be the only true distinction in life—I perfectly agree with Pope when he remarks that '*Worth* makes the *Man*, the want of it the *fellow*. The rest is all but leather or prunella.'"[3]

Although Mills implied that he wanted his work to speak for him, he nonetheless burnished his reputation by presenting himself as the first native born American to study to become an architect. And on several occasions he observed that Thomas Jefferson helped him as a student, and claimed his taste was suited to American projects inasmuch as he never studied or traveled abroad. So despite a professed disinterest in personal history, Mills often linked his background to his work.[4]

The first phase of his training took place in Charleston, South Carolina, where he was born while the city was occupied by the British during the Revolution. His father, William Mills (1750–1802), was a tailor who came to Charleston from Scotland circa 1770. He married Ann Taylor, who counted an early governor of the colony among her ancestors. William Mills was successful. He was able to acquire slaves, to invest in rental property in town, and to speculate in outlying farmland. Before the Revolution his peers elected him Captain of the Volunteer Militia, and when war came, it threatened to unravel everything he had accomplished.[5]

On April 9, 1780, the British fleet crossed the Charleston Harbor bar and anchored off the town. To demonstrate the wisdom of surrender, British Admiral Mariot Arbuthnot elevated the ships' guns and fired 200 cannons into the night sky. An American described the bombardment as "a glorious sight . . . like meteors crossing each other, and bursting in the air; it appeared as if the stars were tumbling down." The next day William Mills joined more than two hundred Charlestonians in presenting a petition to the Continental General, Benjamin Lincoln, asking him to surrender for "it is an indisputable proposition that they can derive no advantage from a perseverance in resistance with everything dear to them at stake."[6]

The Continental forces withdrew, and Charleston surrendered on May 12, 1780. When the British were ashore, William Mills (along with 206 others) signed a public letter repudiating the patriots and welcoming the return of royal authority. The signers were subsequently known as "Addressers" and accepted as British loyalists by both sides. The following September many of them, including William Mills, signed a letter congratulating Cornwallis on British victories to the north. Although he was listed as "a Friend of Government," William Mills did not serve on the civic boards established by the occupation forces, nor did he join the volunteer Royal Militia. On the other hand, he did not slip away and rejoin the harried patriots. He stayed home, and Ann gave birth on August 12, 1781, to a healthy boy. Honoring a paternal uncle, they named him Robert.

During the weeks that followed, the British position deteriorated. There were rumors of evacuation, and many Addressers made plans to flee. Their anxiety was well founded, for only a month after Robert Mills was born the patriot Governor Rutledge proclaimed a pardon for loyalists who returned to the patriots' cause and served six months in the militia. This proclamation specifically excluded the Addressers. Several hundred wavering loyalists quickly enlisted in the American cause, for it was now clear the British would withdraw. A delegation of Charleston loyalists traveled to British headquarters in New York seeking compensation and relocation. In the end, 9,000 people—loyalists from South Carolina, their servants and slaves—took refuge on English ships.[7]

William Mills decided not to go, but he must have taken little pleasure in the celebrations that followed the British evacuation on December 15, 1782. The patriots published a proclamation that Addressers were to be "banished from the state under penalty of death without the benefit of clergy if they returned and their property was confiscated." William Mills was not listed among those specifically charged. Prosecution was arbitrary; nonetheless, ninety-five persons were banished, thirty estates were confiscated, and twenty-one families were fined twelve percent of the value of their property. Hundreds of ex-loyalists—and William Mills must have been among them—sought formally to be pardoned or informally to be excused.[8]

He avoided prosecution and was able to resume his modest role in civic life, serving as one of the petit jurors for the parish of St. Michael's and St. Philips and as a justice of the peace witnessing revolutionary claims against the state of South Carolina. The census of 1790 showed he had weathered the storm,

Thirty-five records related to the property of William Henry Mills are cited in the Combined Alphabetical Index of the South Carolina Department of Archives and History, and his military activities as a loyalist are recounted in Robert Stansbury Lambert, *South Carolina Loyalists in the American Revolution* (Columbia: University of South Carolina Press, 1987), 116, 128–129, 236 and 267. For property owned by William Mills, the Charleston tailor, see note 9 below. Also see Gallagher, 184–186, for a genealogical note on the Mills family. Gallagher, 4, says William Mills emigrated in 1770, as does Laurens Tenney Mills, *A South Carolina Family* (Privately printed, 1960), 28 n4. Also see the *South Carolina Historical and Genealogical Magazine* [SCHGM] 71 (1920): 27, and SCHGM 23 (1922): 31, and the "Hackwood Register," Richard X. Evans Collection, series 2, boxes 1, 3, Georgetown University.

6 David Ramsay, *History of South Carolina* (Charleston: David Longworth, 1809), vol. I, 326. SCHGM 3 (1902): 137. Also see G.M. Gilmer, *American Revolutionary Roster, Fort Sullivan, 1776–1780* (Charleston: Daughters of the American Revolution, 1976), 225.

7 E.P. Levett, "Loyalism in Charleston, 1761–1784,"

Proceedings of the South Carolina Historical Society, 1936, 6–7. Also see G.S. McCowen, *The British Occupation of Charleston, 1780–1782* (Columbia: University of South Carolina Press, 1972), 10.

8 Levett, "Loyalism in Charleston, 1761–1784," 6–7.

9 Department of Commerce and Labor, Bureau of the Census, *Heads of Families at the First Census, 1790, South Carolina* (Washington: Government Printing Office, 1908), 39. G.L.C. Hendrix and M.M. Lindsay, *Jury Lists of South Carolina, 1778–1779* (Greenville: privately printed, n.d.). For the appointment of William Mills as a Justice of the Peace (March 25, 1785), see: L.E. Adams, ed., *Journals of the House of Representatives, 1785–1786* (Columbia: University of South Carolina Press, 1979), p. 268. For the real estate transactions of William Mills, see the Index to *Deeds of the Province and State of South Carolina, 1719–1785, and Charleston District, 1785–1800* (Easley, S.C.: Southern Historical Press, 1977; also see *Charleston Deeds*: E- 5, 113; G-6, 347; G-6, 400; K-6, 193 and 194. For the estate of William Mills, see: *Charleston Wills*, D, 1800–1807, 269.

10 Charles Fraser, *Reminiscences of Charleston* (Charleston: John Russell,

for his household was intact with five free white males over sixteen years of age, two under sixteen, three white females, and eleven slaves.

William Mills' accomplishments after the Revolution were modest, but gratifying. He maintained his niche among Charleston's middle class. He did not build an ancestral seat or establish a business for his heirs, and none of his children married into the agrarian elite. But his family was respectable, on speaking terms with many of the leading local figures of their time. William Mills was able to send the two older boys, Thomas and Henry, back to Scotland to visit relatives and study; he also helped Robert, the youngest, become an architect. He watched his children grow and marked the time on his heavy, silver pocket watch which, in his will, he affectionately called "J. Witherspoon."[9]

Robert Mills left no record of his father's Revolutionary experience or its post-war consequences, so we don't know how it affected his youth. Whatever we can decipher about his childhood and adolescence must be inferred from other sources about life in Charleston.

Charlestonians had a sense of civic pride and public ceremony. Living in the capital of the colony and state, the port of entry and center of trade, they nurtured an architectural setting commensurate with their role in colonial life. Mills' reputation is linked to prominent, evocative public buildings and monuments, and it is reasonable to assume he was influenced by his childhood environs.

In 1791—the summer Mills was ten years old—George Washington made a triumphal tour of the southern states, and Charleston dressed for the occasion. There were balls and speeches and an arch of lanterns capped by "a superb transparency, in the center Deliciis Patriae, and at the top, G.W.," in front of the Exchange Building.[10]

The Exchange was the most imposing secular building in Charleston. It was designed in 1766 by William Rigby Naylor, built of brick covered with stucco and trimmed with imported English Portland stone balusters, urns, and finials. It represented colonial Georgian architecture at its best and reflected the English town and market hall tradition, a formula consisting of an open market space below and civic offices and meeting rooms above. Naylor may have adapted the design from Isaac Ware's *Complete Body of Architecture* (plate 49), or simply drawn upon his memory of similar buildings across the length and breadth of England, from Chipping Camden to the Isle of Wight.

The Exchange played a leading role in the secular life of the community. Its form suggested cultural continuity, and the quality of its design and

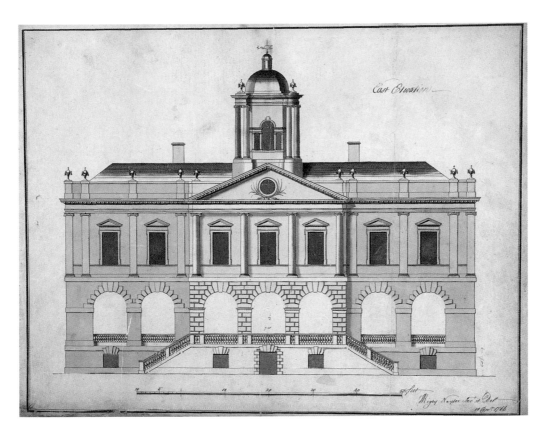

Exchange Building, Charleston, South Carolina, east elevation.
William Rigby Naylor, architect, 1766.

construction projected an image of probity and permanence. In later life Mills often employed an architectural program reminiscent of the Exchange: a raised basement, groined vaults, stairways housed in projecting towers, cupolas, and a concern for ventilation—all these were to become hallmarks of his mature style.

In addition to its physical and visual character, the Exchange was evocative as the site of historic events. It had been erected as a triumphal gesture following the pre-Revolutionary repeal of the Stamp Act. In siting the building, the South Carolina Commons House voted to turn its rear to England. (Cooler heads prevailed, and in the end this vote, rather than the building, was reversed.) The Exchange was still new when patriots broke into its basement and dumped tea stored there into the harbor. Also in the basement, Patriot

1854); State Gazette of South Carolina, March 24, 1791, LIII, 3, 960. Mills mentioned that he had seen Washington "when a boy"; see Robert Mills, *Guide to the Capitol of the United States* (Washington, 1834), 43.

5

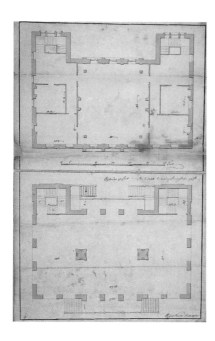

Exchange Building, Charleston, South Carolina, plan. William Rigby Naylor, architect, 1766.

11 John M. Bryan, *The Charleston Exchange* (Columbia: South Carolina Department of Archives and History, 1976); Kenneth Severens, *Charleston, Antebellum Architecture and Civic Destiny* (Knoxville: University of Tennessee Press, 1988), 12–15; Mills Lane, *Architecture of the Old South, South Carolina* (Savannah: The Beehive Press, 1984), 68–70; Jonathan H. Poston, *The Buildings of Charleston* (Columbia: University of South Carolina Press, 1997), 109–111; Beatrice St. Julien Ravenel, *Architects of Charleston* (Charleston: Carolina Art Association, 1945), 33–34, 39–44.

12 Robert Mills, *Statistics of South Carolina* (Charleston: Hurlbut and Lloyd, 1826), 406.

13 Gallagher, 4, 7, 24 n2, 184.

General Moultrie built a brick partition to hide a cache of gunpowder before he evacuated the city. During the occupation the British used the basement as a dungeon (they did not discover the gunpowder), and from here, a week before Robert Mills was born, the patriot martyr Issac Hayne was led to the gallows.[11]

Just down Broad Street from the Exchange, St. Michael's Church also reflected the influence of English architectural pattern books. The *South Carolina Gazette*, reporting the laying of the cornerstone on February 17, 1752, noted St. Michael's was to "be built on the plan of one of Mr. Gibson's designs"—probably a garbled reference to James Gibbs' *Book of Architecture* which illustrated his plans for St. Martin's in the Fields, London (1721–1726). Samuel Cardy, the builder of St. Michael's drew the steeple from Gibbs' plate 29, studied the illustration of the vaulted nave, and decided to simplify the London portico. Mills said St. Michael's "produces a feeling of sublimity and reverence," and his proposal for altering it signaled his early interest in acoustics.[12]

Mills' architectural training began in Charleston. When the Revolution was over, his two older brothers, Henry and Thomas, were sent to Scotland, presumably to study, and Thomas returned with a copy of *The Modern Builder's Assistant* by William and John Halfpenny, Robert Morris, and T. Lightoler. On the frontispiece is an inscription "To Thomas Mills from Robert his Uncle in London November 14th 1789 pr Mr. James Spald." This book is the earliest evidence of an architectural interest in the family.[13]

Unlike his brothers, Robert did not go abroad. Most historians say he attended the College of Charleston and perhaps enrolled in the "evening school, for the instruction of young men in Architecture," advertised by James Hoban. But Hoban, having won the design competition of the President's Palace, or

St. Michael's, Charleston, South Carolina, 1752–1761. Attributed to Samuel Cardy et al.

White House, left for Washington when Mills was only eleven years old, and there is no record of his enrollment in the College of Charleston.

Given the competence of Mills' earliest known drawings (1802), he probably received instruction similar to that offered by Hoban, and there were a number of classes in Charleston during his adolescence. For example, newspapers advertised that Thomas Walker, a stone cutter and mason from Edinburgh "opened an evening school for teaching the rules of Architecture, from seven to nine in the evening (four nights a week)," and M. Depresseville "continues to keep his Drawing School, in different Part of Landscapes, with Pencil or Washed, teaches Architecture, and to draw with method; also the necessary acknowledgements for the Plans."[14]

An advertisement (1795) by Blakeleay White is especially interesting. He offered instruction in the "principals of Modern Architecture, with drawing and designing, not only theoretically but practically" and invited the public to see a "compleat frame of a double two story house in miniature," at a scale of one inch to the foot, executed by a fourteen-year-old student. (Mills was fourteen at the time.) Teaching arithmetic, geometry, and drafting, as well as practical joinery, "from the hours of 6 to 9 in the Evening, five evenings in the Week," Blakeleay White promised to enable "almost any young man" to become "a compleat architect or master builder" in one year.[15]

A similar curriculum was advertised in 1795 by Thomas Mills, Robert's older brother. At his Charleston Academy he offered instruction in every "branch of useful and polite literature," French, Latin and Greek, geometry, trigonometry, and "the principles of modern architecture, with drawing and designing." His announcement also notes he has hired an "ingenious teacher" of architectural principals and that models, as well as "theoretical illustrations," will be employed:

> At the commencement of this very useful undertaking the complete frame of a double three story house, in miniature, will be raised, and lectures given explanatory of the subject by way of exhibiting to the friends of the young gentlemen a specimen of the manner in which this business will be conducted: by this method it will be evident, that a person may soon become a complete architect or master builder.[16]

Similar lessons were advertised in Boston, New York, and Philadelphia, as well as Charleston. The instructors were typically immigrants, like Hoban,

14 *Charleston City Gazette*, October 31, 1793, and April 7, 1797.

15 *South Carolina State Gazette*, November 12, 1795.

16 *City Gazette & Daily Advertizer*, vol XIII no. 2548 (October 7, 1795). Dr. Woodrow Harris pointed out this advertisement to me.

who claimed experience abroad, or, like Blakeleay White, craftsmen hoping to better themselves.

Another influence, more intangible than lessons, may have been the fact that Charleston was a busy seaport. Mills' later interest in navigation, transportation and cartography may reflect a daily awareness of the glinting harbor, the sea breeze, and shipping. Charleston was the gateway to the state. From the interior came tobacco, pelts, lumber and an ever growing tonnage of cotton. Exports on the wharves passed manufactured imports of all descriptions—flour from Philadelphia and Baltimore, iron and hemp from Sweden and Russia, and sail cloth from Boston and England. The Harbor Master's report from January 2, 1797, notes sixty-seven square rigged ships in port and thirty-four schooners and sixteen sloops; there were ninety-one square rigged vessels on February 2nd and fifty-eight schooners and sloops. The schooners and sloops were largely coastal traders, but the bigger schooners and the weatherly square-riggers traversed the globe.

Shipping evoked a wider world. Arrivals unloading brought home the complexity of commerce; departing, they carried the imagination over the horizon. In one of his rare notes about childhood, Mills recalled happy miniature voyages sailing among the barrier islands.[17] Throughout his life, like a mariner, he remained mobile, and his vision was never limited by a commitment to one place. He had a life-long interest in transportation, and this may have owed something to having grown up in a bustling seaport.

After learning what he could in Charleston, Mills went to Washington, in 1799 or 1800, to work under Hoban at the White House. A young Charlestonian without capital could not set himself up as a planter, or go to London to read law, or Edinburgh to study medicine. But he could go to Washington and study to become an architect, and that is what he did.

17 Robert Mills, *Statistics*, 475n.

"View of the City of Richmond from the Bank of James River." Benjamin Henry Latrobe, 1798.

CHAPTER ONE

Early Mentors James Hoban and Thomas Jefferson

Washington, D.C., 1800–1803

THE SECOND PHASE of Mills' education—his active work with profession-als and acquaintance with Jefferson—began circa 1800 in Washington, D.C. Margaret Smith wrote that the new capital, like a magnet, attracted the "active, reflective and ambitious mind," for here America's interests were "dis-cussed by its ablest sons."[1] She and her husband, Samuel Harrison Smith, moved to Washington in 1800 and established the first national newspaper. They reported the grading of streets, the sale of lots, and the construction of public buildings. The work was directed by a federal commission in charge of transforming the forest into a seat of government. The commission's advertise-ments attracted artisans, labor, and materials. James Hoban was soon joined by Pierce Purcell, his former partner, and Robert Given, the stone cutter who offered architectural lessons in Charleston during Mills' youth.

There was much to be done and a chronic shortage of skilled labor. The commission contracted for work by slaves and tried to import European crafts-men. Jobs were made more difficult by inadequate financing, primitive trans-portation, and an uncertain supply of food and building materials. These impediments, and the press of time, placed a premium on the services of able and energetic men. The Residence Act that created the commission required the offices of government be ready by December 1800. Mills arrived during the final flurry of activity. He must have traveled overland, for years later he recalled the view of Jefferson's Virginia State Capitol in Richmond and "the impression it

1 Bayard Smith, *The First Forty Years of Washington Society* (New York: Charles Scribners' Sons, 1906), 94. Also see John W. Reps, *Monumental Washington: the Planning and Development of the Capital Center* (Princeton: Princeton University Press, 1967), 2; and C.M. Green, *Washington, Village and Capitol, 1800–1878* (Princeton: Princeton University Press, 1962), vol. I, chap. I.

made on my mind when first I came in view of it coming from the south. It gave me an idea of the position of those Greek temples which are the admiration of the world." He was soon settled and "pursuing [my] studies in the office of the architect of the President's House."[2]

Mills was probably Hoban's personal apprentice or assistant, for his name is not in the commissioner's accounts. With Henry Munroe, the official apprentice, and perhaps others, Mills experienced office life. They worked amid the bustle of construction. Wagons drawn up from the river passed piles of brick and lumber dotting the ground adjacent to the unfinished Capitol and President's House. Pools of stagnant water marked aborted foundations and excavations for the brick kilns. Clusters of flimsy hovels served as temporary housing for laborers. Nearby were the workshop sheds of the sawyers and stone masons. Acrid smoke and the smell of cooking blended with the resinous tang of green lumber. The rhythmic pounding of stone cutters, like rolling drums, banished the woodland quiet and prompted someone to write a note (grandly titled "Prophecy") in one of the commission's record books: "The time will come when this wide waste of morass and thicket...will resound with the busy hum of industry...all the varieties of animal and vegetable life, before the destructive march of man will gradually disappear, and Art will erect its palaces on the ruins of nature."[3]

Hoban, a joiner himself, was a competent manager, and he directed drawings for wainscot, staircases, and doorways. He kept assistants busy checking the profile of mullions and the progress of the plasterers. In addition to overseeing the construction of the White House, Hoban was directing construction at the Capitol, where the north wing was nearing completion, when Mills arrived. At the White House they were working on the interior. The design of both buildings was fundamentally conservative, and during this period Mills probably learned more about management, construction, and the state of his intended profession than he did about design.

The elevation of the White House presented—albeit on a grand scale—Palladian elements Mills had become familiar with in Charleston. He probably knew plate 47 in Gibbs' *Book of Architecture*, often cited as one of Hoban's sources for the President's Palace, and Hoban may have told him about Leinster House in Dublin, another potential design source which had an appropriately aristocratic pedigree. The Capitol, designed by William Thornton, an Edinburgh-trained medical doctor, was already being criticized for its Georgian

2 Robert Mills, "The Progress of Architecture in Virginia," a fragmentary essay in the collection of Tulane University, which is transcribed by Gallagher, 155–158; PRM 3026A, 3026B.

3 Hugh T. Taggart, "Old Georgetown," *Records of the Columbia Historic Society II* (1908): 141. The quotation is dated January 5, 1795.

"The Washington Capitol under Construction." Benjamin Henry Latrobe, 1806.

detail. Among the harsher critics was the disgruntled Charles Pierre L'Enfant, who dismissed Thornton's design as a pretty residence but inappropriate as "a basilica consecrated to the august representation of the people...it is of too slander [sic] a module...not having sufficient[ly] large masses nor boldness of profile." L'Enfant also declared Hoban's plan for the White House, or the Palace, as it was then known, "hardly suitable for a gentleman[s] country house [and] wholly inconsistent for a city habitation [and] in no aspect...becoming the State Residency of the chief head of a sovereign people."[4]

Observing Hoban and other architects—L'Enfant and George Hadfield (who for a brief time directed work at the Capitol)—was educational. L'Enfant's situation in 1800 also would have been of interest to Mills. L'Enfant had developed the Washington city plan, but had been dismissed by the commissioners in 1792. The French Revolution destroyed his income, and when Mills arrived L'Enfant was destitute, dependent on the generosity of friends. He was often seen at the Capitol, "a tall, thin man, who wore...a blue military surtout coat, buttoned quite to the throat, with a tall, black stock, but no visible signs of

4 Paul H. Caemmerer, *Life of Pierre Charles L'Enfant* (New York: Da Capo, 1970), 402–403.

linen. His hair was plastered with pomatum close to his head, and he wore a napless high beaver bell-crowned hat. Under his arm he generally carried a roll of papers relating to his claim upon the Government, and in his right hand he swung a formidable hickory cane with a large silver head."[5]

L'Enfant's presence was inescapable, for stump-filled swathes hewn through the forest made clear his vision of avenues and promenades. His city plan was much discussed; speculation in lots was rampant, and surveyor's stakes marked the site of future construction like exclamation points upon the land.

The sweeping avenues were a lesson in Baroque composition. As Mills rode the lumbering commuter coach from Georgetown, the "Royal George," drawn by four horses and pitching "like a ship in a seaway" along the rutted, stump-filled Pennsylvania Avenue to the Capitol, or as he walked through the marsh and bogs between the Capitol and the White House, he must have considered L'Enfant's vision "where fancy sees Squares in morasses, obelisks in trees."[6]

Beyond the city plan, the thought of L'Enfant brought professional fees to mind, for just as Mills arrived in Washington, L'Enfant came forward to heckle Congress and the commissioners for money. His petitions presented a disturbing image for an aspiring architect. L'Enfant claimed to have served the country for twenty-two years without compensation. He was offered $2,500 and a city lot as a settlement, but reckoned $95,000 as his due. Moreover, he claimed his city plan had been pirated by an assistant with the knowledge of the commissioners and published without his permission. Adding insult to injury, someone removed his name from the plan, and others profited from its distribution.[7]

L'Enfant argued that a design concept belonged to its creator. He complained that the amateur commissioners "so little versed in the minutiae of such operations" had subverted his work. He wrote bitterly of designers, like Hoban, who "can take side each way as the wind blow, all full of honor and trampling under every honest principle." He emphasized that for orderly coordination and to ensure craftsmanship and economy everyone should be "wholly subordinate to the architect." He said that the commission for the design of the "two main edifices, the capitol and the presidency palace" had been promised to him. He claimed his sketches for these buildings, along with designs for aqueducts, bridges, and canals had been stolen and destroyed. L'Enfant also claimed the commissioners had failed to handle materials and labor efficiently or to act on his advice concerning the development of a canal and "a grand improvement of all main roads through the United States." His wrecked career cast a shadow

5 Ben. Perley Poore, *Perley's Reminiscences of Sixty Years in the National Metropolis* (Philadelphia: Hubbard Brothers, 1886), 54–55.

6 *The New York Advertiser*, January 27, 1791, quoted by P.S. Young, *The Washington Community*, 1800–1828 (New York: Columbia University Press, 1966), 41.

7 Caemmerer, 211, 218, 229, 388–389, 405–406, 408–409.

across the future of the architectural profession. L'Enfant was said to be a difficult person, and Mills may have assumed he was to blame. In fact, L'Enfant's problems stemmed in part from the lack of definition of the profession.

In the middle of May 1800, President Adams ordered federal offices "be opened in the City of Washington for the dispatch of business by the 15th of June." The Purveyor of Public Supplies, Israel Whelen, hired wagons, engaged sailing vessels and moved the government from Philadelphia to the new Capitol for $48,165.57.[8] The arrival of the initial shipments during the first week of June coincided with the president's inspection of the buildings, and we may imagine people gathering at Lear's wharf, near the foot of G Street West, to see the discharge of the public records.

Christian Hines, who was eighteen at the time and lived near Lear's Wharf, recalled "that many of the boxes were marked Joseph Nourse, register."[9] Robert Mills boarded for a time with the Nourse family, and perhaps through them met his future wife, their god-daughter, Eliza Barnwell Smith (1784–1865). The Nourses were politically and socially active. Joseph Nourse (1754–1841), like Robert's father, had come to the colonies before the Revolution. During the war, he served first as a secretary to General Charles Lee, then as Paymaster to the Board of War, and finally as Auditor General. The Nourse family became so firmly associated with the financial affairs of the government that Andrew Jackson was to speak of "cleaning out the Noursery."[10] The year Mills was born, Joseph Nourse became the Register of the Treasury, a post he held for forty-eight years; his home, when Mills boarded there, was one of the social centers of Washington.

The "Joseph Nourse" trunks were trundled to the first office of the Treasury, an undistinguished brick building immediately east of the White House. Robert Mills knew the structure well, for Hoban had unsuccessfully sought the construction contract for the Treasury, and had watched its progress under the supervision of Leonard Harbaugh. It was common knowledge among the building trades that the normally timid architect George Hadfield had balked the commissioners on this project and thereby precipitated his dismissal. He had refused to deliver his plans "for the executive offices" until they promised him control of construction. He informed the commissioners that "what I wish mostly to acquire as an artist depends on successful execution of my production, therefore it is natural that I should feel myself interested in the building of my design. I have long since learnt, that it is possible to be deprived of ones own for the advantage and reputation of others." Going further, he told the

8 J.B. Osborne, "Removal of the Government to Washington," *Records of the Columbia Historic Society III* (1900), 138.

9 Osborne, "Removal of the Government to Washington," 142; also see Wharton, 61.

10 Wharton, 105–106.

commissioners that the relationship of the architect to his creation was "founded upon points that do not appear to be understood in this country."[11]

The commissioners, on the other hand, argued that the plans were public property, for Hadfield produced them while employed by the government (albeit on another project). They used his ground plans and verbal descriptions even though he withheld his drawings, and they saw nothing wrong in seeking bids and entering into a contract without stipulating the treatment of the facade. The exterior of the finished building was predictably drab, brick with small scale Georgian trim—much like the speculative Wheat Row. Hadfield had proposed stuccoed walls, a giant portico based on the north porch of the Erechtheum, and, within the portico, three Adam-Style blind arches to focus attention on the entry.

The commissioners erected a matching brick block west of the White House for the Executive Offices and the War Department. These projects demonstrated the worst aspects of governmental patronage, for here the commissioners showed little or no concern for the aesthetic consequences of their decisions, and ignored the advice of their architect. The result framed the White House and vindicated those who claimed that democracy was inimical to the arts.

Hadfield's protests were futile. Benjamin Henry Latrobe later described Hadfield by saying, "he loiters here, ruined in fortune, temper, and reputation, nor will his irritable pride and neglected study ever permit him to take the station in art which his elegant taste and excellent talent ought to have attained."[12]

Hadfield's Executive Office elevation later came into the possession of Thomas Jefferson; Mills may have seen it there, but even if he never saw it, he must have observed that when Hadfield was dismissed, Hoban picked up the pieces of his shattered career. Subsequently, Mills, like Hoban, was pragmatic and did not view artistic purity as an issue of principle. Instead—again like Hoban—he was typically willing to negotiate and allow clients to modify his work. Latrobe later said Mills was too compliant and that his education (before he entered Latrobe's office in 1803) "had been...misdirected."[13]

Perhaps Hoban did not help Mills as a designer, but his office provided a front row seat, an intense, kaleidoscopic view of American architectural practice. Mills saw more there in a short time (circa 1800–1802) than he could have seen anywhere else in America at the time.

Since July 1792 when his "plan of the palace" had been approved by George Washington, Hoban's role had expanded rapidly, and by the end of the decade his affairs touched virtually every aspect of urban development.

11 Records...Commissioners...Concerned with Public Buildings, 1791–1867 (Washington: National Archives and Record Services, 1964), May 16, 1797, no. 1364; also see G.S. Hunsberger, "The Architectural Career of George Hadfield," Records of the Columbia Historical Society 51–52 (1951–1952): 51ff.

12 Talbot Hamlin, Benjamin Henry Latrobe (New York: Oxford University Press, 1955), 286, n28.

13 BHL to Thomas Jefferson, October 2, 1803. All Latrobe manuscript material cited hereafter is found in The Papers of Benjamin Henry Latrobe, Edward C. Carter II, editor in chief; Thomas E. Jeffrey, microfiche editor, Microtext Edition (Clifton, New Jersey: James T. White, 1976).

Initially he was "retained...to make drawings and superintend the execution of his plan of the palace and such other work of that kind as may be in execution." In addition, however, he soon found himself hiring sawyers and outfitting the surveyor's office. He requisitioned materials: lead, nails, lathe, plaster, slate and lime. And he joined in partnerships to sell materials to the commissioners—with Middleton Belt and William Deakins for 500,000 "good sound bricks" at a price of six dollars per thousand, or again with Edward Williams of Berkeley County, Virginia to "deliver at the President's House...50.000 [sic] good sound merchantable slates." He worried about policing the work, for on April 2, 1796, he wrote to the commissioners that "there is an absolute necessity to protect the materials at the President's House...I have reason to think that the plank scantling etc. is wasting daily for firewood, and unless some method is adopted to protect them, expense will be endless." Apparently the suspicion of pilferage led to the dismissal of Hoban's friend, Pierce Purcell. Among his other ventures, Hoban occasionally sold or loaned supplies, and Purcell bought shingles from him at the President's House; after they were hauled away, Purcell wrote contritely to the commissioners that "there was a few plank under them shingles."[14] He was fired and asked to vacate the housing provided by the commissioners.

Beyond architecture, Hoban exposed Mills to real estate, for he had invested in more than a dozen lots in Washington by 1800 and was involved in the development of a wharf. In short, Hoban was well established and very busy when Mills joined him at the turn of the century. In that last building season the commissioners were being pressed to prepare for the reception of the government. From Philadelphia, Secretary of the Naval Bureau Benjamin Stoddert wrote to Dr. Thornton urging the creation of "something like a garden, at the North side of the President's house," for "that large, naked, ugly looking building will be a very inconvenient residence for a family, without something of this kind...I do not think the com[missione]rs have sufficiently attended to the accommodation of the Pres[ident]. A private gent preparing a residence for his friend would have done more."[15] Reviewing the progress in the spring of 1800, Hoban saw the interior stairs were not installed; not a single room was finished inside, and crowds of curious citizens distracted the workmen and constantly impeded the work. Hoban closed the building to tourists and kept fires burning in the fireplaces to hasten the drying of the plaster. Despite his efforts, the White House was not habitable in

14 *Records of the Commissioners*, roll 14, vol. 12, letter 1255, December 14, 1797; vol. 16, letter 1606, April 3, 1799; also see September 16, 1794, 275–276, March 12, 1798, 14, no. 1304.

15 H.D. Eberlein and C.V.D. Hubbard, *Historic Houses of Georgetown and Washington City* (Richmond: Dietz Press, 1958), 181.

Monticello, Charlottesville, Virginia. Thomas Jefferson, architect.

June 1800 when President Adams visited the capital. He had to take lodgings in Georgetown.

President Adams showed little interest in architecture or in the development of the city, and his wife Abigail was critical about the White House. On the other hand, the Republicans gathering around Thomas Jefferson were generally tolerant about the shortcomings of the capital—the planters among them were accustomed to mud and solitude. If they did not share Jefferson's enthusiasm for architecture, neither did they feel the deprivation of urban pleasures like their colleagues from Philadelphia, Boston, and New York.

In 1800 Jefferson often stayed at Conrad and McMunn's Tavern and sat democratically at the end of the table farthest from the fire. After dinner in a sitting room adjoining his bedroom, he held consultations, and we like to think of Mills meeting him there. Jefferson was an impressive figure, but genial and easy to meet. He was fifty-one, over six feet tall, with sandy hair and piercing hazel eyes. His eccentricities made him appear down-to-earth and accessible. Wearing slippers "without heels" he received diplomats; a pet mocking bird flitted about his room; and he left carpenter's tools on the desk among official papers. Critics saw his informality as "calculated boorishness to win proletarian plaudits."[16]

Edmund Randolph described another of Jefferson's eccentricities when he wrote that his famous cousin "panted" after the arts, and Jefferson himself admitted, "I am an enthusiast on the subject of the arts. But it is an enthusiasm of which I am not ashamed, as its object is to improve the taste of my country-men."[17] His early plans for Monticello included a list of some forty works—paintings and sculpture—for a projected art gallery. The incomplete catalogue of his art collection lists 126 paintings, prints, medals, and other works of art—and it only deals with art in the public rooms of the house. Speaking of the house itself, the Marquis de Chastellux noted that "Mr. Jefferson is the first American who has consulted the fine arts to know how he should shelter him-self from the weather."[18]

Jefferson believed that good design, especially in architecture, was ulti-mately economical. He began his famous collection of books on the arts while still a student at William and Mary. Later reading and travel confirmed his rejection of the English Georgian Style and his affinity for the neoclassicism. He returned from diplomatic service in France and England with eighty-six crates of fine furniture and art objects. Writing of the impact of this trip, one modern scholar has said that "Europe was for Jefferson an altogether enlighten-ing experience...aesthetically it was a veritable revelation."[19] And Jefferson wrote he was "immersed in antiquities from morning to night" and "nourished with the remains of Roman Grandeur." He said he could be found "gazing whole hours at the Maison Quaree [sic], like a lover at his mistress."[20]

Never content as a voyeur, while in France he designed a "carriage and pro-duced the working drawings for its manufacture." To improve architecture in America he sought French and English ideas concerning prisons and commis-sioned a model of the Maison Carrée to guide the development of the Virginia State Capitol. French urban housing impressed him. He approved of the rational planning of the Neoclassicists and their tendency to adapt rather than replicate the antique. Picturesque English gardens also captured his fancy, and he wrote: "The gardening in that country is the article in which it excels all the earth. I mean their pleasure-gardening. This indeed, went far beyond my ideas." After seeing English gardens, he thought of a garden house for Monticello where "the roof may be Chinese, Grecian, or in the taste of the Lantern of Demosthenes at Athens." He also considered building "a small

16 Green, 44–48; Wharton, 102–103.

17 Edward Dumbauld, "Jefferson and Adams' English Garden Tour," in W.H. Adams, ed., *Jefferson and the Arts: an Extended View* (Washington: National Gallery of Art, 1976), 138.

18 Harold E. Dickson, "Jefferson as Art Collector," in Adams, *Jefferson and the Arts*, 122–123.

19 Dickson, 118.

20 Frederick D. Nichols, "Jefferson: the Making of an Architect," in Adams, ed., *Jefferson and the Arts* , 168.

Gothic temple of antique appearance," and noted in his journal the pyramid at Stowe.[21] In short, he had a broad view of current stylistic trends, and he was ideally situated to assist Mills.

Several authors say Mills was Jefferson's architectural protégé, but there is little real evidence concerning the circumstances of the contact between them. In later life Mills wrote on several occasions that Jefferson befriended him and "offered me the use of his library." Mills said this occurred after his "studies in the office of the architect of the President's House" (circa 1801).[22] But he never wrote (as a biographer claims) that "he remained steadily with Jefferson for two profitable and happy years."[23] Mills did visit Monticello (the documented instance was in 1807), but we don't know the conditions under which he studied the famous collection of architectural books, prints, and drawings.

Bits of evidence, like scattered tesserae from a lost mosaic, hint at the pattern of their relationship. Jefferson did not leave us a curriculum for Mills analogous to readings he suggested for Robert Skipwith or the itinerary he prepared for young John Rutledge and Thomas Shippen, but his comments about the value of studying architecture fit Mills' situation like a glove. Jefferson said architecture is "worth great attention. As we double our numbers every twenty years, we must double our houses. Besides, we build of such perishable materials that one-half of our houses must be rebuilt in every space of twenty years, so that in that time houses are to be built for three-fourths of our inhabitants. It is then among the most important arts; and it is desirable to introduce taste into an art which shows so much."[24] Jefferson lamented that

> the genius of architecture seems to have shed its maledictions over this land. Buildings are often erected, by individuals, at considerable expense. To give these symmetry and taste would not increase their cost. It would only change the arrangement of the materials, the form and combination of the members...perhaps a spark may fall on some young subjects of natural taste, kindle up their genius, and produce a reformation in this elegant and useful art.[25]

Jefferson may have met Mills at the White House, for the interior was not finished when he moved in. Mills later wrote that Jefferson wanted drawings of Monticello and "engaged Mr. Mills to make out the drawings of the general plan and elevation of the building," although "the drawing of the details Mr. Jefferson reserved to himself."[26]

21 Dumbauld, 139; also see James Early, *Romanticism and American Architecture* (New York: A.S. Barnes, 1965), 39.

22 Gallagher, 158; PRM 3026A, 3026B.

23 Gallagher, 8.

24 Adams, *Jefferson and the Arts*, 139.

25 D. Gifford, *The Literature of Architecture* (New York: E.P. Dutton, 1966), 77.

26 Fiske Kimball, *Thomas Jefferson, Architect* (New York: Da Capo Press, 1968), 34. Also see W. Dunlap, *History of the Rise and Progress of the Arts of Design in the United States* (New York: Benjamin Brom, 1965), II, 221.

Monticello, Charlottesville, Virginia. Thomas Jefferson, architect.
Drawing by Robert Mills, circa 1803.

For the next quarter of a century Mills cultivated their relationship by informing the president about his projects and publications, and this bore fruit in several ways. First, Jefferson's understanding of European trends must have broadened Mills' perspective; secondly, Jefferson's involvement in public affairs must have encouraged Mills to concentrate on public projects—a focus which became the mainstay of his career, and finally, Jefferson provided letters of recommendation, including one to Benjamin Henry Latrobe when Hoban's work on the White House came to a close.

Drawings done by Mills under Jefferson's direction provide the most vivid record of their interaction. For example, one of Mills' Monticello elevations includes oculi or round windows in the attic, suggesting it was done as part of a study for the addition of another story to the wings, perhaps to accommodate bedrooms on the second floor—Jefferson had noted this as a desirable feature of French residential design. The accompanying plan, also drawn by Mills, develops the Salon into a full octagon with niches and adds curved pavilions at both ends of the central block. These elements, like the sleeping alcoves visible in the plan, took Mills beyond the American vernacular.

The most dramatic example of how Jefferson broadened Mills' perspective is found in the series of Villa Rotunda-like drawings, probably based on Jefferson's Leoni edition (1715) of Vitruvius' *I Quattro Libri dell' Architettura*. Beneath the section Mills signed "Thos. Jefferson Archt." and "Robt. Mills Del." A series of dots on the ribs of the dome indicates a nailing schedule for a system of laminated wooden ribs based on another book, Philibert Delorme's *Invention pour batir les couvertures courbes*. Jefferson had a copy of Delorme's book and used this dome system at Monticello.[27] Mills would later use the system on his auditorium churches. Domes were not part of the American building tradition. The appearance of the Delorme system here is an early indication of Mills' awareness of structural techniques beyond the knowledge of local craftsmen.

In the spring of 1802, during this period of contact with Jefferson, Mills made his first professional venture. Responding to an advertisement in the *Washington Federalist*, he prepared designs for the proposed South Carolina College. This competition prompted Mills' earliest known independent project and produced his first income as a creator. He submitted carefully drawn plans—two of which survive—and split the prize with Hugh Smith, the only other South Carolinian known to have entered the contest.[28]

The diverse backgrounds of the competitors suggest the disorganized state of the architectural profession. Proposals came from Asa Messer, the third president of Brown University; S. Stanhope Smith, who was the president of the College of New Jersey in Princeton from 1795 until 1812; Peter Banner, a carpenter builder then erecting buildings at Yale which had been designed by the painter, John Trumbull; Benjamin Silliman, a scientist at Yale, and Hugh Smith, an amateur from Charleston, South Carolina.

The only professional architect who responded to the South Carolina College competition was Benjamin Henry Latrobe. The trustees apparently wrote him, and he sent a "fair sketch" accompanied by a long letter pointing out that he disapproved of competitions because he found it "inconvenient and humiliating" to prepare drawings which would be judged by non-professionals merely "for the chance of being preferred to the amateur, & workmen who may enter the lists against me." Latrobe said competition winners were usually people "possessing the confidence of building committees, or holding a seat in the committee" and the situation "often made me repent that I have cultivated my profession in preference to my farm."[29]

27 Douglas J. Harnsberger, "In Delorme's Manner: a Study of the Applications of Philibert Delorme's Dome Construction Method in Early 19th Century American Architecture," M.A. Thesis, University of Virginia, 1981.

28 John M. Bryan, An Architectural History of the South Carolina College (Columbia: University of South Carolina Press, 1976), 1–23.

29 Bryan, An Architectural History of the South Carolina College, 123–125.

ABOVE: *Villa Rotunda. Robert Mills, circa 1803.*
BELOW, LEFT: *Villa Capra. O.B. Scamozzi, Palladio (Vicenza, 1778), Book II, Plate XIII.*
BELOW, MIDDLE: *Philibert de L'Orme,* ... Nouvelles Inventions pour dien bastir et a petiz frais.
BELOW, RIGHT: *Philibert de L'Orme,* ... Nouvelles Inventions pour dien bastir et a petiz frais.

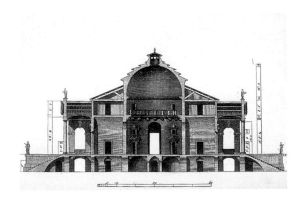

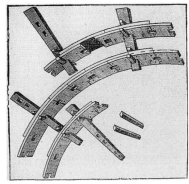

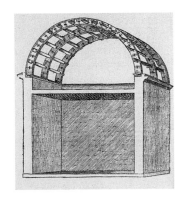

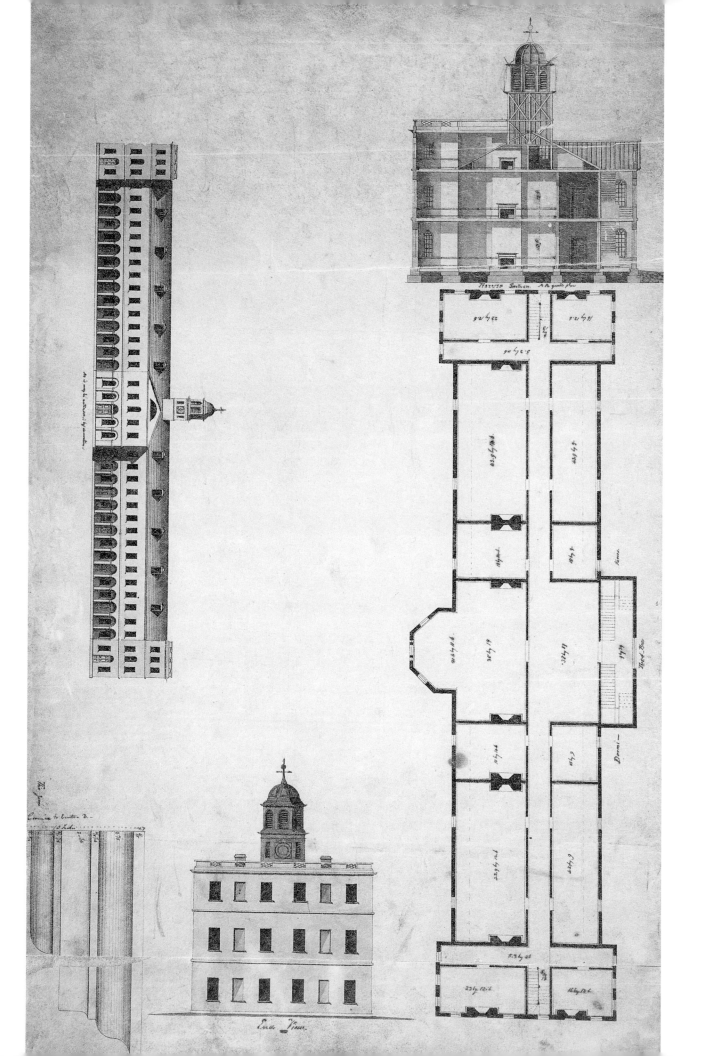

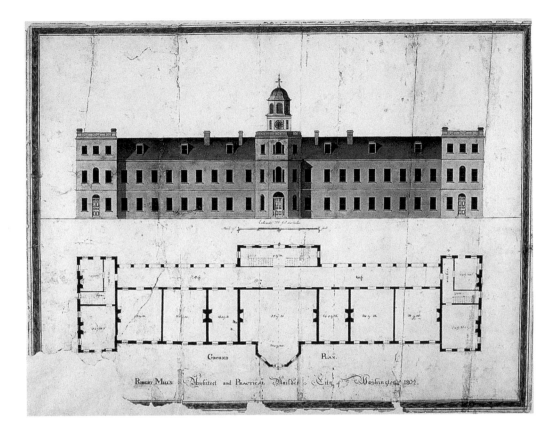

ABOVE AND OPPOSITE: *South Carolina College, Columbia, South Carolina. Robert Mills, 1802.*

The trustees' decision proved Latrobe right. They split the $300 prize between Mills and Smith—two neophytes—and then drew their own plan resembling Nassau Hall at Princeton, where most of them had been students.

Mills' two surviving drawings for the South Carolina College competition had no influence on the buildings (Rutledge and Dessassure colleges) that were erected. Nonetheless, the drawings provide a benchmark of his ability just before he entered Latrobe's office. The drawings present front, rear, and end elevations, plans of the first and second floors, a section, front to rear, through the center, and a detailed cornice profile. Federal Style motifs on the facades—Palladian windows, fanlights, round-headed windows, and the cupola—are awkwardly juxtaposed with projecting Regency features—the central and end bays, stair tower, and parapets. The surviving ground plan ignores some of the criteria required by the trustees, for plans were supposed to provide for student and faculty residences and classrooms. Mills made no provision for closets, water closets, or rooms *en suite*.

The most notable aspect of Mills' design was an open arcade at the base of the rear facade to provide covered access to the ground floor classrooms. Nothing like this existed in America at the time. This concept has become ubiquitous in suburban schools, but Mills proposed it a decade before Jefferson first used it at the University of Virginia.

There are several possible sources for Mills' proposed arcade. He knew the town and market hall building type, and through prints he no doubt also knew the arcaded academic quadrangles of Oxford and Cambridge. He may have discussed the South Carolina competition with Jefferson and adapted the president's earlier (1771–1772) proposal for an addition to the College of William and Mary—an arcaded quadrangle.[30] The Revolution had thwarted the William and Mary project, but the re-appearance of colonnades at the University of Virginia some forty years later suggests Jefferson never lost sight of their usefulness in an academic setting.

After the experience in Hoban's office and contact with Jefferson, the next notable episode in Mills' training was a tour of the eastern seaboard north of Washington. He took this trip during the summer and early fall of 1802, and it is important for several reasons. First, before Mills set out, Jefferson provided a letter of introduction to Charles Bulfinch, and when he got back Mills gave Jefferson two drawings as mementos. Jefferson's letter and Mills' drawings help us understand their relationship. One of the drawings he gave Jefferson was an elevation of Latrobe's Bank of Pennsylvania—the earliest evidence we have of Mills' contact with Latrobe's work—and Latrobe, more than anyone else, would mold Mills as a professional. Mills' trip may be the earliest specifically architectural tour undertaken in America, and also may be the earliest suggestion of the national perspective that would become a distinguishing hallmark of his career. (Insofar as we know, none of his contemporaries toured the seaboard as part of their training.) Finally, Mills went at least as far north as Charlestown, Massachusetts, where he met Jebidiah Morse, who was already famous as the father of American geography. Mills' visit to Morse is the first hint of his later interests in publishing, cartography, and geography.

We have no journal of Mills' trip but know he stopped in Philadelphia, which was the most urbane setting he had ever seen. It had more public build-

30 William Howard Adams, ed., *The Eye of Thomas Jefferson* (Charlottesville: Thomas Jefferson Memorial Foundation, 1976), fig. 23, 19.

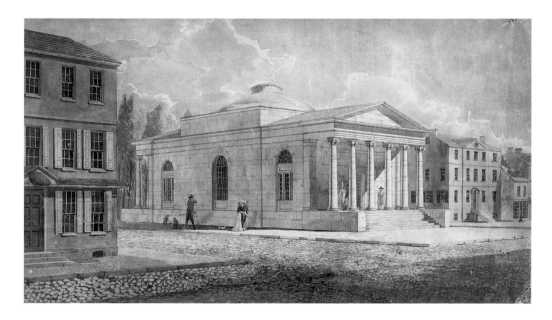

Bank of Pennsylvania, Philadelphia. Benjamin Henry Latrobe, 1798.

ings than Charleston and a walled garden behind the government center that was considered the most distinguished park in the country.

Mills' drawing of Latrobe's Bank of Pennsylvania is meticulous.

The bank was freestanding on its lot, a thing apart; set back some thirty feet from the street behind a forecourt and surrounded by an iron fence mounted on a high stone base. Anyone sensitive to architectural ideas knew it was exceptional. Latrobe's biographer, Talbot Hamlin, who defined the Greek Revival Style in America, was unstinting in his praise: "It was the country's first Greek Revival structure and also the first building in which masonry vaults were used integrally as a major means for achieving architectural effect." Or again, it was

> the first monumental building by Latrobe [and] can justly be called a master-
> piece. In the new country, it was the first building to be erected in which the
> structural concept, the plan conceived as a functional agent, and the effect
> both inside and out were completely integrated, completely harmonious. It
> was also a declaration of architectural independence, and it proved the design
> by a well trained architect could go far beyond the ordinary usage's of the

Bank of Pennsylvania, Philadelphia. Benjamin Henry Latrobe, architect. Drawing by Robert Mills, 1803.

time; its almost universal welcome proved, too, that the popular taste of the period was ready and even eager for this kind of new vision.[31]

The composition was beautifully clear. There was a cubic central block capped by a low, saucer dome. This contained a rotunda—a domed banking lobby. Two opposing wings extended from this block, each ending in a full Ionic portico adapted from Stuart and Revett's illustration of the Temple of Illysis.

31 Hamlin, 157.

28

The major public entry was through the Second Street Portico; the other portico fronted on a garden at the rear of the building and provided access to offices. The whole exterior was marble. The columns were three feet in diameter, and their impact was enhanced by the absence of any diminutive detailing on the elevation. The Second Street facade, for example, which Mills drew, was marked only by the large and simple entry and a single recessed panel above it, a spare horizontal rectangle which served as foil against the vertical thrust of the columns.

The portico entrance opened into a barrel-vaulted hall, flanked by offices, which led to the rotunda with its semi-circular niches, curving walls, and gently swelling coffered dome. Light flooded this spherical space from an oculus and monitor and large, round headed windows on either side. Latrobe's color scheme specified that the walls be painted "pale but warm oker of straw," with a contrasting white bead to outline the niches and recessed panels.[32] The dome was to be set off by a blue-white frieze in which there was to be a russet colored Greek fret. The coffers of the dome, like the recess panels in the wall below, were to be a lighter "oker" than the wall, and the ribs of the dome between the coffers where to be painted a delicate, pale blue.

The rotunda must have been luminous—an impression that was heightened by having entered through the windowless hallway with its warm brown walls and its ceiling of white, red, and blue. It was probably Mills' first contact with the expressive use of spherical forms and the interior expression of masonry vaulting. Several aspects of the bank appeared in his later work—the use of tucked-away spiral stairways, the cupola or monitor, round-headed windows, recessed blind arches, fireproof masonry vaulting, and the reliance on the juxtaposition of forms and masses rather than applied ornament.

Mills' elevation shows he observed the bank closely. There is no record, however, of the visit he must have made to see the already famous, steam-driven Philadelphia waterworks by Latrobe—the first municipal water system in the country. The waterworks offered a glimpse of aspects of engineering that would play a major role in Mills' subsequent career.

Yellow fever had swept Philadelphia in the summer of 1793. The epidemic was blamed on putrid, private surface wells, and the campaign to provide pure water culminated in 1799 when the city retained Latrobe. He built an inlet in the banks of the Schuylkill with a settling basin and pumping station. From here wooden pipes carried water into the center of the city. In Centre Square another pump lifted the water into cisterns located in the raised and domed rotunda of a

32 Hamlin, 155.

pumphouse. These elevated water tanks provided pressure to deliver water by gravity through another network of pipes to hydrants throughout the city. There was no precedent in America for this undertaking, and the novelty of the waterworks, coupled with the prominence of the Centre Square facility, made the system an object of public curiosity.

Escorting visitors to one of the pumphouses, Thomas Cope, a committee-man who monitored the development of the system, recalled:

> While explaining some part of the works to several citizens, I slipped & should have gone to the bottom of the well in the Schuylkill engine house, but was prevented by laying hold of a cross timber & by the assistance of a friend. A slight fracture is the only injury I sustained. A very small matter saved me. I was aware that if I descended, death must have been the consequence.[33]

The pumphouses were dimly lit, and in the gloom the movement, noise, and smell of the engines created an environment that was novel at the time. There were no steam engines south of Philadelphia, and Mills probably had never seen anything like the

> clumsy and apparently...very painful process, accompanied by an extraordinary amount of wheezing, sighing, creaking, and bumping. When the pump descends, there is heard a plunge, a heavy sigh, and a loud bump: then, as it rises, and the sucker begins to act, there is heard a creak, a wheeze, another bump, and then a rush of water as it is lifted and poured out.[34]

Like others, Mills must have been captivated by the inexorable movement of the great balance beam, the dancing push-rods, and the whirling governor, all working tirelessly. He would later serve as president of the Baltimore Water Company, propose a waterworks for Charleston, South Carolina, introduce running water to the U.S. Capitol, design what he hoped was an improved steam engine, and try to participate in the development of steampowered railroads. Latrobe's pumphouses provided a memorable demonstration of an architect's participation in the industrial revolution, a role that went beyond decorative finesse.

The only record of Mills' stop in New York is his drawing of St. Paul's Chapel (1764–1768) by Thomas McBean. This is the other drawing that Mills

33 Thomas Cope, edited by E.C. Harrison, *Philadelphia Merchant: The Diary of Thomas P. Cope, 1800–1851* (South Bend: Gateway, 1978), 59.

34 F.D. Klingender, *Art and the Industrial Revolution* (New York: Schocken, 1970), 5.

LEFT: *St. Paul's Chapel, New York, 1764–1766. Thomas McBean, architect. Drawing by Robert Mills, 1803.*
RIGHT: *Philadelphia Waterworks, 1798–1801. Benjamin Latrobe, architect.*

gave to Jefferson. St. Paul's must have seemed familiar, for like St. Michael's in Charleston, it was based on St. Martin's in the Fields by James Gibbs. But unlike St. Michael's, St. Paul's was built of stone—Manhattan schist and New England brownstone—and the resulting depth and variety of texture and color were new to Mills, for stone was rarely used in the south. Mills' drawing contains a commemorative obelisk under the portico—his earliest recorded contact with Egyptian Revival forms.

Carrying Jefferson's letter of introduction to Charles Bulfinch, Mills must have looked forward to arriving in Boston.[35] Like Charleston, Boston was a peninsula city, confined by water on three sides. Three hills dominated the cityscape. The highest of these, Beacon Hill, was crowned by the golden dome of the Massachusetts State House designed by Bulfinch, who had come to architecture by a circuitous route, pushed, as it were, by a quirk of fate.

Bulfinch represented the eighteenth-century tradition of the designer as a cosmopolitan amateur—a tradition at odds with Mills' determination and sense

35 T.J. to C.B., July 1, 1802; PRM, 0012.

31

of direction. After graduating from Harvard, Bulfinch had taken the European Grand Tour and received advice on what to see from Jefferson, who was in Paris at the time. When Bulfinch returned to Boston, he married and settled down to what promised to be a life of elegant leisure, but his investment in the Tontine Crescent (1793), a disastrous real estate speculation that he also designed, ruined his fortune and forced him to practice architecture professionally. His biographer says difficulties with money marked his face with "a controlled bitterness that testifies to repeated disappointments."[36] Financial pressure also prompted him to accept employment as a municipal official. Bulfinch was potentially an ideal informant about aspects of Boston of interest to Mills.

Mills arrived at a time Bostonians were transforming the cityscape. During the summer of 1799, a real estate syndicate, the Mount Vernon Proprietors, began cutting down one of the three hills adjacent the State House to gain lots for residential development. They altered the landscape by loading the peak of the hill into carts, which slid down a track and dumped their loads into the marsh below, creating land in the Back Bay for further development. This may have been the first use of the gravity railroad in America, and the extensive operation, according to Harrison Gray Otis—one of the Proprietors— "excited as much attention as Bonaparte's road over the Alps." The magnitude of this undertaking was impressive; it was "the largest land transaction ever to have been undertaken in Boston at that time [and] involved a sudden change in the character of an entire region."[37]

The previous year Bulfinch became Chairman of the Boston Board of Selectmen, and under his leadership the town began developing rectilinear streets along the Boston neck, opening the growth of the city to the south. To the north, two bridges crossed the Charles River and provided access to the mainland. The Charles River Bridge was the largest Mills had ever seen. It was 1,503 feet long, carried by seventy-five oak piers. It was forty-two feet wide and had railed sidewalks and street lamps on either side and a drawbridge in the center to maintain navigation. This bridge, and the similar West Boston Bridge, "radically changed the pattern of life in Boston, for regions that had been remote cul-de-sacs suddenly developed into busy thoroughfares to the surrounding world."[38]

From the bridges there was vista of Boston's waterfront with crowded wharves projecting like tines of a comb. From the hinterland, carts and wagons carrying produce and firewood rumbled over the bridges to market. And coming down the Charles River were long, narrow barges carrying waterborne

36 Harold Kirker, *The Architecture of Charles Bulfinch* (Cambridge: Harvard University Press, 1969), 1.

37 Walter Muir Whitehill, *Boston, A Topographical History* (Cambridge: Harvard University Press, 1968), 62.

38 Whitehill, *Boston*, 50.

freight. Upstream, the new Middlesex Canal, twenty-seven miles long, was almost completed (it would open in 1803). Designed to connect the Charles, Concord, and Merrimack Rivers, it was one of the prototypes for the 3,000 miles of man-made waterways that stitched together river systems of the seaboard during the first third of the nineteenth century.

Mills must have crossed one of the bridges to Charlestown on the north bank of the Charles, for he visited Jebidiah Morse there. In Charlestown work was underway on the Massachusetts State Prison designed by Bulfinch. In order to make the prison secure and fireproof, Bulfinch had located a man (a Mr. Tarbox of Danvers, Massachusetts) who knew how to split granite into large, rectilinear blocks. The prison was the first American project to use large blocks of cut granite. Knowledge of Tarbox's technique spread, and precut blocks of granite became a popular building material during the next half century. Mills would later use what came to be called "the Boston Granite Style," and he must have taken note of the prison plan, for the interior conformed to the new theory that solitary confinement promoted penitence (hence the vogue for the new term "penitentiary").[39] The plan called for symmetrical wings flanking a central block. The first floor of the wings was occupied by work rooms, the upper floors by individual cells opening onto a corridor. The central block housed stairwells, a kitchen at grade, and the hospital and keepers' rooms above. In various institutional buildings—hospitals, prisons, and offices—Mills later used elements of this plan.

Jebidiah Morse, the geographer, provided him with a letter of introduction to men in Salem and Newburyport, Massachusetts, Exeter, New Hampshire, Portland, Maine, Providence and Newport, Rhode Island, and Norwich, Hartford, Middletown, and New Haven, Connecticut.[40] Mills may have extended his stay in New England, but we have no record of this final segment of his trip. When he turned south again, he must have thought about Bulfinch and the sustaining hand of governmental employment, the variety of building types to be designed, the topographical impact of the gravity railroad, and the transforming potential of public improvements—canals and bridges—and the integrity of the Granite Style. Judging from his subsequent work, Mills was not drawn to Bulfinch's use of Adam or Federal Style ornament, but he must have found Bulfinch's active, multi-faceted professional life affirming.

39 Gideon Hayes, *Pictures from Prison Life… Historical Sketch of the Massachusetts State Prison* (Boston: Lee and Shepard, 1869), 14–17. John M. Bryan, "Boston's Granite Architecture, c. 1810–1860," Boston University dissertation, 1972.

40 JM to Rev. Dr. Prince, Salem; Rev. Mr. Andrews and Dudley A. Tyng, Newburyport; Rev. Mr. Kellogg, Portland; Mr. Benj. Abbot, Exeter; Rev. Mr. Patten and Jabez Denison, Newport; Rev. Mr. Gans and William Wilkinson, Providence; Dr. Joshua Lathrop and William Lanmon, Norwich; Rev. Henry Channing, New London; Theodore Dwight and Mr. James Stedman, Hartford; the Hon'ble Sam W. Dana, Middletown; Rev. Dr Dana and President Dwight, New Haven, October 18, 1802; PRM, 0016A.

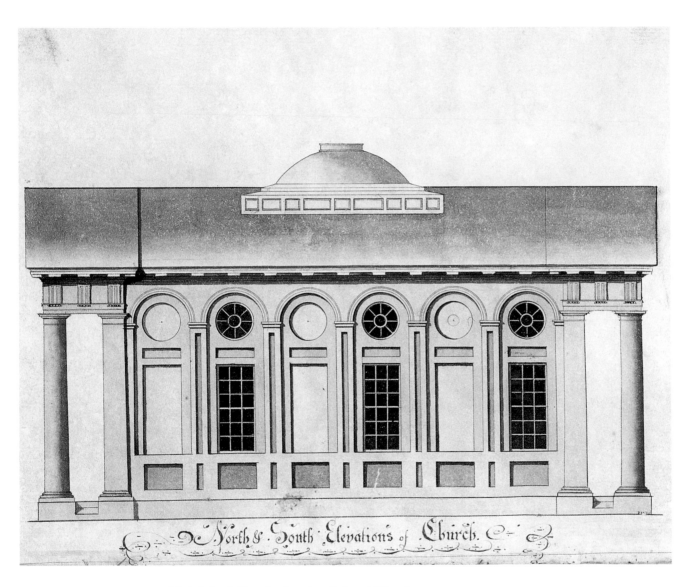

John's Island Church, elevation. Robert Mills, 1804.

CHAPTER TWO

Training with
Benjamin Henry Latrobe

1803–1807

AFTER HIS TOUR, Mills returned to Washington, and his diary suggests a leisurely, unstructured existence. He visited Alexandria and Mason's Island, attended religious meetings, and went sightseeing at the Navy Yard. He must have watched the construction at the Capitol directed by John Lenthall, Latrobe's Clerk of the Works. Jefferson had appointed Latrobe Surveyor of Public Buildings, and he was directing work at the President's House, the Capitol, the Navy Yard, and was designing a canal along what would become the mall. A diary entry indicates Mills did drawings of a lock and bridge for the canal, and this is the earliest indication of any contact with Latrobe.[1]

Mills later wrote that Latrobe was "engaged upon the Delaware and Chesapeake Canal and as an architect of the Capitol at Washington, at which time I entered his office as a student under the advice and recommendation of Mr. Jefferson, then President of the United States."[2]

Latrobe commented on Mills' early days in the office in a letter (October 2, 1803) to Jefferson:

> The young gentleman whom you did me the favor to recommend to me has now been in my office upwards of two months. He possesses that valuable substitute for genius—laborious precision—in a very high degree, and is therefore very useful to me, though his professional education has been hitherto much misdirected. His personal habits and character are very singular. He is

1 PRM, 4001.

2 Gallagher, 158.

an enthusiastic Methodist, devoting many hours of the evenings & mornings to prayer & singing of psalms—and though a temper violently choleric appears through the viel [sic] of religious mildness he has himself so perfectly under command, as never to have exhibited any visible anger [several lost words] provocations to it by the motley crew of my people have been sometimes beyond the common bounds of human patience. I think he will become a very useful citizen, though never a very amiable man. Believe me with the truest respect and attachment

B. Henry Latrobe[3]

Latrobe had no way of knowing Mills would remain with him for six years, or that he would ultimately view Mills as his "professional child" and—despite a low opinion of Mills as a designer—he would lament their parting when Mills matured and emerged as a full-fledged rival.

Latrobe's office was located in New Castle, Delaware. Here he juggled commitments, for he was responsible for the completion of the Capitol and the alteration of the President's House; he was also directing surveys for the proposed Chesapeake and Delaware Canal and was mired in a legal and financial quagmire resulting from investments in the Philadelphia waterworks and an iron rolling mill.

The office was an ideal educational setting for Mills. There were plans for a lighthouse, fireproof details for the Treasury, residential work, and the Baltimore Cathedral. And always there was the example of Latrobe himself—talented, intellectually omnivorous, and a prolific writer about architectural problems. He kept the nibs of the pantograph scurrying as he recorded thoughts on the proper siting of buildings, the use of shadow in design, methods of developing arches, the requirements of institutional buildings, and the role of internal improvements in the nation's future. His clerks took dictation, filed correspondence, worked on drawings, and ran errands. On Latrobe's behalf we find Mills visiting lumber dealers, out surveying, in the office writing to John Lenthall, and traveling to Albany, New York, in search of stonecutters.[4]

In 1803, when Mills entered the office the Chesapeake and Delaware Canal was just getting underway. As initially planned by Latrobe, the canal was to connect the Chesapeake and Delaware bays and allow waterborne traffic to avoid the long trip around the peninsula. Latrobe recommended a route running from the Christiana River near Wilmington, Delaware, on the east to the Elk

3 BHL to TJ, October 2, 1803. PRM, 0025.

4 Hamlin, 264, n9.

River near Frenchtown, Maryland, on the west. At its highest point, the route was seventy-four feet above sea level, and to obtain water for the elevated stages he planned a feeder canal five miles long to bring water from the Elk River into the uppermost locks near Glasgow, Delaware.

By the fall of 1803 Latrobe was in the final stages of negotiating a route with the directors of the canal company. Their regional prejudices and real estate investments forced him to make some thirty different surveys, but in February 1804, he was able to write a mason, Thomas Vickers of Philadelphia, that "the committee has resolved to commence with the feeders." Latrobe noted to Vickers that the route must remain a secret until the right of way was secured, but as work would begin in the spring, Vickers should assemble a crew of masons, carpenters, a blacksmith, and laborers. That spring work began in earnest on the feeder canal. Early in May Latrobe wrote again to Vickers that "yesterday, the day on which five years ago you laid the first brick at the waterworks, I put the first spade into the ground at Elk Forge."[5]

It is not surprising Latrobe compared this groundbreaking to setting the cornerstone of the Philadelphia Waterworks. The initial success of the waterworks had caused celebrations. Now many people had great hopes for the canal, believing it would channel trade and bring prosperity to those, like Latrobe, who were able to buy property along its banks. Enthusiasm was fueled by a growing interest in "internal improvements" in general and canals in particular. Newspapers coupled canals with the promotion of national unity and the defense of the seaboard. Patriotism and greed proved a powerful combination, and many people were swept along by this tide, which did not subside until the coming of the railroads in the 1830s. When Latrobe broke ground nobody foresaw the difficulties, delays, and mounting frustration that would ultimately doom this initial attempt to develop the Chesapeake and Delaware Canal.

Latrobe's work on the canal was evidence of the influence of English engineers. Thomas Vickers, skilled in the use of hydraulic cement (which would harden under water) had previously worked under the direction of William Weston, an English canal builder who worked on the Schuylkill and Susquehanna Canal, the Delaware and Schuylkill Canal, the Northern and Western Inland Lock Navigation in New York State, and the Middlesex Canal—which Mills probably saw under construction near Boston. Latrobe's Clerk of the Works on the Chesapeake and Delaware project was a Philadelphia surveyor named Robert Brooke, who had also worked with Weston. Of the

5 BHL to TJ, May 3, 1804.

eight labor contractors, three had been employed by Weston and two more were Englishmen who had worked on the Grand Junction Canal. Latrobe himself, before coming to America, had worked in the office of the famous English civil engineer, John Smeaton. After leaving Smeaton he worked with William Jessop, once Smeaton's chief assistant, in the construction of the thirty-seven-and-one-half mile Basingstoke Canal. This great work southwest of London had twenty-nine locks, sixty-eight bridges, and two tunnels. In England Latrobe also had planned an alternative route for the Chelmsford Navigation in Essex, but this project did not come to fruition and its failure may have bolstered his decision to emigrate. Upon coming to America he had advised the state of Virginia in matters of navigation and had recently (1802) completed a report for Pennsylvania concerning navigation on the lower reaches of the Susquehanna.[6] In short, Mills found himself among men who talked knowledgeably about inland navigation—one of the great issues of the day—and Mills later used what he learned in writings and in the canals he proposed or designed in South Carolina, Maryland, and Virginia.

The initial surveys for the Chesapeake and Delaware Canal began in July 1803, just weeks before Mills entered Latrobe's office. Throughout the fall and into the winter Latrobe directed the surveyors. For the next ten months crews crisscrossed the neck of the peninsula; they cleared sightlines, stretched chains, and set up transits to establish distances and elevations along alternative routes. We do not know what Mills did during this period—some months later he was working with the surveying crews in what Latrobe complained was "as inhospitable, and wild a country as the peninsula can boast, for no other purpose than to explore it in order to satisfy the public that no canal can be carried over it."[7] Latrobe's impatience with what he considered the inefficiency and indecision of his employers was exacerbated by the fact that he already had a route in mind.

Weather deteriorated as winter approached, but Latrobe pressed on, often spending five or six days a week with his men in the field. When rain drove him indoors, he worked in his New Castle office, writing long letters to John Lenthall, who was working on the Senate chamber. Lenthall's terms of employment, anticipating the architect's absence, granted an extraordinary degree of authority, and although Latrobe had faith in Lenthall's judgement, questions requiring the architect's attention continually arose. Structural inadequacies in the existing building and functional and aesthetic deficiencies in Thornton's

6 Hamlin, 545–566. Ralph D. Gray, "The Early History of the Chesapeake and Delaware Canal," *Delaware History VIII*, 3 (1958–1959): 243, 246.

7 Gray, "The Early History of the Chesapeake and Delaware Canal," 249.

plans plagued Lenthall at each step of the way. Latrobe's other obligations made problems in Washington especially onerous.

On returning from a visit to the Capitol, Latrobe wrote Lenthall that "as I was jolting along in the stage, it occurred to me that I must have been crazy or worse…to have proposed carrying up new flues to receive the smoke of the senate chamber." [8] As an alternative, he suggested adapting new furnaces to the existing flues. Mills saw that decorative detail occupied only a small portion of Latrobe's time, for there were always problems concerning the acquisition of materials and disputes about labor, wages, and contracts. Latrobe believed the difficulties with the Capitol were compounded by his absence, by his need to spend most of his time in New Castle near the canal. [9]

The feeder canal was infinitely less complex than the Capitol. Mills saw gangs of laborers excavate with picks and shovels, using wheelbarrows to remove the earth and shape the banks. He watched the contractors direct the puddling process, wetting and packing the soil which would form the bottom and banks in an effort to deter erosion. Masons directed by Thomas Vickers pried stone from the hillsides and shaped it into voussoirs for the arches of the bridges that were to cross the feeder canal. Carpenters from Philadelphia were soon erecting the centering—temporary wooden staging—that would support the bridges until the mortar hardened. Latrobe and Vickers discussed the preparation of an appropriate cement. Here again, Latrobe drew on his English training, for his mentor, John Smeaton, had conducted experiments to find a water-resistant cement for his famous Eddystone Lighthouse. By increasing the proportion of clay in the lime-pozzolana mortar, he had improved its hydraulic properties. [10] In both America and England, formulas for the improvement of cement were then much discussed; there was a flurry of patent activity, and throughout Mills' career he would be attentive to the innovative use of materials, including asphalt, iron, and heating systems.

In the summer of 1804 Latrobe moved Mills and a surveying team into New Castle to survey streets and establish property lines and elevations above mean high water. The commissioners of the town anticipated growth and asked Latrobe to draw up a city plan. He hoped to finish this work during the summer, but interruptions and delays caused the project to drag on until August 1805. At the outset, Latrobe ordered a "well bound book containing about three quires of the largest elephant paper" in which his assistants were "to record the survey in detail." Onto these pages Mills helped transcribe data from the field. He noted

8 BHL to JL, September 15, 1803.

9 Hamlin, 585.

10 Hamlin, 27, n6. For a note on Smeaton's interest in cement see D. Alan Stevenson, *The World's Lighthouses Before 1820* (London: Oxford University Press, 1959), 126.

the position of the thirty-odd houses then standing, the courses and elevations of the streets, the stones set at intersections and "back sights at high water mark." Elevations were drawn for each streetscape. A perspective view through the town with ships in the background—apparently composed by either William Strickland or by Latrobe himself—was included, and Latrobe wrote a set of notes and submitted the whole to the commissioners.[11]

Several aspects of this project reappear in Mills' own work. He saw here the advantage of a book-like presentation with its forceful integration of graphics and text, and soon he adopted this format for plans of his own. He observed the intellectual scope of Latrobe's explanatory notes, which, among other things, took into account the prevailing winds and the solar orientation of homes.

This village survey, like real estate speculation in Washington, put Mills in touch with rudiments of town planning and popular faith in urban development. On his own he would later lay out streets in Charleston, South Carolina, and would become financially involved in speculative housing in Baltimore and Philadelphia. Now at midsummer in the midst of the survey he once again witnessed the competing demands on Latrobe's time and attention. A family crisis affected the work by keeping Latrobe in Philadelphia. The clerk of the works left the canal. In Washington the Capitol needed supervision. There was much correspondence concerning these problems, and in the spring of 1805 Latrobe wrote to the commissioners of New Castle that "I have...sent over Mr. Mills to make all preparations, so that I may begin on Monday morning very early, if the weather is fair."[12]

Finally, when the work was done, the reaction of the city fathers provided a bitter lesson. Latrobe was paid too little, and his suggestions were ignored. Thinking of New Castle, he later complained that the vices of a small village conspired against the arts and that the only decent man in this community was the hearty innkeeper. The mere thought of the place made him "angry and vexed."[13] Latrobe's frustration did not dampen Mills' enthusiasm for internal improvement projects. Predictably, he too would suffer at the hands of public patrons.

As the new year dawned and just before the New Castle survey began in earnest, Mills went home to Charleston. He had been gone for four years; now he returned as an aspiring professional. He was greeted by his stepmother, Rebecca, his brothers, Henry and Thomas, and their sister, Sarah. There was much to discuss, for William Mills, Robert's father, had died during his absence. Henry and Thomas were managing the estate. Robert had inherited a "brick

11 BHL to John Bird, June 6, 1804; also see Hamlin, appendix 6, 583–585.

12 BHL to John Crow, May 18, 1805.

13 BHL, Journal, August 3, 1806.

house and lot at 30 Elliott Street, my wooden house and lot at 24 St. Phillips Street, my tract of land in St. Thomas' Parish (237 acres), two Negroes, Dundee and Jeffrey, a bond and mortgage amounting to 637 pounds principal given by Johnson Hagood to Charles Glover and legally transferred from him to me, also all my unmade up clothing."[14]

Mills had been earning two dollars a day from Latrobe, and income from his inheritance had allowed him to concentrate on his training. He was now twenty-three years old and had erected nothing of significance to his own design, but he had visited most of the important buildings along the seaboard and met the major practitioners. He had studied many of the basic texts and demonstrated his competence as a draftsman. Having observed both Hoban and Latrobe, Mills had a sense of the building process. And his initial experience with a building committee—the South Carolina College trustees—had been at least partially successful, so when the chance came to design churches in Charleston while he was home, he seized the opportunity.

In the period 1804–1806 Mills produced designs for two churches and a proposal for the alteration of a third. Each of these projects is interesting for different reasons. The proposed alteration of St. Michael's shows his use of Latrobe's ideas about acoustics, and here Mills expressed a commitment to what would become known as "historic preservation." The plans for a new church (never erected) on John's Island near Charleston simultaneously convey his accomplished draftsmanship and his immaturity as a stylist. The only one of the three to be constructed, the Circular Congregational Church in Charleston, is memorable for several reasons: it was Mills' first major building; it was also the earliest of his auditorium churches designed to conform to Latrobe's theory of acoustics using the Delorme dome; finally, his plan was substantially altered by the building committee—a situation he would confront throughout his career.

St. Michael's was already a landmark for Mills. It was a fixture in the cityscape of his youth. He later wrote that it aroused feelings of "sublimnity and reverence" and was "one of the greatest ornaments [of] the city."[15] While he was home in the spring of 1804, "the Church wardens directed Robert Mills to draw up plans for the extension of the church." He presented plans to the Vestry on March 11, and they "resolved unanimously that the foregoing plan and drawings be laid before the church for their approbation." They also passed a resolution thanking him "for the handsome drawings" and "transmitted him … sixty dollars as a further mark of their appreciation." On June 10th the congregation

14 *Charleston Wills*, D-1800–1807, 269, recorded February 22, 1802.

15 Robert Mills, *Statistics of South Carolina* (Charleston: Hurlbut and Lloyd, 1826), 406.

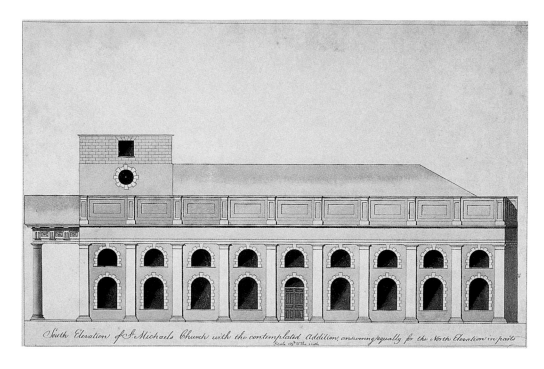

St. Michael's Church, Charleston, South Carolina, elevation. Robert Mills, 1804.

16 See George W.
Williams, "Robert Mills'
Contemplated Addition to
St. Michael's Church,
Charleston and Doctrine
of Sounds," *Journal of the
Society of Architectural
Historians* 12, no. I (1953),
p. 23; also see Rhodri
Liscombe, *The Church
Architecture of Robert Mills*
(Easley, S.C.: Southern
Historical Press, 1985), 5,
41–47.

approved the plans and appointed a building committee, which advertised for bids.[16] At this point the expansion and alteration of St. Michael's promised to be Mills' first major job.

Leaving things in their hands, Mills returned to Latrobe's office near the canal. As summer turned to fall, he had every reason to expect that work on St. Michael's might begin at any time. Word reached him, however, that the vestry was having second thoughts about the structural implications of the plans. In October 1804, he sent them an essay explaining his design.

The immediate problem facing the congregation was the need for more interior space. Mills considered the historic character of the exterior, the new interior configuration, the structural integrity of his additions, and the creation of the curved surfaces required by his understanding of acoustics. In order to add "42 pews below and 12 in the gallery" he planned to remove the apse at the eastern end of the church and elongate the nave by erecting two more bays. Excepting a change in proportion, the resulting north and south exterior walls

LEFT: *St. Michael's Church, Charleston, South Carolina.*
RIGHT: *St. Michael's Church, "Section Showing the Cove & Proposed Situation of the Pulpit." Robert Mills, 1804.*

would resemble the original elevations of 1761. The only exterior detail he suggested altering was the parapet; here he suggested replacing the balustrade with an "Attic Order" of recessed panels. He felt this simplified the elevations, as the resulting parapet would be aligned with both "the first appearance of the tower out of the roof" and the "line of the ridge of the pediment." He wanted the new recessed panels and the diminutive pilasters between them to echo the windows and the giant order of pilasters in the wall below. The powerful Doric portico and the elaborately stepped steeple would be left untouched.[17]

His delicate treatment of the exterior did not prepare the vestry for the extensive alterations proposed for the interior. The interior plan made them reconsider. Mills reasoned they would be able to add more pews if they placed the pulpit, lectern and altar against the wall of the new, extended apse. He also believed the concave ceiling of the new apse would function as an enlarged sounding board, deflecting the voice of the speaker to all areas of the interior.

17 Williams, 25.

43

He explained this unorthodox arrangement, stating that "the present situation of the pulpit is evidently very awkward. It is proposed to place it opposite the center aisle and in the altar niche. The advantage of this is that the speaker will not have his back to any of the congregation....The crown of the niche it is placed in...is the receiver and augmenter of sound, as from its form it immediately disperses it to the cove [of the new ceiling] which conveys it to the farthest end of the church."[18]

St. Michael's was (and is) an Episcopal or Anglican church. Mills was not an Anglican. (Latrobe said he was a Methodist. During the 1820s he was an Elder in the Presbyterian Church.) So he was not constrained by the liturgical tradition which placed the pulpit (for sermons) on the right, the lectern (for bible readings) on the left, and the altar (for the blessing and distribution of sacraments) in the center at the eastern end of the church. He was naïve to think the vestry would jettison the traditional arrangement.

Another major problem was his proposal to remove the existing flat ceiling over the nave and replace it with a barrel vault that would be a continuation of the curve of the apse. This move, prompted by his commitment to acoustics, would require cutting the girders or cross ties that formed the base of the trusses supporting the roof. In his specifications to the carpenter Mills said that "ere you cut the girder, dovetail stout braces into the collar beams and queen posts of the old rafters and strap them well with iron."[19]

The building committee could not bring themselves to authorize such a potentially disastrous course of action. They sought the opinion of Thomas Bennett, a local builder, and there was a delay. Learning of their concerns, Mills sent an essay entitled "On the Subject of the Ceiling of St. Michael's Church and on the Doctrine of Sounds."[20]

In 1797 Latrobe had written an essay on acoustics, and Mills paraphrased it when he described the acoustical aspects of the plans. (Latrobe's essay was later published in the Edinburgh Encyclopedia.)[21] To the St. Michael's vestry, Mills wrote:

> Sound has some of the properties of light. It is radiant . . . and follows the general laws of reflection...it is probably also refracted. Its peculiar properties are not so well understood...its increase by the vibration of the substances thro' or over which it passes, its connection with mathematical forms &c &c.

18 Williams, 28.

19 Williams, 28.

20 Williams, 28.

21 BHL, "Remarks on the best form of a room for hearing & speaking, 1797," an unpaginated manuscript in the collection of the American Philosophical Society, and "Acoustics," *The Edinburgh Encyclopedia*, conducted (sic) by David Brewster (Philadelphia: Joseph and Edward Parker, 1832), I, 104-124, see 121.

Latrobe's 1797 manuscript says:

...sound is also subject to the laws that govern the progress of light, being liable to reflection, perhaps also to refraction. Science I believe has made very little progress on this subject, compared with its extent, for sound has also I think a very intimate connexion with mathematical forms.

They both noted that the ideal acoustic interior was a sphere. On this point Latrobe had written:

...if it could be used when built the best possible room for speaking, and hearing, taking only the direct echo into view, would be a hollow globe. For let the situations of the speaker and hearer be where they will, a ring of first echo perfectly coincident will be produced.

And Mills reiterated:

...if a hollow globe were constructed, a speaker placed in the center would receive echoes from every point of the surface at the same moment, that is, all the echoes would be consonant and primary; of course he would speak with the greatest ease.

Latrobe wrote that "such a room is impracticable," which Mills rephrased as "globular rooms cannot however be constructed." In short, Mills applied the architectural implications of Latrobe's manuscript on acoustics to his proposal for the interior of St. Michael's.

Mills described the interior he envisioned:

The most common room and in many respects the most convenient is the square or oblong quadrangle. It is the cheapest in its construction and adapts itself best to all manner of communications with streets adjacent buildings and contiguous apartments. If such a room have a cylindrical ceiling being either a semicircle or a segment in its section, it will have a great advantage over the same form covered with a flat ceiling especially if the speaker be placed in its axis. In this situation his voice will be assisted by a line of primary consonant echoes, in the perpendicular section of the ceiling exactly over him.

Circular Congregational Church, Charleston. Photograph after the fire of 1861.

In concluding, Mills reduced the functional argument to an aesthetic maxim: "As simplicity in architecture generally produces beauty so is the simplest mode of producing an intended effect commonly the best. A cylindrical ceiling is of those that are not flat, the simplest and cheapest." The same point was made in Latrobe's 1797 draft: "What is...inconsistent with the use of a building can never become ornamental. Simplicity is one of the first of architectural ornaments, and the highest achievement of study and of taste."

Having presented the reason for a coved or curved ceiling, and knowing the vestry was reluctant to cut the beams that supported the roof, Mills described the Delorme system of laminated ribs as an alternative. He instructed anyone with lingering doubts to inspect the Delorme system, which "I have directed in the dome of the Circular Church" just four blocks away. But the St. Michael's vestry remained skeptical, and nothing came of Mills' plans.

The Circular Church was the most unusual of his three early South Carolina church projects. The congregation began discussing the need for a new

LEFT: *"A Round Church...the North Side," James Gibbs,* Book of Architecture *(London, 1728), plate X.*
RIGHT: *"Plan of the Other Round Draught," Gibbs,* Book of Architecture, *plate XIII.*

building in January 1803. Their minister, Rev. David Ramsay, presented the idea of a round church at a meeting on December 19, 1803, and later wrote that his wife suggested the idea and sketched a plan. On February 13, 1804, the building committee thanked Mills "for his ingenious and elegant drawings which had essentially assisted Members and Supporters in forming a correct opinion of the form and plan of their proposed building."[22] (Unless a new cache of papers is discovered we will never know the linkage, if any, between Mrs. Ramsay's sketch and Mills' drawings.) Both Mills and Mrs. Ramsay may have been familiar with English churches with similar plans—Surrey Chapel, Southwark, or the Octagon Chapel, Bath, or illustrations in James Gibbs' *Book of Architecture*.[23]

22 Hamlin, 188; Williams, 23-31; Minutes of the Vestry of St. Michael's Church, I, 298-301, on loan to the South Carolina Historical Society.

23 Liscombe, *The Church Architecture of Robert Mills,* 6.

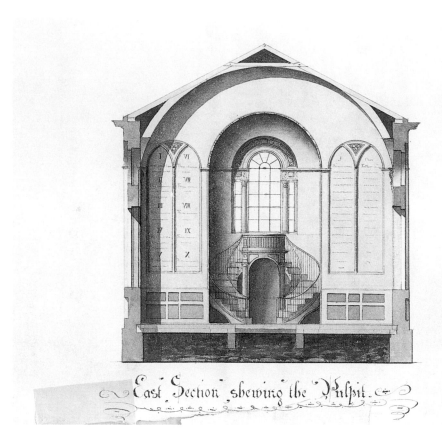

East Section shewing the Pulpit.

John's Island Church,
sections and plan.
Robert Mills, 1804.

Longitudinal Section of Church

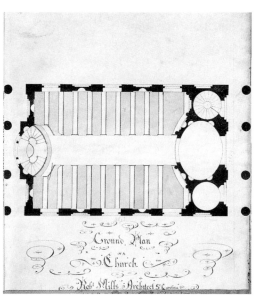

Ground Plan of a Church.
Robt Mills Architect &c Carolina.

The Circular Church *Minutes* make it clear that Mills' plan called for a rotunda eighty-eight feet in diameter and thirty-three feet high, which was to be covered by a hemispherical Delorme dome made of wood and sheathed with copper.[24] This dome was capped by a large cupola. There were twenty-six windows and seven doors in the walls of the rotunda. The church was to be built of brick and stuccoed, a common practice in Charleston. The principle entry was framed by an imposing "Modern Doric" portico extending over the Meeting Street sidewalk, and over this portico Mills wanted a steeple. In effect, he proposed a miniature Pantheon with a Georgian spire rising above its facade like the horn of a unicorn. The steeple and portico over the sidewalk continued the Charleston tradition established by both St. Michael's and St. Phillips.

Inside, the visitor would find a domed, light-filled auditorium, a grand round room accommodating 170 pews on its principal floor and some fifty-two pews in the elevated gallery that swept around the curving walls. At the apex of the dome light from the cupola would flood the room.

When the Circular Church opened on May 26, 1806, it was the first "auditorium style" church in the country. The earliest American art historian, William Dunlap, wrote in 1834 that it was also "the first attempt...to execute such an immense spread of roof without an intermediate support."[25]

Mills' pleasure in the Circular Church commission was short-lived, for without his approval the congregation undertook a series of crippling alterations. They changed the portico from the stolid Doric to an attenuated Corinthian order; they apparently only stuccoed the Meeting Street facade, which emphasized the lack of integration between the portico and rotunda, and worst of all, they altered the dome and thereby ruined the acoustics. As a result of these changes, Mills rarely claimed credit for the Circular Church. In his mind, as built, it was no longer "his" building, and he later wrote that the Baptist Church in Philadelphia (1811–1812) was his first auditorium church.

Drawings for the third Charleston church project, the John's Island Church proposal, are the most complete and elaborate surviving plans from this phase of Mills' career. In these three sections, two elevations, and the accompanying ground plan, the draftsmanship is meticulous, and the rendering of shadow is effective. The elevations, however, present an unresolved juxtaposition of Georgian and Neoclassical elements, for Mills had not yet found his voice as a designer. Conceived as a small rural church, a "chapel of ease," the building was to be forty-two feet by twenty-six-and-one-half feet and was

24 *Idem.* Also see Richard Yeadon, *History of the Circular Church, Its Origin, Building and Rebuilding* (Charleston: J.R. Nixon, 1853), 10.

25 William Dunlap, *History of the Rise and Progress of the Arts of Design in the United States* (New York: George P. Scott, 1834), 222.

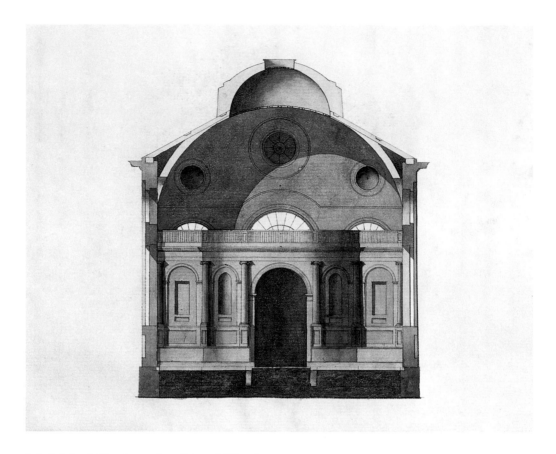

John's Island Church, section. Robert Mills, 1804.

to accommodate twenty pews and a small gallery "purposed entirely for servants." Mills estimated it could be built of brick and stuccoed for $8,000. The budget was never put to the test, for nothing was done with this set of plans.

These early projects brought disappointments, but they also demonstrated he was now able to write specifications and develop drawings on his own. Here too he experienced the cumbersome decision-making process of institutional clients and the difficulty of trying to practice architecture at a distance.

Returning north in 1804 from Charleston by stagecoach, he was accompanied the first day by one of his brothers as far as Georgetown, South Carolina. Mills' described the little town of some 250 houses "mostly of wood, many of them unpleasantly situated.... It was ten o'clock when we arrived here. We partook of a breakfast which was not equal to the price given for it. I had another painful scene to go thro' before I left this place, it was taking leave of my dear Brother who was my companion thus far. The stage horn sounded and I was hurried away from him and with such rapidity we went that the town soon disappeared and we were wrapped in the shade of rural nature." They crossed the Black River on

a raft...which was slipped thro' upright posts...to prevent its being carried down with the stream and by which without oars or poles the flat reaches the opposite shore.... Miles further brought us to our dining place, a small settlement of about a dozen indifferent wooded houses built mostly on one street, and near the banks of the Black Mingo river, a branch of the great Pedee. This settlement is called on the post bill Willtown but around here known by the name of Black Mingo. The depth of the water in the river here is sufficient to admit vessels of 7 or 8 feet draught, and this has made Willtown a place of some business. The produce of the back country, such as cotton, tobacco &c is brought here and transported in vessels sometimes to Charleston. The tavern at the village gave us very indifferent fare, particularly in respect to the cooking, but they took care to make us pay as tho' we had sat down to a table spread with luxuries.... [They continued northward, crossed a flooded causeway through a cypress swamp, and traversed] a cheerless wild seldom interrupted by any kind of cultivation....This day's progress amounted to 54 miles.... [Entering their lodging for the night Mills] thought the driver had made a mistake and stopped at the wrong house, for the people stared at us and hardly would move. The landlady gave us no welcome but seemed rather to say who are you intruders. My companions and I began to look at each other not knowing what to think of this indifferent behavior. However when we saw the driver come in with our baggage we began to think no mistake was made, and without ceremony my companions ordered supper. Soon after the Eastern stage arrived and we all sat down to this meal....This being ended and finding ourselves fatigued we concluded upon going to bed but unhappily we were told that the stage would go on that night. This is not the common practice, but convenience and necessity urged it at this time. Were we to wait until 4 o'clock next morning (the usual time of starting,) we should lose the moonlight....We called for the bill and each had to pay also for the bed which we had never used.[26]

26 RM to Sister, 1804, No. 10; PRM 0027.

When Mills returned to Latrobe's office there were a variety of jobs underway. Latrobe was corresponding with potential clients in New York and Philadelphia. In New York there was discussion of a major drainage system, and he sent an extensive memorandum and estimates, but nothing came of it. In Philadelphia work continued on the alteration of the Chestnut Street Theater, and Latrobe still hoped plans for an Exchange in that city might be realized. Construction was on-going at both the U.S. Capitol and the Chesapeake and Delaware Canal, but for Mills in that fall and winter of 1804, the most important and interesting new work must have been the plan for a Roman Catholic Cathedral to be built in Baltimore. For the next several years he watched its progress and worked on the drawings. In 1806 Latrobe suggested Mills as a potential Clerk of the Works, but the Cathedral Board ignored the recommendation, and Mills remained in the office.

There was much to learn from the Cathedral. Like the Capitol, it was a domed building conceived on a grand scale. The dimensions of its plan were carefully coordinated with liturgical needs; its structure and materials were chosen to reflect the role of the Cathedral in the life of the church and its presence in the city. During Mills' trip south, Latrobe received and reviewed a "plan or sketch of the Main or Cathedral Church proposed to be erected in Baltimore." He had written Bishop John Carroll noting that whether built of brick, stone, or wood, the design was "altogether impracticable." The sketch displayed a forest of Corinthian columns, and Latrobe predicted a cost of "$54,000 for the columns alone." He asked the Bishop to send a building program—size, interior requirements, budget, and site—and promised that "I will then take the liberty of offering you a plan, which though it will probably possess less elegance, shall however not be deficient in practicability."[27]

Latrobe was enthusiastic about the Cathedral. He had offered to design it and supervise the construction at no cost beyond reimbursement of direct expenses, asking only that his design, once accepted, be rigidly adhered to. He wrote the Bishop that "all artists are enthusiasts, I think it my duty as a member of society...to promote as far as my professional talents can promote...the objects of institutions the views of which are not personal emolument, or gratification, or political benefit, but religious and moral instruction, or literary education or charity."[28]

This was not an idle boast. Latrobe donated services on several occasions. Social service, design control, and the recognition of a fee structure were recur-

27 BHL to Bishop John Carroll, April 27 and April 28, 1805.

28 BHL to Bishop John Carroll, April 27 and April 28, 1805

ring themes in his ongoing effort to establish the status of his profession. His offer to the bishop was especially notable in 1804, for by then he had spent most of his inheritance, incurred debts, and had many overdue accounts receivable. He had been forced to accept assistance from his father-in-law, Isaac Hazelhurst, and could ill afford his own generosity. Mills may not have noticed the arrangement with the bishop as part of an emerging definition of the profession.

They worked on the Cathedral in the evening and on weekends, fitting it in between supervision of the feeder canal and visits to Washington and Philadelphia. Latrobe turned at once to the development of a Gothic plan full of arches and deep shadow, lancet and rose windows. It was unlike anything in America and wholly foreign to Mills. But to Latrobe it evoked scenes of youth, village churches in the English countryside. For details, he refreshed his memory, turned to published illustrations, talked to friends, and no doubt discussed the plan with the well-traveled Louis De Mun, who was working alongside Mills as an assistant in the office.

Latrobe wrote Bishop Carroll that a Gothic design was appropriate because of "the veneration which the Gothic Cathedrals generally excite...by the associations belonging peculiarly to that style, and by the real grandeur, and beauty which it possesses, has induced me to propose the Gothic style of building in the first design submitted to you."[29]

Latrobe also submitted a classically derived alternative design, and explained it saying:

> The Gothic style of Cathedrals, is impracticable to the uses of common life, while the Greek and Roman architecture has descended from the most magnificent temples to the decoration of our meanest furniture. On this account, I conceive that the former has a peculiar claim to preference, especially as the expense is not greater in proportion to the effect. The second design which is Roman, has, as far as I can judge of my own works, equal merit with the first in point of plan, and structure, and therefore submit the choice to you entirely, having myself an equal desire to the first or the second executed. My habits rather inclining me to the latter, while my reasonings prefer the first.[30]

Following Latrobe's example, Mills sometimes offered clients alternatives. He worked on both sets of drawings for the Baltimore Cathedral. From Philadelphia Latrobe wrote him "if you could make a complete set of drawings

29 BHL to Bishop John Carroll, April 27, 1805.

30 BHL to Bishop John Carroll, April 27, 1805.

of the Cathedral, leaving out all the windows in the Vellum paper you will oblige me. Everything in my office is at your service, with only this restriction that you permit nothing to go out of your hands into others, a restriction which I am sure is unnecessary."[31] During April, Latrobe wrote Bishop Carroll that "his pupils"—Mills and De Mun—were working on the drawings and both sets were almost ready for consideration.[32] At the end of the month the plans were sent to the building committee; they chose the Neoclassical design and requested some alterations. Latrobe made changes and sent working drawings to Baltimore at the end of the year (December 26, 1805).

During the initial correspondence Latrobe addressed the issue of the visual impact of different materials:

> If the first [Gothic] design be adopted all the walls excepting the projecting piers will be of the flat blue stone found in the neighborhood of your city. The solid, and even rough appearance of this material will rather increase than diminish the effect of magnificence produced by the Gothic style. Brick externally, I hope the committee will reject altogether. Bricks can never produce an effect beyond *neatness*, they are the dress of all our private buildings down to the meanest of them. With a stone building, the idea of strength and permanence is always connected.[33]

Latrobe often argued for stone. He objected when his theater in Philadelphia suffered the indignity of a wooden Corinthian colonnade with capitals made of papier-mache. At one point Jefferson proposed wooden columns in the House of Representatives, and Latrobe wrote Lenthall "the wooden column idea is one with which I never will have anything to do. On that you may rely. I will give up my office sooner than build a temple of disgrace to myself and Mr. Jefferson."[34] And throughout the construction of the Baltimore Cathedral he insisted—often against the wishes of the building committee—that appropriate materials and methods of construction be used. Latrobe's emphasis on permanence and structural integrity must have made an impression on Mills, for it became one of the pillars of his career.

The drawings for the Cathedral may have been the most complex set that Mills worked on in Latrobe's office. "The foundation story" plans were ready in early March 1806, and as Latrobe observed "of course, it was necessary to make drawings of all the upper work in order to determine the foundations."[35] He

31 BHL to RM, February 3, 1805.

32 BHL to Bishop John Carroll, April 8, 1805.

33 BHL to Bishop John Carroll, April 27, 1805 and January 28, 1806.

34 BHL to John Lenthall, November 27, 1803; Hamlin, *Latrobe*, 263.

35 BHL to Bishop John Carroll, March 6, 1806.

later spoke of having made seven different plans in all. The exact measurement of each part of the building was specified—"the length is now on the center line 154 feet 9 $\frac{1}{2}$ inches . . . radius of the sanctuary to the face of the columns 14' $\frac{1}{4}$"."[36] He sent instructions to help the committee understand the plans:

> On studying this plan you will easily understand it. The red parts of the plan represent the foundation, over which is shaded in Indian ink the plan of the body of the Church, by which means, the manner in which the super structure is supported becomes evident at one view.
>
> In one half of the plan you will find in figures all the longitudinal dimensions of the Work, on the other all the transverse dimensions. In setting out the work, you will find the following instructions useful.[37]

Latrobe gave extensive directions for laying out the foundations on the ground. An east-west center line was to be established. This line was to be subdivided into segments of various specified lengths and at the end of each segment, lines running north and south, perpendicular to the center line were to be staked out. Along these perpendiculars, points were located at stated distances from the center line, and these points marked the position of piers, footings and bearing walls. At each crucial point along both sets of lines the builder was to "drive very strong and firm oak stakes in all these central points, marking the points by small nails driven in their heads, and from these set out the whole work agreeably to written dimensions." He emphasized the "absolute necessity of minute correctness" and concluded with one of those hints which reflect experience:

> Before you begin to set out, you must make a pair of ten feet rods very accurately divided into feet and inches, and exactly of the same length. One of these rods must be deposited with the committee to serve in case of accident, the other you will use at the work. For it is a hundred to one, that if you break your rod, you will get another of precisely the same length, by any other method.[38]

Problems arose as soon as work began. The Clerk of the works, George Rohrback, and a member of the building committee, John Hillen, who was also acting as the general contractor, made alterations in the plans without consult-

36 BHL to George Rohrbach, March 8, 1806.

37 BHL to George Rohrbach, March 8, 1806.

38 BHL to George Rohrbach, March 8, 1806.

ing Latrobe. Adding insult to injury, the full committee and Bishop Carroll did little to support their architect. Hillen prepared to thicken the foundation, claiming it would not bear the weight of the walls. Latrobe met this first test tactfully by writing the bishop that "I expected such an objection. For who can think of a Cathedral and keep thick walls out of his head."[39] And he made a distinction between his own work and that of amateurs, like Hillen, who dominated architecture in America:

> The difference between a design made upon scientific principles, and one made by a happy fancy, and a knack of guessing improved by experience consists chiefly in this, that the former admits neither superfluity nor want either in its strength, or its extent, or in its decoration, while the latter, whenever it is in doubt about a sufficiency of strength, or extent, or decoration runs into superfluity.... Nothing therefore is more common than to see mechanical builders, when a great weight is borne, or a great pressure resisted, take care that their walls are big enough, well assured as they are, that too much strength does no harm.[40]

Latrobe wanted his authority confirmed and defined at the outset so that "neither my time nor my temper will be lost by arguing with mechanics about the thickness of walls or any other professional matter." And he wanted the bishop to "establish my drawings as a code of unalterable law." He requested "unlimited control over the manner of execution" and justified this by noting that "My name, my character, and of course my employment and support is now irretrievably consisting [sic] with the success of your work. Should it fail, I am ruined."[41]

Latrobe's anger and concern were prompted by a misreading of the foundation drawings: "ridiculous as it may appear...whoever has first formed the idea that the foundation walls were not solid, but consisted of arches, has studied the section of the church floor *upside down* and has mistaken the vaulted ceiling of the *crypt*...for the foundations."[42]

It was not an auspicious beginning. Having mulled the matter over for a week, Latrobe wrote Bishop Carroll:

> As to the trifling vexation which these things cause me, I ought to be ashamed of it, and in fact it is over, and I cannot resist a most hearty laugh at such blun-

39 BHL to Bishop John Carroll, March 26, 1806.

40 BHL to Bishop John Carroll, March 26, 1806.

41 BHL to Bishop John Carroll, March 26, 1806.

42 BHL to Bishop John Carroll, March 26, 1806.

ders. But to you and to the committee it is of more importance that they should not be committed, and in fact that no one capable of committing them, and who thereby has given such an indisputable evidence of incapacity should have anything to do with the work. While the thing is upon paper, no harm is done, but such blunders executed in freestone [obliterated words] the coarsest workmanship. If Rohrbach is the man, I shall never have the smallest confidence in him, nor will he deserve it.[43]

At this point Latrobe submitted a bill for reimbursement (perhaps thinking he would be compelled to resign); he noted among his expenses $52 paid to Mills as "one of the gentlemen in my office who have been employed in the drawings."[44]

With the drawings finished, work began on the Cathedral, and at the same time the "delinquency of subscribers" stopped work on the canal, so Latrobe redeployed his labor force. He dismissed the head mason at the canal, Thomas Vickers. "What use," Latrobe asked him, "is a general without an army?"[45] Louis De Mun was sent to help Lenthall with the heating of the Senate Chamber and other work in Washington, but Mills stayed with Latrobe. Taking dictation, Mills was soon maintaining the correspondence with various projects, and two of these, the fireproof Treasury wing at the White House and the plan for a lighthouse, influenced Mills' later work.

In early May 1805, Latrobe turned briefly from the canal and Cathedral in order "to overhaul" his "Washington concerns from the lighthouse at the mouth of the Mississippi to the Treasury fireproof at the President's colonnade."[46] Both projects were undertaken for Albert Gallatin, the Secretary of the Treasury under Jefferson. Gallatin requested Latrobe's opinion concerning the proper design for a lighthouse, and at the end of March 1805, Latrobe had written him that his thoughts were "now in the hands of my clerk to be copied." [47] It is possible Mills transcribed the material and working drawings as the lighthouse design evolved. For more than two years—March 1805 through May 1807—documents concerning this project passed through the office, a steady flow creating the foundation of paperwork that was an essential part of a major undertaking—questions from the client, sketches, drawings, letters to the vendors of materials and building contractors, queries concerning transportation, a discussion of funding, contract drafts, the revision of plans, the explanation of delays, and the advertisement for bids.

43 BHL to Bishop John Carroll, March 28, 1806.

44 BHL to the Trustees of the Catholic Church at Baltimore, April 13, 1806.

45 BHL to Thomas Vickers, July 23, 1805.

46 BHL to John Lenthall, May 13, 1805.

47 BHL to Albert Gallatin, March 23, 1805.

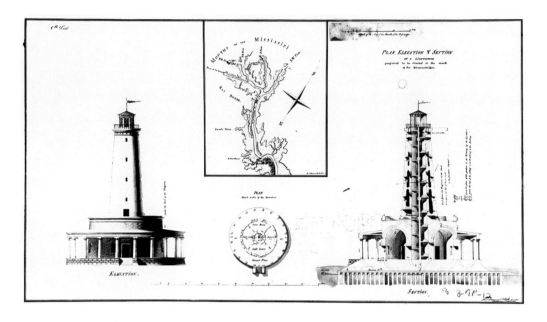

Frank's Island Lighthouse, Mississippi. Benjamin Henry Latrobe, 1805.

As a matter of routine, Mills would have handled many of these items, and the Franks Island lighthouse foreshadows his designs for the Washington Monument in Baltimore, his published plan for the Washington National Monument, and his unrealized proposal for a national mausoleum. Like Mills' designs for the monuments, the lighthouse was a hollow shaft with an internal staircase rising out of an architectural base. Specifications for the fireproof masonry staircase inside the lighthouse could serve without alteration for the construction of similar staircases years later by Mills in his monuments and other buildings.

Mills viewed designs as an inventory to be adapted and re-used. He did this with courthouses, jails, marine hospitals, and customhouses. His tendency to copy his work was part of his habit—whenever possible—of treating individual buildings as part of a larger system. The use of prototypical plans lay at the core of his national vision, and this approach may have owed something to a lesson drawn from Latrobe's lighthouse. Latrobe felt the plan might be useful at Cape Hatteras as well as the mouth of the Mississippi. Going further, he obtained a list of all the beacon sites in the country, apparently hoping to participate in the development of a national network of navigational aids. As it happened, Latrobe himself did not build the lighthouse (it was erected by his son Henry in 1816), nor was it adopted as a national standard. But Mills, in addition to echoing its form in major monuments, later wrote extensively on navigation, published the first complete guidebook to American lighthouses and seamarks, and made good use of the idea of developing prototypical designs.[48]

No sooner was the lighthouse design completed than difficulties arose concerning authorization of contracts. These problems dragged on and construction did not begin until years after Mills left Latrobe's office. But at the time, Latrobe anticipated going to work at once and obtained a federal contract to survey the site and test the soil. The job was awarded to Louis DeMun. With mixed emotions Mills must have watched DeMun prepare for this responsibility. Latrobe assembled the necessary instruments, provided a refresher course in surveying, drew up notes on a tool designed to bore into the earth to take subterranean soil samples. And when the time came for DeMun to go, Latrobe helped him get passage on a navy vessel. Mills, by this time, was looking forward to similar help with his own career.

The Louisiana project assumed an added dimension through Latrobe's relationship with Aaron Burr, who was then spinning a web of intrigue about the western lands. While the office was working on the lighthouse, Burr asked Latrobe to work on a canal around the falls of the Ohio River near Louisville. Latrobe approached contractors, but was reluctant to leave his work in the east. Within months the Ohio canal proved to be a chimera, for Burr never obtained financing. Nonetheless, Latrobe felt obligated, for Burr had purportedly recommended him for work in New York, and when Burr asked him to design a shallow draft river boat, Latrobe sketched a New York periauger, approximately eighty feet long and eighteen feet in beam. He gave Burr six copies of this plan, noting "Mr. Mills and Mr. DeMun each have made three."[49] Soon thereafter DeMun was off to the Mississippi, and within months Burr was charged with treason.

When the scandal broke out in New Orleans, a warrant was issued for DeMun's arrest. (He was never prosecuted.) Latrobe was subpoenaed at Burr's trial, but was never called to testify. In the aftermath of Burr's downfall, Latrobe wrote influential people asserting his ignorance of whatever scheme Burr had in mind, but more than once he and his draftsmen must have wondered what role their little flotilla was meant to play in the western waters.

With DeMun gone, Mills became Latrobe's senior assistant and was put in charge of several projects in Philadelphia. He moved there in 1807, and for

48 Hamlin, 293. Mills' book on navigational aids is discussed in chapter VI below. His use of prototypical designs is discussed in chapters V and VI.

49 Hamlin, 222.

almost two years served as Latrobe's Clerk of the Works. The first of these projects was the William Waln House on the southeast corner of Chestnut and Seventh streets. Two years earlier Latrobe had received a letter from J. S. Wilcocks requesting a design for a townhouse. He typically avoided private clients, but when he learned this request was made on behalf of Wilcox's sister Mary, "more loved and esteemed by Mrs. Latrobe than any other of her friends," he complied.[50] Mary Wilcox was then engaged to marry William Waln, a wealthy China merchant, and Latrobe found that in this case sentiment was bolstered by his desire "to see a rational house built in Philadelphia."

Nonetheless, he carefully spelled out to Waln how an architect should conduct private practice. First he would submit a "book" of "two designs in order to give you a choice of two perfectly different modes of arrangement." If either were chosen he would make "such alterations as you may point out to me," and then produce a set of detailed working drawings. Latrobe stressed to Waln, as he had to Bishop Carroll, that "I hope you will see how necessary it is to my reputation, as I assure you it is to your interests, that I should control its execution and especially draw your contracts, in order to prevent unnecessary expense, the blame of which will inevitably fall upon my shoulders."[51] In subsequent letters Latrobe reiterated that design control protected both client and architect; furthermore, he said, any lack of authority would cause untold problems.

Construction began on the Waln House in the spring of 1807, and Latrobe sent Mills to monitor "the execution and the charges" and to certify the quality of the materials and labor. He also arranged for Mills to serve as Clerk of the Works for the Bank of Philadelphia, and his description to the bank directors of Mills' role provides a detailed view of this final phase of Mills' training:

> I mentioned the necessity of appointing a Clerk of the Works, whose duty it is to be constantly on the spot, to see that the contracts are faithfully fulfilled, to watch over the progress of the work, and take care that the different contractors are ready to do their part of the work at proper times, so as to prevent collision between them and delay in the building, to give from the office drawings the detailed and full sized drawings to each, to set out the work and to keep such accounts as grow out of the undertaking. He is also to report and explain to the committee the progress and the object of the work during its execution, and in fact, represent the interest of the institution, perpetually and on the spot. For his conduct and skill the architect is in all respects

50 BHL to James S. Wilcocks, March 12, 1805.

51 BHL to Willliam Waln, May 6, 1805.

responsible. At the Bank of Pennsylvania, the salary of the Clerk of the Works was 600 dollars per Annum, at the Waterworks 900 dollars. A less salary would be proper at the Philadelphia Bank, and the Gentleman I formerly proposed to you, Mr. Mills, is willing to do this duty for 450 dollars per Annum. Mr. Mills has been 4 years in my office, and is perfectly competent to the duty. He does not depend entirely for support on his industry, having a competence of his own, and therefore is willing to devote himself to your service for this compensation, for the sake of the experience he will gain in the work.... I have delayed this appointment as long as possible chiefly because I can ill spare the assistance of Mr. Mills in my own office.... But the state of the work already requires constant inspection, and I respectfully request you to decide on this point.[52]

With Mills running what amounted to a branch office, the nature of his relationship with Latrobe began to change. Now Mills had to interpret the drawings, discuss things with clients, and sometimes make decisions without being able to consult Latrobe, and Latrobe was not always pleased. For example, concerning another residence, he wrote Mills:

The manner in which you propose to finish the windows of Captain Meany's dining room appears to me very unfortunate. I cannot possibly imagine what can occasion the necessity of a circular head to the center part of the Venetian Window. It is an increase of expense, a loss of light, and what is worse it is absurd in its construction." Or again, "panels externally in brickwork, as proposed in Captain Meany's house are merely receptacles for dust and dirt, which is washed by the rain over the face of the wall, and which by degrees accumulates so as to produce a crop of fine green moss; and that they besides are so many means of soaking the wall with water, and bursting off the plastering by the frost. They are therefore inadmissible." On this job Latrobe finally lost patience and wrote Mills that "Captain Meany must do just as he pleases about his house, I care very little about its appearance. Please tell him that the design I made is I think the best thing he can make of it. But if anything else pleases him better, I hope he will adopt it.[53]

The Bank of Philadelphia (1807–1808) was the largest commission Mills directed for Latrobe. From Washington, Latrobe sent long letters and sketches,

52 BHL to President and Directors of the Bank of Philadelphia, May 25, 1807.

53 BHL to RM, July 2, 1807.

and in Philadelphia Mills took charge of the construction. It is a credit to them both that the Bank—full of intricate Gothic detail—was completed on schedule and within budget. In many respects the Bank was especially meaningful for Latrobe. His Gothic proposal for the Cathedral had been rejected; the Bank of Philadelphia, as a new rival to the Bank of Pennsylvania, which Latrobe had earlier designed in a well-received Neoclassical style, suggested a different stylistic identity; and the Gothic Style reminded him of home. In a letter to his brother in England, Latrobe said he never expected to see England again and "your fondness for Gothic Architecture has induced me to erect a little Gothic building in this city, the Philadelphia Bank. Externally it will not be ugly, but internally I plan it to be a little cabinet. The board room is a Gothic Octagon Chapter house with one pillar in the center. You shall have the drawings in the course of the next 2 months, and when I publish the works, I shall inscribe this plan to you." He was proud of the boardroom, and told Mills it was "the handsomest thing I ever designed." Latrobe confidently told George Clymer, the president of the bank, that he would "predict that the Board room...will acquire more fame than any other rooms in Philadelphia."[54]

The bank was built of brick with granite trim. Its facade was symmetrically arranged with a central entry, two pinnacles, battlements at the cornice line and pointed arches capping all doors and windows. He sent Mills detailed explanations for the construction of elliptical forms. Molds for intricate plaster items—bosses, "roses," and the pendant in the lobby were made in Washington and Baltimore by Andrei and Franzoni, Italians employed by Latrobe at the Capitol.[55]

Everything went smoothly until the very end, when an argument erupted between Latrobe and two contractors. According to Latrobe, they "considered the profession of an architect as an intrusion on their province as builders." Latrobe resigned, but was prevailed upon to return. Immediately thereafter, he was struck by two tragedies: his friend and Clerk at the Capitol, John Lenthall, was killed by the collapse of a masonry vault, and Mrs. Latrobe gave birth to a still-born daughter. Then the directors of the bank delayed his final payment. He wrote a friend that it was an "irritating and humiliating...injustice" and that he had "been treated...as if I possessed neither knowledge of my profession nor integrity."[56] None of the records suggest that Mills, as Latrobe's representative, was drawn into the disputes, but tension must have been palpable as work drew to a close. It sullied what should have been a happy ending.

54 BHL to George Clymer, August 25, 1807.

55 BHL to RM, April 17, 1808; BHL to William Thackara, April 21, 1808.

56 BHL to Samuel Hodgdon, August 26, 1808.

Although he owed Latrobe a great deal, Mills was growing restless. He was in his late twenties and wanted to establish a family and career, and he was in love.

On a sweltering Sunday in July 1800, after church near the Capitol, he had met Eliza Barnwell Smith. When they met, she was sixteen, attractive, petite, with dark hair and dancing eyes. She had the soft accent and social ease of the Virginia gentry. Her home was Hackwood Park near Winchester in the Blue Ridge, but her father, General John Smith, brought the family to Washington when he came to serve in the House of Representatives. They often stayed with Joseph Nourse, who was Eliza's godfather and uncle, her mother's brother.

Although Eliza would later write of their first meeting, their frequent correspondence appears to have begun in 1805, and their protracted courtship was conducted largely by mail. They both saved letters, and the collection offers a two-point perspective, an in-depth glimpse of their anguish and anticipation. From circa May 1806 until their marriage (November 15, 1808), the correspondence records pendulum-like swings of emotion between a fear of rejection and the elation of affection. The prose trembles with the heightened sensitivity of courtship: meanings are attached to casual phrases; circumstances are mulled over and assume unwarranted significance; there is an evolution of tone and content as their relationship deepens. They become increasingly open and forthright and move away from stylistic formula. An anecdotal record of little things emerges: conversations at table, social plans, the demeanor of the postman, the opinions of relatives, and the impact of Mills' professional prospects on his private life.

Custom dictated that Mills and Eliza needed her father's blessing, and this seemed an insurmountable obstacle, for Mills had little money and no secure employment, and nobody in the General's circle knew Mills' family. To marry Eliza, he needed work and references that would impress General Smith.

Lancaster-Schuylkill Bridge. Lewis Wernwag, engineer, and Robert Mills, architect of cladding and toll house, 1813–1814. Engraving by J.G. Martins.

CHAPTER THREE

Philadelphia

1808–1812

A COMMISSION FOR A jail helped Mills leave Latrobe and marry Eliza Barnwell Smith. While visiting Charleston in 1806, Mills learned the governor of South Carolina was urging the legislature to create a penitentiary. Acting quickly, before returning to Philadelphia, he submitted plans and offered to obtain information about prisons in other states. He wrote Jefferson and Latrobe seeking advice on penitentiaries and sent drawings of the proposed prison to Jefferson. Mills used this correspondence to obtain a letter of introduction from Jefferson.

Capitol Hill Washington Hill Octr 3rd 1806
Thomas Jefferson, President of the United States
City Washington

I take the liberty of presenting Mr. Jefferson...the drawings accompanying this, being designs for a penitentiary house, which have been laid before the governor of South Carolina and met with his approbation's (sic), and which the next legislature of that state will take into consideration for execution. Your acquaintance with architecture will preclude the necessity of a further explanation of the designs than what is laid down in the drawings. I therefore will not take up your time on this head....

I will intrude myself no longer than to make a request of Mr. J. My time admits at present of taking a little recreation excursion into the country, and which my health in a measure calls for. As in every species of amusement I take, I endeavor to combine edification therewith & in the one before me have laid out a route that I trust will [?] this to my mind. My design is to go into the country to Winchester in VA to cross from that to Harper's Ferry or to the [passage] of the Potomac thro' the Blue Ridge of which you have given so sublime & fascinating a description, and to return (God willing) by the way of Hagar's and Fredericktown to the City. The favor I would request of you Sir, is, that you would honor me with a letter to Gen. John Smith who resides in Winchester (a representative in Congress from that place) and to any gentleman at the U.S. works at Harper's Ferry you may think proper. My going out a stranger into the country, and the diffidence of my nature, would tend to place me in a very awkward situation, and would prevent me from reaping that benefit I should otherwise, were I acquainted. It is this that emboldens me to solicit the favor of a few lines of recommendation to the above gentleman. Mr. Smith being a public character I could mention him to you more Particularly....[1]

Mills later wrote Jefferson that "we stand indebted to you" for the introduction. Following his visit to Eliza's home, their correspondence became less guarded as they waited for the South Carolina legislature to act. A study committee praised Mills' plans, but the legislature rejected their report and chose to increase the use of corporal punishment instead of erecting a prison.

Visiting Charleston that spring, Mills raised $5,000 by selling three houses he had inherited from his father.[2] This simultaneously provided money to establish a household and severed ties with home. South Carolina was now the scene of several disappointments, and he took his money and sought his future elsewhere. Judging from Eliza's letters, he must have kept his disappointment about the legislature to himself, for two months after he had returned to Philadelphia, she wrote: "Have you succeeded in your expectation of business in that country [South Carolina]? I rather suppose not from your silence on the subject. The desire you expressed to obtain it, and the society of my dear Friend would alone have reconciled me to the distance."[3] Mills responded with a letter which juxtaposes—in a breathless rush—the prison and their marriage bed:

My mind, as you may reasonably suppose feels more and more anxious every day, to be settled, and to claim my "sweet mountain girl" to cheer me in the scene of domestic life. I still am in doubt where it would best suit my plans of

1 RM to TJ, October 3, 1806; see RM to TJ, June 4, 1810, PRM 0254.

2 Charleston County Register of Mesne Conveyance, Deeds, 1806-1807, T-7, 298-300, Robert Mills to Thomas Mills.

3 EBS to RM, February 27, 1808.

professional emolument to become resident. My desires tend to the place I now am at [Philadelphia] but [I] am dubious of success. I got a letter a few days ago from one of the commissioners appointed by the Legislature of S. Carolina on the subject of the Penitentiary who remarked that "much business of an unusual and unexpected sort prevented that of the Penitentiary from being taken up the last session, (which adjourned on that account to May next when it is expected twill come fully before the house)." Thus you see my dearest E. how things stand relative to us. If you think proper it would not be amiss for us to arrange matters relative to our house & its conveniences. As you are much the best judge of what is proper, will you be so kind as to devote a little of your time to giving me information on the subject? In respect to beds do you not think (as well as on the score of cleanliness and goodness) that these had better be obtained up about your neighborhood? The feathers mostly used in cities by the upholsters are taken from old beds bought up at vendues, they sometimes mix with them new feathers but the proportion is not very great.[4]

Several months after the Carolina legislature decided not to build a prison, the Freeholders of Burlington County, New Jersey accepted Mills' plan for "A Debtor's Gaol and Work-House for Felons."[5] This commission was a milestone for Mills. It was his first major work as he was leaving Latrobe, and his first secular, institutional building. The materials he prepared for this jail are more thorough than any that survive from this stage of his career. The drawings include eight plans, four elevations, and two sections. Mills bound the drawings with a descriptive essay addressed to the building committee which paraphrases and expands his letters to Governor Hamilton of South Carolina.

The essay presents the rationale for the plan and contains a descriptive tour written in the present tense to engage the reader's imagination: "We enter the building (after ascending a flight of steps) thro' a strong door way into the vestibule or waiting Hall. Before us is the keeper's office." Mills walks the reader through the building and points outs how the plan promotes health, safety and efficient operation. He discusses the "principles on which prisons should be instituted," the first of which is "strength and permanency," which requires construction "distinct from a common house." He then describes fire-proof masonry vaulting (the hallways are barrel vaults, and perpendicular to them spring the vaulted ceilings of cells, offices and communal rooms).[6]

4 RM to EBS, March 9, 1808.

5 Reproduced in G.J. Giger, *A Model Jail of the Olden Time: Designs for a "Debtor's Gaol and Work-House for Felons" for Burlington County, State of New Jersey, by Robert Mills, Architect, Philadelphia, May, 1808* (New York: Russell Sage, 1928); see also PRM 6039, 0233.

6 Giger, *A Model Jail of the Olden Time: Designs for a "Debtor's Gaol and Work-House for Felons.*

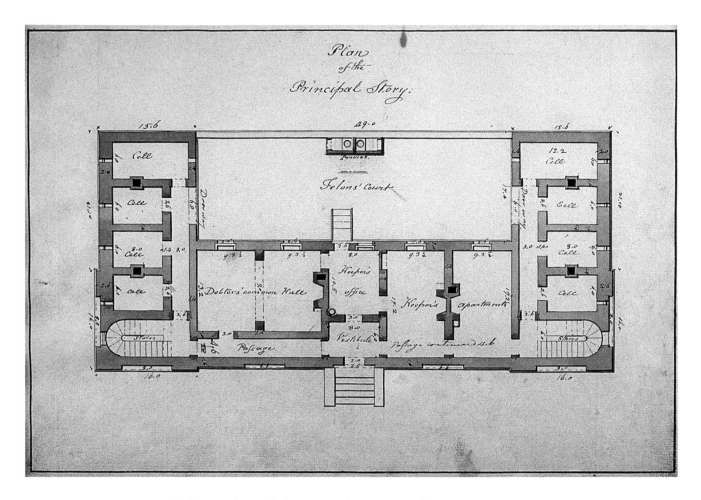

Burlington County Jail. ABOVE: *plan;* BELOW: *elevations.*

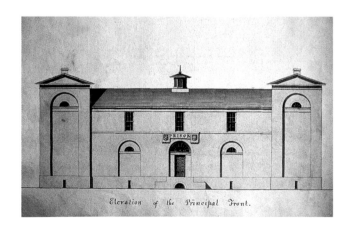

General section from East to West, thro' the Debtors' & Keeper's apartments.

Burlington County Jail, section.

Masonry vaulting was unusual in America, and Mills would advocate it throughout his career. He had seen Thomas Vickers build a simple, segmental arch over the fifteen foot wide feeder canal at Elk Mills, Delaware (1804); he had observed vaulting erected by Latrobe at the Treasury Office wing of the White House (1805–1806) and the Capitol; and as Latrobe's Clerk of the Works, Mills had directed construction of the elliptical, segmental arches (1807) at the Bank of Philadelphia.

Beyond its plan and structure, the jail foreshadowed the fact that utilitarian public buildings would be a major pillar of his career, for despite the fact that he is typically remembered for participating in the design or construction of half a dozen major projects in Washington, D.C., much of his work entailed the design or construction of smaller public buildings—courthouses, jails, customhouses, and hospitals.

Mills had corresponded with Latrobe about the South Carolina jail, and aspects of Mills' jail resemble Latrobe's first major work in America, the Virginia Penitentiary in Richmond. Both had multi-storied wings embracing an exercise yard; the courtyard elevations of both had loggias. (The Mount Holly

ABOVE AND OPPOSITE:
Burlington County Jail.

loggias were deleted from the final plan—perhaps the climate made them impractical.) Administrative functions were centralized in both plans, and both used blind arches to express closure and confinement. Latrobe's plan was based on drawings and letters that Jefferson sent from Paris. Jefferson said his proposal for a Virginia Penitentiary was based on a published prison by Pierre Gabriel Bugniet of Lyon.[7] So by way of Jefferson and Latrobe, Mills' Mount Holly jail had a cosmopolitan pedigree.

While the jail was getting underway, Mills was readying a home in the city. He and Eliza wrote about painting, furnishings, and suitable servants. In October he went to Hackwood to marry. The stage for Georgetown started before dawn, and jostling along in the dark there was ample time to think about his prospective in-laws. Eliza's mother, Animus or Anna Bull Smith, was a forceful woman. She managed the plantation when General Smith was in Washington. She arranged family vacations to the medicinal springs and was outspoken about the affairs of those around her. She disliked Latrobe (whom she had met socially), offered advice about deportment to Eliza and spoke of politics with her husband. Except for short social outings, Anna Smith rarely traveled beyond her sphere of influence. During a visit to Hackwood, Mills had witnessed her temper—a scene that had left her embarrassed, Eliza in tears, and Mills discomfited. But he knew she lived with the stress of bereavement, for she lost four children. And although she sought solace in religion, the trauma of these deaths affected her deeply, and Hackwood became a haven for children in need. She raised fifty foster children there before her death in 1831. In this bustling household she orchestrated events to coincide with the agricultural and political comings and goings of her husband.[8]

General Smith was an impressive—even forbidding—figure. He had been a justice for the Royal government and fought in Dunmore's war against the Indians. During the Revolution he was responsible for many Scotch and Hessian prisoners; after the war he was elected to the Virginia Senate. Now he was a fixture in the national House of Representatives, serving from the Winchester district, 1801–1815. He built Hackwood before the Revolution of limestone quarried on the site. General Smith moved in influential circles and counted Patrick Henry, James Monroe, Henry Clay, and Henry Lee among his acquaintances. Perhaps he considered Mills a poor match for Eliza, for he had not encouraged the young man as a suitor. It would take time for Mills and his father-in-law to feel at ease with one another.

7 John M. Bryan, "Robert Mills, Benjamin Henry Latrobe, Thomas Jefferson, and the South Carolina Penitentiary Project, 1806–1808," *South Carolina Historical Magazine* 85, no. 1 (January, 1984): 1–21.

8 For Anna Smith's lament for her dead children see AS to EBSM, n.d. [circa 1811], in the Richard X. Evans collection, Georgetown University.

Whatever Mills' emotions were during the three-day journey to Hackwood, his protracted courtship was coming to an end, and on October 15, 1808, he and Eliza were married. Although he professed to be shy and retiring, Mills now had a reputation and a letter of introduction from Jefferson; he could point to the Burlington County Jail and to his work for Latrobe. His early career (circa 1808–1815) was productive. He continued to work for Latrobe at the Bank of Philadelphia (1807–1808) and supervise the construction of a residence designed by Latrobe for John Markoe on Chestnut Street (1808–1810). But he became increasingly absorbed in his own affairs. Soon he was responsible for another circular church, the Sansom Street Baptist Church (1808–1811), a meeting hall, the Washington Hall (1813–1816), an eleven-unit housing project, the Franklin Row (1809), wings for Independence Hall (1809–1812) and the cladding and a toll house for the Schuylkill Bridge (1812). He also became involved in the Pennsylvania Academy of Fine Arts and the Society of Artists of the United States. Beyond Philadelphia, construction began on his Monumental Church in Richmond (1811–1814) and the First Presbyterian Church in Augusta, Georgia (1807–1812).

Marriage did not alter his professional schedule. He apparently had an office at home, for clients and tradesmen called for him there. Eliza ran the house, but Mills managed, or mismanaged, the money. (His failure to discuss their financial situation with Eliza would cause the only recurring bitter note in their domestic correspondence which spans some forty years.) During the hottest months—May through October—she took their children, Sarah Zane (1811–1894) and Jacqueline Smith Mills (1814–1859), to Hackwood to escape the fever-ridden city. Mills typically remained behind, tended to business and received long letters about the childhood illnesses and housekeeping concerns.[9]

The mail often brought queries and instructions from Latrobe, and through these we can trace Mills' growing independence. The letters concerning the Markoe House are a case in point—some thirty letters spanning several years. After the death of John Lenthall (1808), Latrobe was increasingly confined to Washington. He worked on Markoe's drawings for a year, and work on the house began in the spring of 1809, for Mills checked the configuration of the cellar walls in May. As the end of the year approached, the walls were up, but the house was not habitable; questions arose concerning the complicated stairways and pipes in the watercloset. Latrobe, in Washington, was frustrated to find that Mills was off at Hackwood for the Christmas season. Construction

9 Other authors have called the eldest daughter Sarah Jane, but she was named after a family friend, Sarah Zane; see PRM 0243, 0471, and so forth.

73

dragged on that winter and spring. By mid-summer Latrobe, becoming impatient, wrote Mills:

> I have not a line from you since I left you and as the time draws nearer I begin to be exceedingly anxious that Mr. Markoe should not be even in appearance likely to be disappointed of his expectations as to the completion of his house in time for the accouchement of Mrs. Markoe, which is expected in November.[10]

And Latrobe wrote Markoe:

> As soon as I hear from Mills I will again write to you. In the meantime pray assure Mrs. Markoe that no exertion on my part shall be wanting to enable me to bow to her most respectfully in her own little dressing room in full view of the geraniums, Oleanders, Jessamines and sensitive plants that decorate her balcony.[11]

At the end of the summer Latrobe urged Markoe to:

> ...peep through the telescope of hope, into the fair prospect of the accomplishment of all your wishes and promises, and hear in advance the first squall of your fourth baby, half drowned by the rattle of coaches of your Chestnut Street neighbors. For not withstanding my believing that the pious Robert Mills is not absolutely the most minute inspector into the proceedings of your workmen, as in good faith and consideration of good pay he ought to be, yet his answers to my string of queries are so detailed that it would have been more trouble to have invented the state of things he has reported than to have copied them from observation. From the actual appearance of forwardness which he minutely reports, I take for granted that you will certainly be able to move into the house in October.[12]

But Christmas 1810 found Mills still supervising the installation of iron railings at the Markoe House, and Latrobe sent instructions on riveting and leading the balusters and cap. That winter the Markoe family moved into the upper two stories, but they had to use the back stairs, for the front entry and principal rooms below were unfinished. In February, the job was complete. The

10 BHL to RM, July 25, 1810.

11 BHL to John Markoe, July 29, 1810.

12 BHL to John Markoe, August 10, 1810.

 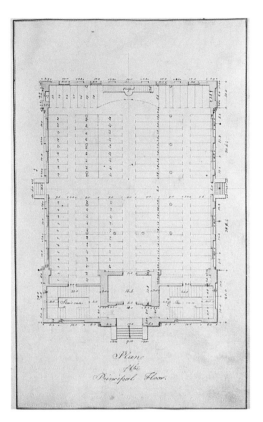

First Presbyterian Church, Augusta, Georgia. Robert Mills, architect, 1807–1812.

workmen packed their tools and departed, and the dust settled. Latrobe's last letter to Mills on the subject conveyed the client's satisfaction and several personal notes, indications that although this project may have strained, it had not destroyed, their relationship. In years to come they would correspond, but Mills never again worked closely with or for Latrobe.

Some months before leaving Latrobe, Mills responded to an advertisement for design proposals for a Presbyterian church in Augusta, Georgia. He obtained this commission in 1807, but construction only began in 1809, and the building was not put into service until 1812. The work was underway during Mills' early years in Philadelphia, and it is doubtful he ever visited the site. This is notable, for the Charleston projects and Latrobe's difficulties with remote business prompted Mills to devise a procedure for distant projects. For the Augusta Presbyterians he

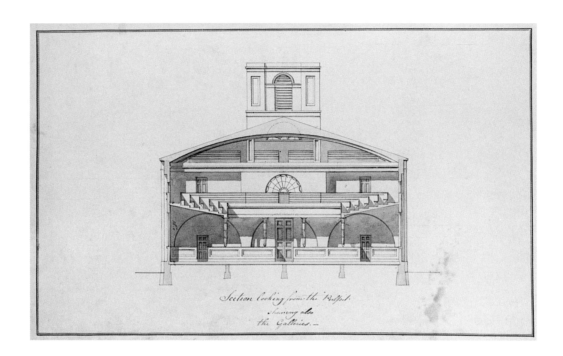

Section looking from the Pulpit, showing also the Galleries. —

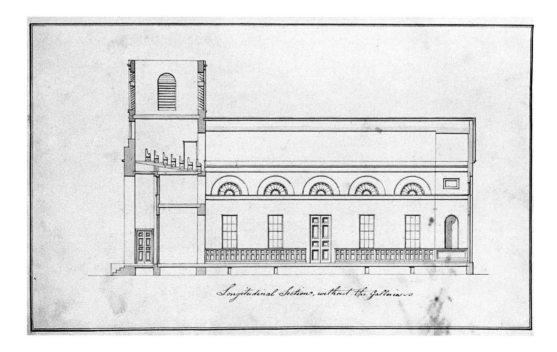

Longitudinal Section, without the Galleries.

First Presbyterian Church.

prepared and bound a set of eleven drawings, a short essay for the Elders and a set of notes addressed to the craftsmen—the stone mason, carpenter and joiner, plasterer, glazier, blacksmith, and painter. It was in effect a builders' manual.[13]

Mills did not insist on design control or the appointment of his own clerk of the works or the right to review and approve the contracts and budget. On the contrary, his admonitions are diffident. For example, he advises that "if you have any kind of freestone in your neighborhood it would be advisable to make use of it for the sills of your doors and windows." He gently notes the blind arches within the elevations will prove as cheap as a common wall "because of their rendering unnecessary a large mass of material which would be requisite to fill up the voids they make."[14] Throughout the presentation he never makes demands.

Latrobe would have considered this unprofessionally lax, perhaps expedient in obtaining the work, but fraught with the danger of uncontrolled construction, and he had pointed this out to the board of trustees of the South Carolina College and reiterated it directly to Mills when reviewing the acoustical problems at the Circular Church in Charleston. The Baltimore Cathedral correspondence—which Mills knew—was studded with Latrobe's insistence on professional prerogatives. But Mills ignored or rejected the lesson of these examples.

Mills already had reason to know that meddlesome amateurs threatened professional standards. But throughout his career he seldom asserted himself or complained. Certainly he did not make a habit of resigning in a huff as Latrobe did at some point in virtually every major project. Instead, Mills was instinctively pliant and diplomatic, traits that would have both positive and negative effects on his career.

The elevations of the Augusta Church show Mills still relied stylistically upon Latrobe, for the church resembles an amalgam of Latrobe's unrealized plan for a hotel and theater complex in Richmond and his Virginia State Penitentiary. In the evolution of Mills' taste, the Augusta church stands between the John's Island elevation and the facade of the Burlington Jail. Two structural features of this church are notable. First, plans for the foundations specify inverted arches below grade carrying the piers flanking the recessed arches. This method of transferring the load with reversed arches was the system used in Latrobe's plans for the Mississippi lighthouse and under the crossing of the Baltimore Cathedral. And secondly, the specifications for the coved ceiling of the Augusta church call for Delorme-type ribs to serve as rafters.

13 The manuscript "Designs for Augusta Church, State of Georgia by Robert Mills of South Carolina Architect. Philadelphia—July 22d 1807" is owned by the First Presbyterian Church, Augusta, Georgia; a transcription appears in Liscombe, *Church Architecture of Robert Mills*, 47–53.

14 Liscombe, *Church Architecture of Robert Mills*, 47–53.

While the Augusta Church and the Burlington County Jail were underway, Mills designed a large, speculative housing project for Captain John Meany, whose house he had superintended for Latrobe. As conceived, Franklin Row (1809) was to consist of forty-two three-story dwellings disposed as "four blocks of buildings" occupying a lot on 9th Street between Locust and Walnut Streets in Philadelphia.[15]

In 1811 Mills exhibited the project in the annual exhibition of the Philadelphia Society of Artists. His drawing presented two alternatives for the principle facade, an end elevation, and a ground plan. The three facades, and the design ultimately built, are dominated by the repeated use of the Adam Style recessed arches framing entries and windows on the principal floor. The repeated arches made each block appear to be a single unit. Mills favored a design that grouped the entries into pairs, allowing the arches framing the entries to equal the width of the arched triple windows; the net result resembled a shallow arcade. The second proposal alternated single entries with triple windows, each framed by an arch. This pattern was not as powerful.

The exhibited designs were not used for Franklin Row. Captain Meany or Mills opted for the single-entry version with the arch over the doorway being narrower and lower than the arches framing the tripartite windows. This alternation in height and width created a staggered impression—like a row of working pistons—and destroyed the illusion of an arcade. This unfortunate result was furthered by removing basement windows which had contributed to the sense of an arcade springing from the ground. A final change, the insertion of another tripartite window at the second floor, destroyed the horizontal harmony. These changes admitted more light to the front room on the second floor, and that is probably why they were made.

Floor plans were apparently uniform throughout the project: the entry, hall, and staircase were on the right; two rooms on each floor opened onto the hall; the kitchen and dining rooms were located in the basement. Each dwelling was twenty-three feet wide and forty feet deep. There was nothing innovative in these ground plans. Indeed, a number of similar projects were readily available to Mills and Meany. In Philadelphia, Latrobe and Thomas Carstairs had erected the Sansom Street Row (1800–1803); there were speculative rows of dwellings on Pine Street (1805–1809), Spruce Street (1804–1808), and the York Row on Walnut Street (1807–1808). None of these used recessed planes or large forms to create a visual unity, in this respect Mills' proposal for the Franklin Row was a departure from the norm.

15 Kenneth Ames, "Robert Mills and the Philadelphia Row House," *Journal of the Society of Architectural Historians*, XXVII, 2 (May, 1968): 141.

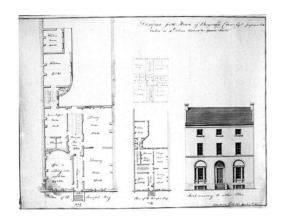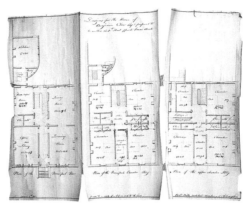

Benjamin Chew House, Philadelphia. Robert Mills, architect, 1810.

Our understanding of Mills' residential work is limited by the loss of private records. One of his most thoroughly documented houses is the Benjamin Chew residence, a product of his early career in Philadelphia. In April 1810, Mills drew plans for a Philadelphia row house for Chew "to be erected on 4th between Walnut 48 and Spruce Streets."[16] It was designed as a complex, three-story dwelling. The facade, forty-four feet wide, featured a central entry with a delicately detailed fanlight balanced by a pair of triple windows framed in recessed arches. Much of the facade was predictable: the diminution of the windows on the second and third stories, a simple string course and cornice. The interior, on the other hand, reflected the energy Mills invested in the undertaking. Several versions of the plans survive.

The Chew House was to be fifty-four feet six inches deep with four principle rooms on each story grouped around a central corridor. The plans are notable for the incorporation of a fireproof cabinet in the "office & library," a generous closet, or "recess for clothes & hats &c" in the "principal staircase," as well as other storage closets throughout the house. Two of the plans suggest that the office or library and the staircase might each have one hemispherical wall; all the plans call for the central corridor to be well lighted and end in a rear entry. The service wing is connected to the body of the house by a narrow hyphen, which contains a private stairway, a separate service entrance, and provides space for windows facing the courtyard. In the angle between the connecting hyphen and the service wing he placed a bow with a pantry next to the

16 Benjamin Chew Papers, Historical Society of Pennsylvania. Four sheets of drawings and related documents make this one of the most thoroughly documented example of Mills' domestic work.

kitchen with a bathroom above it on the chamber level. Two of the drawings show this bathroom. In one of these the bathtub is separated by a non-bearing partition wall from the toilet. Several of the floor plans show revisions in Mills' hand, and there are measured drawings for a "Coach house and Stables."

Construction began almost at once. Bills and receipts note that lime, brick, and stone were delivered to the site during the month of April 1810. By late summer the windows were ready to be glazed with glass from Boston (Harrison Grey Otis assisted Benjamin Chew in arranging the purchase). The interior was being plastered in August; hardware was installed in September; and this was followed by the fitting of guttering, marble mantels, bell pulls, and "one copper bath kettle."

Although the construction went smoothly, Mills had problems with the client. His bill was rejected, and Chew wrote that $160 was "very widely differing from my own sentiment and expectations" and implied he never requested such an elaborate plan and suggested submitting the dispute to three arbitrators.

Mills responded with his most forceful written comment about his profession:

> To give you a general view of the basis upon which the reasonableness of my charge is exhibited, I would at present observe, that the commission allowed architects in England—1st on the whole expense incurred in executing their designs is 5 per cent. 2d—for furnishing drawings & descriptions alone, without any further direction of the work either personally or by letter—2 1/2 per cent, upon the estimate whether the work be executed or not. All the English architects of eminence charge 5 guineas per day, & no surveyor or measurer less than one guinea per day. My charge upon the estimate of your house does not amount to one per cent.
>
> For designing more common houses than yours I have been allowed 100$ to 150$—and I should presume that in a house of the magnitude of yours, that the arrangement of its plan for comfort, convenience & beauty was worth at least 150$ or that the profession of an architect was not deserving of attention. Your profession Sir of the Law above all others must point out to you, what ought to be the reward attached to the practice of a profession that required an expensive education....
>
> I may venture to assert that no profession requires a more expensive education than that of the architect. If in the practice of this profession he is to receive his reward merely in proportion to the bodily labor he bestows, he had

better quit the profession & pursue in preference the meanest mechanical employment....

I should Sir feel no hesitation in referring our difference to two or more persons, if competent judges settlement of could be found to undertake it. But as my profession is novel in this country, and there are no cases that can be referred to for decision, it is impossible that a correct view can be taken of the subject to found a correct opinion.[17]

Chew finally paid Mills $100.55.

Fortunately, there were public successes to offset the argument with Benjamin Chew. During his years in Philadelphia, Mills completed three churches similar to the Circular Church in Charleston. For the Baptist Congregation on Sansom Street, he designed his second round or "auditorium" church—a rotunda ninety feet in diameter with walls fifty feet high and a low, saucer dome with a cupola "upwards of twenty feet in diameter." It was designed to seat 2,500 people. On the exterior, "in front and rear of the rotunda, square projections, of sixty feet extent, come forward; that in the rear, to provide space for vestry rooms, rising only one story; that in the front, to accommodate the stair cases of the galleries, rising on a marble basement to the common height of the walls. The front projection comes to the line of the street, in the form of wings, separated by [a] colonnade, and are crowned by two belfries or cupolas."[18]

This facade, with its pair of ionic columns in antis, was notable for its severity. Mills juxtaposed the deeply shadowed portico with broad areas of specifically defined planes. The protruding bays containing staircases were articulated with recessed blind arches like the Burlington Jail facade. Above the columns both frieze and parapet were unadorned and emphatically horizontal.

Local antecedents for the Sansom Street facade included the Waterworks (1797) by Latrobe and the Academy of Fine Arts (1806), attributed to John Dorsey, both of which were domed, centrally planned, and had similar porticoes. Within the Sansom Street portico, doors opened left and right into the stairways. In the center was a "great Venetian door into the grand aisle."[19] The pulpit, opposite the entry, was raised to the level of the balcony as it had been in his southern proposals.

Only two working drawings by Mills have survived, and one of these depicts the Sansom Street Church dome. First and foremost, this drawing was intended to be intelligible: ribs, purlins, and the framing of the monitor are all

17 RM to Benjamin Chew, August 2, 1810.

18 James Mease, *The Picture of Philadelphia* (Philadelphia: B.&T. Kite, 1811), 326–327.

19 Mease, *The Picture of Philadelphia*, 326–327.

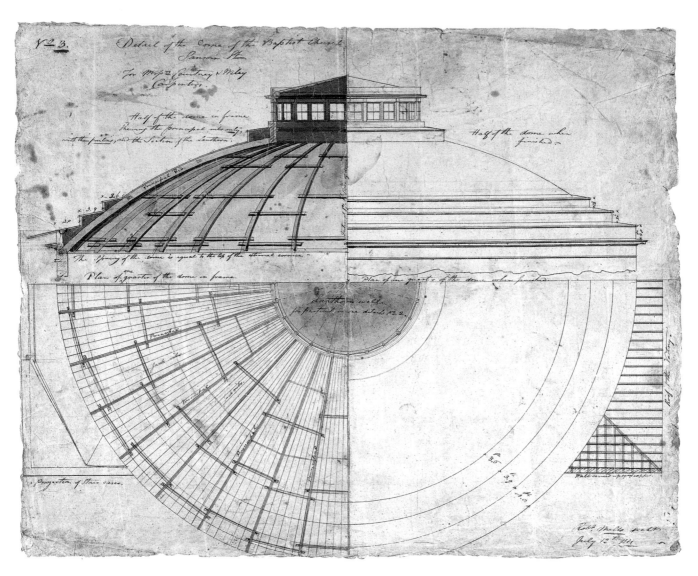

Sansom Street Baptist Church, "Elevations, plans and sections of the framing and exterior of the dome." Robert Mills, 1811-1812.

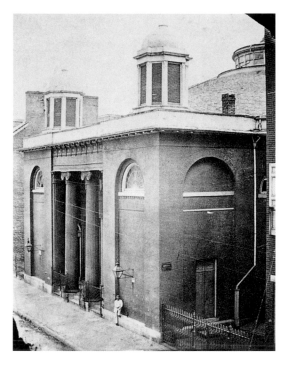
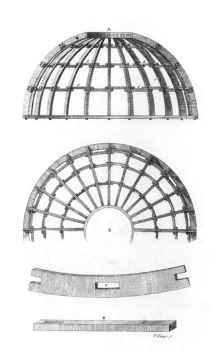

LEFT: *Sansom Street Baptist Church, Philadelphia. Robert Mills, architect, 1811.*
RIGHT: *"Dome of Boards and Plank," Owen Biddle, Young Carpenter's Assistant (1805), Plate 26.*

clearly legible. Having divided the sheet into quadrants and established relationships by juxtaposition, Mills presented four points of view concisely and simultaneously. The shadow and shape of the "principal ribs" in the section are the only indication that he was tempted by the spherical form to indulge in perspectival illusion. The fusion of the quadrants into an imagined form must take place in the mind of the viewer, so the impact of the drawing is primarily cerebral rather than sensual. As Mills' drawing was intended for the carpenters, it is not surprising that it resembles the illustration of the Delorme system published by Owen Biddle, *Young Carpenter's Assistant*, Plate 26. Mills' use of the dome antedates Biddle's publication, but the description of this technique in a popular handbook may have encouraged its adoption at Davidge Hall, University of Maryland (1812) by Robert Cary Long, Sr. (1770–1833), a Baltimore carpenter-builder, and by Alexander Parris at the

Massachusetts General Hospital (1823) and the Quincy Market (1825) in Boston. Maximilian Godefroy, who used a Delorme dome at the Unitarian Church in Baltimore (1817) and possibly at the City Hall in Richmond (1816), may have been familiar with Delorme's *Inventions* and the Halle au Blé, which, with its dramatic skylights, had sparked Jefferson's interest in promoting this system in America.[20]

Mills' early career in Philadelphia (circa 1808–1815) was a time of professional and personal definition. His domestic life coalesced into a gratifying pattern. Eliza was a competent manager of household affairs. Her letters recount relationships with the servants who came from Hackwood, dealings with tradesmen, bulk purchases of seasonal foods, the renovation of the house, and her cultivation of Robert's brother Thomas, who settled near Philadelphia in 1808. Eliza was an amiable companion and soon had a circle of friends. During the hot months (circa May to October), she moved with the children to Hackwood to avoid the coastal fevers, and this annual migration prompted much of their early domestic correspondence. In 1810, having taken her to Hackwood and returned alone to the empty house, Mills wrote:

> My dearest Eliza,
> How sensibly I feel your absence. On my entering our dwelling all seemed cheerless and without those means of pleasing which your presence never fails of imparting. My mind appears lost as it were to the pleasures deduced from surrounding objects, and I experience mentally those emotions which they do who are left to the solitude of retirement far from the fascinations of sense. When the evening advances with mournful tread and the business of the day [is] over, when solitary I return to the couch of rest, oh! Then I double feel the absence of my loved wife. But sweet is the anticipation that our absence is best for a little while & that ere many days are elapsed (thro God's blessing) we shall fold one another again in the arms of affection.[21]

If Robert missed his family, Eliza's extended visits were welcomed by her aged parents, who were mourning the death of Peyton, one of Eliza's younger brothers. Mills had reason to think fondly of the brothers, Augustine and Peyton, who had aided their sister in the campaign to win their father's consent. Now the memory of Peyton was rueful, for on the morning of November 28, 1809, he was mortally wounded in a duel with another young man from

20 Harnsberger provides the most thorough treatment of the Delorme dome in America. Also see Bryan, ed., Robert Mills, Architect, 31, n44 and n45, and Bryan, "Le developpement de la charpente à la Philibert Delorme aux Etats-Unis," a chapter in *Le bois dans l'architecture* (Paris, Association pour la Connaissance et la Mise en Valeur du Patrimoine, 1993).

21 RM to EBSM, May 8, 1810.

Winchester. Peyton had accepted a challenge resulting from an argument among a group of William and Mary students "much affected with spirit." His death had helped ensure the passage of Virginia's anti-dueling statute the following year, but that was little consolation to his parents.[22]

Anna wrote to Eliza in Philadelphia:

Time passes on so imperceptibly...say what comfort I can have in this wale of sorrow. Alas none, and I can truly say that never has a day been counted by me but has witnessed the tears shed for my dear Peyton...but for Peyton does the sigh heave and the incessant tear flow. To his memory have I dedicated a part of my flesh, my memory, my eye-sight, and indeed my hair has for the most part come out, and all my delight is, to use the words of Sister Young's favorite author:

When busy memory retraces
Scenes of bliss forever fled,
Lives in former times and places,
And holds communion with the dead

As I love to talk of Peyton, I believe I will tell you a dream Jacqulina had the other night. She thought she beheld him again in the house, but on the point of being removed to his own narrow dwelling in the orchard; & while the throng was waiting to attend he took a pen and wrote in large letters these three words: VIRTUE—MODESTY—MEEKNESS—which he put in her hand and vanished. I begged her to make [these] a rule of her actions through life. And as you equally [illegible] I will also recommend those emphatic words to your consideration.[23]

Correspondence suggests Mills' relationship with his in-laws was mutually satisfying, but he never entered fully into their social orbit, where seasons turned on visits to medicinal springs, house parties, and balls in Washington. Mills recoiled with all the force of his Scotch Presbyterian background against what he called the "frivolous & volatile manners of the world," telling Eliza "most of the luxuries of life are a species of refined barbarism."[24]

Mills' social life seems to have revolved around educational activities. In Philadelphia he participated in professional and philanthropic societies and

22 Evans, "The Smith-Holmes Duel, 1809," *William and Mary Quarterly* XV, 4 (October, 1935): 413–423.

23 Anna Bull Smith to EBSM, 1811.

24 RM to EBS, n.d., "4th letter, rough copy". Also see RM to EBS, October 15, 1807, and the Diary of RM, July 4, 1803.

proudly noted to the biographer William Dunlap that he was one of the artists "who shall be called Pennsylvania Academicians." Mills often signed himself "Robt. Mills, P.A." It was an honor, for "the architects and engravers together shall never exceed one fourth of the whole number of Academicians," and membership was national—even international if one included Benjamin West and John Singleton Copley—and was dominated by painters. The "first body of Academicians" included William Rush, Charles Willson, James, and Rembrandt Peale, Thomas Birch, Gilbert Stuart, John Vanderlyn, Washington Allston, John Trumbull, Latrobe, Godefroy, and Mills.[25] Both organizations sponsored classes and exhibitions.

As Secretary of the Society of Artists Mills published one of his earliest essays (1815). Writing would become an important part of his professional life, and under the somewhat misleading headline of "On Painting," the *National Intelligencer* reprinted from a Philadelphia paper an article by Mills on the state of the arts in America.

The War of 1812 had disrupted the affairs of the Society of Artists and caused the cancellation in 1815 of what would have been their fifth annual exhibition. Explaining the situation, Mills wrote that "in a republic the artist is rewarded only as he is useful. Our political institutions having a tendency to a more equal distribution of wealth than can possibly exist under monarchical or aristocratical governments, leave the artist but little to expect from individual patronage." He noted that the Society had been formed to draw artists together, but that the war wreaked havoc with their plans, for "artists are but tender plants, although they are sometimes able among weeds, briars and thorns to raise their heads, and for awhile enjoy the sunshine of public favor and patronage; yet it more frequently happens that they are destroyed by the insects of an hour, or, nipped by the chilling wind of poverty, they languish, wither and die." Despite a gloomy portrait of the present, Mills observed that "deeds of patriotic bravery…call loudly to be recorded by every art within the reach of men. The genius of the only republic on earth calls upon her artists to do justice to her heroes."[26]

Mills always sought civic work, and "On Painting" is his earliest published argument for public patronage. It concludes noting that the Society planned to seek a state appropriation to support a building, classes, and exhibitions. He had several designs in their first exhibition, including "Design of the Public Buildings now erecting at Harrisburg," "The New Baptist Church building in

25 *Charter, By-Laws, and Standing Resolutions, of the Pennsylvania Academy of Fine Arts* (Philadelphia: Office of the United States Gazette, 1813), 17–18; RM, "The Art of Painting," *National Intelligencer* (April 1, 1815): 3–4.

26 *Charter, By-Laws, and Standing Resolutions, of the Pennsylvania Academy of Fine Arts* (Philadelphia: Office of the United States Gazette, 1813), 17–18; RM, "The Art of Painting," *National Intelligencer* (April 1, 1815): 3–4.

George Street between 8th and 9th," "The Utilitarian Church, now building at the corner of Tenth and Locust Streets," "Arrangement of a square lot of ground situated on Walnut Street and Locust Street, between Ninth and Tenth Sts with the design of four block buildings, comprising 42 houses, proposed to be erected thereon," and, finally, "Design for the bridge now erecting at the Upper Ferry, Schuylkill River." These designs were credited to "Robt Mills, F.S.A. [Fellow of The Society of Artists] Architect and Engineer, 45 Sansom Street, Philadelphia." In the same exhibition were elevations of the capitol by Latrobe, Godefroy's sketch of "Mercury in the Clouds," numerous illustrations adapted from the popular literature of the day, and a "Landscape painted by holding the brush in the mouth by Miss Sarah Rogers."[27]

Perhaps it was through the Society of Artists that Mills met Charles Willson Peale, then the most colorful figure in the local artistic community. And it followed that Mills should become involved in some of Peale's many projects; no one had more irons in the fire. Peale wrote Jefferson, for example, that he had a drawing of the gardens at Monticello by Mills and that a set of such drawings "might be made to give a profit to some artist." Peale wrote to his son Rembrandt that Mills had "given in a plan and estimate which meets my idea very nicely" for an exhibition and classroom building and "the additions proposed to accommodate the museum in the State House."[28] Peale thought it was an optimistic moment for the arts in Philadelphia, observing that "The rage of building in the city does not abate, houses are springing up, somewhat like mushrooms in every Quarter."[29]

Peale wanted to enlarge his own museum, the first natural history museum in the country, which was housed on the upper floors of the State House, known today as Independence Hall. In the same letter to Rembrandt, he noted that "the Academy of Fine Arts have had the last year a visitation of about 1000 and the year before 1200." He told his son that "I have drawings made by Mr. Mills (architect) of the additions proposed to accommodate the museum in the State House and if I find the legislature (on feeling the pulse of mankind) are disposed to adopt my proposals, I shall make my address to them in the ensuing season."[30] Mills' drawing for Independence Hall was exhibited at the Second Annual Exhibition of the Society of Artists with the caption:

The State-House in Chesnut-street, agreeably to its original design, and with certain *proposed* improvements; together with the *wing buildings* now erecting

27 Anon., *First Annual Exhibition of the Society of Artists of the United States*, 1811 (Philadelphia: Tho. L. Plowman), no. 36, 331, 339, 482.

28 Charles Willson Peale to Rembrandt Peale, October 28, and November 17, 1809 (one letter, having been interrupted and completed on the later date), Lillian B. Miller, ed., *The Collected Papers of Charles Willson Peale and His Family* (Millwood, N.Y.: Kraus Microform, 1980), IIA/48A8-B10.

29 Charles Willson Peale to Rembrandt Peale, October 28, and November 17, 1809.

30 Charles Willson Peale to Rembrandt Peale, October 28, and November 17, 1809.

Alternative designs for wings for Independence Hall, Philadephia. Robert Mills, architect, 1812.

(fireproof) for the accommodation of the *public offices*, and the Court-houses on 5th and 6th streets, the whole extending 400 feet.

R. Mills, F.S.A. & P.A.[31]

31 Anon., *Second Annual Exhibition of the Society of Artists of the United States and the Pennsylvania Academy* (Philadelphia, 1812), 5–6.

32 For Mills' signature on the petition and the need for the new construction, see *Collected Papers of Charles Willson Peale*, XI A 5D4-E8, n.d. [1811]

33 Charles Coleman Sellers, *Mr. Peale's Museum* (New York: W.W. Norton, 1980), 194–195. See also *Journal of the House of Representatives of Pennsylvania* (1810–1811): 202, 276, 469, 652, quoted by Edward M. Riley, "The Independence Hall Group," *Transactions of the American Philosophical Society*, New Series, 42, part 1 (1953): 31, n193.

As a result of Peale's activity, a petition signed by more than 500 persons (including Mills) was presented to the Pennsylvania House of Representatives requesting that Independence Hall be renovated, and that fireproof wings be added to either side. The memorialists lamented the vulnerability of the public records; they said that the state of Independence Hall was "inconvenient, unsightly, exposed to improper uses, and disgraceful to the venerable edifice." They noted also that "the well known Museum of Mr. Peale, an establishment dear to science, useful to the arts, and reflecting honor on the state in which it exists [had] by the activity and zeal of its proprietor...so increased that the rooms in which it is contained are not sufficiently spacious for its full display, or to render it as useful as a greater extension would make it."[32] The House committee endorsed this request.

The city government, however, wanted to expand its offices within the State House complex and became alarmed by Peale's ambitions. In January 1811, their representative presented a counter-proposal to the legislature that would allow the city and the county to "pull down the east and west wings of the state-house...and to erect in their place, suitable buildings for the deposit of the records of said City and county."[33] Their request was approved March 24, 1812, and Robert Mills' new wings were built on either end of the State House.

The wings were designed to house offices and connect the Old State House, the Supreme Court, and Congress Hall buildings. No provision was made for expansion of the museum. This was the first time Mills worked on a building with national historical associations, and he approached the exterior like he had treated the elevations of St. Michael's. Offering alternative elevations, conservatively adapting existing motifs, he employed recessed decorative panels, belt courses, and keystones to align the new and lower wings with the facade of the Old State House. But he made no attempt to copy the historic building; instead, there was a distinct expression of modernity in his grouping of the windows and entries into triple units and in the low profile of his cupolas or monitors. The wings were built (1812–1814) using the square-headed entries shown on the right-hand side of Mills' drawing. Both wings contained the masonry vaulted, fireproof offices that would become a hallmark of his work.[34] Beyond the new wings, the original Peale-Mills proposal included extensive alterations to the State House itself, for changes are described in the Society of Artists catalogue of 1812:

> The improvements proposed to the main building are, 1st. The restoration of its ancient *steeple*; 2d. The projection of a *portico*, at the entrance in front crowned with a *balustrade*, which encloses a rostrum for public speaking; 3d. The removal of two blank windows under the portico, and putting in their place niches for the reception of the statues of Wisdom and Justice; 4th. Changing the scite of the clock, and placing it in front.[35]

The exhibition of 1812 must have been satisfying for Mills. The drawing of Independence Hall associated him with an historic public shrine, and his "Design for the bridge now erecting at the Upper Ferry, Schuylkill River. Span 330 feet" linked him to visions of the future.[36]

The bridge suggested economic growth, westward expansion, and the marvels of engineering. In 1811 the Lancaster Schuylkill Bridge Company had been chartered to undertake the project. The company advertised (September 1811) and initially received two designs from Mills and one from Thomas Pope. The advertisement called for a plan "not to have more than one pier (a single arch would be preferred)" with a road and walkway thirty-six feet wide, provisions for a roof, abutments, specifications, and cost estimates, as well as a bond for the performance of the contractor. Mills' drawings do not

34 The wings were demolished in the late nineteenth (Alexander says 1896) or early twentieth centuries (Liscombe says 1912–1913); Liscombe, 38; Alexander, 60, in Bryan, ed., *Robert Mills, Architect.*

35 *Second Annual Exhibition*, 5–6.

36 *Second Annual Exhibition*, 5–6.

Lancaster-Schuylkill Bridge. Engraving by Klinokowstrom.

survive, but in a letter to the managers of the company he estimates the cost of the bridge to be $36,674. A roof and toll house would increase the cost, he thought, to $44,174. The managers never signed a contract with Mills for the construction of the bridge, although on November 14th they passed a resolution that apparently paraphrased his proposals. But the following month, on December 5th, 1811, they voted to rescind their resolution of November 14th and determined that "Mr. Wernwags plan of a bridge with one arch of 330 feet chord be adopted." They entered a contract with Lewis Wernwag, a millwright, for the construction of the bridge. It is clear that Mills did not design the accepted plan, which arched "like a scarf, rounded by the wind [and] flung over the river."[37] The drawing Mills exhibited may have been his unsuccessful competition entry. Despite the fact that his proposal had failed, he was proud of his effort, for his response had required research and faith in his economic and structural projections.

The public was interested in this undertaking. During the winter of 1812, stock in the company was quickly subscribed, Lewis Wernwag gathered materials, and Thomas Pope, the third competitor, accused Wernwag of patent infringements and waged a publicity campaign on behalf of his own design. Pope exhibited his model, published broadsides, and threatened litigation. He ultimately forced Wernwag to make minor modifications, but the real result of their dispute was only to keep the subject before the public. Quarries were opened in March on the bridge site, and in April with great fanfare the cornerstone was laid. On the copper plate "engraved for the occasion" it said, "Louis [sic] Wernwag, Architect."[38]

We do not know how Mills proposed to erect the bridge. Wernwag's plan consisted of five laminated wooden arches (later reduced to three) with a superstructure of kingposts and diagonal braces. On the soft western bank, footings for the arches were achieved by driving some 600 pilings into the mud and framing these within a heavy masonry revetment. Wernwag built a machine to drive the pilings and constructed an immense floating scaffold on which to erect the arches. Neither Mills, nor anyone else, had ever seen so great a wooden span; it was the longest wooden arch in the world.

Mills must have followed the project with great interest, for by comparison, his earlier experience at the Chesapeake and Delaware canal was merely child's play. Wernwag knew success was assured on January 7, 1813, when a crowd gathered to watch the removal of all temporary supports. It was a dra-

37 Frances Anne Butler [Kemble], *Journal* (London, 1835), II, 29–30, quoted by Nelson, 177.

38 Lee H. Nelson, "The Colossus of Philadelphia," in Brooke Hindle, ed., *Material Culture of the Wooden Age* (Tarrytown: Sleepy Hollow Press, 1981), 168.

matic moment—perhaps the most notable spectacle during Mills' years in Philadelphia. Workmen drove the wedges from beneath the bridge; the arches held and the span stood free. There was a ceremony. The directors marched across, and then the thoroughfare was opened to the public.

Much, however, remained to be done. Only the roadway, or deck, had been completed. During the spring, Wernwag labored to correct a flaw in the western abutment, which showed a disconcerting tendency to slide into the river. The managers also wanted to cover the bridge with a roof and sides for protection from the weather, to build a residence for the gate-keeper, and to erect a toll booth. On March 22, 1813, they contracted with Mills to undertake these projects, since Wernwag had moved up-river to manage the Phoenix Nail Works. Mills was to execute the work to his own designs in six months for $4,520. The specifications stipulated a shingled roof, tongue and groove siding, portals with columns at either end of the bridge, and three coats of paint on all exterior surfaces. The scope of Mills' contribution in the "general finishing" of the bridge is clear; he would "furnish the finished design, bills of scantling, supervision, and labor to complete the work."[39]

Two points need to be made concerning the Schuylkill Bridge. Although the ambiguous exhibition caption has often been cited—either in attributing the whole structure to Mills, or accusing him of claiming credit for Wernwag's work, Mills did not maneuver to undermine Wernwag's reputation in 1813. At that time their relationship must have been amicable, for several years later Wernwag approached Mills concerning another project. On the other hand, Mills initially did nothing to correct the impression that he was solely responsible for the bridge, and several times in later years he did claim credit for the design, always noting the span of the arch and never defining the scope of his contribution. He referred Jefferson, without comment, to an article which credited him with the entire design, and he allowed William Dunlap to cite the bridge as his work in the *History of the Rise and Progress of the Arts of Design in the United States.*

If Mills improperly took credit for the Schuylkill Bridge, it is ironic that his real contribution has not been appreciated. The portals and tollhouse he designed were effective solutions to problems for which there was no local precedent. We catch glimpses of these elements in illustrations. (Mills' drawings have not survived.) One contemporaneous print includes a view, a plan and an approximate scale. The tollhouse stood in the middle of the road at the eastern end of the bridge. It was conceived as a peripteral temple, its cella or

39 Nelson, "The Colossus of Philadelphia," 170.

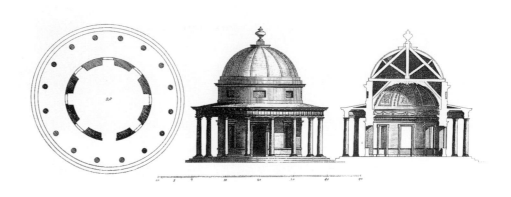

LEFT: *Joseph Manigault House, Garden Gate Lodge, Charleston, South Carolina. Gabriel Manigault, architect, circa 1802–1803.*

RIGHT: *A temple for the Duke of Bolton's Garden at Hackwood. James Gibbs,* Book of Architecture *(London, 1728), Plate 72.*

core (approximately ten feet in diameter) served as a booth for the toll collector. The projecting peristyle extended the total diameter to about sixteen feet. The cella was capped with a low dome and sheathed with a metal roof. The early Roman Temple of Vesta is an apt prototype, and as the Tempietto-like toll booth had a total height of about twice the width of its cella, its proportions coincided with the Vitruvian proportions for this building type. Mills' diminutive temple by the river was analogous to similar structures that had appeared like mushrooms in English and French Neoclassical gardens. He was no doubt familiar with Jefferson's plan (1794) for such a retreat at Monticello. Latrobe's base of the Mississippi lighthouse had demonstrated the adaptability of the peripteral temple, but peripteral temples were rarely built in America, and neither Jefferson nor Latrobe had seen their plans realized. Round temples appeared in the standard illustrated texts. James Gibbs' *Book of Architecture*, for example, contains elevations, plans, and sections for more than a dozen garden pavilions with a variety of plans—circular, octagonal, cruciform—intended to present formal facades from all directions. One of these resembles the toll booth in plan and scale, and reading its caption we see why Mills may have smiled at the thought of using this source:

> A circular building in form of a Temple, 20 feet in Diameter, having a Peristylium round it of the Dorick order, and adorned with a cupola; erected in his Grace the Duke of Bolton's Garden at Hackwood, upon the upper ground of an Amphitheater, backed with high Trees that render the Prospect of the Building very agreeable.[40]

If Mills used the Hackwood pavilion plates, he probably concluded that the high drum and hemispherical dome would have to be sacrificed on the altar of economic utility. This pressure to simplify reshaped virtually every classical plan executed in America. From personal experience, as well as from literary sources, Mills could advocate the use of such a pavilion, for he knew the gate house designed by Gabriel Manigault (1758–1809) for his brother Joseph in Charleston (circa 1803). When Mills visited Charleston "to check on his churches," this adaptation of the tholos was new and exciting. In Mills' experience it may have been unique, and it demonstrated the usefulness of an ancient type. Strictly speaking, the Charleston example had neither front nor back; it was effective for the visitor both coming and going, and this was the principal requirement to be satisfied by a toll house for the bridge. Mills' use of triumphal arches for the entries to the bridge was as notable as the toll booth. The arches separated pedestrian and vehicular traffic, divided east and westbound travelers, shielded the ends of the trusses from the weather, and dramatized the crossing of the river. Here he adapted freely from Roman types—the city gate, the fortified bridge, the triumphal arch. The approaching traveler saw a pair of central portals that were flanked by smaller doorways for pedestrians. Columns framed these entries and carried an unadorned entablature and parapet. The effect was similar to the Porta Maggiore in Rome, which also channeled traffic through two central archways, possessed secondary entries, and displayed similar columns and a simple attic story. The Porta Maggiore marked the confluence of two great aqueducts, so, like the Schuylkill Bridge, it expressed a water-related triumph.

Travelers entering the Schuylkill Bridge found light spilling into the roadway through large openings both up and downstream. These windows were arched and framed with columns. At both ends of the bridge piers at each corner gave the effect of an in antis elevation, and these piers were raked or battered at an angle which reflected the diagonal iron braces anchoring the trusses into the abutments. The resulting angle expressed the tension within the arch. Battered

40 James Gibbs, *A Book of Architecture* (New York: Benjamin Blom, 1968), xix.

94

piers were part of the idiom of the Egyptian Revival, and by juxtaposing them against columns and voids Mills accentuated their prominence. Permanence and stability were attributes ascribed to Egyptoid forms, and these side elevations resemble an "Egyptian Garden Temple" illustrated by Sir John Soane. (Mills had recently adapted his Franklin Row from the same book.) The north and south portal elevations, like Soane's garden temple, combined Doric distyle in antis openings with an Egyptian frame.

Whatever his source of inspiration, Mills' design was part of the tradition of ceremonial bridges. He seems to have been the first to use this tradition to dramatize an American bridge. In addition to potential European sources, it is possible that Mills simply may have recalled temporary arches erected during Washington's triumphal tour of 1791. Bulfinch had designed an arch in Boston. And Mills would have seen the Charleston version which stood in Broad Street before the Exchange. In Philadelphia arches of greenery had decorated both ends of the Upper Ferry Bridge that then spanned the river near the site of the "Colossus" by Wernwag and Mills. Perhaps even more to the point, in 1783, to celebrate the end of the Revolution, the city government of Philadelphia directed that an arch be erected in Market Street (between 6th and 7th streets). It was described as being forty feet high and fifty feet wide, its central portal being fourteen feet "in the clear" and its secondary archways nine feet wide. Its "pillars are of the Ionic Order" and adorned with "Festoons of Flower in their natural Colours."[41]

The exterior of the bridge was not completed within the six months allotted by the contract. Indeed, years later the managers complained that Mills still had not finished the job. First weather caused delays, then another project took him, like it had Wernwag, away from the bridge.

41 For an illustration and discussion of the Washington Arch in Boston, see Harold Kirker, *The Architecture of Charles Bulfinch* (Cambridge: Harvard University Press, 1969), 23–24. For an illustration of the Schuylkill floral arch, see Martin P. Snyder, *City of Independence: Views of Philadelphia Before 1800* (New York: Praeger, 1975), fig. 77. The description of the Market Street arch is contained in a printed broadside, "In Assembly, Tuesday, December 2, 1783, A.M.," reproduced in the *Collected Papers of Charles Willson Peale* IIA (Add.)/3D5.

Washington Monument, Baltimore.

CHAPTER FOUR

Diversification and Maturity

Richmond, Philadelphia, and Baltimore 1810–1820

O N T H E N I G H T of December 26, 1811, during a popular pantomime, the Richmond theater burst into flame. Pandemonium ensued, and seventy-one people died. A committee, chaired by Chief Justice John Marshall, was organized at once to select a design and erect a memorial, and the resulting Monumental Church marks Mills' maturity as an architect. This is the last of his projects in which his mentor Benjamin Henry Latrobe played a major role—this time as a competitor.[1]

John Wickham, a member of the selection committee, contacted Latrobe, who responded by observing that earlier plans to build a church nearby might be revised "on the supposition...that the erection of a Church and of a monument to the deceased...proceed on the same plan, and on the same spot." But he concluded that available funds were inadequate to erect a church.

Latrobe wrote the committee about a memorial: "the first quality should be permanence. There should be unbroken surfaces to allow for the engraving of the names of the dead, and "as to sculpture, the less of it the better. Allegory is a most equivocal mode of description, plainness in design...character of permanent duration in appearance...is all I think is required."[2] He submitted an Egyptian Revival composition reminiscent of Soane's pyramidal temple (mentioned above in connection with Mills' treatment of the Schuylkill Bridge). Here, "the remains of those who were destroyed" were to be "deposited about the center of the pit and occupy an area of perhaps 18 or

1 Margaret Pearson Mickler, "The Monumental Church," MA thesis, University of Virginia, 1980; George D. Fisher, *History and Reminiscences of the Monumental Church* (Richmond: Whittet & Shepperson, 1880); Rhodri Windsor Liscombe, *The Church Architecture of Robert Mills* (Easley, S.C.: Southern Historical Press, 1985).

2 BHL to John Wickham, January 21, 1812.

Monumental Church, Richmond, Virginia. Robert Mills, architect, 1812–1817.

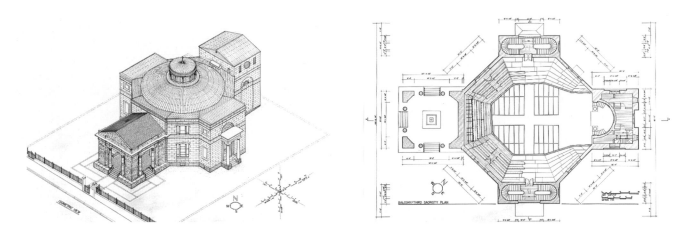

Monumental Church. Measured drawings by Historic American Buildings Survey.

20 feet square." He recommended covering the pit with a "plan...about 32 feet square."

Latrobe's proposal called for a raised basement five feet high to serve as a vaulted crypt. A chamber "20 or 24 feet square" would rise from the platform created by this raised basement. The exterior of this chamber would be severe, broken only by a distyle in antis entry and a heavy cavetto cornice. Above the cornice, and set back behind its parapet, Latrobe proposed a stepped pyramid forty-eight feet high. Within the dimly lit chamber the visitor would read the names of the dead on marble panels reaching from floor to ceiling; opposite the entry a niche would contain "a kneeling figure...mourning over an urn containing the ashes of her children." The interior was to be lighted by clerestory windows hidden on the exterior by the parapet.

Latrobe concluded, "I would by all means advise the church to be on the same spot behind the monument."[3] He urged the committee to avoid brick, wood, or other expediencies and suggested, as he had to Bishop Carroll of Baltimore, that they raise money by selling crypts.

Mills' plan, despite its innovative features, suggests he knew of Latrobe's proposal. Mills placed his church directly behind the monument; his monument is distyle in antis and contains a funerary urn. Like Latrobe he proposed marble tablets to record the names of the dead, and—perhaps most telling— made his monumental porch thirty-two feet square.

3 BHL to John Wickham, January 21, 1812.

Letters allow us to reconstruct some of the interplay between Mills, Latrobe, and the committee. Both architects submitted more than one proposal. Henry Clay, on journeys between Richmond and Washington, conveyed letters to Latrobe from the committee. Mills also used Henry Clay as a conduit, but through the intermediary of Gen. John Smith, who often saw Clay in Washington. Latrobe too, on at least one occasion, discussed his plans with Gen. Smith, and later came to believe Smith had passed along information to his son-in-law. Latrobe soon realized that he had been naive in speaking openly with General Smith; he also felt he had misjudged Henry Clay. Latrobe's irritation during this episode must have been fueled in part by the awareness that he had contributed to his own defeat.

Latrobe assumed his design had been approved, and he offered to retain a contractor. He was unaware Mills was submitting designs until the committee informed him that a plan by Mills had been approved. Mills plan combined a monument and a church, and the committee invited Latrobe to submit a comparable design. Embarrassed, Latrobe declined, and wrote the committee:

> Mr. Mills, who as you have rightly been informed, was several years in my office, and for whose feelings and interests I have the highest consideration, has furnished you with designs, one of which you approve.—You wish for a design of a Church,—a monumental church, from me also,—in order that you nay decide between us. I confess that knowing the exact rate of Mr. Mills' talents and powers, I feel exceedingly reluctant to enter the lists against my own professional child,—contrary to the established rule of the profession, even in cases of actual and profitable benefit, especially, when the principal on which Mr. Mills has made his design, is my own idea communicated to him; though much modified. This bids me to point out to you what I think fatally exceptional in his design, as far as you have enabled me to understand it.
>
> Of Mr. Mills I cannot however speak but in term of respect. He is a man of the strictest integrity and virtue and of talents which close study have much improved. He is of a religious turn of mind. Whatever design you ultimately adopt, it would be infinitely to your interest to endeavor to engage him to direct its execution on the spot, which I doubt not he would undertake at very reasonable terms, although how his engagements in Philadelphia might influence him. In the design of private houses he is uncommonly excellent. In

the design of public works he wants experience, as yet,—to a sufficient extent,—but his rigid integrity in the conduct of their execution has been highly useful and honorable to me in the superintendence of more than one great work.

I have said this much of Mr. Mills, least I should be thought to be influenced by unworthy motives in the general opinion I have given of his above plans. I would now propose to you to inform me what are your own ideas, as expressed by the words, "A Monumental Church" as you have explained Mr. Mills' design to me—it is a monument, so placed in front of a Church, as to serve as its vestibule. The Monument, if constructed of freestone may be made at a great expense, very permanent. The Church itself has no trace of a monumental character, and as the roof built on the construction of that of the house of Representatives in this city must be of boards and probably covered with Shingles, it has every property in a superior degree to that of permanence.

A Monumental Church ought to be such monument as that in extent and arrangement it could serve as a Church. There are such churches in Europe. Westminster Abbey has been converted into such a one. But such a one your funds cannot build, and I am very certain that allowing a superficial foot to each inscription, and considering Mr. Mills' circular vestibule surrounded with columns of permanent materials and of an impressive size his estimate of $35,000 would fall infinitely short.

If you will favor me with the idea of the Committee on this subject, and are at all desirous of my further assistance, I will prepare a design in which they shall be embodied and transmit to you as soon as possible—together with a tolerable accurate estimate.

In the meantime, as the design I sent you was my first rough sketch of which I have no copy, you would oblige me by returning it to me thro the address of Mr. Clay.

I beg, Sir, that you and the Committee my be assured that the interests I take in your [illegible word] and in your feeling is unabated, and that I should always be sensible of the honor your having [illegible word] to consulted me confers upon Me

Respectfully B. H. Latrobe[4]

Obtaining title to the site caused delays, and throughout the spring of 1812, General Smith kept Mills informed. At the end of April he was able to

4 BHL to John Brockenborough, March 22, 1812.

announce "your temple, I understand is approved of." That spring and summer Mills looked for marble, again with the help of his father-in-law who directed him to Mr. Leferre's quarry fifty-three miles from Lancaster on the Lancaster-Philadelphia road.

Just before construction began, Mills and Latrobe were apparently reconciled. Having found drawings by Mills in the Washington office, Latrobe wrote from Washington on May 26, 1812:

> Dear Sir
>
> In searching over Mr. Lenthall's papers again I have found the lined drawings herewith sent. I have not looked into them. They were rolled up as you will receive them.
>
> I take this occasion to express my regret that after knowing that I Had been consulted on the Monument once proposed to be erected at Richmond You would have transmitted to them a number of Ideas and drawings, which rendering decision difficult has I believed defeated the object. I am far from supposing you intended me an injury yet you have not only injured but disgraced me because I had already made a conditional contract with respectable men, whom I have had to disappoint with an explanation not very creditable to myself, namely that your plan was preferred. I am very far from being jealous of the preference given to your design by such judges, but I am most sensibly hurt that you should not have become aware of the indelicacy towards any artist, which other transaction involves in it during your studies with respect and delicacy of which no inducement of profit could have made me guilty toward you and which in service of sentiment only [illegible] to have been impossible.
>
> It is also singular that you should propose inserting marble panels into freestone margins exactly in the same manner in which I had proposed without being informed of my intention. It is however impossible to suppose that you were so informed because you would hardly have waged war against me in my own armor.
>
> Had you had the special information on the subject which the Committee furnished to me you would have given a different design. I am respectfully
>
> B. H. Latrobe[5]

5 BHL to RM, May 26, 1812.

Mills apparently replied that he had been unaware of Latrobe's efforts, for Latrobe wrote again on July 22, 1812:

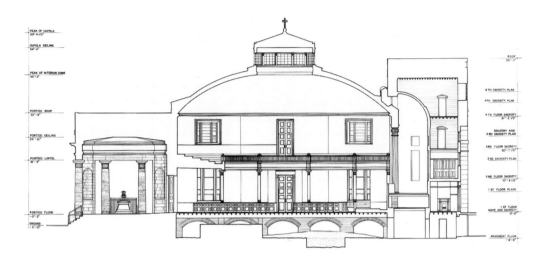

Monumental Church. Measured drawings by Historic American Buildings Survey.

Dear Sir,

Your letter requesting me to write to you [illegible] reached me on Monday, no letters being delivered here on Sunday. Therefore it would have been inelegant to have announced it as you were here already yesterday.

As to the subject of the letter, I can only say that as you did not know that I was consulted by the Richmond Committee, & had given them a design & were wholly unapprised of my intentions as to the mode of recording the names of the sufferers, although your father in law told me that he should write to You on the subject, before you sent in your different plans, then all ground of offense is certainly removed, & nothing remains but the astonishment that in so novel a mode of setting Marble in Freestone as Your and my method certainly are we should both have invented the same thing at the same moment. But such an extraordinary coincidences do actually happen sometimes.

As to permanent displeasure I am not capable of it. I shall always endeavor to serve you, & altho' my period of ability is passed for the present, it may again arrive.

I am with much truth
[illegible]
B. H. Latrobe[6]

6 BHL to RM, July 22, 1812.

Monumental Church. Engraving by William Goodacre.

And that is where they left it.

Mills plan consists of an emphatic "monumental porch"—thirty-two feet square as Latrobe had proposed—grafted onto an auditorium style church. The porch, which Mills called "the vestibule," dominates the south elevation, and fronts upon the street. The body of the church is an octagon, one facet of which abuts the rear of the monumental porch. Within the church directly across from the doorway from the monumental porch, the pulpit stands within an acousti-cally conceived apse, which balances the porch. This bay projects from the northern facet of the octagon and was intended to serve as the base of a steeple (never executed). To the east and west corresponding bays project; these contain stairways to the balcony that circumscribe the interior, excepting the pulpit apse on the north face of the nave. A low saucer dome caps the nave, and its center is pierced by a round monitor or cupola.

In earlier auditorium churches Mills had used saucer domes, built in the Delorme method. These buildings also shared similar balconies, elevated pulpits, occulae and interior plans based upon theories of acoustics. Both the Circular Church and the Monumental Church were designed for steeples. Like James Gibbs' Plates VIII–XV, they joined the central plan with a Baroque spire.

It is the Monumental Porch that sets the Richmond building apart. Here he used shadow, void, and contrasting forms to create an impact, and his reliance on large forms rather than upon a proliferation of detail is evidence that by 1812 he was thoroughly conversant with Rational Classicism. Excepting lachrymatories within the frieze and the acroteria (a typical Greek anthemion often used at the apex of funereal stele), the exterior of the monument is virtually unadorned; its solemnity is reinforced by the brown tones of the Aquia stone. Broad piers throw the interior of the porch into deep shade. Against the darkness, the columns thrust boldly into the light. These Doric columns with fluted drums at top and bottom may derive from those at Delos; their splayed capitals and projecting echinus blocks suggest the form of Archaic Greece. The proportions of the porch and the clear geometry of its parts connote stability and permanence. The composition is forthright and direct like the rigging of a sailing ship or the exoskeleton of an insect.

THE WASHINGTON MONUMENT, BALTIMORE

The cornerstone of the Monumental Church was set on August 1, 1812. Civic sentiment, the unusual design, and the role of Richmond as a regional center all insured its prominence. It was a major commission, and soon there were signs that Mills had attained a new measure of status and credibility, and he capitalized on this success. Commissions came from influential citizens in Richmond.

In Philadelphia he exhibited a drawing of the church at the Society of Artists in 1812 and set about publishing an engraving, "a handsome picture, capable of ornamenting any room." His advertisement noted that the drawing was to be exhibited in Richmond in the Capitol and that he wanted "to give to bereaved relatives and friends an opportunity of possessing same domestic memento of the respect and sympathy manifested by a generous public for the loss of so much worth, talent, and beauty."[7]

Mills had William Strickland do the drawing, for he recognized his own limitations as a draftsman and rarely attempted evocative, perspectival draw-

7 *The Enquirer*,
Richmond, VA
(December 5, 1812): 3–4.

*Washington
Monument, Baltimore,
Maryland. Robert
Mills, architect,
1813–1842.*

ings. The Monumental Church print is one of the earliest American architectural illustrations intended for distribution, and the promotional and sentimental aspects of this idea are characteristic of Mills. It marks the beginning of his use of publication to present his work. He was aware that to be successful he must do more than design buildings.

Mills had exhibited—if not distributed—drawings before. In 1811 his drawings of Franklin Row, Independence Hall, the Schuylkill Bridge, the garden front of Monticello, the Monumental Church, the Unitarian Church in Philadelphia, and competition drawings for the Capitol in Harrisburg all hung in the Academy with those of other architects, including Maximilian Godefroy's proposals for a monument to George Washington—the project which would shape the next phase of Mills' career.

Mills knew Godefroy as a member of Latrobe's circle during the New Castle period. Latrobe's son was then studying under Godefroy at Saint Mary's College in Baltimore, where Godefroy had executed a celebrated Gothic Revival chapel. Latrobe had written Godefroy about the Cathedral and collaborated with him on the Baltimore Exchange. When the exhibition opened in Philadelphia in the spring of 1811, Godefroy was the most sophisticated architect working in Baltimore. The proposal he exhibited for the Washington Monument was evidence of his European training and included a triumphal arch that framed an equestrian statue, a domed rotunda crowned by a statue of Washington, and a fountain within a round Ionic temple. Godefroy presented the monumental potential of Neoclassicism and portrayed civic sculpture on a scale that was literally and figuratively foreign to American experience. Congress had authorized a monument to Washington as early as 1783 (it was never executed). North Carolina and Virginia had commissioned pedestrian statues, but nothing as imposing as Godefroy's proposals had been contemplated.[8]

Godefroy's drawings had been done for the Board of Managers of the Washington Monument in Baltimore. In 1810 the State of Maryland authorized the Board to raise funds by lottery to erect a monument. The Board solicited Godefroy's ideas, but did not settle upon a design, for they were preoccupied with securing funding and a site. The unsettled political situation, culminating in the War of 1812, caused further delay, but as soon as victory was assured they resolved to select a design and get underway, and they did not feel compelled to adopt Godefroy's suggestions. Instead, they decided to start over, to advertise in

8 For a succinct review of earlier monuments to Washington see Pamela Scott, "Robert Mills and American Monuments," 143–144, in Bryan, ed., *Robert Mills, Architect*. For Maximilian Godefry, see Robert L. Alexander, *Maximilian Godefroy* (Baltimore: The Johns Hopkins University Press, 1974).

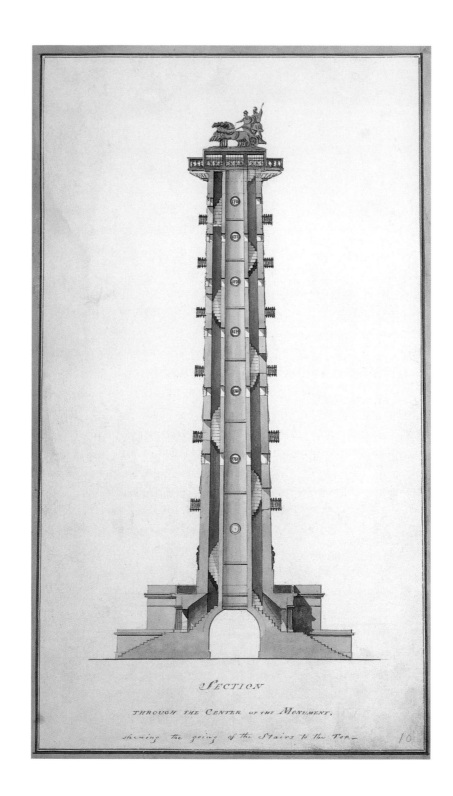

SECTION

THROUGH THE CENTER OF THE MONUMENT,

shewing the going of the Stairs to the Top.—

Washington Monument,
Baltimore, Maryland.

Europe and America, offering a prize of $500 and setting a deadline of January 1, 1814, for the submission of proposals.[9]

Here was a golden opportunity. The resulting monument—the first major work dedicated to Washington—was sure to be nationally significant. Moreover, it offered the chance to design on a grand scale, to build for eternity and be unabashedly inspirational. If the Richmond Church was a dirge, this monument could be an epic paean. Mills set to work enthusiastically.

He ultimately submitted at least a dozen drawings and many pages of explanatory notes. His earliest surviving composition (November 1813) contains six rough sketches and an essay of some 3,000 words, which offers insight into his attitude about ornament. The initial drawings were little more than notations, but the narrative is notable. He first thought of the monument as an octagonal column divided into four stages, each being about eight feet high. Each of these levels displayed a series of bas-relief panels intended "to represent the public character and important events connected with the public transactions of General Washington from the commencement of the revolutionary war to the time of his death." An equestrian statue of Washington, made of gleaming brass, "as large as life, to face the rising sun exactly," was to top the column. An octagonal paved courtyard would encircle the monument, enclosed by a fence composed of "eight white marble posts about six feet in height, the tops of which to be formed into virgin heads and bosoms—their countenances to be highly finished and turned towards the spectators, displaying features [of] modesty & innocence."[10] His plan included the placement of gates, trees, and gravel walks. He noted six or seven variations of this scheme, including an octagonal column surrounded by a diminutive peripteral temple—eight detached pillars carrying a cornice "eighteen inches in width and six inches in thickness."[11] This last alternative recalls both Latrobe's lighthouse and Mills' own proposal, years later, for the Washington Monument in the nation's capital.

At first glance the early schemes bear little resemblance to his competition drawings or to the completed monument. But in fact, from the first moment the essence of his idea was a column with its crowning statue and emblematic decor. From the outset, he was working in the tradition of the columns of Trajan and Hadrian, Sir Christopher Wren's memorial to the Fire of London, or Nelson's Column (Dublin 1808).

In the initial sketches of November 1813, Mills' most elaborate version had thirty-two panels, eight on each of the four levels of the column. Because the

9 Alexander, *Maximilian Godefroy*, 71–75. Also see J. Jefferson Miller, "Baltimore's Washington Monument," MA Thesis, University of Delaware, 1962.

10 James W. Foster, "Robert Mills and the Washington Monument in Baltimore," *Maryland Historical Magazine* XXXIV 2 (June 1939): 144–160.

11 Foster, "Robert Mills and the Washington Monument," 145.

angles of the octagon were obtuse, he envisioned the viewer seeing two panels at once, like pages of a book. Each level depicted a significant chapter in Washington's career; for example, the panels around the base depicted "the former colonial dependence and military achievements of the United States by which they acquired their national independence" and included "13 lam[b]s with a lion to watch them & by Dr. Franklin agent for the Colonies humbly presenting a petition in their behalf to his Britanic Majesty to repeal obnoxious acts of parliament." Another image on this level presented "the gloomy state & doubtful issue of American affairs in the fall of 1776. By the shabby starved looks of a few officers & soldiers retreating before the enemy." The second course concerned Washington's presidency, and here Mills aimed to depict "the languishment of commerce and the lack of public credit. By a ship in the harbour stripped of her sails and cordage—ship carpenters with their hands folded, idolling [*sic*] about & soldiers in tattered uniform selling public securities to speculators."[12]

The panels were designed to appeal to Everyman. Mills proposed a sentimental realism instead of the classical allusions then in vogue. Gods and goddesses, however, occupy center stage in his final alternative. After describing the panels, he offered alternative systems of ornament, both entailing a similar column with only a single band of bas relief. Having suggested three plans for the applied ornament, he concluded with the accommodating, pragmatic concession that "the designer and the artist may select from the various devices I have presented, or such others as he may himself conceive, or design, may form such new groups or combinations as can with the most facility, be laid out & executed." He added, "if, to save expense or for any other purpose it should seem most proper, all devices and inscriptions may be ommitted [*sic*]." The passage is prescient: "a simple column without any devices or inscriptions may be erected, if such as have been suggested should seem too numerous, complex, expensive, inappropriate, or inexpedient."[13]

He must have regarded these notes and sketches as a draft—important enough to save but not polished enough to submit in competition—and as the deadline approached he requested and obtained an extension. He knew of Godefroy's drawings and may have been aware that another Frenchman, Joseph Ramée, had submitted a triumphal arch. (Latrobe, out of deference to Godefroy, decided not to compete.) Mills revised his plans and took great pains with new drawings and explanatory prose. On January 12, 1814, he sent to the Board a "book of designs" containing an essay and seven tinted drawings (three exterior

12 Foster, 152.

13 Foster, 150.

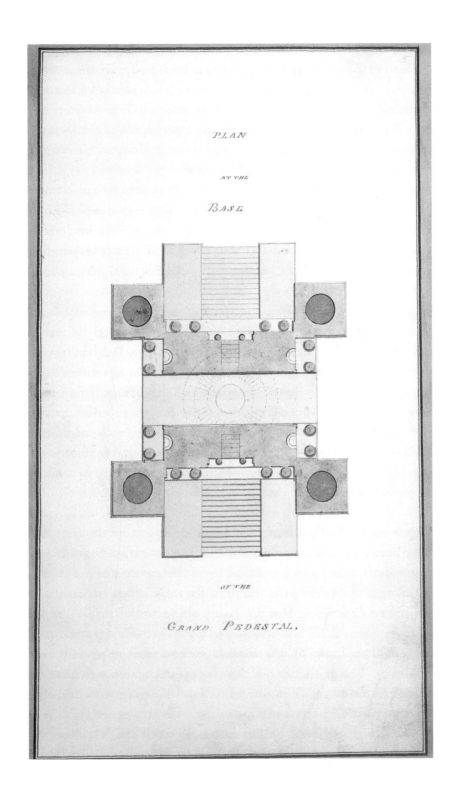

PLAN

AT THE

BASE

OF THE

GRAND PEDESTAL.

*Washington Monument,
Baltimore, Maryland.*

III

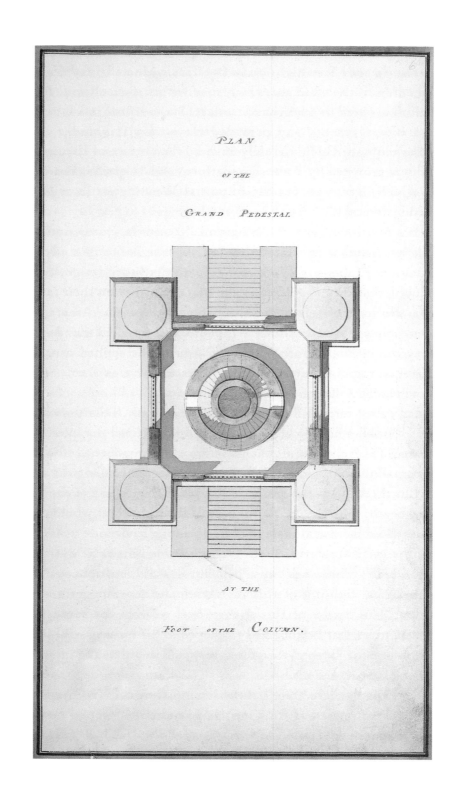

PLAN

OF THE

GRAND PEDESTAL

AT THE

FOOT OF THE COLUMN.

Washington Monument,
Baltimore, Maryland.

the Board on April 6th that his concept "admits of any extension or retraction of expenditures."[18] But economy was not uppermost in mind as he drew the column with its brick core, marble exterior, and metal ornament. This is his most polished surviving presentation. The drawings are delicate and self-explanatory; the prose is forceful and concise. He had every reason to be optimistic.

The Board promised to select a design at their May meeting, and during the long wait Mills kept in touch. Several weeks before they convened he sent a perspective drawing (which has not survived) to their secretary, Mr. Eli Simpkins, and wrote to Robert Gilmore, an influential member of the Board. The new drawing, Mills noted, would give a better idea of the "character and mass" than his earlier efforts. He stressed the potential for economy if required and suggested that the base be of granite and the bas-relief panels of marble. (Latrobe had used this combination in the Congressional cenotaphs, and Mills would later use it again in the Maxcy Monument.) He pointed out that the column could be constructed of freestone and suggested acquiring Revolutionary cannons to incorporate in the ornamental scheme.

Mills' plans encountered opposition. Some members of the Board expressed doubts about expense and others feared that the column might topple onto their homes. And the design itself was called into question. Latrobe, writing to the disgruntled Godefroy, said Mills' "Christian monument is an imitation of the design proposed for Lord Nelson. It is anything but a fit mausoleum for Washington. Mills is a wretched designer. He came to me too late to acquire principles of taste. He is a copyist, and is fit for nothing else. But he also has merit. He is an excellent man of detail, and a very snug contriver of domestic conveniences and will make a good deal of money. He wants that professional self respect which is the ruin of you and me, and therefore we shall go to the wall, while he will strut in the middle of the street."[19] Godefroy called the design a pagoda, and Rembrandt Peale, writing years later, recalled that objections to the design prompted the subsequent modifications. But Mills' papers reflect no hesitancy or doubt, and when he was informed of his victory he moved ahead promptly.

On May 2, 1814, Isaac McKim wrote to Mills announcing the award and noting that the $500 prize would be deducted from his salary if he directed the construction, for the Board felt that "the adoption of your design is presumed to be a sufficient compensation for what you have already done."[20] The prospect of a major project in Baltimore was welcome, for Mills could not find enough

18 Mills' essay, bound with the competition drawings, is in the collection of the Maryland Historical Society and has been published by Foster, "Robert Mills and the Washington Monument in Baltimore," *Maryland Historical Magazine* vol. 35 no. 2 (June 1939):144–160.

19 BHL to Maximilian Godefroy, October 10, 1814. Also see C.B. Davidson, "Maximilian Godefroy," *Maryland Historical Magazine* vol. 24 no. 3 (September 1934): 209.

20 Foster, 159.

work in Philadelphia. He had confided to Jefferson that "since my professional establishment in Philadelphia I have had my time completely occupied but [am] finding much difficulty in receiving pecuniary returns as suffices reasonably to my trouble."[21]

Jefferson provided a letter of recommendation to President Madison, for Mills hoped to participate in rebuilding the federal buildings following the War of 1812, but Latrobe got the job. The war also affected the plans of the Baltimore Monument Board. First there was a delay as the hostilities focused upon Baltimore; then, following the British defeat (September 12–14, 1814), civic leaders decided to erect a Battle monument designed by Godefroy in the Courthouse Square, the site previously set aside for the Washington Monument. The Board of Managers released the site because Robert Gilmore, now Chairman of the Building Committee, had already begun negotiations for a more dramatic site on the summit of Belvedere, the hillside estate of Col. John Eager Howard at the western edge of the city.

Waiting in Philadelphia, Mills accomplished little that winter. In several respects it was a season of disappointments. Just before Christmas his application for membership in the American Philosophical Society was rejected. In January nagging details at the Schuylkill Bridge required his attention, and he wrote to the Board of Managers of the bridge accepting full responsibility for things left undone, "which certainly come within the engagement of my contract with you."[22] The exterior trim, portions of which had structural implications, was still unfinished; window sills were not properly canted to shed water, and the roof was poorly shingled. Multiple commitments had diverted his normally attentive supervision, and shoddy work at the bridge was the result of his preoccupation. Through the end of the year Mills and Gilmore corresponded concerning Howard's site. Mills made a visit and "stepped the ground to ascertain the extent of each part" and drafted four ground plans. He recommended plan "No. 2," because it offered maximum lot frontage "upon the principal streets" and best met the needs of pedestrian and vehicular traffic. Mills added a postscript, broaching the subject of altering the design, asking Gilmore for his "ideas on the small sketch I left with you relative to certain minor alterations in the base of the monument."[23]

The sketch does not survive, but Gilmore responded that he preferred a solid pedestal, which suggests that this alteration was discussed long before expense became a consideration. Gilmore also gently rebuffed Mills' request for

21 RM to TJ, October 8, 1812.

22 RM to The honorable the Board of Managers of the Lancaster Schuylkill Bridge, January 28, 1815; PRM 0502.

23 RM to Robert Gilmore, November 7 and 16, 1814.

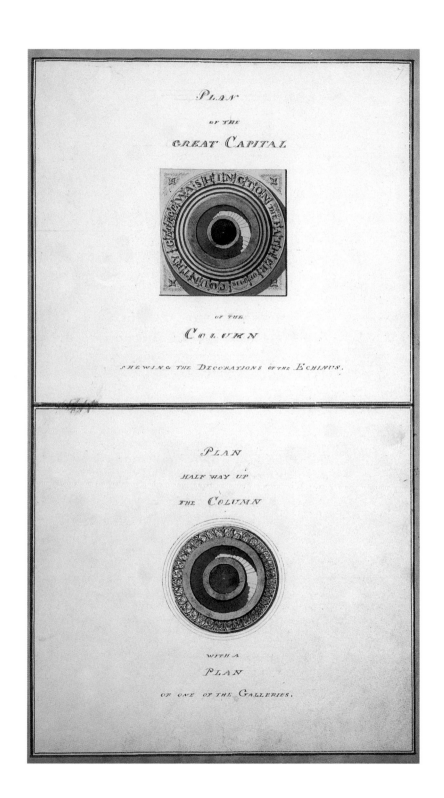

PLAN

OF THE

GREAT CAPITAL

OF THE

COLUMN

SHEWING THE DECORATIONS OF THE ECHINUS.

PLAN

HALF WAY UP

THE COLUMN

WITH A

PLAN

OF ONE OF THE GALLERIES.

Washington Monument,
Baltimore, Maryland.

an advance, saying they did not have enough money on hand to incur expenses of any kind and hoped the model Mills proposed would prove unnecessary; moreover, they did not want to settle upon "the precise final plan" until they were ready to begin construction.

Despite these uncertainties, both Mills and Gilmore pressed forward, making preparations for the commencement of operations in the spring. Contracts were signed with Sater Stevenson for the masonry in the foundations and base, with a carpenter named Robert Tunworth who was to serve as a general laborer and to be the general caretaker of the building site, and with Thomas Towson and William Steuart for marble. Materials were located, and Col. Howard's hilltop was obtained. April 1815 found Mills traveling often to Baltimore. Excavations were underway by the first week in May. Additional contracts were executed with John McNulty for excavations, with Clackner and Foss for stone for the foundation, and with William Constable for lumber. Mills drafted specifications for materials, readied the building site, coordinated construction, had full authority in questions of quality, served as paymaster, and maintained financial records for the Board.

From Philadelphia Eliza kept him abreast of family affairs. Little "Sarah sends her love. She says frequently 'Pa's come' when a stranger knocks at the door." And "I think of weaning Jacqueline this night if my heart don't fail me— a hard task."[24] Their domestic correspondence also recounts the star-crossed liaisons of Betty, a Black housemaid, and news of neighbors. As the tempo of work increased Mills spent more and more time in Baltimore. Everything progressed smoothly. The Board soon announced that the ceremonial setting of the cornerstone would take place at noon, July 4, 1815.

Eliza and the children moved to Baltimore; it was an auspicious new beginning. The celebration, like the monument itself, was planned on a grand scale. More than twenty-five thousand people assembled; a band played martial airs; the militia marched, flourished banners and fired a thirty-nine-gun salute (one for each year since the Declaration of Independence). Dignitaries gathered at the excavation, where a portrait of Washington and a large painting of the projected monument "formed an appropriate Trophy for the occasion." The crowd hushed and speeches began.

James A. Buchanan, President of the Board of Managers, spoke at length and turned to the Grand Master of the Masons, who tested the corner stone with plumb, square, and level; he pronounced it "true and trusty." Mills and the

24 EBSM to RM, April 15, 1815.

118

"operative Masons," William Steuart and Thomas Towson, set the stone. Their duty done, they stepped aside, and the Grand Master, the Mayor, and officers of the Society of the Cincinnati tapped the stone to settle it. The Grand Master asked the blessings of the "Grand Architect of the Universe," poured wine and oil, and scattered corn upon the stone. Mr. Buchanan then addressed Mills and presented him with the square, plumb, and level, and Mills made a speech that was carried in the newspaper accounts of the event:

> The honor, sir, you have been pleased to confer upon me I hope to prove that I duly appreciate by a faithful performance of the duties incumbent on me as your architect. I feel a double inducement to use my best exertions to execute faithfully and with ability the important duty entrusted to me from the recollection that the work to be performed is the execution of a monument to perpetuate our country's gratitude to the father of her liberties, and that you have given a preference to native genius in the choice of a design for the work.

More prayers and music extended the program into the summer evening. The finale must have been effective: "Yankee Doodle," another volley from the militia, and then "our evening sky was beautifully bespangled by rockets [which] rose in a brilliant line…forming a graceful arch turning into stars as they descended."[25]

BALTIMORE, 1815–1820

Robert Mills' residency in Baltimore (1815–1820) coincided with a critical period in the history of the city. When he arrived it seemed on the verge of a period of dramatic growth; its population had more than trebled since the Revolution (13,000 in 1790; 31,514 in 1800; 46,555 in 1810; and 62,738 in 1820). There were, as William Wirt then wrote to his daughter, "more than twice as many people as there are in Washington, Georgetown, Alexandria, and Richmond, all put together." The most dramatic growth took place among the white-collar and professional classes—people like Mills. In the decade prior to his arrival the number of attorneys had grown from sixteen to forty-three (a 168 percent increase), doctors from thirty-six to fifty-six (a sixty percent increase), clergymen from six to twenty-two (a 266 percent increase) and accountants from four to thirty-eight (an 850 percent increase). During these years Baltimore became

25 *Maryland Gazette*, June 29, 1815.

First Baptist Church, Baltimore, Maryland. Robert Mills, architect, 1816–1818.

the first American city to install gas street lights, and the establishment of corporations, factories, and the use of steam engines all increased dramatically. The stage seemed set for a period of sustained prosperity. In fact, however, a devastating depression was lurking in the wings.[26]

In 1815 Baltimore basked in a prosperity based on twenty years of European warfare. Baltimore merchants with their sophisticated clipper ships had excelled in blockade running and privateering, and their skill and daring had been richly rewarded. Two members of the Board of the Washington Monument, Robert Gilmore and Isaac McKim, exemplified the venture capitalists of Baltimore. McKim's schooner "Rossie" carried the first commission issued to a privateer by President Madison. McKim would later build the "Ann McKim," the largest and fastest of the Baltimore clippers. During the War of 1812 the merchants of Baltimore financed 126 privateers and captured 556 British vessels, accounting for fully one third of the British losses during the war. Equally significant, these privateers brought some sixteen million dollars into Baltimore. This lucrative period of seafaring culminated with the repulse of the British forces that had burned Washington. Victory prompted a surge of civic pride, a mood which resulted in the Battle Monument by Maximilian Godefroy, the initiation of work on the Washington Monument, and the instant popularity of the new "Star Spangled Banner," sung to the tune of "Anacreon in Heaven," a popular English drinking song.[27]

Architecture flourished in this environment, and Mills was busy for the first several years he lived in Baltimore. In addition to the on-going work at the

26 Hamilton Owens, *Baltimore on the Chesapeake* (Garden City: Doubleday, 1941), 149, 161, 201, 220, 253; also see Gary Browne, *Baltimore in the Nation, 1789–1861* (Chapel Hill: University of North Carolina Press, 1980), 58.

27 Owens, *Baltimore on the Chesapeake*, 201.

Washington Monument, he completed a series of residential projects (a porch for James A. Buchanan, 1816; a house for James Sloan, 1819; a house for Robert Oliver, 1819–1821; a house for John Hoffman, 1821–1822). He was responsible for at least two row houses (Waterloo Row, 1816–1819, and Courtland Street Row, 1819), designed several monuments (the Winchester Monument, 1816, the Aquilla Randall Monument, circa 1815, and the Calhoun-Buchanan Tomb, circa 1819), and served (1816–1817) as President of the Baltimore Water Company. He installed at least twenty furnaces and submitted plans to the city for the improvement of Jones Falls and its environs, participated in the competition for the Baltimore Exchange (1816), and drew plans for a library and several shop fronts.

Unfortunately, peace was an economic disaster for Baltimore. Tranquility in Europe permitted foreign goods to flood the American market. England and France reasserted control of their colonial trades. Black markets evaporated, and these problems were exacerbated by a simultaneous failure of the American banking system, which, in Baltimore, entailed the trial (and acquittal) of James A. Buchanan, then president of the Baltimore branch of the national bank. The recession and Buchanan's trial (and his resignation as President of the Board of Managers of the Washington Monument) halted virtually all construction, including work on the monument. Mills went bankrupt and was forced to seek work elsewhere in 1819.

FURNACES, THE MERCHANT'S EXCHANGE, THE FIRST BAPTIST CHURCH

During the latter half of 1815 Mills was busy establishing himself in Baltimore. Lacking documentation, we know little about his daily schedule, but it was during this autumn that he installed a furnace at the Patapsco Factory, adding heating systems to his repertoire. Furnaces were noteworthy as a new technology, and a Baltimore newspaper published a full account of Mills' work, so "the public may be benefited, and the merits of this most deserving and modest individual may be more generally known."[28]

The furnace was made of brick and soapstone. An access door with an adjustable grate or damper opened to the outside of the building allowing the firebox to be filled with "dry oak wood." Hollow brick flues passed through the firebox. Fresh air entered at one end of these flues and was heated as it passed through the section of the flue within the firebox. The heated air then rose within the flues to exit through vented registers throughout the mill. Adjustable

28 *Supplement to Nile's Register—Scraps*, n.d., 183.

dampers allowed regulation of the air within both the firebox and the flues. The writer noted that at three in the morning the fire was lighted and that the furnace was full of glowing coals by six. The flow of air into the firebox was then restricted and the furnace, without further tending, operated throughout the day keeping the mill at an even seventy degrees Fahrenheit. The smoke was separately vented; there was no odor, and throughout the factory the furnace maintained "the mild temperature of May." The article concluded with a comparative cost analysis of Mills' furnace and an alternative steam system and noted that the new furnace requires less than a cord of wood per week, or less than one seventh of the amount formerly consumed.

The emphasis on economy is taken directly from Daniel Pettibone's *Economy of Fuel*, the source of Mills' Patapsco plan. Pettibone appears in Mills' 1816 diary, but he was aware of the inventor before coming to Baltimore, for Pettibone's work was published in Philadelphia in 1812 and was endorsed by both Latrobe and George Clymer, President of the Bank of Philadelphia. On January 31, 1812, the latter wrote that a Pettibone furnace heated the lobby of the bank that had been constructed under Mills' supervision. Mills must have been impressed, for he obtained a license from Pettibone to build more furnaces and made the installation of furnaces a sub-specialty during the Baltimore years. His 1816 diary lists twenty-two such jobs, including residential, commercial, and institutional systems. Furnaces were demonstrably more efficient than fireplaces and radiant stoves; moreover, furnaces could be located outside the area to be heated, which often meant they were both safer and easier to maintain.

Construction normally slowed in midwinter, and Mills' first winter in Baltimore was no exception, but now there were several major and numerous minor projects to occupy his attention. On New Year's Day he completed the first of numerous competition drawings (none of which survive) for the proposed Baltimore Merchants Exchange. The Exchange Trustees wanted a prominent building; it was the most significant commercial architectural commission during the post-war boom in Baltimore, and for several weeks Mills actively sought this prize. He competed as he had for the Monumental Church and the Washington Monument; he got in touch with members of the Exchange, including Robert Goodloe Harper, a fellow South Carolinian. Several weeks later there was an exhibition of the contestants' drawings. Mills studied these then wrote the building committee and drafted "Plan No 4 of Exchange on a large scale with alterations."[29]

29 RM, "Diary, 1816," January 22, 1816; approximately sixty percent of this manuscript is transcribed in Richard X. Evans, "The Daily Journal of Robert Mills," *Maryland Historical Magazine* vol. 30 (1935): 257–271; PRM 4002.

He continued to refine his presentation, making more drawings and an estimate, which he submitted at the end of the month. (Latrobe later wrote to Godefroy that Mills had presented nine designs.) Mills noted in his diary on February 2, 1816, that "Mr. Latrobe (my old preceptor's) design for the Exchange approved."[30]

It is a measure of Mills' reputation that Latrobe had written Godefroy:

the fact is, that Ramee will be the Architect or Mills, and all we are doing is vain. Yet we can not avoid it. In such is the deplorable state of the arts among the mushrooms of fortune upon whose vile patronage they depend, that we must submit to the only means that exist to get employment at all & bread for our families. We are put into a dark room, in which we are to grope among straw for a pin. Instead of what we seek, we may encounter the bite of a rat, or the poison of a snake, or the slime of a toad.[31]

Sketches in Mills' diary are the only record of his proposals for the Exchange. As the most detailed elevation and plan depict different schemes, these notations present only a suggestion; nonetheless, it was clearly intended to be his most imposing building to date. The principal facade consisted of projecting central and end pavilions linked by lower blocks. The focal point of the facade, the central pavilion, is a bold example of the modern French use of a triumphal arch crossed by a screen of columns. Behind these columns the entry is sheltered in a large semi-circular niche that culminates in a coffered hemispherical dome. It is as if he had removed the raised basement from the elevation of his Washington Hall (Philadelphia, 1808). In the Baltimore proposal the arch dominates the pavilion rather than being used as a decorative adjunct, and the effect promised to be more monumental than it had been in Philadelphia. The Exchange proposal was the last major project in which Mills attempted to incorporate the full drama of Romantic Classicism. In the Washington Hall facade Mills had exploited the dramatic contrast of light and shade created by the screened recess to present statues of Washington, William Penn, and Alexander Hamilton. He also placed "on the blocking over the entablature, in front of [the] canopy, an Eagle...descending with a wreath of victory."[32]

Few American patrons favored sculptural embellishment, and Mills' later uses of the screened, recessed entry niche (St. John's Episcopal Church, Baltimore, 1817; Ainsley Hall House, Columbia, South Carolina, 1823) are much

30 Richard Evans, "The Daily Journal," 258.

31 BHL to Maximilian Godefroy, July 19, 1815.

32 Anon., *Washington Benevolent Society* (Philadelphia: U.S. Gazette, 1816), 101.

simplified, more akin to the appearance of this motif in Jefferson's Pavilion IX, West Range, at the University of Virginia than to the work of Ledoux.

Mills did not brood on his loss. Instead, he apparently drew a lesson from the experience; after this—except for major federal commissions—grandeur plays a diminished role in his work. Never again would he attempt to combine projecting pavilions, a triumphal arch, and dome; indeed, he would move away from the domed central plans that had been the hallmark of his early career. In Charleston, Philadelphia, and Richmond, his domed churches were unique, but after 1815, only one more of this type would be built to his design, and in the future he would increasingly restrict the use of grandiloquent, complex, or unusual forms to projects which were obviously symbolic.

Despite losing Baltimore's most prestigious commission of 1816, Mills was busy. The focal point of his work remained the Washington Monument, where he directed a crew of some forty laborers preparing its foundations. He was responsible for disbursing funds for both labor and materials and maintaining an account for the Board of Managers of the Monument.

While drafting plans for the Exchange, he also erected furnaces at the Monument smithy (a complete blacksmith's shop was necessary to maintain the stone cutting tools and to prepare metal cramps). Simultaneously he was involved with the installation or adjustment of furnaces at Rembrandt Peale's museum and at a "Mr. Bachonne's" academy. During the first weeks of the new year he drew a house plan for James Williams of Baltimore and worked on the "sarcophagus" [memorial urn] within the monumental porch of the Richmond church. Much of his work during the year entailed the renovation or remodeling of homes and offices. He also initiated the development of land owned by the Water Company and traveled to Richmond and Philadelphia on business.[33]

His professional life consisted of a variety of activities, and these early years in Baltimore were the most financially successful period of his career. He had a base salary of $1500 as President of the Water Company (August 1816–October 1817), and a salary of $1500 for directing the construction of the Monument; in addition, on December 28, 1816, he computed that he was owed $5,201 for twenty-two jobs either completed or underway during the year.

On February 3, 1816, the day after learning that he had lost the Exchange competition, he noted in his diary that he had "commenced the study of the designs for the Baptist Church, proposed to be built corner of Sharp & Lombard Sts." He also jotted that he was "consulting with Mr. Wilson about Baptist

33 See Mills' "Pocket Memorandum Book, 1816," PRM, 4002.

Church designs."[34] William Wilson, an influential parishioner, would prove to be Mills' contact in this situation, as Robert Gilmore had been during the Monument competition. Mills pursued this opportunity, and the diary records conversations, sketches, letters, presentations, and estimates.

On February 8th he wrote to the building committee and offered to superintend the construction, whether or not his plan might be selected. Two days later he noted that he had finished his design, and on February 12th he showed his proposals first to "Messrs Wilson" and later that evening to the whole committee. On February 15th he "called on Mr. Wilson who informed me of the adoption of my plan for the B Church."[35] Within a week he had advertised for bids, and initial trenching for the foundation began on February 26th.

The First Baptist Church of Baltimore is the last of his five domed auditoria. The simplicity of its elevation presents his mature and idiosyncratic interpretation of the Greek Revival. His earlier designs for "round" churches had included Adam Style spires, thermal windows, an array of recessed panels, blind arches, and projecting porches and pavilions—all of which tended to obscure the auditoria within. Here the reference is the Pantheon instead of James Gibbs' Georgian central plans. The exterior walls are a smooth, virtually unbroken expanse of stucco over brick. The only significant decorative element is a broad frieze, which extends around the projecting hexastyle Ionic portico and unifies the composition. This was Mills' first monumental use of the Ionic order; it was, perhaps, the realization of his thwarted vision for the Circular Church in Charleston (1804). The columns of the Baptist Church were unfluted and Palladian in proportion, being nine diameters high; the six capitals were executed by Capellano for $250. The portico framed a projecting vestibule, which contained a stair at either end leading to the gallery that swept around the auditorium. Upon passing through the vestibule and into the auditorium, the visitor found a central aisle leading to a sunken baptismal pool before the pulpit. The pulpit, dramatically elevated, was much like those he had designed for St. Michael's, Charleston, First Presbyterian, Augusta, the Johns Island Church proposal, and the Monumental Church in Richmond. Indeed, such a pulpit was invariably the focal point of his acoustical plan. Other elements recurred here too: the circular floor plan, approximately 110 feet in diameter, a low saucer dome, and a crowning cupola or monitor.

The dome of the Baptist Church, like the domes of his earlier auditorium churches, was based upon the use of laminated wooden ribs. The First Baptist

34 Evans, "Daily Journal," 258.

35 Evans, 259.

Church in Baltimore was a success, even drawing a compliment from Latrobe, who wrote Mills that "the portico of the Baptist Church is a beautiful thing." And Latrobe's son in his guide to Baltimore called it "an ornament to [its] part of the city."[36] Equally important to Mills' reputation was the fact that the construction proceeded in an orderly, timely fashion. The excavation for the foundation began during the last week in April, and for the next several months he supervised construction at the church, the Monument and his own home. In early April, with the danger of freezing past, masonry work began, the foundations for the columns were laid on October 28, and on November 18th Mills delivered sketches of the church to George Strickland, brother of William, the architect, in Philadelphia to enable the artist to produce a "prospect" or perspectival drawing. December found Mills drawing the pews, decorative details, and the Ionic capitals. The building was ready to enclose that winter, for on February 20th Eliza wrote to Robert (who was in Richmond on business) that men from the church had stopped by the house seeking drawings for the construction of the dome. Mills' method was to produce drawings as work progressed, and his diary notes drawings made for the church during the whole span of construction (February 20, June 6, August 20, and November 14). Smaller jobs during these months included the design of a shop front for Fielding Lucas, a bookseller and publisher who would later publish much of Mills' writing, the "alterations of Mr. G.s house," and the "examination" of the home of "Mr. Walsh." He was also working on his own house on St. Paul's Lane; he installed a furnace and built an addition during the winter and early spring, and by April 3rd he and Eliza were able to select wallpaper. On May 11th he "moved all the family into new house where I humbly trust the blessing of God will accompany us."[37]

During the Baltimore years Mills' family responsibilities increased. Their oldest daughters, Sarah Zane Mills (1811–1894) and Jacqueline Smith Mills (1814–1859), had been born in Philadelphia. Two more daughters, Mary Powell Mills (1816–1894) and Anna Mills (1819–1864), were born in Baltimore. His eldest brother, Thomas Mills (1774–?) had moved to Philadelphia, but there is little surviving evidence concerning contact between the two families (Thomas and his second wife, Elizabeth Diana Humphreys, had twelve children—seven girls and five boys). Robert's other brother, Henry Mills (1777–1806), had died in Charleston leaving his widow, Mary Phillips Mills and at least one child, Henry (b. 1805), destitute. Mary depended on the generosity of friends. Both

36 BHL to RM, November 20, 1817; John H. B. Latrobe, *Picture of Baltimore* (Baltimore: F. Lucas, Jr., 1832), 137.

37 PRM, 4002; Evans, "The Daily Journal of Robert Mills," *Maryland Historical Magazine* 30 (1935): 261.

Thomas Mills and Robert's sister Sarah Mills Lusher, who lived in Charleston, disapproved of Mary's way of life. In 1817 Robert invited Mary to come and live with them in Baltimore. She declined. The following year (April 1818) she sent young Henry to Baltimore, and he remained with Robert and Eliza until they moved to South Carolina in 1820. Life was hard for Mary. She was living in the orphan asylum in Charleston in 1819. Ostracized by old friends, she argued with the matron, burned herself badly, and may have become an alcoholic. Robert's younger sister, Sarah Mills (1787–1846) had married George Lusher in 1805. By 1817 he had become an abusive drunkard. Sarah wrote to Robert that "death would be a deliverance for me." And "my cup of sorrow is full I have drank its dregs."[38] She lived for her children, five of whom were alive in 1820 when Robert and Eliza moved to South Carolina.

SEEKING WORK IN RICHMOND

On March 1, 1816, Mills received a letter from a friend in Richmond, Col. John Ambler, informing him that plans were afoot for a city hall and courthouse. Mills acted decisively, despite numerous commitments in Baltimore. Deciding to go to Richmond and put his hat in the ring, he left Baltimore on March 5th, traveling, presumably by stagecoach, overland to Washington, then "by hack" to Alexandria where he spent the night. The next night found him in Fredricksburg, and he arrived in Richmond on March 7th "by early candle-light." The following day, having taken up residence with the Ambler family, he began sketching plans for the courthouse. He spent the morning of his second day in Richmond refining his drawings and that afternoon he presented them to "the committee." The third day, being Sunday, he attended services in the Monumental Church.[39]

Throughout the following week he was "engaged in designs for Court-house," but he took time to dine with Governor Wilson Cary Nicholas on Tuesday, to meet again with the Court House Committee Wednesday evening, to dine with Judge John Wickham on Thursday and Dr. John Brockenbrough on Friday. On Saturday he "Began a study of a proposed route of a canal from the Basin to Rockets without locks," wrote to Eliza, and spent time on the courthouse plans. The following Monday he met with the "Commissioners of the Court H." who approved the plans; he also "met the Town Hall who confirmed it." For the remainder of the week he worked on his canal proposal, which he

38 Sarah Mills Lusher to RM, January 23 and February 3, 1830.

39 Evans, "The Daily Journal," 260–261; City of Richmond, VA, *Records No. 5, Common Council, 1814–1816*, March 18, 1816, 150; *Virginia Patriot*, Richmond, June 13, 1814; *Daily Compiler*, Richmond, July 9, 1814, 3–4.

directed to the "Commissioners of navigation." Leaving the canal material with his friend Ambler, Mills departed for home on March 23, noting that the "commissioners of the Court House agree to give me $400 for my design." He left Richmond confident work would soon begin on the courthouse, as in June and July he advertised for bricks, lime, and lumber. The advertisement noted "that no heavy timber is required," so the courthouse was probably designed to be fireproof, masonry vaulted, structurally similar to the Burlington County Jail or the courthouses he proposed for South Carolina during the 1820s.[40]

The Richmond excursion is one of the best documented examples of Mills' decisiveness. He had promptly determined to undertake the journey and set to work immediately upon arrival. He quickly assessed the situation, settled on a plan, and produced a convincing set of drawings. He used spare time to re-establish relationships with potential patrons; his suggestions for the Capitol grounds and the canal were probably prompted by these social contacts. Little is known about his canal proposal, but it seems to have been his earliest effort in an area that absorbed much of his attention during the 1820s. Clearly, he felt his brief contact with the Chesapeake and Delaware Canal qualified him for such work.

The Virginia legislature authorized renovation of the Capitol and landscaping of the site on February 28, 1816, some two weeks before Mills' decision to go to Richmond. If he went seeking these commissions, he was disappointed, for Maximilian Godefroy was retained in June to work on the Capitol—he arrived in Richmond two months after Mills' departure. Throughout that summer Godefroy maintained an office in the Capitol, and in addition to his work for the state, he received a commission to integrate two bank facades from Mills' friends Wickham and Brockenbrough. Worse yet, from Mills' point of view, work was halted on the foundations of the courthouse, and in August 1816, Mills' plan was replaced by a design by Godefroy. Thus the Richmond excursion, once bright with promise, bore bitter fruit.[41]

Mills' plan for the courthouse survives only as a sketched plan and elevation in the 1816 diary. He apparently proposed a square, two-story central block capped by a saucer dome and flanked by lower wings. Aspects of his plan and elevation are not congruent. Nonetheless, it is clear he intended porticoes on the southeast and southwest elevations, and beneath the dome, an oval courtroom with a gallery and an elevated bench or dais reminiscent of the pulpits in the auditorium churches. The flanking wings were to contain offices. The sketch indicates vaulted, fireproof construction. He placed stairways in the southeast

40 Evans, "The Daily Journal," 260–261; City of Richmond, VA, *Records No. 5, Common Council, 1814–1816*, March 18, 1816, 150; *Virginia Patriot*, Richmond, June 13, 1814; *Daily Compiler*, Richmond, July 9, 1814, 3–4.

41 For Godefroy in Richmond see Robert L. Alexander, "Maximilian Godefroy in Virginia: A French Interlude in Richmond's Architecture," *Virginia Magazine of History and Biography* vol. 69 no. 4 (October 1961): 420–431.

corners of the central block; the northwest corners contained offices for judge and jury. The only decorative elements clearly shown are four niches flanking entries in the courtroom, and, in the elevation, a Doric portico, occulae or roundels in the central block, and as fenestration on the wings the familiar shallow arch framing thermal windows. The roofline of both the central block and the wings was to be hidden by a parapet based on a bold entablature.

Mills' proposal for the Richmond Courthouse provides an example of his tendency to rework his designs, for in proposals for two libraries he later rearranged the elements of this proposal: fireproof offices and the domed rotunda. For a proposed library at the corner of Monument Place and Church Street in Baltimore, he submitted (July 19, 1817) a plan to John Hoffman that consisted of a raised "Basement or office story" containing fireproof, vaulted attorneys' offices (the intended site was adjacent to the courthouse) and a library on the principal floor in a rotunda that rose "above the main walls of the building and is crowned with a dome."[42] His description of this plan—which was not executed—is similar to his proposal for the Caroliniana Library (1836–1840) at the South Carolina College. As discussed in the next chapter, the Caroliniana was drastically altered, but sketches and a set of measured plans by Mills are similar to the library he described to John Hoffman in Baltimore. Jefferson's library at the University of Virginia no doubt prompted Mills to adapt the Pantheon rotunda for these library proposals, and the Charlottesville rotunda may have influenced his proposal for the Richmond Courthouse and the U.S. Bank he unsuccessfully proposed for Baltimore (1817). Be that as it may, Mills must have drawn a lesson from the failure in Richmond, for his subsequent courthouses do not include rotundas.

With Robert away in Richmond Eliza found herself tending to loose ends left by a distracted husband. The day he left (March 7, 1816) she discovered the woodshed empty. Clients came to the door: "one of the Baptist gentlemen called but who, Nancy did not know. She said you had gone to Richmond." Or again, "I have never known you so much called upon when absent." She confronted creditors and chided him, "I wish you at home when you could answer these things—as usual I know nothing about them."[43] And she dealt with a rental house that he had purchased in Baltimore. His activity gave every appearance of success. He had private, governmental, and institutional patrons; he had completed twenty-five projects in five states; his drawings had been exhibited and won competitions. But to their sorrow he often found patrons prone to haggle and slow to pay. The competitions rarely paid the prizes advertised, and among

42 RM to John Hoffman, July 19, 1817; PRM 0671.

43 EBSM to RM, March 9 and 12, 1816.

the architects he knew, only James Hoban flourished (and this was a special case, for Hoban's prosperity was grounded in real estate and federal work). Mills' correspondence makes it painfully clear that there was a chronic shortage of money to operate the household. Eliza's laments may be due in part to their method of managing income and expenses. She had to constantly ask for money to pay the grocer, the woodcutter, the children's doctor. Whatever their problems, they were always able to own their own home, and Robert felt able to invest modestly in rental housing in Philadelphia and Baltimore and raw land in Bath County, Virginia.

In 1816, Robert and Eliza purchased and remodeled a home on Saint Paul's Lane, Extended, in Baltimore. Work on this house and on the Washington Monument occupied much of his time following the return from Richmond. He supervised the laying of the first marble at the Monument (May 1st) and ordered curved molds for the brick interior core. Work on the First Baptist Church continued, and he undertook several smaller residential and commercial projects. June found him travelling again, this time to Philadelphia. On June 24, 1816, he took the steamboat to the head of the Chesapeake and crossed overland to Wilmington, Delaware, where he arrived at midnight. Reaching Philadelphia "by 11 o'clock" the next day, he made a "drawing of vestibule of Washington Hall" and visited the Academy of Fine Arts. He consulted on the heating of the Marine Asylum; then, on July 3rd, accompanied by his sister and her son, he took the steamboat down river and retraced his steps to Baltimore. He now planned a series of drawings "in prospect," perspectival views of the Washington Monument with its altered base, the Richmond Courthouse, the First Baptist Church in Baltimore, and Washington Hall. (The elevation of Washington Hall by George Strickland is the only one of this set known to have been produced.)[44]

In 1813 the Washington Benevolent Society, of which Mills was a member, had solicited plans for a meeting hall to be erected adjacent to a renovated hotel on Third Street. They received "from different artists a great variety of plans," and from "Robert Mills, Esz. They received no less than ten or twelve."[45] Mills' approved elevation was a complex pastiche of Adam Style and French motifs. Sculptural niches, bas-relief ornament in recessed panels, piers and columns in antis, and crowning shallow coffered dome-like niches created what must have been—for the building was designed for public meetings and entertainment—an intentionally festive and theatrical elevation. The facade was seventy-three feet

44 Illustrated by Gallagher, opposite 42.

45 Peter Hastings Falk, ed., *The Annual Exhibition Record of the Pennsylvania Academy of the Fine Arts, 1807–1870*, a reprint of Anna Wells Rutledge, *Cumulative Record of Exhibition Catalogues* (Madison, CT: Sound View Press, 1988), 142–143.

wide, and the building was 138 feet nine inches deep. Four marble steps led into a round vestibule, twenty-six feet in diameter and crowned by a dome. Behind the vestibule and to the right was a large meeting room—117 feet long and thirty feet wide. This room was much like the typical convention room in a late twentieth-century hotel. One long wall consisted of folding doors that could be opened to expand the floor area by incorporating a flanking corridor; thus extended, the room was said to accommodate 3,000 people. The narrow ends of this assembly room were semi-circular, and there was a "music gallery" or balcony above the entry from the vestibule. Across the central corridor, which extended the full depth of the ground floor, were committee rooms and a fireproof closet. The principal staircase opened to the right as one entered the vestibule and ascended to a second vestibule, the lobby for the "Grand Saloon." This second-story lobby or vestibule was lighted by a floor to ceiling window within the great niche on the facade. The "Grand Saloon" must have been one of the largest private meeting rooms in North America. It was 120 feet long, sixty-nine feet nine inches wide. Its vaulted ceiling rose to a height of forty-five feet. A gallery carried by an Ionic colonnade surrounded the room. It was estimated to accommodate 4,000 people on the floor and an additional 2,000 in the galleries.

The interior hallways and exterior piazza of the Washington Hall (1813–1816, burned 1823) linked the meeting rooms to the adjacent hotel—thus people using the meeting rooms had access to kitchen facilities, bar, hairdresser, pastry room, and lodging. Mills considered it an important commission.[46]

PROFESSIONAL DIVERSIFICATION

On August 2, 1816, Mills was elected President of the Baltimore Water Company. This job paid $1,500 a year and thrust him into urban development. The Water Company had been established in 1805, so Mills' role was not analogous to the part played by Latrobe in Philadelphia; instead, he only had to keep things running and concentrate on developing company property. Upon being hired, he toured the works with John Davis, his predecessor, who had designed the system. They walked along the sluice that carried water from Jones Falls to a waterwheel. The waterwheel drove pumps that lifted the water into reservoirs near the corners of Calvert and Centre Streets and Franklin and Cathedral Streets. A steam-driven pump had been installed near the Belvidere Bridge, but it was only used as a back-up system.[47]

46 Alexander, 61–62 n49, in Bryan, ed., *Robert Mills, Architect.*

47 "Autobiography of John Davis, 1770–1864," *Maryland Historical Magazine* 30 (1935): 23–24.

Mills knew Davis, an English immigrant who had served as Clerk of the Works for Latrobe at the Philadelphia waterworks. In 1805 Davis was called to Baltimore, where topography and his penchant for simplicity enabled him to create a system which proved less prone to break-downs and cheaper to operate than its Philadelphia counterpart. He was soon sought after and became involved in the Susquehanna Canal and numerous mills in the Baltimore area, including a three-mile mill race with four large flour mills at Gwynns Falls and two more mills on Jones Falls. He designed the City Spring Fountain on North Calvert Street and completed a famous well, approximately 100 feet deep, within the walls of Fort McHenry. For such work his fee was ten percent of costs, and as the waterworks no longer needed the attention of a fulltime engineer, Davis concentrated on consulting and arranged, circa 1808, to take a reduced salary as President of the Water Company. It was this post that Mills obtained.

The Water Company job did not require daily oversight of operations, and five days after assuming his new responsibilities Mills left town to accompany Eliza and the children to Hackwood. He returned briefly then went back to Virginia at the end of the month, for little Jacqueline was ill. Not until September 9th does his diary reflect participation in Water Company business and then for the next several months all entries mentioning the company concern the surveying of streets and lots, the presentation of plans to the Board, and finally, "Dec. 20. Finished drawing of Col Buchanan's house. Also drawing of range of houses for water company."[48]

Clearly, from the outset he was charged primarily with real estate development, but this occupied only a portion of his time. As he prepared the plans that would result in Waterloo Row (1816–1819) he simultaneously sought to finalize the decorative detailing of the Washington Monument, designed the tomb for the Monumental Church, continued to supervise construction at the First Baptist Church in Baltimore, and made four more drawings of Washington Hall. He also accepted residential work and made another quick trip by steamboat to Philadelphia (November 16–21, 1816).

The Philadelphia trip was apparently related to the completion of Washington Hall rather than a new commission, for his association with Philadelphia was drawing to a close. William Strickland, formerly his office-mate under Latrobe, now dominated architecture in Philadelphia. Prior to Mills' departure, Strickland had been responsible for only one building—now he had several underway. In Philadelphia Mills made a quick sketch in his diary

48 Evans, 269.

of a Swedenborgian church, The Temple of the New Jerusalem (1816–1817), at George and Twelfth Streets, designed by Strickland.

This sketch is the only one known that year by Mills of a building designed by somebody else. He rarely recorded his impression of work by others. Strickland's application of Saracenic and Gothic detail to a domed central plan must have seemed worth remembering.

Later that winter, during a spell of bitterly cold weather (February 10 through March 15, 1817), Mills made a longer trip. Travelling overland by stage to South Carolina, he wrote Eliza from Fredricksburg, Virginia (February 12), and Fayetteville, North Carolina (February 16), before arriving in Charleston on February 18th. The first stagecoach broke an axle seven miles south of Baltimore, and the eight passengers walked four miles before being picked up by a passing carriage. In Washington that evening Mills chanced to meet Dr. Thornton. (Thornton offered him the use of a horse in Charleston, if he would ride it back to Washington. Mills declined.) Also by chance he dined with Samuel Lane, Superintendent of Public Buildings, and he noted to Eliza that Lane had inquired about his practice. The next morning before dawn (4:30) he took the stage for Alexandria and then south to Richmond, Fayetteville, and Charleston.

Mills accepted the hardships of travel as routine, only observing that he wished he had "2 or 3 days to spare [as] I should have liked to have gone to Charleston by way of Camden & Columbia, a part of my native state I have never seen." In Charleston he "perceived great alterations...but not such as I have been accustomed to see in Pha. or Baltimore." After having been there a week he "found the improvements or I may say the additions...so extensive that it was with difficulty I could distinguish places I was formerly familiar with. The population of this City has increased amazingly & with good reason, as it ranks now the 3rd city in the Union—and (would you believe it), is more healthy than either Baltimore Pha or New York—a proof of this is that the proportion of deaths here is less than in either of the other cities, according to population. It is a delightful winter climate, but the heats of summer are powerful, but this would be bearable if the muskitoes could be excluded."[49]

Reading this, it may have occurred to Eliza that he was thinking of relocating, and perhaps their move to South Carolina in 1820 was influenced by this trip. Mills must have noted that Internal Improvements, a state-wide network of canals, courthouses, and jails was a topic of public discussion. Another

[49] RM to EBSM, February 16, 21, and 27, 1817.

possible result of this journey was a plan for a jail in Richmond, Virginia. On March 17, 1817, the Common Council in Richmond voted to "pay Mr. Mills and Mr. Manson twenty five dollars each for plans furnished by them, of a jail for the city."[50] Mills had passed through Richmond the previous week on his return trip, but the plans he apparently submitted have not survived.

From Charleston he wrote Eliza that he would delay his return in order to work on plans for "one or two churches which are contemplated to be built here."[51] One of these was probably the First Baptist Church (1818–1822), which demonstrates his evolution toward the Greek Revival and the use of large expanses of unbroken plane, clear geometric form and a pronounced horizontality. Consisting of a Doric portico and rectangular nave, it reflects the Gibbsian tradition of its neighbors, St. Michael's (1752–1761) and the Second Presbyterian Church (1809–1816). Here Mills put aside his auditorium plan and returned to the traditional, rectangular plan he had used in Augusta (circa 1807–1812) and proposed for Johns Island (circa 1803). He considered it "Greek" and published a description that unequivocally expressed his satisfaction:

The Baptist church exhibits the best specimen of correct taste in architecture of the modern buildings in this city. It is purely Greek in its style, simply grand in its proportions, and beautiful in its detail. The plan is of the temple form, divided into four parts; the portico, vestibule, nave, and vestry rooms. The whole length of the building is 110 feet, and breadth 60.

The facade presents a portico of four massy columns of the lightest proportions of the Doric, surmounted by a pediment. Behind this portico (on the main walls) rises an attic story squared up to the height of the roof, and crowned by a cupola or belfry. The side walls of the building are opened by the requisite apertures for windows and doors, and a full cornice runs round the whole.

You enter the vestibule by three doors, on each side of which the gallery stairs ascend; by three opposite doors you pass into the aisles, dividing the pews into blocks; at the extreme end of the nave of the church are the baptismal font and pulpit, lighted by a large vaulted window.

Around three sides of the nave a double colonnade extends, rises up to the roof, and supports the galleries. The lower order of the columns is Doric, the upper Ionic; each with their regular entablatures; the whole finished in a rich chaste style, and producing from the unity of the design, a very pleasing effect.[52]

50 City of Richmond, VA, *Records No. 6, Common Council 1816–1819*, March 17, 1817, 48.

51 RM to EBSM, March 5, 1817.

52 RM to EBSM, March 5, 1817.

Very few statements by Mills survive expressing satisfaction with his own work. The description of the First Baptist Church is all the more remarkable as he had little or nothing to do with its construction. The Church advertised for bids in the spring of the following year; the cornerstone was set on September 16, 1819, and the building was dedicated on January 17, 1822, two years after he and Eliza had moved to South Carolina.[53]

Mills' travels and work for the Baltimore Water Company made him experience first-hand the country's need for improved transportation to facilitate growth and trade. Support for roads, canals, and waterworks became one of the major political topics of the 1820s, and during his years in Baltimore he began writing about regional transportation. An early indication of his growing interest appears in notations at the end of the 1816 journal in reflective end-of-the-year paragraphs under the headings "Railroads" (in reality a method of building roads based upon tramways used in quarries in New England) and "Water" (here he sketched a development plan for Baltimore, a modification of the flood plain below Jones Falls to extend and maintain the navigable channel, to provide additional mill sites and create commercial streets with frontage on the stream). His musing about Jones Falls soon appeared prophetic.

PROPOSALS FOR PUBLIC WORKS

In the summer of 1817, as was their habit, Mills accompanied Eliza and the children to Hackwood. While they were traveling, torrential summer rains prompted him to mention his anxiety about potential flooding in the Baltimore area, and as he was returning home a friend told him about the disastrous flood of August 9, 1817. When he reached Baltimore he wrote Eliza of the devastation: "Many families were actually taken out of the 2d story of their houses, where the water had reached them—at the place where Mrs. Launy lived the water in the street was as high as her head."[54] The normally placid Jones Falls flowed through the city, its banks closely lined with mills, privies, houses, and streets. Its typical depth was only three feet, but on the morning of August 9th, a flash flood caused it to rise rapidly twenty feet above its banks. Trees, buildings, and bridges were swept downstream. Flotsam lodged against the arches of the stone bridge, and water fanned out into the streets.

Baltimore was still picking up and drying out when City Council called for the inevitable report; they turned to the president of the Water Company,

53 *City Gazette*, Charleston, April 20, 1819; also see Liscombe, *Church Architecture of Robert Mills*, 14, 54.

54 RM to EBSM, August 14, 1817, PRM 0681.

and Mills' plan (September 25, 1817) is one of the few documents that he signed simply as an "Engineer." His essay is more than an analysis of flood control, for he seized the chance to address the larger issues of urban design, land use, transportation, active and passive recreation, property values, and green space.[55] He saw that impediments could be removed from the streambed in a manner that would create a constellation of civic benefits and spoke of the plan as being "ornamental" as well as "useful." He proposed to straighten the water course between John and Bath streets by taking enough land from the west bank to make Holiday Street a waterfront boulevard. Below Pratt Street he suggested moving the channel east and into under-developed land, thus creating more commercial property in the East Market-Union Street area. As Jones Falls needed dredging he recommended using the excavated sand and gravel to build wharves along both banks from the harbor inland to Madison Street. These wharves and the boulevards behind them would serve as a defined flood plain in times of high water. He wanted to place a canal lock at the mouth of Jones Falls, where it emptied into the Basin (harbor). The lock would make the improved waterway navigable at any stage of the tide. To keep the channel free of sediment he suggested digging pits in the bed of the stream. The pits would trap sediment, which could be periodically mined and sold by the city. To avoid obstructions in the channel he argued that new bridges should all be of a single span like those over the Seine and the D'Oise, masonry bridges of comparable span and rise to those he had in mind. (He did not cite the Lancaster Schuylkill Bridge in Philadelphia—perhaps because it was wooden or perhaps because its designer, Lewis Wernwag, also submitted a proposal for Jones Falls.) Having dealt with the waterway itself, he pointed out that the wharves would foster the development of a new business district, and that this should prove inducement enough to secure the cooperation of property owners in the area. Finally, he urged that the new streets be "planted with a row of trees" to create "a place of public recreation, a promenade" with "romantic scenery and waterfalls...associated with this walk a recess here and there could be added, planted with trees and provided with seats, no city in the Union could...vie with it."[56] This last boast was correct, for there was nothing to match his plan in America.

The City Council found the transformation of the flood plain appealing, but balked at the cost. Their sense of urgency subsided as the water ebbed, and they only resolved that the next Council should decide what to do. The next Council did advertise for designs (March 5, 1818) and offered a $500 prize. Mills resubmitted. He

55 Robert Mills, "Report on the Survey of Jones' Falls," *Baltimore American* (October, 3, 1817): 2.

56 Robert Mills, "Report on the Survey of Jones' Falls," *Baltimore American* (October, 3, 1817): 2.

was in good company, for both Lewis Wernwag and Benjamin Henry Latrobe offered proposals, as did eight other aspirants. The Committee on the Harbor reviewed the plans and reported "they feel themselves not authorized to recommend definitively any of the plans," but that "your committee are of opinion that the plan No 2 in Mr. Robert Mills' Map is under all circumstances of the case, that which is most suitable to their views."[57] The committee did not give the prize to anyone, but that was not the end of it, for by doing nothing they guaranteed the problem would rise again. Twenty years later the stream flooded portions of the inner city, and both Mills and Wernwag wrote to remind a new set of Councilmen that their plans were on file. This Council, like their predecessors, decided not to decide, and the final flurry of correspondence (1837) is notable only insofar as it illuminates the first round of designs (1817–1818). During the second round, Wernwag complained that Mills' initial plan was copied from a draft he had entrusted to Mills immediately after the flood of 1817.[58] Unfortunately, we cannot judge the merits of Wernwag's charge, since his plan is unknown. Excepting his accusation, the only relevant fragment of evidence is the "Water" passage in Mills' 1816 diary, and if this paragraph was indeed written during the winter of 1816, then Mills had the major elements of his own plan in mind six to eight months before Jones Falls flooded on August 8, 1817.[59]

Mills' association with canals dated from his earliest contact with Latrobe—the Washington canal lock and the Chesapeake and Delaware feeder canal project (both circa 1803). He cultivated this interest in Baltimore as he looked to engineering as an alternative source of income, and—in addition to the Jones Falls proposal—immediately before moving to South Carolina, he published a pamphlet titled *A Treatise on Inland Navigation* (1820).[60] This essay suggested a canal uniting the waters of the Susquehanna and Potomac and linking Baltimore to "the country west of the Allegheny mountains." He claimed that with "a perfect navigation of the Susquehanna to Baltimore, a preference would be given to this river, rather than to the canal of New York." Having noted that the Potomac at Shepherdsown, West Virginia, was 310 feet above sea level and that the Susquehanna at Middleton, Pennsylvania, near the falls of the Conewago, was 160 feet above the tide, he proposed a canal flowing northeastward along the eastern face of the mountains. A spur from this canal, near Emmitsburg, Maryland, would descend to Baltimore along the ridge dividing the Gunpowder and Patapsco Rivers. To bolster this proposal he cited canals in New York, Pennsylvania, Virginia and South Carolina as well as examples in

57 "Report & Resolution on the Petition of B.H. Latrobe," March 24, 1830, Baltimore City Archives.

58 Lewis Wernwag to S. Smith, Mayor, July 15, 1837, Baltimore City Archives.

59 RM, Report on the Survey of Jones' Fall," *Baltimore American,* October 3, 1817, p. 2, addressed to the mayor and city council of Baltimore, September 25, 1817. See also Bryan, ed., *Robert Mills, Architect,* 102 n15.

60 Robert Mills, *A Treatise on Inland Navigation, Accompanied by a Map* (Baltimore: F. Lucas, 1820).

China, Russia, Egypt, Europe and England. The essay reviewed construction and transportation costs, ancillary social effects, and the possibility of transcontinental communications based on railroads and canals. Much of Mills' *Treatise* was drawn from Albert Gallatin's *Report on Public Roads & Canals* and from letters by Robert Fulton and Benjamin Henry Latrobe that were reprinted as appendices in Gallatin's *Report*.[61] The Susquehanna-Potomac canal pamphlet is Mills' first published canal proposal. Nothing came of it.

Mills' attention was drawn like a compass needle to public issues which entailed potential construction—fireproofing, flood control, transportation, civic monuments—and on October 4, 1817, while he waited for a decision on the Jones Falls proposal a gunpowder factory, Levering & Company, located eight miles from Baltimore, exploded. Buildings in the vicinity were destroyed, others "3 miles off had their window glass broken," a concussion was "sensibly felt" in town, and the following week Mills wrote City Council concerning public safety and the production, transportation and storage of munitions.[62]

From this accident Mills drew a grim lesson. Despite the scope of destruction, the Levering Company contained less than one-tenth of the gunpowder then stored in the Federal Hill Arsenal within the city. He pointed out that the practice "in Europe is to deposit the powder in different parts [of the city] and not to collect it all into one magazine." Even better, he said, would be to locate a group of magazines out of town on navigable water as "the transportation of powder by water is much less liable to accident than by land." He suggested a site surrounded by hills and thought that such criteria could be met on the Patapsco River. He said he would be happy to submit a design "embracing strength with economy...made fireproof [and] on a circular plan."[63] Today there are no known plans for a circular magazine by Mills, but in 1817 the issues he addressed were familiar to all thoughtful people.

As early as 1719 the English Parliament had passed an "Act for Preventing the Mischief's which may happen by keeping too great Quantities of Gunpowder in or near the Cities of London and Westminster or the Suburbs thereof."[64] Closer to home there were precedents for the fireproof, brick-vaulted, circular magazines advocated by Mills. Latrobe's first federal work (1798) was a survey of fortifications at Point Nelson and Fort Norfolk, Virginia. His sketches included the ruined foundations of a circular powder magazine. The renovations Latrobe proposed there also incorporated a circular magazine, and he wrote to Jefferson that these plans were used and complained that the

61 Albert Gallatin, *Report of the Secretary of the Treasury on the Subject of Public Roads and Canals* (Washington: R.C. Weightman, 1808), 104–123.

62 RM to the Honorable Mayor and City Council, October 12, 1817, Baltimore City Archives.

63 RM to the Honorable Mayor and City Council, October 12, 1817, Baltimore City Archives.

64 International Congress of Applied Chemistry, *Rise and Progress of the British Explosives Industry* (London: Whittaker, 1909), 142.

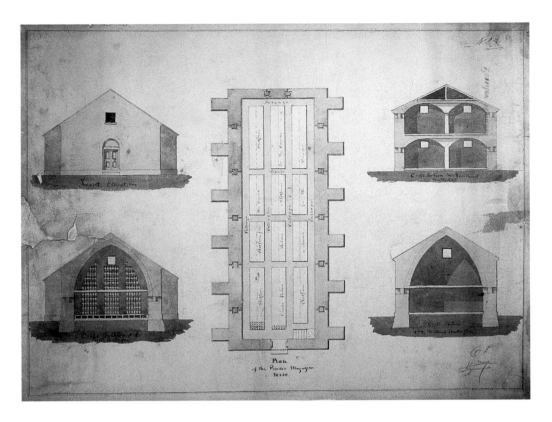

Proposed Powder Magazine. Robert Mills, 1817.

work was taken from him for political reasons. As he mentioned no alterations, his powder magazine was presumably built. Ten years later he recommended a similar brick-vaulted magazine, "an octagon externally and a circle internally," for naval stores in Gosport, Virginia, and these designs subsequently influenced a magazine erected in Washington on Judiciary Square (1812). Mills knew these projects, and they must have influenced his preferred plan, but hedging his bets he drew at least three alternatives. The one surviving drawing depicts three versions of a rectilinear, vaulted, fireproof magazine and includes his earliest design for a pointed masonry arch. The surviving section depicts a two-story plan, the upper floor of which is carried on fireproof brick arches. The plan is shown both with and without buttresses—adjustments being made in the thickness of the walls and the pitch of the roof to reflect these possibilities.

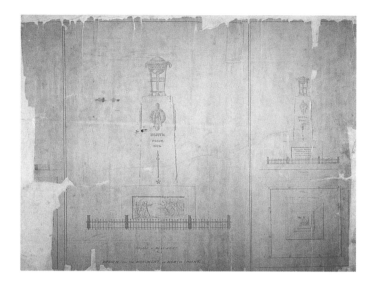 

LEFT: *Proposed North Point Monument. Robert Mills, 1816–1817.*
RIGHT: *North Point Monument, Baltimore, Maryland. Jacob Small, Jr., architect, circa 1817.*

Nothing came of these proposals, but years later when he found himself in a position of responsibility in South Carolina he erected a cluster of nine magazines on Charleston Neck. These magazines—discussed in the next chapter—were out of town, sited on navigable water, all made of fireproof, vaulted masonry, and circular in plan.

During Mills' final years in Baltimore, the Washington Monument remained the pillar about which his work revolved, but he also made plans for another monument, and although it is small and relatively simple, the Aquilla Randall, or North Point Monument, proposal is notable, for it contains his earliest complex use of Egyptian Revival forms. The North Point Monument commemorates the repulse of the British in the War of 1812. It is among the earliest handful of obelisks in America and thus foreshadows Mills Washington National Monument in Washington, D.C. Today the North Point Monument only vaguely resembles Mills' elevation, for a simpler obelisk designed by Jacob Small, Jr., (1772–1851) was adopted. A decade later, however, Mills adapted his Baltimore proposal for the Jonathan Maxcy Monument in South Carolina (Maxcy Monument, Columbia, S.C., 1827). Obvious similarities between the two monuments include the cubical plinth, bas relief, inscriptions, the truncated obelisk and the bronze tripod supporting an orb.

A newspaper account of the dedication of the Maxcy Monument noted that it was "perhaps the second instance of a monument being crowned by a tripod, the first being that of Lysicrates, or as it is better known, the Lanthern of Demosthenes." The author—probably Mills himself—was mistaken, for in Classical Greece there were many monuments conceived specifically to support tripods, and of these Comte de Caylus, then an authority on such matters, says "On est quelquefois surpris de la prodigieuse quantite de Trepieds qu'on voycit dans la Grece." Mills wrote—in an essay on the column version of his unsuccessful proposal for the Bunker Hill Monument in 1826—"a Tripod crowns the whole and forms the surmounting of the Monument. The tripod is the emblem of immortality."[65]

Both tripod and obelisk were readily available to Mills in 1817. Jefferson, during his tour of English gardens in 1786, had taken note of obelisks at Twickenham, Leasoves, and Chiswick. Mills had examined the obelisk mounted upon the facade of Thomas McBean's Saint Paul's Chapel and was familiar with obelisks in architectural texts. In explaining the Bunker Hill proposal he cited "Kercher" concerning "obelisk(s) that were celebrated above the rest, namely that of Alexandria; that of the Barberins; those of Constantinople; of the Mons Esquilinus; of the Campus Flaminius; of Florence; of Heliopolis; of Ludorisco; of St. Makut, of the Medici of the Vatican; of M. Coelius, and that of Pamphila. The highest on record mentioned, is that erected by Ptolemy Philadelphus in memory of Arsinoe."[66]

Mills was referring to the work of Athanasius Kircher (1601–1680), famous as a writer on geology, mathematics, and the study of hieroglyphics, several of whose books present the proportions, construction, origin and ornament of obelisks and passages similar to Mills' historical recitation. Kircher's *Romani Collegii*, for example, illustrates more than twenty examples and opens with a view of obelisks crowned by Christian symbols in the Jesuit museum. A number of other books available to Mills presented the tripod and its significance; Bernard de Montfaucon's *Antiquity Explained* illustrated several examples and traced "the meaning of the tripod" to the worship of Apollo at Delphi. Comte de Caylus, in the definitive work on Egypt before the Napoleonic era, also may have been a formative influence. He writes that the origin of the form is lost in antiquity, that it is discussed by Homer and is imbued with religious significance.[67] When Mills designed the ornament for the base of the Washington Monument in Baltimore, he produced tripods similar to Caylus' introductory illustration.

65 Comte de Caylus, *Recueil d'Antiquites* (Paris: Chez Duchesne Libraire, rue S. Jacques, 1756), II, plate LIII, 161; Gallagher, 205; PRM 1015A.

66 Comte de Caylus, *Recueil d'Antiquites* (Paris: Chez Duchesne Libraire, rue S. Jacques, 1756), II, plate LIII, 161; Gallagher, 205; PRM 1015A.

67 Bernard de Montfaucon, *Antiquity Explained* (London: J. Tonson and J. Watts, 1771), I, plate 18, 85–86.

The severe geometry of Mills' obelisks reflects an awareness of the memorial tradition in post-Revolutionary France. Godefroy had introduced this type to Baltimore with his Battle Monument (1814–1825), and it melded, as did most of Mills' work of this type, Egyptian, Greek, and Roman motives. Mills' smaller obelisks recall illustrations of the then new Parisian cemetery, Père-Lachaise (1804). There the Comte de Peluse rested beneath a mausoleum "d'un style Egyptien" with a cavetto cornice and a winged sun disk or orb; nearby were variations of the small Roman pedimented tombs, their eaves adorned with antefixae, like those on the Maxcy Monument; among these the widely published monument to Massena, Prince d'Essling, was crowned by an obelisk and was twenty-one feet high, the height of the Maxcy Monument obelisk.[68]

In addition to monuments and other public projects, more mundane residential work occupied much of Mills' time during the Baltimore years. The frequency and nature of these commissions is probably typical of his career as a whole, but the loss of private papers, especially in contrast to the survival of public and institutional records, has tended to obscure this side of his professional life. If the Baltimore years are a reliable guide, he was constantly engaged in the upgrading, remodeling and design of homes. Waterloo Row (1817–1819), twelve rowhouses built on land belonging to the Water Company, was his major residential project in Baltimore. He had become President of the Water Company on August 2, 1816, and the following autumn he surveyed the route of what was to become Calvert Street through Company property near the Monument. On December 20th he wrote in his diary that he had finished plans of a "range of houses for W Company grounds." The range is memorable for the harmony of its facade and for the joint venture he organized between the craftsmen and the company to finance the construction. In the elevation he achieved a unity, rhythm, and interest which had eluded him in earlier rowhouses. Above a partially raised basement, the treatment of arched openings on the principle or entry level resembled the rejected elevations for Franklin Row (Philadelphia, 1809–1810). Tripartite Venetian windows set in blind arches alternated with entries framed by sidelights and fanlights within matching arches. These entries and windows created the rhythm of an arcade, a horizontal movement that was reinforced by a watertable designating the first floor, a beltcourse on which the second-story windows were based, and a continuous cornice. Vertically he aligned Venetian windows from the basement to the cornice, and on the upper two stories, single windows aligned vertically above the entries

68 F.G.T. de Jolimont, *Les Mausolées Français* (Paris: Firmin Didot, 1821), n.p.

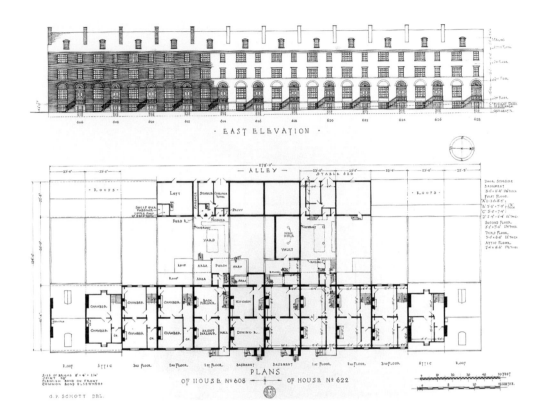

Waterloo Row, Baltimore, Maryland. Robert Mills, architect, 1817–1819.

provided a contrasting width that lent interest to the elevation as a whole. The basement and principle story of the elevation were similar to his plans for the Benjamin Chew House (Philadelphia, 1810–1812), and although he had previously incorporated the Venetian window in the upper stories of earlier work in Philadelphia (the Richard Willcocks House, 1810, Eighth Street Houses, 1812–1814, and Franklin Row, 1809–1810), he had never attained the undeviating, harmonious vertical and horizontal unity of Waterloo Row.[69]

The interior plans were not exceptional. The main block of each house was forty feet deep and twenty-three feet wide. A hallway containing a staircase ran front to back along the south wall of each unit. On each level two rooms, all nineteen by sixteen feet (excepting the bedrooms on the third floor, which were smaller to accommodate the pitch of the roof), opened onto this hallway. In the basement the dining room was in the front, the kitchen in the back; two parlors

69 For Mills' row houses see Kenneth Ames, "Robert Mills and the Philadelphia Row House," *Journal of the Society of Architectural Historians* 27 (1967): 140; also see Alexander, "The Young Professional in Philadelphia and Baltimore, 1808–20," 35–72, in Bryan, ed., *Robert Mills, Architect.*

Waterloo Row, Baltimore

with double doors between them occupied the principle floor, and the bedrooms were located on the second and third floors. Each room had a fireplace on the north wall. At the rear of each house an ell contained a back door and service stair to the basement and first floor. The rear of each lot was spanned by a stable and privies. The interior molding was restrained and angular. Baseboards, cornices, and mantels were composed of fewer, larger elements than had been common in the Adam Style. The severity of the black veined marble mantels and the discrete forms of the parlor ceiling medallions reflected the Greek Revival.

The Waterloo Row records are our best record of Mills' participation in the organization of a speculative project. It was not uncommon for contractors to pool resources and exchange labor and expertise for equity in the completed work. Mills may have done the same thing in earlier row housing. At the end of his 1816 diary he had jotted alternative ways to finance development along

Calvert Street: the directors of the Water Company could each develop a lot; the craftsmen employed by the Water Company to build houses on every other lot could be required to build for themselves on the intervening lots; or the craftsmen could form an association, lease the land, and build the row using financing provided by the Water Company. The Company would be paid back through the sale of the houses. A variation of this last scheme was adopted, and the Calvert Street Building Company was formed on January 22, 1817. [70]

Mills and his partners (Jas. Hinds, Moses Hand, Thos. Towson, Chas. Hammell, Chas. Constable and Company, John Ready, Peter Mason, Joseph Bonner, and John H. Rogers) agreed to finish the exterior of the twelve houses according to his plan. When the row was roofed against the weather they would divide the houses among themselves by selling each to the highest bidder, that failing, division would be based upon drawing lots. Once the row had been divided, each of them would be responsible for finishing the interior himself. The Articles of Association indicate that the Water Company intended to limit its construction financing to the estimated value of the two houses it was to receive when the work was done ($16,100). Despite the fact that the company eventually committed $43,000, a stone contractor, Thomas McCoy, filed a claim for $8,200 against the Association and the Water Company on August 5, 1819. The finished row stood forlorn and empty on the outskirts of town, through the recession of 1819. The Association was in arrears to its suppliers and perhaps to the Water Company, for the ground rent was $6 per foot per year of frontage along Calvert Street. The failure of Waterloo Row was a major factor in Robert Mills' bankruptcy, which was announced in the Federal Gazette on April 2, 1821. The houses (demolished in 1979) were sold at a loss and then acquired by the Water Company, but by then Mills had moved to South Carolina where he hoped to make a fresh start.

Waterloo Row was not the only reversal Mills experienced during this phase of his career. Like Latrobe and Godefroy before him, he found it difficult to make a living as an architect. He had attempted and failed to become the supervising architect for the Baltimore Cathedral; his application to be appointed Surveyor of Public Buildings in Washington was rejected; he lost several public competitions including the U.S. Bank in Philadelphia (won by William Strickland), and the Baltimore Exchange (won by Latrobe and Godefroy). Other proposals—the Jones Falls improvements, the Baltimore powder magazines—had fallen on deaf ears, and the construction of his major work, the Baltimore Washington Monument, was halted by the depression of 1819.

70 Alexander, "The Young Professional in Philadelphia and Baltimore, 1808–1820," 44–46, in Bryan, ed., *Robert Mills, Architect.*

On October 30, 1820, Mills reported to the Board of Managers of the Monument that the column was finished to the base of its capital, or 140 feet four inches above the street. The cornice, parapet, interior and exterior trim of the base remained to be completed, as did the landscaping, paving, and fencing of the grounds. Unfortunately, the colossal statue was neither complete nor in place, none of the trophies or inscriptions (which Mills regarded as being essential) had been prepared, and more than $96,000 had been spent (against an estimated budget of $100,000–$150,000). Lotteries had failed to produce the anticipated revenue and construction was halted. Mounting expenses had already prompted Mills to suggest in 1820 deleting the balconies and much of the bas relief depicted in the approved design. For the next two decades he would correspond with the Board of Managers as the monument inched toward completion in 1842.

The halt of work on the Monument combined with the failure of Waterloo Row was more than Mills could bear financially. He wrote the Board of Managers that if they would not advance his salary for 1820 he "did not know how to obtain means to go to market."[71] To Eliza he observed that "if this stagnation of business continues, I know not what numbers of persons are to do except they go to farming. The only professions that find business now, are those of law and physic. If commerce does not flourish, there will be no improvements in our cities—and it is a question whether the government will enter into those interior improvements which are of such vital importance to the prosperity of the country."[72] Hoping to find work on "those interior improvements," Mills sought Jefferson's help in securing an appointment as an engineer in Virginia. Emphasizing his experience as an engineer, Mills lied to Jefferson about his role in the Lancaster-Schuylkill Bridge, taking credit for the whole design:

> Since I removed to Baltimore (when I was invited to put my design for the Washington monument into execution) I have been engaged in various public works especially in the Engineering department. Being under the impression from the circumstance of the disposition of our people, and the local situation of our country that a better prospect opened for the encouragement of the Engineer than the architect, I have since my engagements in the Delaware & Chesapeake canal with Mr. Latrobe, turned my studies & practice particularly to this branch of my business . . . I have directed my attention also a good deal to the subject of Bridges, and was fortunate enough to have a design of mine executed of a single arch of the greatest chord line in the world, being 340 feet &

71 RM to the Board of Managers of the Washington Monument, April 8, 1820.

72 RM to EBSM, October 20, 1819.

upwards versed sine only 19 feet. You will find a brief notice of it in the last edition of Gregory's Encyclopedia under the head of Schuylkill & with a plate.[73]

It would be wrong to end a review of Mills' early career on a wholly somber note. Professionally and personally these were formative years. His domestic correspondence reflects a warm and stable family life. As an architect, his working methods crystallized. He responded quickly to potential clients, often by submitting alternative designs. He invariably stressed economy and utility and willingly altered plans in consultation with patrons. Once a commission was secured, Mills usually offered to superintend construction, producing working drawings as work progressed. His full services included the drafting of contracts, the acquisition of materials and labor, the certification of craftsmanship and the disbursement of funds. He considered himself competent to direct all aspects of construction, and he undertook a broad range of tasks, including the design of bridges, furnaces, waterways, and the creation of a variety of building types. Mindful of the need to promote himself professionally, he exhibited and published drawings, was active in the Philadelphia Society of Artists, and wrote for the periodical press.

As a designer, he rejected Georgian and Adamesque forms learned from Hoban and pattern books. Instead, he began adapting the spare geometry of Sir John Soane and the Neoclassicists as advocated by Latrobe. Mills also embraced Jefferson's belief that architecture and engineering were vital to the development of the Republic. Consciously seeking an American architecture, he gravitated toward the use of plane and the juxtaposition of solids and voids as organizing principals. He relied less and less upon applied ornament. The Doric became his preferred order, although he was never concerned about archaeological exactitude. He wrote, "I have always deprecated the servile copying of the buildings of antiquity; we have the same principles and materials to work upon that the ancients had...Study your country's tastes and requirements, and make classic ground here for your art."[74] He was eclectic and quick to modify useful prototypes to suit the job at hand. These traits lay behind his creation of the auditorium churches and the Baltimore Washington Monument, which established his reputation along the seaboard. Despite his architectural accomplishments, he concluded that America's "taste and requirements" called for "interior improvements," so he set out to refocus his career.

73 RM to TJ, June 16, 1820. Mills corresponded with William Dunlap concerning the entry on Mills' career in Dunlap's *History of the Rise and Progress of the Arts of Design in the United States* (New York: George P. Scott and Co., 1834), 221–226. For Dunlap's notation of letters to and from Mills, 1833–1834, see: *Diary of William Dunlap* (New York: New York Historical Society, 1930), 760, 774–777, 784, 786. Mills must have drafted the sketch of his career, and it says that the bridge "which has the largest chord of arch in the world, is the design of Mr. Mills." Dunlap, *History*, 223.

74 RM, "The Progress of Architecture in Virginia," transcribed in Gallagher, 155–158; PRM 3026A, 3026B.

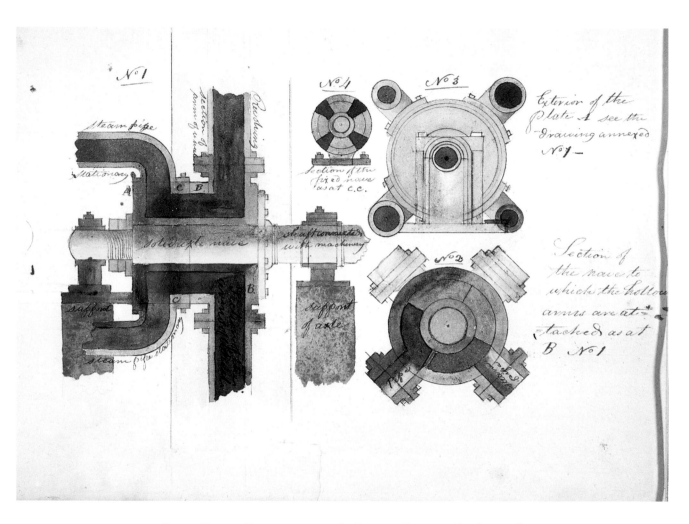

Rotary Engine. "Improvements in the Rotatory Engine . . ." Robert Mills, engineer, 1824.

CHAPTER FIVE

South Carolina

1820–1830

IN 1820, WHEN prospects were bleak in Baltimore, opportunity beckoned in South Carolina, for Mills' native state had initiated an Internal Improvements program in 1819. The appropriation—one million dollars to be spent over ten years—was the largest per capita commitment made by any state for the creation of canals and public buildings. The program precisely matched Mills' aspirations, and he returned to Carolina and worked there throughout the 1820s.[1]

In several respects this decade served as a prelude to the final phase of his career in Washington (1830–1855). In South Carolina he refined his use of fireproof masonry vaulting. Here too he developed a series of institutional interiors based on modular, groin-vaulted offices flanking barrel-vaulted corridors, which became a hallmark of his later federal buildings. Beyond their structural significance, the functional interiors of the fourteen courthouses and thirteen jails he designed in Carolina foreshadowed his advocacy of prototypical federal customhouses and marine hospitals. Mills' mature expression of an American Classicism also crystallized, as he increasingly avoided ornament and relied instead on raised basements, belt courses, broad entablatures, and boldly projecting porticoes. Although this period was important in his professional development, it did not bring financial security, for Internal Improvement proved a costly delusion, and public disenchantment quickly led the legislature to dismantle the program and remove Mills from office on December 31, 1823. For the remainder of the decade he worked on a building-

1 David Kohn and Bess Glenn, eds., *Internal Improvement in South Carolina, 1817–1828* (Washington: privately printed, 1938). Also see: N.G. Raiford, "South Carolina and the Issue of Internal Improvement, 1775–1860," Ph.D. dissertation, University of Virginia, 1974.

by-building basis and turned seriously to writing and cartography to supplement his income. After ten years of struggle he left South Carolina—as he had Baltimore—seeking greener pastures.[2]

INTERNAL IMPROVEMENT, THE SOUTH CAROLINA PROGRAM

One of the policy debates in the Early Republic centered on whether or not the federal government could—or should—create interstate roads and canals. After the Revolution, Alexander Hamilton, Secretary of the Treasury, and James Madison, then a Representative from Virginia, failed in attempts to promote a system of national roads. They argued that good transportation was necessary for defense, postal delivery, economic growth, and inter-regional cooperation. Subsequently, the Louisiana Purchase, the admission of Ohio to the Union, and the westward drift of settlement made the need increasingly obvious, and in 1806 Congress authorized a turnpike from the upper reaches of the Potomac at Cumberland, Maryland, to the Ohio River at Wheeling, West Virginia. Additional roads were approved for Illinois, Georgia, Louisiana and Tennessee. These first national roads were not finished when the British blockade during the War of 1812 gave new urgency to arguments for interior lines of communication, and Madison, now as President, urged Congress to consider "the great importance of establishing throughout our country the roads and canals which can best be executed under the national authority."[3]

While Congress wrestled with the cost and constitutionality of a national program, many seaboard states moved ahead, and until states' rights clouded the issue, South Carolina was a leading proponent of roads and canals. Her most prominent spokesman, John C. Calhoun, justified national investment in transportation saying that "whatever impedes the intercourse of the extremes...weakens the union.... Let us bind the republic together with a perfect system of roads and canals. Let us conquer space."[4]

Calhoun spoke from personal experience. His father, Patrick Calhoun, had led a band of settlers south along the eastern slope of the Appalachians to the South Carolina Piedmont. Growing up in Abbeville, a back country county seat, John C. Calhoun saw the hardships caused by obstacles between his community and distant centers of power and commerce. Patrick Calhoun advocated state-supported access to banks, courts, and markets. Increased settlement in the back country and the establishment of an inland cotton culture at the turn of the cen-

2 For difficulties encountered by the internal improvements program see Daniel W. Hollis, "Costly Delusion: Inland Navigation in the South Carolina Piedmont," *Proceedings of the South Carolina Historical Association* (1969): 29-43.

3 F.L. Israel, *State of the Union Messages, 1790–1966* (New York: Chelsea House, 1966), I, 138.

4 *Annals of the Congress, Debates and Proceedings,* 14th Congress, 1st session, 854, quoted by Raiford, 7.

tury finally convinced the coastal planters that improved inland navigation would channel commerce to Charleston and stem the westward flow of capital.

In 1817, Governor Andrew Pickens convinced the South Carolina Legislature to retain an engineer to submit a report on potential canals and roads, superintend construction of public buildings, and "recommend repairs and alterations, whenever the same may be required." The engineer was to be paid $4,000 per year. The following year one million dollars was appropriated to carry out this work. John Wilson (1789–1832) was appointed Civil and Military Engineer, but he found it impossible to manage the forty-odd projects dispersed across the state. He was dismissed and replaced in December 1819 by a Board of Public Works with five members. Abram Blanding (1776–1839) was the paid Acting Commissioner for Roads, Rivers, and Canals, and by virtue of his industry, he became de facto head of the public works programs. Thomas Baker (n.d.), a contractor, was salaried Acting Commissioner for Public Buildings; other members included Joel R. Poinsett, politician and an influential proponent of internal improvements, who was President of the Board; William Jay (1794–1837), an English-trained architect based in Savannah, from whom the Board purchased designs for courthouses and jails; and Robert G. Mills, a contractor—no kin to Robert, the architect.[5]

The Board of Public Works held its organizational meeting on January 24, 1820; they carried on the work begun by John Wilson, but by the end of the year their efforts were called into question, and on December 20, 1820, Robert Mills, who was living in Baltimore, was appointed as a salaried Acting Commissioner for Public Buildings. He replaced Thomas Baker and was thus in a position to modify or replace the plans by William Jay, whose seat on the Board was taken by Nicholas Herbemont (d. 1836), tutor of French at the South Carolina College. Led by Blanding and Mills, its two salaried Acting Commissioners, the Board was to direct the creation of canals and to erect courthouses and jails throughout the state. Officially, Mills served the Board of Public Works as Acting Commissioner (December 20, 1820–December 31, 1822), then as Superintendent of Public Buildings (January 1, 1823–December 31, 1823) and finally as a private architect often employed by the state (1824–1829).[6] At first, however, he worked both as an architect and as an engineer, and the ambitious program promised to be an ideal outlet for his talents and training.

5 Robert G. Mills (d. 1843) was not related to Robert Mills, the architect. Robert G. Mills was a farmer from Chester County, S.C., member of the S.C. House of Representatives and Senate, and a member of the Board of Public Works. In 1836 Robert G. Mills became a director of the Cincinnati and Charleston Railroad. The probate record of his estate spans nine years and contains circa 400 transactions—none of which involve Robert the architect nor any of his known relations. See S.C. Probate Court, John A. Bradley, Administrator, February 28, 1843, Apartment No. 51, Package No. 813, Book A, 22.

6 Bryan, ed., *Robert Mills, Architect*, 76; Kohn and Glenn, xiii.

The details concerning Mills' move to South Carolina are not clear, for only a few, isolated letters survive from the winter of 1820–1821. In March 1821, Eliza installed furniture in their new home in Columbia, the state capital, while Mills returned to Baltimore to attend bankruptcy hearings and then traveled throughout the low country for the Board of Public Works. During the spring and fall of 1821 he participated in plans for canals. His reading, early experience, and the *Baltimore Treatise* are apparent in the essay *Inland Navigation: Plan for a Great Canal between Charleston and Columbia*, which introduced him to the citizens of South Carolina.[7]

Mills' essay proposed a canal 110 miles long. Beginning at Columbia on the north bank of the Congaree River, the canal was to be carried by an aqueduct across the river (to avoid swamps downstream) and proceed to Charleston along the ridge between the Congaree and Santee and Cooper Rivers. This canal was designed as the principal link in a chain of canals he envisioned stretching from Charleston to the foot of the Appalachian Mountains in the northwestern corner of the state where you could stand at the crest of a narrow ridge and "pitch a stone with ease" into streams flowing east (into the Green River) or west (into the Mud River, which joined the French Broad, which in turn flowed into the Ohio River). He described connecting South Carolina canals to the Ohio, Mississippi, and Missouri Rivers, opening "2000 square miles of trade" and making Columbia the "great thoroughfare from the west to the seaboard." Charleston, he wrote, "is better situated than New York for a commercial intercourse" with the "western country." At the height of his optimism he imagined a canal system providing access to the Columbia River and the Pacific: waterborne transportation from Charleston to India.[8]

Mills cannot be blamed for the collapse of the canal program in South Carolina. The state had committed to canals before he arrived, and there was no attempt to build any of the routes he recommended. His actual work on South Carolina canals consisted of preliminary surveys for a canal to connect the Savannah and Broad Rivers (the Broad River in Jasper County) and participation in the supervision of construction of the Columbia Canal and certification of work on the Landsford Canal. By 1823 support for canals was waning, and Mills focused wholly on the creation of public buildings. As was

7 Mills, *Inland Navigation: Plan for a Great Canal between Charleston and Columbia and for Connecting Our Waters with Those of the Western Country* (Columbia: Telescope Press, 1821).

8 Mills, *Inland Navigation*, iii, 35.

Columbia Canal, Columbia, South Carolina. Robert Mills and Abram Blanding, engineers, 1821–1824.

the case in Baltimore, his writings are the principal legacy of his brief engagement with canals.

Albert Gallatin, as Secretary of the Treasury, had written a *Report on Internal Improvements*.[9] Gallatin's *Report*, the foundation of Mills' writings on canals, concentrates on costs and anticipated revenues and notes that transportation is vital to internal unification and external defense. But with the whole nation as his canvas, Gallatin never illustrated in detail the effects of canals and turnpikes upon daily life. Gallatin included an appendix by Latrobe, which went into detail concerning matters of civil and military engineering, but it did not attempt to evoke an image of canals in service. A letter by Robert Fulton, the final element of the Gallatin *Report*, presented calculations based on the transportation cost of staples—salt, molasses, coffee—and compared labor costs per mile of men, boys, and horses on canals and turnpikes. Fulton's examples all concerned money.

9 Albert Gallatin, "Report on Internal Improvements," American State Papers, Miscellaneous, I, 740; Alexander Balinky, *Albert Gallatin, Fiscal Theories and Policies* (New Brunswick: Rutgers University Press, 1958), 96; also see Gallatin, *Report of the Secretary of the Treasury on the Subject of Public Roads and Canals* (Washington: R.C. Weightman, 1808).

Mills' canal essays are different, for he often added passages concerning the impact of canals on patterns of life. Having lived in both Philadelphia and Baltimore, cities which then boasted the major municipal water systems in the United States, and having served as President of the Baltimore Water Company, Mills argued that his canal could provide water for similar systems in South Carolina. Such a canal would lead to fire protection, pure drinking water, cleaner streets, urban fountains, and irrigated gardens; it would also promote bathing and hygiene. By providing both drainage and irrigation, canals would increase the value of the agricultural lands through which they passed. Inland navigation would remove the burdens of overland transportation, and laborers would therefore became more productive; finally, 1,280,000 acres of reclaimed swampland would become an agricultural "goldmine" instead of a source of disease.[10]

Mills suggested that inland navigation projects could be used to finance an end to slavery. In *Internal Improvement* (1822), he wrote that "slavery is an evil" and that "the day will come when we must part with our black population." To achieve this, he reasoned the state could buy 6,000 slaves, whose labor would drain 2,000 square miles of swampland in ten years. Proceeds from the sale of this land would fund the repatriation of 120,000 slaves (at a cost of $400 each), and the state would still realize a profit of $42,624,000. Of slavery he wrote, "If the evil be of fearful magnitude now, what will it be fifty years hence?" The more commonplace—and complacent—viewpoint in South Carolina was the opinion voiced by John Drayton: "if it [slavery] is an evil, it will sooner, or later, effect its own cure."[11] In condemning slavery and advocating repatriation Mills was not alone, but he was out of step with most powerful Carolinians.

THE SAVANNAH & BROAD RIVER CANAL PROPOSAL

Because it was grandiose, Mills' dream of transcontinental navigation is memorable, but his more plausible proposal concerning the Savannah River has been forgotten. The Savannah originates on the eastern slopes of the Appalachian Mountains and for 314 miles forms the boundary between Georgia and South Carolina. Savannah, Georgia, strategically sited near the mouth of the river, virtually monopolized waterborne trade from the 10,500 square mile drainage basin. For thousands of South Carolinians—including the Calhouns in Abbeville—the river made Savannah the most accessible major market. In 1819

10 Mills, *Inland Navigation*, 7.

11 Robert Mills, *Internal Improvements in South Carolina* (Columbia: State Gazette, 1822), 12, 16; John Drayton, *View of South Carolina* (Charleston: W.P. Young, 1802), 145.

the South Carolina legislature directed their engineer to report on the feasibility of a canal to divert Savannah River traffic northward into South Carolina and create an inland link between the Savannah River and Charleston. Mills never received authorization to develop his initial proposal—probably because it would have entailed at least fifty miles of canal, aqueducts, and locks. He never advocated half-measures, and his initial plan was characteristic of his tendency to think on a large scale and go back to first causes. He presents the geological history of the river basin, describes the erosion of soil into ridges and valleys, the inclination of the coastal plain, and evidence of a prehistoric riverbed once occupied by the Savannah. This proposal, like his earlier suggestions for the James River canal, the Susquehanna-Potomac canal, and the Columbia to Charleston canal, seems to have fallen on deaf ears.

He crisscrossed the state in the course of his work. Passages in his domestic correspondence present pleasurable moments. For example, he spent a rainy day in March 1821, at Fairfield, the home of Col. Pinckney on the Santee River. They watched

> the steam boat from Columbia loaded with cotton with her tow boat alongside also loaded with this article…P's house commands an extensive prospect of what may be called the gold mines of the state namely rice fields. The Santee river glides majestically by silent and slow. A number of handsome country seats stretch along its banks, each fronted by rice fields—the verdure is beautiful, the weeping Willow, Wild Orange, sweet orange and mock orange, besides innumerable evergreens.[12]

The following spring he wrote of a trip from Columbia to Charleston on the steamboat with his wife's Aunt Jacquelina:

May 7, 1822
Steam boat So. C. off Sullivan's Island

My Dearest Eliza,
We are now endeavoring to force the steam boat thro' the narrows of this island. The tide is falling fast, and it is very questionable whether we shall not be obliged to lie here until next high tide. This is exactly the seventh day since we left you. We had a fine run down the river, & experienced no delay until

12 RM to EBSM, March 6, 1821.

we got into the salt water, when the tides & wind regulated our movements. We got within a day's ride of Charleston on Tuesday, I may say, but we were obliged to lay in Bulls bay, (the terror of all the boatmen) two days before we could cross it. This delay however has given an opportunity to Jacquelina of witnessing several natural curiosities of a marine nature, and for myself I have learnt more of the difficulties of this navigation than I could have known by volumes of description which experience will enable me to represent the subject of improving this navigation to the Legislature with more effect.

Jacquelina had "a surfeit in eating oysters & crabs." The first day the boat had traveled thirty miles before tying up for the night. On the second day they covered 100 miles, and when the boat stopped to load wood for fuel, they visited planters along the riverbank. Visiting Sullivan's Island, Jacquelina walked along the beach collecting seashells, and Mills observed that "the salt air has been of much service to her." John Mills, two years old, was with them, and in Charleston he "strayed out into the street and could not be found anywhere.... The boys servants & Mr. Reed spread themselves in every direction and towards 8 o'clock, the news was brought that the lost was found, and he was soon in doors again. Apprehensions were entertained that he might have strayed down to the water where the steam boat lay, which was close by and I went down accordingly to inquire, but he had followed his nose, and kept straight up the street [and] playing with [some] children."[13]

Mills' most enthusiastic reactions are reserved for the mountainous northwest corner of the state, which he described as being "sublime and beautiful in the extreme; the eye is never tired with a mountainous view; the landscape is forever varying, and every variation affords matter to interest or to delight."[14] But such pleasures were coincidental, for apparently he never traveled strictly for pleasure during his years in South Carolina.

THE COURTHOUSES

The legislature did not adopt any of Mills' plans for the improvement of navigation, and in January 1823, he became Superintendent of Public Buildings, while Blanding, as Superintendent of Public Works, retained responsibility for canals, roads, and bridges. The creation or rehabilitation of courthouses and jails in twenty-one counties now occupied much of Mills' time. He modified

13 RM to EBSM, May 7 and 12, 1822.

14 Mills, *Statistics*, 37–39, 51.

Kershaw County Courthouse, Camden, South Carolina. Robert Mills, architect, 1825–1830.

two courthouses that had been designed by William Jay, designed fourteen others, and strongly influenced seven more for which others were responsible.

Prior to his arrival the lateral stairways were compressed within the portico itself and screened from view by the raised basement. The Kershaw County Courthouse, the only fully developed temple plan, was without a raised basement and originally had a giant Ionic portico; its entry opened into a vestibule that contained the staircase to the courtroom on the piano noble. The Chesterfield County Courthouse was an anomaly; its interior included the basic elements of Mills' pattern, but its portico was on one of the long sides of the building and was perpendicular to the axis of the gable roof. The courthouses were without applied ornament. Stairs, porticos, belt courses, and recessed panels (which articulated the side elevations) comprised the austere vocabulary of this set of buildings.

ABOVE: *Horry County Courthouse, Conway, South Carolina. Robert Mills, architect,*
1823–1825.

OPPOSITE: *Williamsburg County Courthouse, Kingstree, South Carolina. Robert Mills, architect,*
1821–1825.

159

Functionally, Mills' courthouses offered security against fire and segregated uses in a manner which insured quiet for the court. Waddell and Liscombe have suggested the Villa Arsiero as a prototype for Mills' courthouses—he owned a copy of Scamozzi's Palladio—and have noted the Worcester County Courthouse (1801–1803) by Charles Bulfinch as a possible precedent.[15] Pamela Scott has pointed out similarities between Mills' program and Asher Benjamin's "Plan and Elevation of a Courthouse," a probability bolstered by the fact that in the Benjamin plan the lower offices are sixteen feet square and sixteen by twenty-one feet. Mills used similar dimensions for the offices in his courthouses (Kershaw, sixteen feet square; Alexandria, fifteen by twenty feet and twelve by twenty feet; and nineteen feet square for Lancaster; and eighteen feet square for offices in the proposed Caroliniana Library).[16] Latrobe's work on the south wing of the U.S. Capitol may also have influenced Mills' courthouse plans. Latrobe's revision of the original plan included vaulted fireproof areas for offices and record storage below an elevated meeting hall. A description from Latrobe's "Report" (February 1804) is applicable to Mills' formula for the courthouses: "The great feature of this alteration is to raise up the floor of the legislative hall...and to use the whole lower story as the situation for committee rooms and offices."[17]

Masonry vaulting on the first floor, or raised basement, was an essential characteristic of the courthouses and would become a hallmark of Mills' subsequent public work. In Charleston as a youth he had known the vaulted basement beneath Naylor's Exchange, but it was probably the practical experience directing construction of Latrobe's Bank of Philadelphia (1807–1808) that allowed him to use vaulting in the Burlington County Jail (1808–1810) and the fireproof wings at Independence Hall (1812). Latrobe's most famous vaults were spherical. But the system Mills refined in South Carolina was different. It consisted of a central, barrel-vaulted corridor flanked on either side by a series of groin-vaulted offices. The lateral thrust of each vault was opposed by the thrust of the adjacent vault. Piers in each corner of the offices carried much of the vertical load. Plaster was applied directly to the interior surface of the masonry to avoid the use of any wood, and whenever the budget allowed it, Mills specified iron window sash to further enhance the fireproofing. In South Carolina he had to work with common mortar and irregular hand-made brick (in the 1830s the availability of hydraulic cement would speed the work and enable him to reduce the thickness of the walls). In any given building, he repeated the size

15 Gene Waddell and Rhodri Liscombe, *Robert Mills's Courthouses and Jails* (Easley: Southern Historical Press, 1981), 11.

16 Pamela Scott, review of Waddell and Liscombe, *Winterthur Portfolio* 20 (Winter 1985): 299–301.

17 BHL, "Report of the Surveryor of the Public Buildings," March 6, 1804, 12, 172/D11.

and shape of most of the groin-vaulted spaces; this allowed the disassembly and re-use of the centering, the wooden forms which supported the vaulting until the mortar hardened. Despite Mills' work, fireproof construction never became commonplace in South Carolina, for it was three times more expensive than traditional timber framing and required special knowledge to build the centering and arches.

During the 1820s in South Carolina the creation of courthouses and jails began with a petition to the legislature. An appropriation, typically $10,000 for a courthouse and $5,000 to $8,000 for a jail, initiated Mills' involvement. He provided "plans, specifications, and estimates, of the quantities and quality, of both materials and work to be furnished" and advertised for bids. He received proposals and participated in drafting contracts for construction, which often cited "plans and specifications signed by Robert Mills." Surviving documents do not suggest that he, or anyone else, considered siting except insofar as the sale of an obsolete courthouse might make way for or defray the cost of new buildings. As work got underway, he corresponded with contractors concerning alterations of plans and the quality of materials and workmanship. He reviewed invoices. Payment was usually made in three installments: one-third upon execution of the contract, one third when the walls were finished, and a final payment upon acceptance of the work. Cost was a function of quantity as determined by measurement of the finished building and set out in the specifications.[18]

Each judicial district had a Commission of Public Buildings, which reported to the Legislature. The Commissioners were Mills' primary clients. His immediate superior, the President of the Board of Public Works, submitted annual reports to the Legislature, and the report for 1821, Mills' first full year of service, reflects his critique of "the usual course of contracting for public building" and changes he instigated to conform with the "practice prevailing in Europe and in several of our Northern cities."[19]

In South Carolina contracts had been let to general contractors, who might or might not be skilled "mechaniks" and whose profit was a percentage of the cost of labor and materials. Mills proposed "the Board be authorized to engage a fit person, a mechanic, who has no interest in the contracts, to superintend personally the faithful execution of such contracts as might be made for materials or work, with the several persons Employed about the buildings." This latter system was adopted and reflected his own experience working for Latrobe in Philadelphia, 1804–1811. Correspondence between Latrobe and his Clerks of the

18 *Charleston Courier*, April 25, 1822, for fireproof offices. See also the *Courier*, February 21, 1822, for the Williamsburg, Newberry, York and Greenville courthouses and the Union, Spartanburg, Lancaster and York jails; the issue of March 20, 1822, contains the announcement for the Charleston jail. See also Timothy D. Williams to RM, May 18, 1822, and John B. Miller to RM, August 16, 1822, proposals for the Laurens and Sumter buildings in the South Carolina Department of Archives and History.

19 Kohn and Glenn, 109.

Works—Mills in Philadelphia and John Lenthall in Washington—epitomizes
the frustration Mills experienced in directing widely separated projects; superintendents and Commissioners often lamented Mills' absence when a decision
needed to be made or work certified for payment.[20]

The procedure adopted for the courthouses was used in the construction of
district jails, the other building type for which he developed a prototypical plan.
Of the thirteen jails that can be attributed to him, only those in Union and
Lancaster survive. His interior plan for jails was in many respects like that of
the courthouses; the lower floor consisted of a central corridor that contained
the staircase and was flanked by rooms used as lodging for the keeper and confinement for debtors; the upper floor contained cells for felons. Judging from
the Union and Lancaster jails and documents concerning the jail at Pendleton,
it is probable that the upper floor was typically constructed as an open span
(analogous to the courtrooms) and then subdivided into cells through the use of
non-bearing, wooden partitions. If this was the case, then the Carolina district
jails differed from his Mount Holly, New Jersey jail (1808–1810), which was
vaulted throughout, and from his initial proposal for a district jail in South
Carolina (Marlboro, 1821), for which he recommended fireproof construction.
Cost, no doubt, was the determining factor. Only the Lancaster jail is known to
have been vaulted on its lower level; its second floor cell-partitions have been
removed, which makes the relationship between its plan and that of the courthouses self-evident. The elevations of the jails lacked projecting elements that
might have diminished the impression of enclosed volume; he further emphasized closure through the liberal use of rough hammered granite sills and lintels,
by reducing the size of window openings on the second floor (two feet four
inches by three feet eight inches at Lancaster), and, at Union and Spartanburg,
by recessing the entry behind three arches carried by monolithic granite piers
(eighteen inches wide, fourteen deep, and seven feet two inches high at Union).
Although the jails varied in detail, the basic plan was often repeated with little
modification, for the Union jail is said to have been based upon the Marlboro
jail, and the specifications for the Edgefield jail called for it to be "in every particular and after the model of the Union jail;" the Newberry jail, in turn, was to
be "in all respects similar to the present [jail] at Edgefield."[21]

Problems arose despite the relative homogeneity of the plans and the
establishment of standardized procedures. Rural counties could not support resident craftsmen; consequently, contractors, masons, and carpenters typically

20 Kohn and Glenn, 109.

21 Waddell and Liscombe,
12, 34, 38.

Union County Jail, Union, South Carolina. Robert Mills, architect, 1822–1823.

Lancaster County Jail, Lancaster, South Carolina. Robert Mills, architect, 1821–1822.

moved from job to job. Mills sometimes found it difficult to induce men to work in the fever-ridden low country during the hot months. John M. Miller, for example, wrote Mills that he would work on several Piedmont courthouses, but "the other court house at Williamsburgh is in a sickly part of the country for that reason I should not feel willing to go there."[22] Much of the back country was far from centers of supply, and this affected every aspect of construction. Robert Leckie, an experienced contractor, told Mills that bids for the York courthouse were twenty-five percent higher than low country prices. Concerning independent minded up-country laborers, Leckie observed that they must be well paid, for

people you know here do not sail so near the wind [and] if they do not get a liberal price for every thing both of labor & produce they will fold their arms

22 John M. Miller to the Board of Public Works, February 28, 1821, South Carolina Department of Archives and History.

& look on; and at present it would be extremely difficult to find subsistence for either man or horse. My foreman has just returned from sweeping a segment of the circle of the horizon of 90 degrees, with a radii of 100 miles from Landsford, and has not been able to purchase a barrel of flour, nor a bushel of corn in all that distance. I am getting my provisions & flour from Charleston at an advance for carriage of between 50 & 55 percent on the Charleston prices.[23]

The Greenville County Courthouse is the best documented instance of structural problems caused by poor materials. Locally made bricks were so porous that the walls had to be taken down and rebuilt twice, and the contractors, Pond Graham and Charles McCullough, finally agreed to stucco the exterior of the raised basement to prevent further spalling and erosion. And that was not all: before the building was accepted the roof had to be replaced and money deducted for defective flooring, missing shutters, flues, forty-two windows, and a defective judges' bench.[24]

SEARCH FOR WORK, 1823–1830

Although he was very busy, Mills quickly realized that popular support for the internal improvements program was waning, and as early as 1822 he wrote Bernard Peyton, Secretary of the Board of Public Works in Virginia, because "the uncertainty of anything like permanent employment here in my profession, induces me to look out for a situation elsewhere."[25] Several weeks later he applied formally to the Virginia Board, but nothing came of it. He also applied without success to be appointed "one of the officers of Engineers" of the Federal Board of Engineers for Internal Improvement, and hoping to return to Baltimore, he contacted Robert Gilmore, but Gilmore was unable to promise either railroad work or a position superintending the completion of the Washington Monument.[26] Mills' search for work was prompted by the reorganization of the administration of internal improvements in 1822. The commission was abolished; Blanding took control, and Mills foresaw that support for architectural projects would diminish. His concern was justified, for in December 1823, the legislature removed him from office, and Roederick Evander McIver, a clerk of court and sometime contractor, was appointed in his place.[27]

23 Robert Leckie to Robert G. [sic.] Mills, Architect, April 9, 1822, South Carolina Department of Archives and History.

24 New Courthouse, Greenville, Terms of Settlement, Charles McCulloch, Isaac P. Pond, Daniel Graham, Robt. Mills, June 7, 1824.

25 RM to Bernard Peyton, December 23, 1822; also see RM to George Tucker, January 8, 1823; John Smith to James Pleasants, January 17, 1822, PRM 0942A; TJ to RM, June 22, 1820, PRM 0886.

26 RM to Alexander Macomb, September 12, 1826.

27 David Kohn and Bess Glenn, eds., *Internal Improvement in South Carolina, 1817–1828* (Washington: Privately printed, 1938), xiii; Bryan, ed., *Robert Mills, Architect*, 76.

Mills accomplished a great deal in South Carolina after he was removed from office, but the painful consequences of a catch-as-catch-can living are a constant refrain in his domestic correspondence. Eliza's letters are eloquent:

> I am placed in a very awkward & unpleasant situation dun'd on all sides, it is almost more than I can bear, and I am some times on the point of making my escape from, the scene of turmoil, & with my Children to share the fate of my Parents in the country that gave me birth, but then my beloved husband, your image rises to my view...we have been toiling for years, & still met with trials of every description, poverty and hardship still keep in view, as if willing to humble our pride & vain glory, whilst the substantial good things of this life, like tempting baits have only allured us to follow them, only to end the chase in disappointment [and] fear.[28]

The diverse nature of his efforts after his removal from office suggests a dogged persistence. He continued to work for the state on a contract basis and sought private commissions; he dabbled in applied technology and proposed internal improvement schemes. Writing occupied a major portion of his time, and he said that from 1822 to 1826 he had "devoted all his time, talents and means" to the preparation, publication, and distribution of his *Atlas* and *Statistics of South Carolina*, works as ambitious as his dreams of transcontinental navigation. Mills' *Atlas* presented the first systematic mapping of any state, and his *Statistics*—an 808-page volume—contained a statewide, county by county, description of flora, fauna, cultural history, and topography.

THE *ATLAS*, *STATISTICS*, AND OTHER WRITINGS

The winter Legislature of 1823 did not re-appoint Mills as Superintendent of Public Buildings, but they softened the blow by placing him on the two commissions then directing state construction in the Charleston District. The legislators also ratified (December 19, 1823) a provisional contract he had made with Abram Blanding for the publication and sale of maps each of the twenty-eight counties.[29] This agreement authorized Mills to use state-owned district surveys as a data base; he was to provide twelve atlases to the state free of charge, and the Superintendent of Public Works was to purchase another fifty copies for six hundred dollars. With this subscription to defray publication costs, Mills hoped to

28 EBSM to RM, January 23–24, 1825.

29 Report of the Joint Committee on the Report of the Superintendent of Public Works on the Map of the State, December 19, 1823, and Report of the Superintendent of Public Works on the Map of the State, December 19, 1823, General Assembly Misc., 1823, no. 6, South Carolina Department of Archives and History.

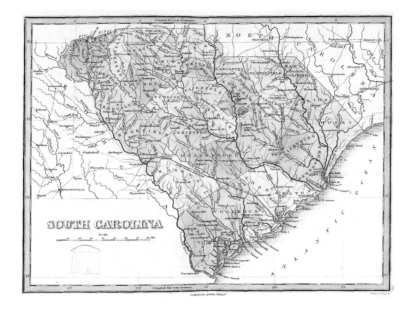

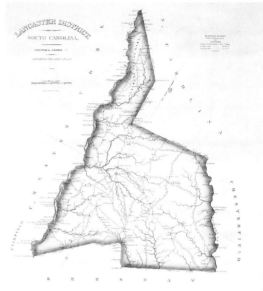

LEFT: *Frontispiece,* Atlas of the State of South Carolina. *Robert Mills, cartographer, 1825.*
RIGHT: *Lancaster District Map,* Atlas of the State of South Carolina. *Robert Mills, cartographer, 1825.*

sell single maps and bound atlases at a profit. Beyond financial need, several factors must have reinforced his interest in producing an atlas. He had crisscrossed the state for three years and knew the collection of surveys which John L. Wilson, as State Civil and Military Engineer, had used to publish a state map in 1822. Five of these district maps had been published (Fairfield, Lexington, Newberry, Union, and York) but were on a scale of one inch to the mile, too large to be useful in the field. Finally, his canal work had entailed cartography. His manuscript Report (1821) concerning the potential Savannah River canal, for example, conveys a sense of history and geology and a first-hand topographical knowledge. In short, his involvement with canals, before his responsibilities focused upon architectural projects, laid some of the groundwork for the *Atlas* and The *Statistics.*

The *Atlas* contains twenty-eight maps, on a scale of two miles to the inch. The district maps Mills used were the result of an 1816 appropriation to create a state map. George Blackburn, Professor of Astronomy at the South Carolina College, initiated this project and made observations of latitude, but his contract was not renewed in 1817; instead, the Legislature commissioned surveys of each county as a more efficient approach. Nineteen surveyors were hired to produce county maps, which were reduced and consolidated by Wilson. The resulting state map was published by Henry S. Tanner of Philadelphia in two printings, 1821–1822. There was little demand for Wilson's map or the printed county maps, so the legislature declined to fund the publication of an atlas in 1821 and again in 1822, but they were willing to allow Mills to undertake it as a speculative venture.[30]

Eighteen of the original county surveys survive, and the scope of Mills' contribution and his use of other sources can be determined by comparing these with those in his *Atlas*.[31]

The *Atlas* maps differ from earlier surveys in format and often in scale and detail. Notations in Mills' hand on the original surveys indicate additions and corrections. Standardization of cartographic conventions and typography in the published work may represent his collaboration with Tanner or Tanner's editorial contribution, for the plates from which the *Atlas* was printed were engraved in Philadelphia by "H. S. Tanner & Assistants." The legend of each map bears the name of the surveyor(s) and notes that the map was "improved for Mills' Atlas, 1825." Improvement meant redrawing the surveys that were not on a scale of two miles to one inch, adding a legend to each map noting "geological position," the bearing and distance of the county courthouse from Columbia, the latitude and longitude of the county seat, and sometimes adding, deleting, or otherwise altering place names and topographical features that appeared on the original district surveys. For example, to the manuscript survey of the Richland District, which is signed by Marmaduke Coate, Mills added [Columbia] "Canal 30 foot fall" and "Saluda Canal fall 31 feet." On the published map his note about the fall of the Saluda Canal does not appear, but his addition of "or Brisbane's" as an alternative designation for "Garner's Ferry" was retained. Revisions probably continued through publication. On the Richland map, as on other surveys, he deleted mileposts, substituted his own legend, and supplied a standard scale. On the Fairfield manuscript survey he added shoals and islands in the Broad River, supplied the names of "the Old York Road" and "Grubs Road," converted roads from faintly dotted to perceptible solid lines, and added a conventional grid to indicate the town of Winnsboro. Throughout the state he added details to existing surveys; in Pendleton, the westernmost district, he added the home of "Gen Earle" and the "Big Esatoe Creek," and on the Darlington survey to the east he supplied the names of land owners and topo-

30 Gene Waddell, "Robert Mills, Cartographer," *Mills's Atlas of the State of South Carolina, 1825* (Easley: Southern Historical Press, 1980), I, xii.

31 The surviving original surveys are in the collection of the South Carolina Department of Archives and History.

graphical features which had not appeared on earlier maps and altered other names he thought were incorrect.

The *Atlas* was presented to the South Carolina Senate on September 29, 1826, and was commended as a "fine specimen of American Science and Art." The *American Farmer* touted it as better than comparable European publications.[32] But acclaim did not bring financial success. Mills hoped to sell atlases for $16 and single maps from $2 to $3; however, the lack of subscriptions and the need to pay the printer induced him to petition the legislature to subsidize the distribution of the maps in order to "disseminate correct geographical information of its territory among the people." He offered to cut the retail price in half, "provided your honorable body would make your petitioner a compensation in some measure commensurate to the sacrifice of interest he would have to make, which may not exceed the sum of one thousand dollars." His request was denied on the same day that the Senate complimented the *Atlas*. Periodically for the next twenty-two years he asked the state for help in disposing of maps, atlases, and finally the plates themselves.[33] (The state never helped, and the whereabouts of the plates is unknown.)

The detailed knowledge presented visually in the maps is articulated in the encyclopedic *Statistics*, which Mills called "an appendix to the *Atlas*." Here he recounts the natural history of the state, including flora, fauna, and all aspects of topography, with an emphasis upon minerals, timber, and navigable waters. He dwells on the social and military history of European settlers, the folklore and way of life of the Indian population; he describes economic development and opportunities for internal improvement and discusses the relationship between health and topography.

To gather material on each county and major settlement, Mills sent a questionnaire throughout the state and compiled the information under fifty headings: "History of settlement, origin of its name, situation, boundaries, soil adaptation to particular products" etc., and two-thirds of the book consists of a recitation of these characteristics. The *Statistics*, unlike Jefferson's *Notes on Virginia*, is primarily descriptive rather than analytical; nonetheless, within this restrictive format his interests are evident. There is no trace of bitterness in his repeated support for internal improvements projects. The benefits of canals and reclamation of swampland are leitmotifs, as is his support for scientific farming. He integrates and paraphrases his earlier writing on these topics and often emphasizes the Revolution as having conferred meaning on scenes of action. Detailed accounts of

32 For Mills' presentation, see General Assembly Papers, 1826, no. 23; for acceptance and commendation by the Senate, see Acts and Resolutions of the General Assembly, Senate, December 1, 1826-14-01, South Carolina Department of Archives and History. Also see *American Farmer* 8 (1826): 231; and Walter W. Ristow, "Robert Mills' Atlas of the State of South Carolina, 1825, the First American State Atlas," *Quarterly Journal of the Library of Congress* vol. 34 no. 1 (January, 1977): 52–66.

33 General Assembly Petitions, 1826, 117; General Assembly Petitions, November 30, 1827-93-01; Manuscript Acts, 1837, no. 2742, SCDAH. Mills had the plates in his possession in 1852, for he offered to sell them to the state: see RM to Governor Means, August 18, 1852.

numerous engagements, taken largely from David Ramsay's *History of the Revolution in South Carolina* (1785), illuminate Mills' interest in public monuments.

Mills' response to picturesque or sublime aspects of landscape is Romantic. This is especially obvious in passages describing the mountainous northwest corner of the state, where he speaks of the "wildness of the steep and rugged rocks—the gloomy horrors of the cliffs—the water falls." Excepting his domestic correspondence, descriptions of landscape contain his most openly emotional writing. Passages about geology often attempt to reconcile Biblical and scientific literature, for he accepts both as sources of proof. In his discussion of marine fossils, for example, he cites "Genesis i, 2,9; which clearly proves the Neptunian origin of this globe." His theology—an acceptance of the fallibility of Man and redemption through Grace—is evident in discussions of socially funded programs for the poor, the infirm or the criminal. Other recurring themes include anecdotes presenting the Indian as noble savage, in terms familiar to readers of James Fenimore Cooper. He also savors local customs which define a sense of place and provide "an evidence that the primitive simplicity of former days is not entirely passed away" such as the "general turn out of all the villagers on a whortleberry expedition once or twice a year" in Edgefield.[34]

The *Statistics* is aptly named. Expressions of emotion, bias, or opinion are the exception here. The bulk of the text is a prosaic recapitulation of facts—the names of Indian towns, a listing of native flora, its habits of growth and potential uses, a survey of mineral resources; it is, as he intended, a verbal equivalent to the landscape presented in the *Atlas*.

Mills often used his publications to promote himself professionally, and he did this with the *Atlas*. In 1827 he sent a copy of the Lancaster District map to Andrew Jackson at the Hermitage. Jackson (who modern historians have said was born in North Carolina or Tennessee) thanked him for the "map of the district of Lancaster within which I was born.... Pointing to the spot that gave me birth," and commented on place-names he remembered from his youth. Two years later, after Jackson had become President, Mills sent him a bound copy of the *Atlas* along with the *Statistics*. This time Mills noted that he had been working for "our native state," but was now seeking employment with the Topographic Corps of Engineers and hoped that Jackson might "mention my name" to the Secretary of War, Joel R. Poinsett, another South Carolinian.[35]

34 Mills, *Statistics*, 51, 37, 8, 9. At this writing the whortleberry has been entirely forgotten. Prof. John Nelson, botanist at the University of South Carolina, suggests that the whortleberry may have been Vaccinium stamineum.

35 Andrew Jackson to Robert Mills, July 8, 1827, PRM 1080; RM to AJ, August 15, 1829, PRM 1117.

LEFT: *Robert Mills, "Plan of a Rail-Road,"* Baltimore Gazette and Daily Advertiser, *July 7, 1827.*
RIGHT: *Henry R. Palmer, "Description of a Railway,"* Description of a Railway on a New Principle *(1824).*

THE ELEVATED MONORAIL AND THE STEAM ENGINE

Mills' other essays from this period concern railroads and steam engines. These essays record his interest in technology and his attempt to participate in developments that soon would make canals obsolete. None of his writing resulted in employment. Shortly after the South Carolina Senate accepted the *Atlas,* Mills sent an essay on railroads, "A Plan of a Rail-Road," to John McLean, U.S. Postmaster General, proposing a mail route via an elevated, horse-drawn, monorail from Washington to New Orleans.[36] As he had done earlier with canals, he estimated the cost of construction, calculated operating costs and concluded that savings resulting from the advantages of his suggestion would pay for the project in fourteen years. Here he rejects canals and embraces railroads.[37]

The essay breathes enthusiasm, as if having finished the dry *Statistics,* he found the new subject vivifying. "Happy is it for our country that this system of improvement has been so early substituted for that of canals. What an honor will redound to that city which shall first accomplish the great work of throwing a chain of connection like this, between the east and west!" The railroad he proposed "differs entirely from those commonly used." It was to be a single rail a minimum of three feet above the ground supported on posts every nine to fifteen feet. The cars were to consist of two boxes suspended on either side of the rail, like saddlebags, connected by a frame and attached to wheels running on the top of the rail. Theoretically, the concave rims of the wheels, the convex surface of the rail, and the equilibrium established by the low center of gravity of the "saddlebag" cars would keep the cars level.

36 RM to John McLean, December 26, 1826, PRM 1058B and PRM 5006 and 1058A.

37 Dated "Columbia, S.C., December 16, 1826," published in the National Intelligencer and republished in the *Baltimore Gazette and Daily Advertiser* 68 (July 7, 1827): 10323.

Mills pointed out several advantages. The elevated track virtually removed the need for grading during construction and minimized maintenance during use, for debris and damp would not be in constant contact with the rail. Elevating the track also reduced the risk of accident and (by reducing friction) would "diminish the quantity of animal torture." He said it took twenty-six days to deliver the mail from Washington to New Orleans, but using his system "if the case was urgent, it would be possible to accomplish the route in four days, (the nights inclusive)." When Mills made this proposal there were no steam-driven railroads in America, and he did not consider steam as a motive power. He did note that similar railroads were in use in England, and his monorail is probably based on the work of Henry R. Palmer, whose published specifications match Mills' proposal.[38]

Discussing friction, for example, Palmer notes the problem of "extraneous substances lying upon" the rails and the "resistance occasioned by dust lying upon the rails." On the same subject Mills said that an elevated rail is not liable "to be covered with dust, or any extraneous matter." In discussing the optimal harness Palmer says that the "horse is connected by a towing...length of rope which will enable him to vary his height without much altering the angle of draught," and Mills says "a track rope is required, which enables them to draw without material alteration of the angle of draught."[39]

The "Plan of a Rail-Road" was used by Mills in his attempt to find work as an engineer, and although he played a small role in one major railroad project, he did continue to circulate his writings and to develop his ideas. In 1827 he wrote General Macomb, Chief Engineer of the War Department, offering to dedicate a "Manuel on Rail Roads" to him, and in 1853, at the end of his career, an updated version of the 1826 plan appeared in the *Scientific American*; he proposed an elevated, suspended, steam-driven train capable of traveling a hundred miles per hour for the "New Pacific Railroad Line." And he added that if "it is wished to combine architectural effect with this construction, the space between the posts or pillars, under the rail, may be arched, and while thereby strengthening the mass, will give them the effect of a continuous arcade." This would also "furnish the means of providing a series of dwellings below, for the operatives and others on the roads, especially in the crossings of ravines and sinkings in the country."[40]

Nothing came of the monorail idea, and the following year Mills sought employment with what would become the Baltimore and Ohio Railroad. In the spring of 1827, when he requested a recommendation from Robert Gilmore, Mills wrote that he had sent a manuscript on railroads to Fielding Lucas for

38 Henry R. Palmer, *Description of a Railway on a New Principle* (London: J. Taylor, 1824).

39 Palmer, *Description of a Railway on a New Principle*, 16–17.

40 *Scientific American* (August 6, 1853): viii, 47. The *Charleston Courier*, September 8, 1853, republished a review of Mills' plan from the *Baltimore American Times*: "...to us it appears better calculated to amuse the fancy, than for practical use."

publication. That summer Mills wrote Eliza that he hoped to find railroad work and to move the family to Baltimore, but prospects there did not materialize.[41]

The only railroad-related work Mills did during the 1820s appears to have been the preparation of estimates in 1828 for the South Carolina Canal and Rail Road Company—whose engine, the "Best Friend of Charleston," was the first American-built steam locomotive (December 1830). Their track from Charleston to Hamburg, South Carolina, 136 miles, was the longest in the world when it opened in 1833. Beyond preparing estimates, Mills is not known to have participated in the development of the Charleston to Hamburg line, nor was he successful in his application to Joel R. Poinsett for a position with the new Charleston to Cincinnati Railroad in 1836. Despite these rebuffs, for years he suggested improvements to those who were busy in the field. In 1834 he suggested that "steam carriages on common roads" would replace canals and railroads, and he wrote Congress in 1852 concerning a route to the Pacific and suggested that a telegraph cable ought to be sheathed in rubber and laid inside the hollow of a rail line.[42]

THE ROTARY PISTON ENGINE

Although there were no steam locomotives in America in 1826, it is surprising Mills did not consider steam in the monorail essay, because in 1824 he had prepared a manuscript for publication, which presented "Improvements in the Rotatory Engine."[43] This presented plans to replace the reciprocating piston with a rotary piston. He suggested several ways this might be accomplished and argued it would be a great improvement, for the traditional reciprocating engine expends three-fourths of its power in reversing the stroke of its pistons and transforming the rectilinear energy of the piston into the circular motion of the drive shaft. The energy saved would mean that a "Rotatory Engine upon either plan stated before, if only 8 horse power (so called) will be equal in effect to a Reciprocating Engine of 20 horsepower." He said additional advantages would include the elimination of vibration, an increased fuel efficiency, and smaller, lighter engines. The advantages would mean that the rotary engine could be adapted "in navigating and propelling wheel carriages."

Ten drawings—plans, sections and elevations—illustrate the engine and are the most complex set of surviving mechanical or engineering drawings by Mills. The illustration, for example, of an "End View of the Rotatory Steam Engine" depicts an engine "in operation acting immediately upon the axle of

41 RM to Robert Gilmore, April 22, 1827; RM to EBSM, August 4, 1827.

42 For Mills' estimate, see *First Semi-Annual Report, South Carolina Canal and Rail Road Company* (Charleston: A.E. Miller, 1828), 18, 19. RM to Joel R. Poinsett, March 17, 1836. Robert Mills, *Substitute for Railroads and Canals* (Washington: James C. Dunn, 1834), 1–12; *Senate Reports 32d Congress, 1st Session* (August 18, 1852), no. 344, 13.

43 A forty-four-page manuscript, "Improvements in the Rotatory Engine; or several modes by which a Direct Circular Motion may be obtained, using either as an Agent, Steam Air Water Gunpowder or any other Propelling Power," by Robert Mills, Engineer and Architect, Columbia, State of South Carolina, 1824, in the collection of the Franklin Institute, Philadelphia.

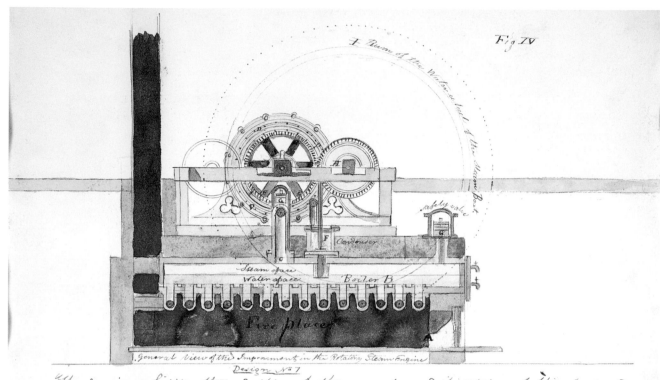

Fig IV

General View of the Improvements in the Rotatory Steam Engine

Design No 1

The drawing exhibits the adaption of the several modifications of the proposed improvement, to practice; where A represents the fire place B the boiler C the steam pipe feeding the Engine DDD the stationary wheel EE &c arms of the moveable wheel with cogs F the condenser — GG the two safety valves H the gearing cog wheel driving the shaft of the water wheel I Tho' as is evident, the shaft of the steam wheel could be used for that of the Water wheel ———— For the operation of the wheel see

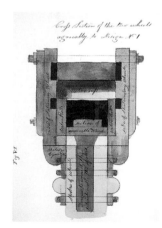

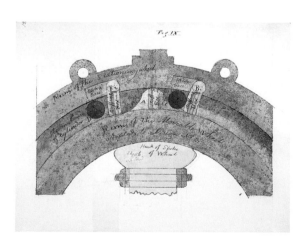

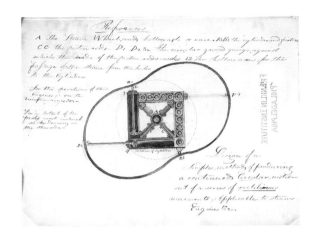

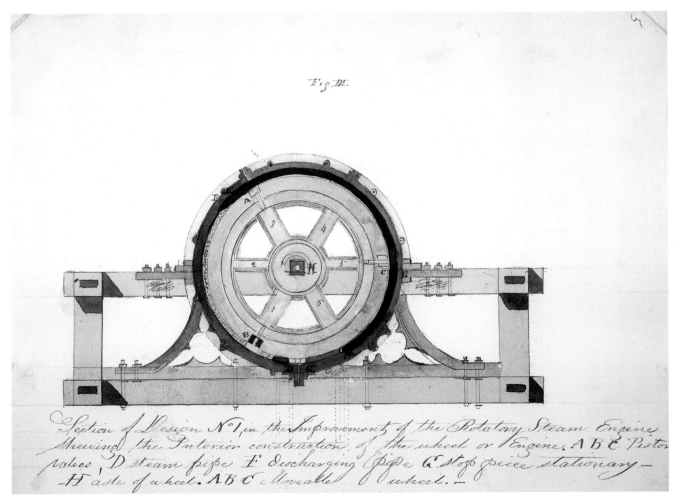

Section of Design N.º 1 in the Improvement of the Rotatory Steam Engine Shewing the Interior construction of the wheel or Engine. A B C Piston valves, D steam pipe F Discharging Pipe G Stop piece stationary — H axle of wheel. A B C Moveable wheel. —

175

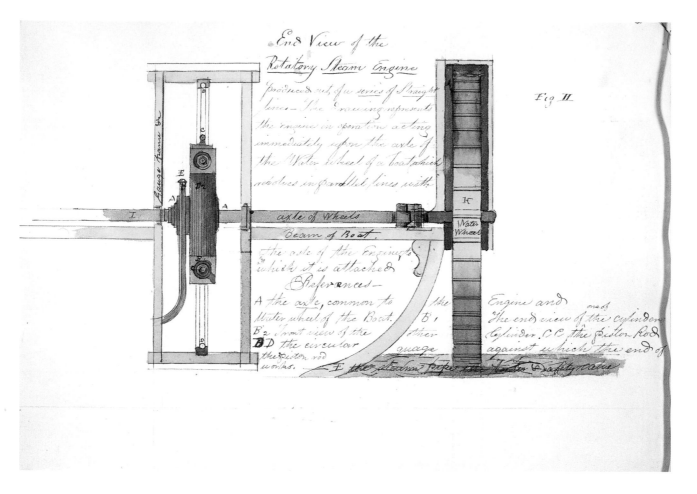

ABOVE AND PAGES 174–175: *Rotary Engine. "Improvements in the Rotatory Engine…"*
Robert Mills, engineer, 1824.

the Water wheel of a boat;" the frame, beam, and engine housing of the boat are
shown in section. Beyond the hull water is indicated to establish a context. The
exterior of the engine housing is stripped away to provide a view of the cylin-
ders and piston rods, and the mechanical apparatus is drawn of straight lines to
emphasize the parallel action of the rotary engine and the water wheel.

Rotary piston engines did not go into production until the early twentieth
century; nonetheless, Mills' idea was not revolutionary. Inventors, including James
Watt, Samuel Boulton, and Oliver Evans, had tried for more than two centuries to

design steam engines using essentially circular internal motion, and approximately 2,000 patents for rotary engines were applied for in the U.S. prior to 1900. Nothing we know about Mills suggests he had the experience to design an engine, and circumstantial evidence indicates his manuscript reflects the work of James Wallace (circa 1783–1851), a professor of mathematics at the South Carolina College.[44]

Viewed from any perspective, Wallace is a fascinating figure. An Irishman and a Jesuit priest, he came to South Carolina after attending Georgetown College. Using the South Carolina College observatory, he established the latitude and longitude of Columbia for the state map, and his report to the Board of Public Works was signed by Robert Mills. Wallace's publications included "New Algebraic Series," "Geometry and Calculus," "Steam Engine and Railroad," and "Canal Navigation." More to the point, on September 25, 1824, he obtained a patent for a "crank, wheel motion." Unfortunately, all records concerning this invention were lost in the Patent Office fire of 1836, but an 1832 reference to it suggests he had patented "the use of two or more pit men, or connecting rods, in place of one, which saves most of the power lost by the use of the crank."[45] This configuration of piston rods appears in the first of several ways Mills described building a rotary engine. Mills gave partial credit to Wallace by saying that the professor had "discovered a great improvement in the Crank motion which he is preparing to lay before the public" and by noting that Wallace had created the "diagram and calculations" in the essay computing the relative force of rotary and traditional reciprocating engines. Neither Mills nor Wallace pursued the idea. Neither tried to develop the engine commercially, and—whoever deserves credit for the idea—Mills' essay is memorable mainly as his most thorough presentation of an avant-garde engineering concept.

Mills' optimistic interest in mechanical engineering was similar in many respects to that of Latrobe; Latrobe used a horse-drawn railroad during the construction of the Chesapeake and Delaware Feeder Canal (1805), and although involved in the manufacture of steam engines, he never considered their application to railroads. Like Mills, Latrobe failed in his attempts to profit from the new transportation technologies. William Strickland, on the other hand, was actively engaged in the development of railroads in Pennsylvania during the very years that Mills was struggling in South Carolina.[46]

44 Jennifer Tann, ed. *The Selected Papers of Boulton & Watt*, vol. I, *The Engine Partnership, 1775–1825* (MIT Press, 1982), 3; Oliver Evans, *The Abortion of the Young Steam Engineer's Guide* (Philadelphia: Fry and Kammerer, 1805), 93–94, 97; "A History of Rotary Engines and Pumps," *The Engineer* (January 13, 1939), 43–45, the first of a series of articles on the topic. For a brief biography of Wallace, see John Hammond Moore, *Columbia and Richland County, A South Carolina Community, 1740–1990* (Columbia: University of South Carolina Press, 1993), 132–133.

45 "Report of the Board of Public Works for the Year, 1821," Kohn and Glenn, 99–100, for Wallaces' role in the preparation of the state map. The title and date of Wallace's patent appears in the *Subject-matter Index of Patents for Inventors Issued by the United States Patent Office from 1790 to 1873, inclusive* (Washington: U.S. Patent Office, 1874), 251, 586. The description appears in a note in *The Southern Review*, vol.8 no. 15 (November, 1831 & February 1832): 20.

46 Agnes Addison Gilchrist, *William Strickland, Architect and Engineer, 1788–1854* (Philadelphia: University of Pennsylvania Press, 1950), 69–71.

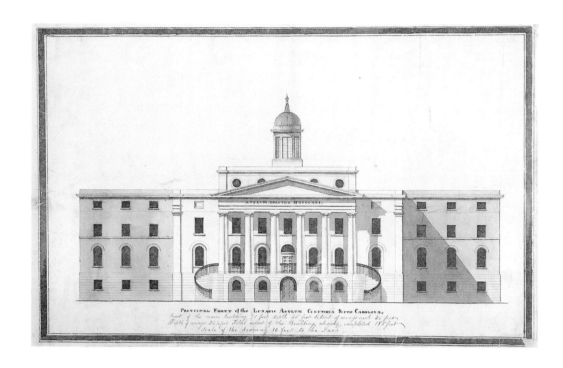

PRINCIPAL FRONT of the LUNATIC ASYLUM COLUMBIA SOUTH CAROLINA.

South Carolina Asylum. Robert Mills, architect, 1822–1828

South Carolina Asylum, Columbia, South Carolina. Robert Mills, architect, 1822–1828.

THE SOUTH CAROLINA ASYLUM

Mills' most important public buildings in South Carolina—the Asylum (1822–28) and the County Records Office (Fireproof Building) (1822–27)—spanned his employment as Acting Commissioner of the Board of Public Works, Superintendent of Public Buildings, and finally as an architect in private practice. The cornerstone of the Asylum was laid on July 22, 1822. Everyone present basked in "sentiments of sociability, humanity and benevolence." The building was to be the largest in the state and was based upon avant-garde theories of psychiatric care. Mills' design replaced an earlier plan by John L. Wilson and was intended to be fireproof and to further therapeutic practices advocated by William (1732–1822) and Samuel Tuke (1784–1857), English Quakers who were instrumental in psychiatric reform. Knowledge of the Tukes' work had already influenced psychiatric hospitals in America. The Friends' Asylum, Frankford, Pennsylvania, 1817, the Asylum for the Insane (later called the McLean Asylum), Charlestown, Massachusetts, 1818, by Charles Bulfinch, the Bloomingdale Asylum, New York, 1816–1821, by Thomas C. Taylor, and the Retreat, Hartford, Connecticut, 1821–1824, all reflected English precedents described in writings by the Tukes which were republished in Philadelphia, 1813–1815.[47]

The South Carolina Asylum differs from its American predecessors in the degree to which its ground plan, structural detail and proposed landscaping realized ideas promoted by the Tukes. Nothing is known concerning the asylum plan by Mills' predecessor, John L. Wilson, except that it had been intended to serve both as a lunatic asylum and a school for the deaf and dumb. Mills' involvement coincided with the decision to create an institution specifically to serve the insane, to make the building fireproof and incorporate gardens within the plan—all of which increased the initial estimates $28,932 to $46,500.[48]

During Mills' participation as supervising architect (1822–1824) the exterior of the central block and the first segments of the obliquely angled flanking wings were enclosed. Costs escalated to $91,000, and the legislative committee was quick to note that the project had been "directed in the plans, calculations, and production, by Mr. Mills who was the Architect of the State when the work was commenced."[49] After Mills was removed from office construction slowed to a crawl. The first patient was admitted on December 12, 1828, but the Asylum had long since lost public support, and to save money the legislature deleted all of the plumbing and landscaping.

Mills' initial plans called for a central block forty feet by eighty feet, five stories high, having a raised basement and fronted on the north by a hexastyle Doric portico on an arcade. As with the courthouses, access to the service areas (kitchens, laundry, store rooms, furnaces, and refectories) was through the arcade beneath the portico. At either end of the portico, winding lateral stairs provided access to the main floor. The entry hall was flanked by offices, and at its rear was the main staircase which projected from the rear of the building. The wings, each composed of a series of wards, were to sweep back to the south and enclose a semicircular garden 500 feet in diameter. The garden was to be subdivided into segments accessible to the various wards. Samuel Tuke had noted that large activity rooms were needed to accommodate groups of patients (these were located in the central block) and private bedrooms were beneficial (these were located on the south side of the wings). Tuke also advocated sepa-

47 *Charleston Courier*, August 3, 1822. William Tuke established the Retreat in York, England, 1792; his grandson, Samuel Tuke, published tracts on the design of asylums, including *Practical Hints on the Construction and Economy of Pauper Lunatic Asylums* (York, England: William Alexander, 1815) containing the plans for the Wakefield Asylum by William Stark.

48 Report of the Committee on the Lunatic Asylum, S.C. Senate, December 16, 1822, South Carolina Archives and History.

49 Report of the Commissioners of the Lunatic Asylum, n.d. [December, 1824], South Carolina Department of Archives and History.

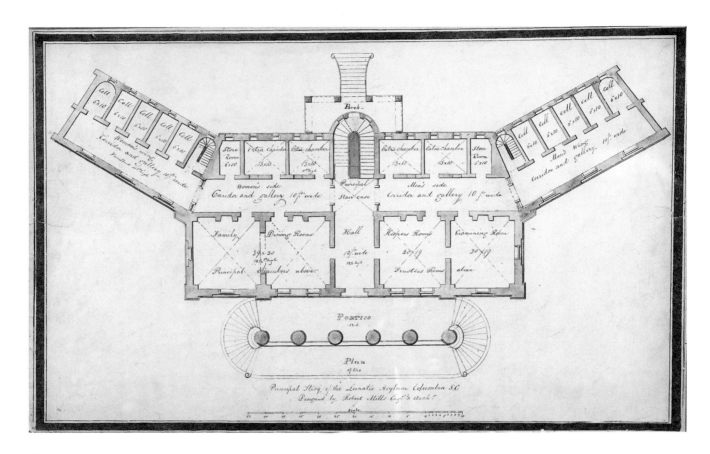

South Carolina Asylum.

rating the sexes, but avoiding any impression of constraint. Mills accomplished this by angling the ward corridors, effectively blocking visual contact without having to resort to physical restraint. Wide corridors were to serve as "exercise galleries during inclement weather" (each of Mills' bedrooms opened into such a corridor); metal sash, Tuke said, and concealed hinges should provide security unobtrusively (this was done at the Asylum where "security is agreeably deguised [*sic*] under appearances familiar to the eye in every private house"). Samuel Tuke stressed the beneficial effect of orientation and landscape, and in these respects the Asylum is Mills' most notable work in South Carolina. He was criticized for facing the building away from the town, but did so in order that the dormitories might have a southern exposure. The grounds to the north

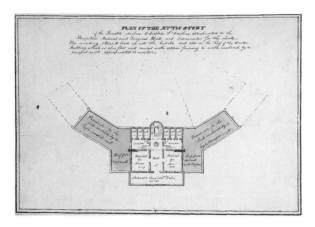 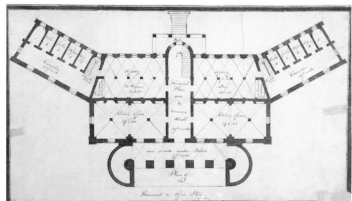

South Carolina Asylum.

were to be "laid off in walks, with trees, shrubbery, and seats" for "the respectable class of patients." To the south within the semi-circular embrace of the wings the grounds were to be "divided into sections for the several classes, and for the requisite domestic accommodations of the Institution." The roof of the central block was used as a "walk...which is surrounded by a parapet wall, is appropriated exclusively to visitors. It overlooks those [on the flanking wings] of the patients, as well as all the courts of the Institution."[50] This may be the earliest roof in America designed for recreation, and like the walled court-yards, it was Mills' response to the need for controlled access to nature for patients in an urban setting.

Technologically, the most exceptional aspects of the plan were the heating and ventilating systems. A system of underground drains connected with ducts in the corridor floors to cool the building by convection. Jefferson had used an underground ventilating tunnel at Monticello, but insofar as is known, the Asylum was the first instance of its use in Carolina. The heating system can be reconstructed from Mills' plans and writings, as well as from contemporary accounts and fragments that survive *in situ*. Two separate furnaces were used to heat the building; each consisted of three elements: a firebox, a heat chamber, and a system of flues and dampers, or registers, which distributed the heated air throughout the building. The fireboxes were located at one end of the refecto-ries, the long and narrow (thirty-eight feet by twenty-one feet) rooms that

50 *The Pioneer*, Yorkville, South Carolina, March 20, 1824.

occupied the southern side of the basement of the central block. To facilitate the delivery of fuel and the removal of ashes, each of the fireboxes was located near an exterior entry. The furnaces, which shared a common wall and flues with the fireplaces used for cooking, were approximately four feet wide, four feet high, and six feet deep and were made "mostly of brick." They had one or more hinged metal doors, through which wood was loaded, fires stoked, and ash removed. They also had at least two adjustable metal dampers, one of which controlled the flow of air into the fire chamber to regulate the rate of combustion. The other damper(s) controlled the flow of air into flues (probably cast iron), which passed through the firebox. Air heated in these flues passed by convection into a "heat chamber" or reservoir—a sealed, vaulted brick chamber (five feet seven inches wide, six feet ten inches deep, and six feet seven inches high) resembling a kiln, which contained a series of interconnected flues. Here it was thought that the heated air, like water flowing within a constricted course, would gather momentum. The flues within the reservoir opened into a network of flues, or channels within the walls, through which the air rose to dampers or registers located in each corridor throughout the building.[51]

The most unusual exterior feature of the Asylum were the curving staircases at either end of the portico. Mills used similar staircases at nine of his courthouses, and may have drawn upon the river facade of Palladio's Villa Foscari (1570) as a prototype. The flanking, or lateral, stairs of the Horry County Courthouse most nearly resemble those of the Villa Foscari; others resemble the curving stairs designed by the English Palladians—Isaac Ware for Wrotham Park, Middlesex (1754), or Robert Adam for Kedleston Hall (1761) or the west front of Osterley Park. These staircases were an important element of the courthouses for Horry, Greenville, Orangeburg, Union, Lancaster, Williamsburg, Georgetown, and Sumter counties, as well as at the Fireproof Building, the Asylum, and the later Alexandria, Virginia courthouse. These stairs allowed the lower entry to be framed within the basement arcade, they expressed the functional separation of the floors, maintained a firebreak between floors, buffered the court from noise and traffic, and conserved interior space.

The United States Bank (1800) (which became the Charleston City Hall), attributed to Gabriel Manigault, may have introduced this Palladian motif to South Carolina. In New York Mills had seen a similar staircase at the Government House. Palladio described both solid and hollow core "winding stairs." Mills used both types. The ascending spiral twisted around a solid core

51 For a review of early heating systems in America, see: Samuel Y. Edgerton, "Heat and Style: Eighteenth-Century House Warming by Stoves," *Journal of the Society of Architectural Historians* 20 (March, 1961): 20–26; also see Eugene S. Ferguson, "An Historical Sketch of Central Heating: 1800–1860," in Charles E. Peterson, ed., *Building Early America* (Radnor, Pennsylvania: Chilton, 1976), 165–185.

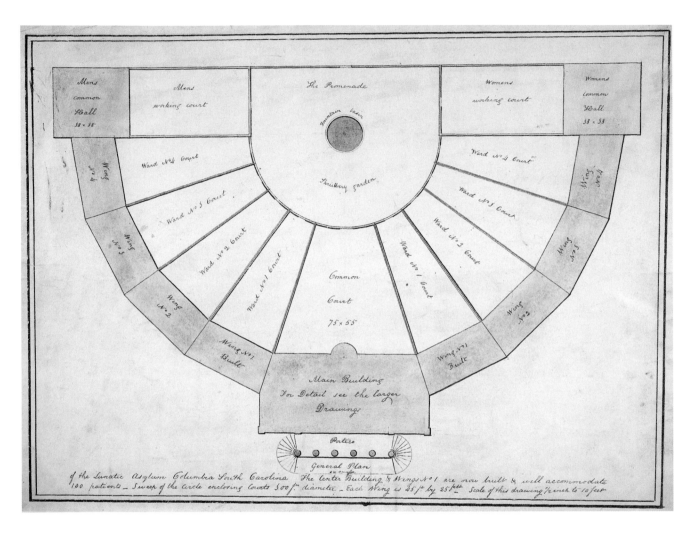

South Carolina Asylum.

184

on the facades of the courthouses at Georgetown, Williamsburg, and perhaps Greenville and Union as well as at the Fireproof Building and the Alexandria courthouse. The service stairs of the Asylum, located in the angle between the central block and the wings, were also designed with a solid core, with the inner end of each tread serving as a drum of the central column. The solid-core spiral also appears in his project for the South Caroliniana Library (1836). The cylindrical space defined by the staircase, which Palladio called the "column in the middle," was open and the treads cantilevered from the wall in the central staircase inside the Fireproof Building. The porticos of the Orangeburg courthouse and the Asylum were also flanked by hollow-core spiral stairs.

Only three of the exterior stairways have survived intact (at the Asylum, the Horry and Georgetown County courthouses); among them, only the Asylum steps feature the exposed, curving form he used most frequently. The Asylum plans and elevations differ from the stairs as built, for the drawings indicate projections from either end of the portico, which served as footings for the outermost columns and as a cylindrical solid core around which the staircases would have turned. As drawn, the staircases were visually integrated into the portico; the face of each tread was designed as a radius originating at the center of the column and common to the concentric circles formed by the base of the column and the inner and outer arcs of the staircase. The projections, however, were deleted (perhaps during the final stages of construction, when landscaping, plumbing, and the fireproofing of the upper floors were all cancelled to save money), and this change made the stairs a disharmonious appendage.

THE FIREPROOF BUILDING, OR COUNTY RECORDS OFFICE

Perhaps the best known of Mills' public buildings in Carolina is the County Records Office, or Fireproof Building, Charleston, 1822–1827. In 1819, prior to his return to South Carolina, the legislature had noted the need for fireproof repositories in both Columbia and Charleston, and Mills acted while the project was in its formative stage; he corresponded with the City Council of Charleston concerning such a facility in October 1821.[52] Two months later the legislature appropriated $25,000–$10,000 for the purchase of a site and $15,000 for the construction of fireproof offices. On May 20, 1822, the City Council voted to pay Mills $200 for plans concerning the improvement of the square adjacent the City Hall. Mills' plan entailed siting the new building within an open space

52 Gene Waddell, "Robert Mills' Fireproof Building," *South Carolina Historical Magazine* vol. 80 no. 2 (April, 1979): 105–135.

County Records Office (Fireproof Building), Charleston, South Carolina. Robert Mills, architect, 1822–1827.

53 Waddell, "Robert Mills' Fireproof Building"; also see Committee on Public Buildings, *General Assembly Papers, Reports*, 1819, no. 86.

which would serve simultaneously as a firebreak, and as a linkage between the City Hall, the state offices, and a proposed federal courthouse and academy of fine arts; the open space would also be Charleston's first professionally designed park. His plan called for paired walkways dividing the lot into quadrants; one pair formed the east-west axis, entered the park perpendicular to Meeting Street and separated the new building from the existing City Hall; the north-south axis consisted of another pair, which extended through the park from Chalmers to Broad Street and was intended to set off the proposed courthouse and academy. The prominent site and the fact that the building was to be occupied by ten state offices induced Mills to design the most complex of his Carolina buildings. The plans were completed during the spring of 1822, for he advertised for bids from April 21–May 13, 1822.[53]

The funding of Charleston County Records Office was prompted by the need for fireproof storage for public records. As Mills was getting the Charleston project underway, he seized the moment and presented a plan for Columbia, the state capital. He proposed "to convert the present [Columbia] Court House into a jail, which may be easily accomplished; to surrender up the present State House to the use of the courts, and to erect a new building for the use of the legislature, with fire proof offices within it."[54] Mills' drawings (which have not survived) for a new state capitol were exhibited in the House of Representatives in 1822, but he was nearing the end of his tenure, and there is no evidence that his suggestion was officially discussed.

Mills was removed from his post as Superintendent of Public buildings in December 1823, but he was appointed as one of four "Commissioners for completing the Fire Proof Buildings" on December 13, 1823. The following week he was also appointed a Commissioner of Public Buildings for Charleston District, a group which had "full Power & Authority to design, construct & finish the Public Buildings authorized by law." Insofar as work in Charleston was concerned, these appointments mitigated his loss of office, especially since his fellow commissioners "found it requisite to have some skilful architect to superintend the work & inspect the contracts and appointed Mr. Robert Mills for that purpose." He was retained by the Commissioners of the Fire Proof Offices, and for $500 took bids, drafted contracts, checked construction (but was not continually on site), and measured and certified completed work for payment. The pace of application for payment and certification of work suggests that construction progressed smoothly.[55]

Mills was living in Columbia (120 miles from Charleston) and travelling throughout the state in conjunction with his work variously on the *Atlas*, courthouses, and jails, so the Commissioners hired John Spidle to direct construction of the Fireproof Building. Together Mills and Spidle approved the work of the principal brick mason, John Gordon, including the interior plastering and the exterior stuccoing of eaves and cornices, on May 5, 1825. The work of James Rowe and John White, the stone masons—cutting and installing the cantilevered interior stair treads as the brick walls rose, facing the basement with brownstone, setting the flagstone flooring and brownstone sills, thresholds, capitals and parapet—was measured periodically from November 23, 1823, through February 16, 1826. A blacksmith, John Johnson, was paid for fabricating and installing metal balusters and other trim on October 4, 1826, and at year's

54 Kohn and Glenn, 34. Also see John M. Bryan, *Creating the South Carolina State House* (Columbia: University of South Carolina Press, 1999), 11.

55 Report of the Commissioners of Public Buildings for Charleston District, n.d. no 59-1; see also Report of the Commissioners of the Fire Proof Offices, General Assembly, December 11, 1826, no. 172-05.

end, Robert Downie was paid for "souldring conducting pipe" on the roof. The Commissioners of the Fire Proof Offices reported on December 11, 1826, that the interior was ready for occupancy (Benjamin Hunt, Commissioner in Equity, had been for "some time" in rooms assigned "by Mr. R. Mills the Architect"). They said the exterior was within days of completion and observed that they had exceeded their budget because "there had been two Architects one counteracting the other." The final cost for the building and lot was $53,803.81.[56]

The elevations did not conform in several respects to Mills' drawing and descriptions, and some of these alterations are attributable to Spidle. Mills envisioned a Palladian block five bays wide on a raised basement. The principal facades (north and south) were designed with projecting Doric porticos elevated on arcades and bracketed by winding lateral stairs, like those planned for the Asylum. Mills' surviving elevation shows that the columns were to be fluted, but Spidle left them unfluted and covered them with rough cast.[57] He also affected both the proportions and horizontality of Mills' elevation by using quoins in lieu of continuous horizontal channeling, and by doing so he diminished the visual effectiveness of the basement as a podium. (Mills' use of channeling is seen at the Asylum and the Georgetown Courthouse as well as in the Fire Proof Building elevation.) Equally significant was the deletion of the belt course between the second and third floors and the lengthening of the third floor windows, changes which erased the illusion of an attic story and the closure this had provided in Mills' elevation. This latter alteration adversely affected the east and west facades, which Gene Waddell has observed were to resemble triumphal arches. These elevations consist of three bays, the central bay being recessed and vertically integrated through the use of a Latrobean triple window on the main floor and a thermal window above.

The exterior changes did not affect the interior plan. The ground plan had to satisfy three primary criteria: the secure storage of governmental records, accessibility to diverse offices without the disruption of other tenants, and adequate lighting and ventilation. Meeting these goals Mills modified the concept he used repeatedly in the lower floors of his courthouses and jails by inserting a central bay flanked on either side by hallways that extended through the building from north to south.

This fireproof central bay contains a vault at grade secured by wrought-iron doors, several rooms without fireplaces or combustible materials of any kind, and an oval stairwell with cantilevered brownstone stairs and balconies.

56 Waddell, 110, 115–120; see also Report of the Commissioners of the Fire Proof Offices, General Assembly, December 11, 1826, no. 172-05.

57 Waddell, 118–119.

As the stairwell is crowned by a skylight, it provides circulation of light and air as well as vertical access throughout the building. Mills had planned a fireproof vault in the home of Benjamin Chew (Philadelphia, 1810), but there is no direct precedent in his work for the double hall and central stairwell. The stairwell recalls a Palladian rotunda reduced to a utilitarian scale, and it represents a creative solution to the design criteria.

THE POWDER MAGAZINE COMPLEX

During construction of the Fireproof Building, Mills also designed an addition to the Charleston Jail (1822–1824) and a complex of nine powder magazines, barracks, and a gatehouse (1822–1827). The advertisement soliciting bids for the jail (March 20, 1822) noted that his plans and specifications would be "in the hands of the commissioners" the following week. This jail (demolished circa 1855) was a rectangular addition to the Charleston County Jail and was described by Mills in the *Statistics* as being four stories high, "divided into solitary cells," and "the whole made fireproof." The description suggests it incorporated features he described in his earlier unsuccessful proposal for the South Carolina Penitentiary.[58]

The Charleston powder magazines also represented ideas he had used previously. He described the magazines as "brick, rough cast, and made fireproof...all of a circular form, with conical roofs, and disposed in three ranges, 130 feet apart." The central magazine was the largest and was reserved for the storage of publicly owned gunpowder, and its roof was made "bomb-proof."[59]

Plans for the Charleston Magazine have not survived, but the need for secure arsenals was noted in the Board of Public Works Report for 1821 and resulted in an initial appropriation of $8,000. From this appropriation in September 1822, Mills paid Mrs. Anne Langstaff $1,000 in partial payment for Laurel Island, a five-acre site adjacent to the Charleston Neck and New Market Creek, a tributary of the Cooper River. The island was located in the salt marsh and "a bold navigation extends up to the spot, and affords every convenience to the importers of powder."[60] By the end of the year the Board reported that contracts had been let and that the buildings "are in a state of forwardness." Additional appropriations were made in 1825 ($17,380) and 1827 ($2,000). In 1824 Mills solicited bids for the construction of a Palmetto log embankment "not to

58 *Charleston Courier*, March 20, 1822; Robert Mills, *Statistics*, 420; also see Waddell and Liscombe, 32.

59 Mills, *Statistics*, 421–422.

60 Kohn and Glenn, 105. Also see Nora M. Davis, "Public Powder Magazines at Charleston," *Yearbook of the City of Charleston*, 1942, 186–210.

Powder Magazine Complex, Charleston, South Carolina. Robert Mills, architect, 1822–1827.

Powder Magazine Complex.

exceed 340 feet" along the margin of the creek, but this aspect of the work proved too expensive and was abandoned.[61]

Judging from rubble on the site in the early 1970s, the eight smaller magazines were sixteen-and-one-half feet in diameter and the larger public magazine was approximately twenty feet in diameter. The walls of the magazines were of Charleston gray brick covered with rough cast and were two feet thick. Lintels, thresholds, and door jambs were made of brownstone; all the magazines had slate roofs. The most architecturally notable part of the magazine complex was the gatehouse. Mills said it was a barracks "two stories high, and covering the grand gateway leading into the magazine court." It was apparently a triumphal arch incorporating a residential interior in the manner of Ledoux. Shortly before its demolition (circa 1940) it was described as "a most picturesque ruin of

61 Mills, *Statistics*, 421, 422; Kohn and Glenn, 105, 150, 156; Nora M. Davis, "Public Powder Magazines at Charleston," *Yearbook of the City of Charleston, 1942* (Charleston, 1944), 208.

College of Charleston Gatehouse. Edward Brickell White, architect, 1852.

a building distinguished from all other structures around Charleston by two Roman arches through the center and an up and down stairs room in each wing. Obviously a gate yet the parapet gables and absence of battlements gave it the appearance of a home rather than a military structure."[62] We know just enough about it to conclude that it was one of Mills' most unusual buildings. It foreshadowed his 1836 proposal for the South Carolina College library and his design, circa 1850, for lock keeper's quarters in the piers of a unrealized monumental bridge over the Potomac. Mills' gatehouse for the magazine complex probably inspired the triumphal arch and porter's lodge that Edward Brickell White designed for the College of Charleston in 1852.

 Mills' public work in Charleston—the Fireproof Building and the Powder Magazine complex—was completed after he lost his job with the Board of

62 *Charleston News and Courier*, May 5, 1929.

Public Works. There is no public record of the criticism or debate that led to Mills' dismissal. An anonymous writer, however, came to his defense, argued for the architectural expression of civic dignity, urged recognition of architects as professionals, and lamented the way Mills was treated by the state:

CHARLESTON COURIER, FEBRUARY 27, 1824
Architecture-Economy in the creation of public buildings, and the display of taste in their structure and appearance, are among the legitimate objects of public concern. It was the boast of Augustus, that having found Rome composed of brick buildings, he had rebuilt it with stone.... It is thus that the broken fragments of Grecian arts convey to modern times, the most distinct memorial of her greatness, and we judge from the foot of Hercules the muscular energy of the tout ensemble.

We, in this country, gained nothing in the beauty of our public buildings by the revolution that achieved our liberty. Economy is the republican rule—and the utmost of pride is sometimes seen in the disdain of ostentation. There can be no doubt that Diogenes in his tub, was a prouder man than Croesus on his throne. Yet something would seem to be due to the majesty of a state, when so much is required for the majesty of a monarch. Our public edifices should partake somewhat of the grandeur of our political and civil institutions, and should not be allowed to form a beggarly contrast to the buildings of Europe.

...the principles of architecture...as a science, can accurately be known by those only, who have studied it professionally. Such men are invaluable citizens of a state, contributing where they are successfully employed to its character for refinement as well as its facilities for convenience. We have such a man, a native of South Carolina. We invited him from Baltimore, where he was profitably employed and remunerated, into the service of this state. As superintendent of public buildings, Mr. Mills, the gentleman alluded to, saved the state upwards of $30,000 and yet erected very superior edifices. Upwards of a year since, the Legislature thought proper to substitute another gentleman in his place, without the shadow of any imputation against him, and at the last Session, they abolished the office altogether—leaving the design and superintendence of public buildings to gentlemen not professional men, but chosen because they enjoy the good opinion of the Legislature.

We regret this for many reasons. It was ungrateful treatment towards Mr. Mills—it will injure the tasteful character of our public buildings, and we know from facts communicated to us, that it will increase their cost at least 20 per cent. So much for false economy![63]

PRIVATE COMMISSIONS IN CAROLINA

During the second half of the decade Mills received new commissions for five courthouses (Chesterfield, Kershaw, Orangeburg, Anderson, and Abbeville counties) and four jails (Edgefield, Newberry, Orangeburg, and Greenville counties), but his major work for the state was over. Few documents survive concerning his private work during the 1820s. The Ainsley Hall House, Columbia (1823–25), is a notable exception, for the client died during construction, and contracts, accounts, and lists of materials were preserved as probate records. Only scattered papers and glancing references confirm other private commissions including the Bethesda Presbyterian Church, Camden (1821–23), St. Peter's Roman Catholic Church, Columbia (1824), the DeKalb monument, Camden (1824–27), the Maxcy Monument, Columbia (1824–27), and a Presbyterian Parsonage in Columbia (1828). But if the Baltimore years can be taken as a guide, he no doubt had private projects in South Carolina that have been forgotten.

The earliest record of the Ainsley Hall House is the masonry contract that Hall signed with John Davis on April 4, 1823. Davis agreed to lay the brick for $3 per thousand (all materials were to be supplied by Hall). The following month (May 6th) Charles Beck, carpenter, contracted to complete "agreeably to the designs and instructions of Robert Mills," all necessary woodwork. Mills witnessed the carpentry contract and no doubt wrote the specifications, which Beck promised to execute for not more than $2,500. The surviving ledger does not record payment to Mills, but includes expenses spanning the period April 5,

63 *Charleston Courier,* February 27, 1824.

Ainsley Hall House, Columbia, South Carolina. Robert Mills, architect, 1823–1825.

1823, through September 18, 1824. The total cost was $19, 414.36, or almost twice that of a typical county courthouse.[64]

    Ainsley Hall had purchased an entire city block, and Mills sited the house with its principle facade facing north and its garden facade facing south. The house was aligned with Hall's former residence directly across Blanding Street, which he sold to Wade Hampton. This latter building, now known as the Hampton Preston House, is set close to the street, and Mills created a more monumental image by setting the new Ainsley Hall House in the center of its four-acre block. He also planned service buildings—a stable, kitchen, wood house, privy, and a gardener's house—and estimated the cost of a wall around the entire block, for he conceived the new complex as a Palladian manor with its dependencies. The house consists of a full raised basement, a principal floor, and a "chamber" or bedroom floor. The basement contains a central hall and four rooms, each having a fireplace and windows on two sides. Intended as a service area, it was "plain and neatly" finished with an unglazed brick floor and

64 James C. Massey, "Robert Mills Documents, 1823: A House for Ainsley Hall in Columbia, South Carolina," *Journal of the Society of Architectural Historians* 22 (December, 1963): 228–232.

ABOVE AND OPPOSITE: *Ainsley Hall House.*

197

Bethesda Presbyterian Church, Camden, South Carolina. Robert Mills, architect, 1821–1823.

rough plastered walls. An unobtrusive hall perpendicular to the central hall contains a service stair and an exit on the east facade.

Formal access to the principal story is provided by the two-story Ionic portico and central doorway. The interior end of the entry hall is curved and establishes a play of arcs that makes the house unique in the midlands of South Carolina. An apse-like niche within the curved end wall is flanked by doorways opening into matching parlors, and these parlors have curved walls which are echoed by a double niche in the south facade. Mills' use of arcs continues in the arcades that support both the piazza and the portico, as well as in the prominent round-headed windows framed by blind arches on the principal or north facade. It has been suggested that the plan of the principal floor is based upon Latrobe's design for the home of Senator John Pope, Lexington Kentucky (1811). The windows on the south facade are Latrobean triple windows, which Mills had used often in earlier residential work. The interior staircase is Jeffersonian inasmuch as it is placed in an enclosed hall and is functionally rather than ceremonially conceived.

Functional details include a piazza shading of the southern facade, the use of interior shutters and triple windows in the public rooms, sash windows hung with counterweights, base boards mortised into the floor, durable cypress specified for the eight columns of the piazza, and hinges with linch pins set in diagonally canted sockets so that doors rise slightly as they open to clear carpets and lower flush upon the thresholds in closing.

In several instances functional considerations are outweighed by the Mills' Neoclassical instinct for symmetry: a false door in the entry hall—a mirror image of the staircase doorway; a window intersected by the staircase landing, placed so that it is in its "proper" place on the east facade; the contorted arching of the flues in the attic, allowing the chimneys to rise symmetrically through the hipped roof. Ultimately it is symmetry and balance that make the house memorable. The clarity of its vertical definition, provided by belt courses and a broad entablature, is counterbalanced by the elevated, two-story Ionic portico and the flanking bays containing round-headed windows framed by blind arches. The dignity of the elevation is enhanced by the English raised basement, a feature common in Carolina low country houses, which Mills had made a hallmark of public buildings throughout the state.

In addition to the Ainsley Hall House, documents exist for two churches, the Bethesda Presbyterian Church, Camden (1821–1823), and St. Peter's Roman Catholic Church, Columbia (1824). They demonstrate his stylistic breadth, for

St. Peter's Roman Catholic Church, Columbia, South Carolina. Robert Mills, architect, 1824.

they have nothing in common with, nor do they resemble, his contemporaneous governmental work. The temple-form Camden church has a pedimented Doric portico at either end and an elevated pulpit, much as he had proposed for the John's Island Episcopal Church (circa 1803). In Camden he placed the belfry and spire above the rear facade, as he had suggested for the Monumental Church in Richmond (1812–17), and in doing so he may have remembered the steeple at the rear of St. Paul's Chapel, which he had drawn carefully during his study tour before joining Latrobe.

For the Catholic congregation in Columbia he designed the earliest Gothic Revival building in South Carolina. Built of brick and covered with stucco to imitate stone, St. Peter's (1824) was in the form of a Greek cross, its nave eighty feet long and forty-four feet wide and its transepts spanning sixty feet. Balconies above the nave were supported by a double range of "four clustered" columns, which rose above the balconies to support the "vaulted roof or ceiling, intersected with groin arches." The nave terminated in a semi-circular apse with a hemispherical dome, and within the apse an elevated altar was dramatically lighted by skylights in the dome. Mills sent a description of St. Peter's to the *Charleston Courier* in 1824. Citing Britton's *Antiquities of Great Britain* on the Gothic, he observed, "there is a sublimity in this species of Architecture that particularly adapts it for sacred uses. Its simple elegance, lightness and grandeur, excite an interest in the mind of the beholder, that neither the Greek nor Roman temples could."[65] In Mills' hands Gothic elements, the towers, crenellations, finials, and pointed arches were usually symmetrically arranged, and if he understood the "sublimnity" of the style, his work suggests little affinity for the irrational, asymmetrical nature of the Gothic Revival as it would be developed by the next generation of designers.

65 *Charleston Courier,* September 22, 1824; also see Liscombe, *The Church Architecture of Robert Mills,* 56–57.

THE BARON DEKALB, JONATHAN MAXCY,
AND BUNKER HILL MONUMENTS

The Maxcy Monument in Columbia (1824–1827) and the DeKalb Monument in Camden (1825) reflect his ongoing interest in history, his unremitting search for work, and a tendency to adapt designs with which he was familiar. The bases of the Maxcy and DeKalb monuments are similar to cenotaphs designed by Latrobe for the Congressional Cemetery, and the Maxcy monument was essentially a re-use of his suggestion for the Aquilla Randall Monument in Baltimore. Mills' two Carolina monuments are modest in scale and design, and both are specifically local in meaning, but in his eyes they were part of an important national phenomenon. First, like other designers of his generation he associated Egyptian forms with monuments as reflexively as he used the Gothic Revival for major churches and institutions of higher learning. The Maxcy and DeKalb monuments join his earlier obelisks in foreshadowing the Washington National Monument, his most famous work. Secondly, he believed monuments promote citizenship by serving as "beacons of virtue."

While the Maxcy monument was being erected, Mills drafted a proposal for a more elaborate (never built) monument to South Carolinians who participated in the Revolution. He wrote that although "no tongue can express" the gratitude owed to the Revolutionary generation, "hands will one day rear for the instruction and admiration of a grateful posterity the Monumental cenotaph enrich'd with the names of that galaxy of heroes and statesmen which graced our State and advanced the glory of the Union." Mills believed monuments stimulate an awareness of the shared ideals and experiences that sustain the Union.

In 1824 the Clariosophic Society, a student literary and debating society, decided to erect a monument to Jonathan Maxcy (d. 1820), the first president of the South Carolina College. The society contacted George McDuffie, U.S. Representative from South Carolina. The students sought McDuffie's advice and requested him to write an epitaph; they also worked with William K. Clowny, the professor of mathematics at the college. Clowny obtained plans from Mills and arranged for Mills to direct the work. Clowny also kept McDuffie informed. (This second-hand contact with McDuffie proved important, for in 1830 McDuffie helped Mills obtain his first federal work.) It took three years for the students to raise the money for the monument. The

TO
DE KALB

ABOVE: *Maxcy Monument, Columbia, South Carolina. Robert Mills, architect, 1824–1827.*
OPPOSITE: *DeKalb Monument, Camden, South Carolina. Robert Mills, architect, 1824–1827.*

cornerstone was laid on December 15, 1827, and the stonework, including McDuffie's epitaph, was completed that spring by William Brown for $873.[66]

The Maxcy and DeKalb monuments are dwarfed by proposals Mills submitted in the competition for the Bunker Hill Monument. From Columbia he sent (March 20, 1825) drawings, a description, and specifications for two designs—a column and an obelisk—both hollow, both containing stairs, and both to be crowned by a tripod. His presentation assured the committee that he had devoted years to the study of monuments, had been entrusted with the creation of the Washington Monument in Baltimore, and that his aim was to combine "economy with good taste [as] simplicity I have always considered the groundwork of beauty." He wrote that of the two designs he preferred the obelisk, for "the obelisk form is peculiarly adapted to commemorate great transactions from its lofty character, great strength, and furnishing a fine surface for inscriptions. There is a degree of lightness and beauty in it that affords a finer relief to the eye than can be obtained in the regular proportioned column."[67]

The granite obelisk proposed by Mills was to rise 220 feet above its plinth. Similar to his plan for the Baltimore Washington Monument, "the shaft is divided into four great compartments for inscriptions and other decorations, which come more immediately under the eye by means of oversailing platforms, enclosed by balustrades, supported as it were by winged globes." The ornament was to include inscriptions and bronze shields and stars representing each state. Here, as in Baltimore, wreaths were to frame round windows lighting the interior of the monument. The crowning tripod was to be a functional eternal flame—a gas-lit beacon for mariners entering Boston Harbor. Concerning cost, he assured the committee that "it will be easily seen from the nature of the annexed design that its expense may be increased or diminished at pleasure in the ratio of the decorations introduced," and in closing he casually mentioned he had recently assisted the aged Lafayette "to lay the first corner stone of a monument to one of the worthies who fell in the defense of our liberties (General DeKalb) at Camden."[68]

Mills heard nothing from the committee in Boston, but he learned an obelisk without ornament was under construction and that it seemed to be his "naked pillar preserved in all its original proportions." He asked Richard Wallack, a friend who was going to Boston, to look into the matter and at least retrieve his drawings "finished in oil colors with a distant view of Boston in the background." Wallack was apparently unsuccessful, and the Bunker Hill Monument traditionally has been attributed to Solomon Willard, a Bostonian.

66 Bryan, *An Architectural History of the South Carolina College,* 63–69.

67 RM to the Monument Commission, Boston, Mass., Accompanying His Competitive Plans for the Bunker Hill Monument, March 20, 1825, transcribed in Gallagher, 204–207.

68 RM to the Monument Commission, Boston, Mass., Accompanying His Competitive Plans for the Bunker Hill Monument, March 20, 1825, transcribed in Gallagher, 204–207.

From the outset there was some question as to who should receive credit for the design. The selection committee did not award the $100 premium to anyone. Alexander Parris, who participated in the competition and was in charge of the cornerstone ceremony (June 17, 1825), had his own name engraved as architect on the plate placed beneath the cornerstone. Willard, retained as architect and superintendent by the committee (December 1, 1826), considered himself the creator. Mills' claim relies upon the fact that basic measurements of the finished work match dimensions stipulated in his specifications. The advertisement had suggested a height of 220 feet, so this similarity is natural, but beyond this Mills had described the base of his design as being thirty-one or thirty-three feet square, the circular interior stair as having a diameter of ten feet, and the top of the tapered shaft as fifteen feet square. An undated construction estimate submitted to the committee by Loamni Baldwin, an engineer, a "Memorandum and estimate of an obelisk, of thirty feet base, fifteen at the top, and two hundred and twenty feet high, with a winding stairway round a circular hollow newel," may have been an analysis of Mills' proposal. Summarizing the dimensions as built, Willard wrote "the obelisk is thirty feet in diameter at the base, fifteen at the top of the truncated part, and two hundred and twenty feet high. . . . The diameter of the hollow cone is ten feet at the bottom, and six feet at the top."[69] Willard's biographer sidesteps the issue by saying the obelisk-form belongs to history, not to an individual; nonetheless, Mills' chagrin is understandable.

Mills' problems with the Bunker Hill Committee followed on the heels of the loss of his state job in South Carolina. A month after he sent the drawings to Boston, a notice appeared in *The Charleston Courier* (April 27, 1825) that Lafayette and the President of the United States were expected to attend a cornerstone ceremony for the Bunker Hill Monument. On a brighter note, in the same column was a brief article concerning a water company Mills hoped to organize for the city of Charleston. But like his plans for the elevated railroad and the rotary engine, the Charleston water company never materialized and is only memorable as another example of Mills' energetic pursuit of work beyond architecture.

Several years earlier, in conjunction with his proposal for a canal from Columbia to Charleston, he had pointed out the benefits of running water. In 1825 the Charleston City Council passed an ordinance granting him the right to form a company and lay pipe beneath the city streets, provided the company be incorporated by the state and begin its operations within one year. Although he applied to the legislature, the company was never incorporated. Mills never lost faith in

69 William W. Wheildon, *Memoir of Solomon Willard* (Charlestown: Monument Association, 1865), 88. RM to Richard Wallack, July 1, 1822, quoted by Wheildon, 87–88. Solomon Willard, *Plans and Sections of the Obelisk on Bunker's Hill* (Boston: Chas. Cook, 1843), 11, 16, 22.

the idea, however, and twenty-five years later, with his fortunes again at low ebb, he published a series of articles in the *Charleston Mercury* urging Charlestonians to support the creation of a municipal water supply.[70] He argued that fire protection, health, comfort, and economic growth required Charleston to follow the other major cities along the seaboard. As a water source he suggested a canal to the Edisto River, but nothing came of his proposal this time either.

Equally fruitless was his participation in an attempt to convince the federal government to fund harbor improvements to make Charleston a suitable site for the establishment of a naval depot. During the spring of 1824, Mills and several others charted the harbor bar and surveyed the channels, and the following September Mills submitted a plan to Secretary of War, John C. Calhoun and the Topographical Corps of Engineers, but Congress did not fund the proposal.[71] (Federal support for dredging the harbor was secured in 1852; the Charleston Naval Yard was established in 1901.)

Mills' persistent interest in public water-related projects also prompted him to write (December 27, 1827) to DeWitt Clinton, Governor of New York, suggesting a way to make the Erie Canal more productive. When the canal was frozen (typically several months each year), it was closed to navigation. Mills observed that "nature has converted it into a perfect road in lieu of a river," and "we must resolve to use the canal at this season as a road." With his characteristic optimism, he wrote, "a canal in a northern winter presents the most perfect road that can possibly be devised, and offers facilities of communication greater even than...when its waters are in a state of fluidity." Skids or runners could be attached to the boats to convert them into sleds. Inclined planes or tramways could be installed at the locks to move the sled-boats from one level to another. If the skids and the tracks of the inclined planes were all carefully installed a consistent distance apart, then the canal "would possess all advantages of a rail road." Mills hoped to establish a connection with Governor Clinton and closed saying "I hope I am not unknown to your Excellency in my professional capacity."[72] No response from Clinton is known.

70 RM, *Charleston Mercury*, August 7, 17, 22, 1850.

71 RM to EBSM, May 23 and September 25, 1824.

72 RM to De Witt Clinton, December 27, 1826, PRM 1096.

WASHINGTON MONUMENT, BALTIMORE
The lack of work in Carolina during the late 1820s forced him to look elsewhere, and after 1825 the search became more urgent as his financial situation grew increasingly desperate. Eliza was harassed by creditors. She was forced to settle

bills by offering the *Atlas* and was distressed in 1827 to learn they were more than a year behind in their pew rent at the First Presbyterian Church in Columbia. For several years Mills had sent periodic queries to Richmond, Baltimore, and Washington. Contacting James Barbour, Secretary of War, and General Alexander Macomb, Chief Engineer of the U.S. Board of Internal Improvements, he sought federal employment as an engineer, but was told there were no vacancies.[73] Beginning in 1825 he wrote with increasing frequency to Robert Gilmore in hopes that construction at the Monument would resume and require his attention in Baltimore.

In Mills' absence work on the Monument had continued under the direction of William Stewart, the marble contractor. Between 1820 and 1827 Stewart completed the interior staircase, repaired the construction scaffolding and finished the capital. The column itself was finished, but much remained to be done. Designs had not been approved for the fencing, landscaping, or inscriptions. No decision had been made about the "trophies" (sculptural groups Mills planned for each corner of the base) or the crowning statue of Washington. The Board was reluctant to make design decisions, for they were perennially unsure of receipts from the state lotteries. They were in debt to Stewart for marble and masons' work, and consequently resisted all but the most necessary expenses. If Mills was aware of their financial situation, he disregarded it. In August 1826 he sent Gilmore a description of inscriptions and ornament he considered essential for the completion of the monument. He suggested the inscriptions be brief, but in four languages (English, Latin, Greek, and French) so as to be "comprehended by all, in every age," or, at the very least, in Latin as well as English. There were to be symbols of all existing states in the frieze and banners or shields as emblems of the thirteen original states ringing the base of the column. Each corner of the parapet of the base was to be crowned by "trophies of war stacked in groups, the reward of valor," and encircling the column above the emblems of the thirteen original states would be text recounting Washington's supreme act of "disinterested patriotism"—the resignation of his commission at Annapolis.

The Board did not resume Mills' salary as Superintendent, but they did agree to pay his expenses in coming to Baltimore, and an advertisement appeared over Mills' name,

> for executing the various decorations contemplated for this structure. The decorations proposed consist, 1st, of a colossal marble statue of

73 RM to James Barbour, circa September 12, 1826; PRM 1044, 1065, 1068. RM to Alexander Macomb, PRM 1045, 1046, 1047, 1070, 1089.

Washington...surmounting the monument—2d, bronze or marble trophies at the four angles of the great base or socle, 3rd, civic wreaths and stars in the frieze of the base—4th inscriptions on the four faces of the socle—and 5th, tripods on each front of the blockings of the steps of entrance, all of bronze.[74]

The Board intended to review proposals on May 1, 1827, and Mills wrote Gilmore that he hoped to return to Baltimore to participate in the selection. At the same time he asked for a recommendation "to the Directors of the Railroad Company," for he had studied "this branch of my profession particularly anticipating the adoption of this system in our country in lieu of canals."[75]

Mills ultimately obtained only minor survey work with the Baltimore railroad, but was successful in his contacts with sculptors concerning ornament for the monument. The Board considered three proposals, all solicited by Mills (they refused a request from a fourth sculptor, Luigi Persico, for an extension of the deadline). Each of the entrants was responsible for one or more of the historical bas-relief panels in the rotunda of the U.S. Capitol. Enrico Causici, purported to be a pupil of Canova, bid $9000 for the statue of Washington. He informed the Board that he would accept responsibility for purchasing the marble, carving the statue and hoisting and securing it in place atop the column. He did not submit a bid for the creation of the other embellishments. Antonio Capellano, another pupil of Canova, offered to carve the colossal statue for $12,000, but this was not to include the acquisition of the stone or setting the statue in place. Capellano, like Causici, offered no bid for other decorations mentioned in the advertisement. The most detailed bid was submitted by Nicholas Gevelot: $1,000 as an allowance for purchase of the stone, $11,000 for creating the statue, $5,000 for hoisting and setting the statue and $1,200 for the four sculptural "trophies." Predictably, Causici's low bid won, but the Board informed him they could not execute a contract until January 1828, when they anticipated receiving lottery money from the state treasurer.

Throughout the summer and fall of 1827 Causici wrote from his residence in New York, eager to begin. Mills came to Baltimore for an extended period; letters to Eliza suggest that he left South Carolina in July and did not return until October. He told her of his hopes for employment with the railroad and mentioned promising experiments with a model steam engine and a surveying instrument. He undertook small jobs for members of the Monument Board and

74 *Niles Weekly Register*, September 30, 1826, quoted in full by Miller, 108–109.

75 RM to Robert Gilmore, April 22, 1827.

ventured that the family might be able to move to Baltimore in the spring of 1828. While he was away Eliza must have written of a chance to move from Columbia to Abbeville and establish a school, for he wrote her that "I replied to your letter which mentions your plan of the Abbeville establishment. Really it is difficult to determine what course to pursue."[76]

He was frustrated by his inability to find work. It was a period of personal crisis. He wrote Eliza:

> Innumerable cares occupy my bosom, and harass my mind in consequence of being out of business. We must all get wise by sad experience, and in the mean time suffer for our folly. I was too ambitious in past days to be careful in the world, when my means were totally inadequate to support it. I neglected too much our pecuniary interests or ventured imprudently into speculations which a change of times in business totally destroyed. The beaten plodding path is after all the surest end. Not to be known in the world but only to enjoy the domestic scene [is] the safest to our happiness.[77]

Without much delay, Eliza acted on her plan to move, for on January 2, 1828, her mother sent a letter to her in Abbeville urging her not to open a school. Eliza ignored this advice, rented a house in Abbeville, and took pupils—including the children of John C. Calhoun. She and the children lived in Abbeville from circa January 1828, through April 1830. For months at a time, especially during the fall of 1829 and the winter and spring of 1830, Robert was away seeking work. They kept their house in Columbia, for there were no satisfactory offers for it.

Whenever Mills was underemployed, his thoughts turned to writing. The end of his 1829–1830 journal contains notes for numerous possible publications. He thought of writing a religious manual titled "Pearl of great Price," containing "selections from the New Testament under different heads embracing the fundamental doctrines of Christianity." Perhaps prompted by Eliza's school, he also considered a series of textbooks including a geography of South Carolina, a history of South Carolina, a United States history, and "Epitomes" of Chemistry, Natural Philosophy, Rhetoric, Arithmetic, and the Bible. He went so far as to prepare a prospectus and price a printing press for a possible newspaper titled "the Abbeville Journal & Peoples Friend (price 2$ pr annum in advance)," and he jotted down "headings" and a rough outline for a book on architecture, a project that resurfaces several times throughout his career.[78]

76 RM to EBSM, September 30, 1827.

77 RM to EBSM, September 2, 1827.

78 Robert Mills, Diary, December 28, 1828–May 4, 1830.

Before leaving Baltimore, he thought about writing a "comprehensive" book titled the "Principles of Architecture" for Philadelphia publisher Joseph Delaplaine, who distributed a handbill seeking subscribers in 1817. Delaplaine's advertisement promised a book adapted "to the demand of this country," written simply for the carpenter, stone mason, bricklayer, plasterer, blacksmith, "and all other mechanics." Mills' undated notes in the 1829–1830 journal, like a preliminary sketch, only hint what he thought should be included in such a book. He began with a "Memoranda" on the "Origin of Architecture." "The great Architect divine created Man," he wrote, and placed him in a paradise where shelter consisted of "rural palaces" formed by "the plastic hand" of nature. After being expelled from Eden, "our unfortunate first parents were called into action, and compelled...to provide a shelter & food for themselves & their offspring. Urged by necessity one improvement succeeded another until the stately palace grew out of the humble hut."

The fragmentary introduction is the only narrative portion of his notes; the remainder consists of lists of "Heads of work, begun"—including the "Rise of Architecture Progress in different ages...Different Styles of building." Styles listed included Persian, Indian, Chinese, Asiatic, German, French, Spanish, Russian, American, and Modern. Proposed sections followed dealing with the "Orders & general proportion" of the styles; there was a section on building materials, another on the construction of various parts of buildings (foundations, arches, groins, domes, vaults, floors, etc.), another section on types of bridges, another on the prices of different types of work, and another on the design of public and private buildings (itemized by type). He concluded with a list of skills related to engineering (surveying, leveling, locks, aqueducts, tunnels, canal boats, and railroads) and a section on heating and ventilating. The book outline is followed in the journal by a list of topics for "a Course of Lectures on the practice of Architecture & Engineering." He later advertised architectural lessons and did leave several incomplete, draft accounts of his career, but he never completed a book on the principles of architecture.[79]

Enrico Causici had moved to Baltimore. After vexing delays and complaints to the Board (he felt his bid was far too low), he carved the statue from three blocks of marble in a wooden shed on the monument grounds. By September 1829, the statue was ready to be approved, hoisted, and secured atop the column. Now it became imperative that Mills return. The Board wanted him to inspect the statue, and Causici, whose contract obligated him to hoist the

79 Advertisement of architectural lessons cited in Liscombe, *Altogether American* (1994).

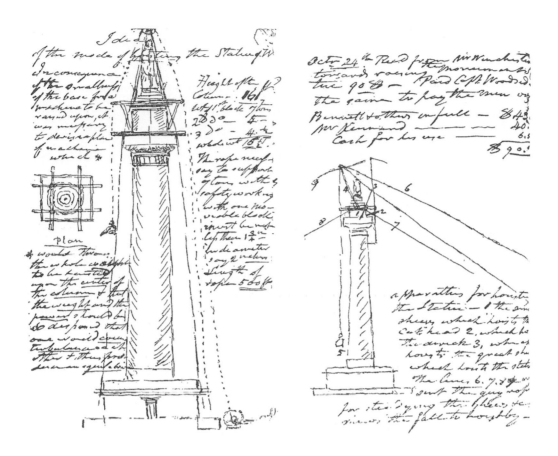

"A Plan for Raising the Statue of Washington" for the Washington Monument, Baltimore, Maryland. Robert Mills, architect, 1813–1842. From the *"1829–1830 Journal"* of Robert Mills.

statue—which weighed sixteen-and-one-half tons—was in fact relying upon Mills to do it. From Abbeville Mills wrote to David Winchester, Treasurer of the Board, explaining his subcontract with Causici for the hoisting of the statue. Mills sought an assurance that he would be paid "out of the balance" to be released to Causici upon completion of the work, and said "I believe I have accomplished the great desideratum to be able to raise the statue with safety, and comparative ease, as the machine acts upon the principle of equalizing the power & weight, and thus throwing the whole weight upon the center of the Column where there is sufficient capacity to bear anything that can be put upon it."[80]

The plan devised by Mills consisted of erecting a derrick and adjustable shear legs on the capital. The base of these shear legs would be secured in the

80 RM to David Winchester, September 11, 1829.

"stirrups" of a chain ringing the capital; the apex of the shear legs was to be held in position by cables attached to trees in Monument Square. Block and tackle would be used to hoist the statue in three sections.

Not long after he outlined his plan to Winchester, Mills arrived in Baltimore. He hired Captain John D. Woodside, whom he had known during his early days in Washington, "and confiding to him his plan of operations, left it to his ingenuity and practical knowledge of machinery to carry out and perfect the same. The complete success which attended the operations proved the efficiency of the plan."[81] Chain and sheave blocks were borrowed from the U.S. Navy, new rope was purchased. Woodside first raised a small pair of shear legs and used them to raise a small derrick. With this apparatus he hoisted the large derrick (seventy feet long and sixteen inches in diameter) and then the large shear legs (forty-five feet long and forty-five inches in circumference). The base of the statue, a block weighing seven tons, was raised without fanfare or incident. Only when the second block was also safely in place did Mills invite the public and Board to attend a ceremony (noon, November 25, 1829) celebrating the ascent of the bust of Washington.

Many of those present must have recalled the laying of the cornerstone fourteen years earlier. Now again there was the crowd, a band, and artillery. Everything went smoothly, but for those associated with the work there was no sense of closure or resolution. Causici would petition unsuccessfully for more money, and Mills, who was paid $1,500, "on closing the accounts relating to the work [found] that he not only had expended that sum, but fell indebted to the persons Employed by him upwards of $500, without any compensation for his risk & labor." Beyond this onerous debt, Mills knew it was going to be difficult to fund the ornament which he still considered essential, for Gilmore reported that the "balance of funds at the disposal of the Managers" was only $928.45.[82]

Both Robert and Eliza must have been relieved that the statue was safely in place, but their joy would have been tempered by pressing needs. Immediately after learning all went well Eliza wrote to ask if he would apply to be caretaker of the monument as "every little [bit] that is certain is so much gain." (He did apply but was turned down.) She wanted to buy a modest house in Baltimore, for "the unsettled manner in which we live seem hard" and asked when he planned to return to South Carolina.[83]

Their correspondence indicates he did not return to Carolina before the end of February 1830. Having gone north in September 1829, he remained based in

81 Anonymous [RM], *Washington Monument, Baltimore, Account of laying the corner-stone, raising the statue, description, &c.* (Baltimore, 1849), 28.

82 Robert Gilmore to George MacKeebin, Treasurer of the Western Shore, January, 4, 1830.

83 EBSM to RM, December 3, [1829].

Baltimore for at least six months, leaving Eliza to wind up their affairs in South Carolina as best she could. In Abbeville she was forced to trade furniture to settle accounts. He was able from time to time to send small amounts of money, and her acknowledgments record her circumstances: "your last enclosure of $10. came to hand by the last mail, and served a very good purpose in helping me to a barrel of flour, we have been about six weeks without flour which made it the more acceptable to us."[84] She had given notice that she intended to close the school on April 1, 1830, the end of the spring term; consequently, pupils began to leave and creditors grew insistent. Blanding held a note secured by the Mills' home in Columbia and informed Eliza he planned to foreclose in March 1830. After struggling all fall with Mills away, she wrote him in Baltimore:

> I am not in favor of your Northern plans, and I do most sincerely wish that you would drop all idea of a removal to that country, it appears to me, 'following the shadow, and losing the substance'....I would by no means depend on the visionary prospect of a little business which may occasionally offer.... [She admitted she was] in a wretched state of mind...in a kind of purgatory at present, which it is impossible for me to stand much longer, I am not left merely to support the family, but to pay back debts and it is too much for a woman to be harassed in this way, and I do assure you that I cannot support it.... Dear husband I have but one objection to make to you, and that is that you *want decision*, and keep me in a wandering state of mind. I love practical minds, and I trust that you will fall on some plan that may be realized soon. God grant it. You must excuse the dark tenor of this letter. I feel *discouraged*.[85]

In February she wrote Robert that "the school is getting small as I expected it would & my time is progressing to its crisis in business, how little do the quiet & stationary know of the tumultuous passions, the shifting scenes of life occasion, I almost envy them their repose & wish to find a calm retreat undisturbed by bustle & turmoil."[86]

In Washington Mills' persistence finally bore fruit. He went to the capital "with three or four objects in view" in mid-January. He hoped to sell copies of the *Atlas* to the Library of Congress, to discuss the grounds around the Baltimore Washington Monument with John Eager Howard, and to meet General Gratiot, Chief Engineer of "the Engineer department to ascertain the prospects of professional employment." He also planned to propose modifica-

84 EBSM to RM, Friday Night [April, 1830].

85 EBSM to RM, December 14, 1829, PRM 1140.

86 EBSM to RM, February 13, 1830.

tions to the U.S. House of Representatives to improve its acoustics. Elated by the results on this last count, he wrote Eliza an uncharacteristically detailed account. Both John C. Calhoun and George McDuffie had taken an interest in his suggestions for the House, and McDuffie encouraged him to "draw up a memorial." Mills gave memoranda and drawings to McDuffie and then he

went up into the gallery of the house to witness the course that this business would take. I saw Mr. McD. deliver the papers to the Speaker & speak with him. I saw the Speaker open the roll, look at it, turn over to the plans, examine these and as an opportunity occurred while speakers occupied the floor he commenced from the beginning of the MMS and continued reading it regularly thro'. I thought this indicated an interest in the subject, and might result favorably.

After reading a communication from the President & Secretary of war, and before the regular business of the house commenced, the speaker announced to the house that he had received a letter from Robt. Mills Architect communicating a plan for improving the Hall of Representatives &c and wished to know the pleasure of the house concerning it. A member moved that it should be referred to the committee on Public buildings and be printed. One member asked what would the cost of the alteration be. The speaker observed that the plan was very simple and would cost very little to put in execution as the plan drawings were necessary to be attached to the printed document, it was inquired what the cost of the engraving would be, the Clerk of the house informed the speaker it would not exceed $20. Mr. McDuffie then rose and made a few remarks in relation to the plan which he said he had examined and it appeared to him to be the most feasible plan that had yet been offered to effect the object intended. The subject I observed excited some interest in the house, and one member who probably felt a little sore from the noise remarked that a cheaper plan than the one proposed for hearing he could offer, namely that the house should be made to keep silence. This occasioned a smile. The speaker then put the original motion before the house for printing and engraving the plans, 'and referring it to the Committee on Public buildings, when it was agreed to. As soon as the Speaker handed it to the Clerk of the house, I observed him examining it very minutely, then others got it from him & examined it, and so it passed thro' many hands. I then went down and requested Mr. McDuffie to procure me the paper that I might revise them for publication, as I had no idea that they would take this course, which he did.[87]

87 RM to EBSM, January 17, 1830.

This was the opportunity Mills had been waiting for. He studied plans of the House in the Clerk's office, spoke with the Superintendent of Public Buildings, and visited with the Nourse and Woodside families before returning to Baltimore to have his plan printed for presentation to the House. A month later he wrote to tell Eliza that his plan was "unanimously adopted." As a test, a temporary partition was to be erected in an arc immediately behind the columns in the gallery, for Mills believed this would diminish echoes caused by the irregular wall surface at the rear of the gallery. He was optimistic:

> if I succeed (which I trust I may) then it is probable I shall be engaged to have the improvement perfected during the recess of Congress—in which case there are other improvements I intend to suggest to be done.
>
> Tell the girls I attended the Presidents Levee on Thursday evening, which was crowded to excess with the fashionable, the gay and many of the plebian cast. I saw here the republican principle carried into effect. The heads of the government mingling with the sovereign people. It was an amusing scene. The room was splendidly furnished & lighted and all appear'd pleased.[88]

Eliza and the children did not leave Abbeville until May 1830, and she wrote Robert (May 10, 1830) from Savannah that their leave-taking was difficult. She had raised a pittance by selling the coach ($75) and horse ($21). Friends, Col. Bowie and Col. Noble, each gave her $30. Her elderly slave, Nanny, told everyone on the day of the sale that she was eighty years old and "very sickly" so that nobody bid for her. "Gen Hodges offer'd $75 for her, and I accepted his offer & deducted the $50 due him, thus I recde. but $25 for myself, I had no other alternative, and therefore was obliged to sacrifice the old woman. She objected to every master that applied & to leave her, as our property would have been a weighty consideration."[89]

Three wagons carried their furnishings to Augusta where they boarded the steamboat, the *John David Mungin*, to Savannah. Eliza planned to proceed to Charleston and remain there "until we get assistance from you." Despite past difficulties and an uncertain future, she was resolute. "The Girls send their love to you & long to see you and to be *at home* again. I am in hopes our home will prove a reality to ourselves during our pilgrimage—do think of my business, I must do something, for the world pinches hard, when you are pennyless [sic]."[90]

88 RM to EBSM, February 19, 1830.

89 EBSM to RM, May 10, 1830.

90 EBSM to RM, May 10, 1830.

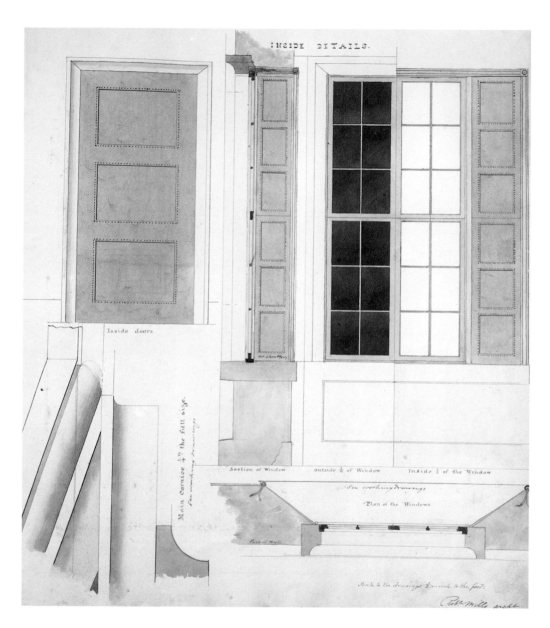

Custom House, New London, Connecticut. Robert Mills, architect, 1833–1835.

CHAPTER SIX

National Practice

Washington, D.C. and Elsewhere, 1830–1835

MILLS HAD WANTED to work in Washington for many years. In 1814 he had written President Madison in hopes of being hired to restore the White House, Capitol, and executive office buildings, which the British had burned during the War of 1812. Mills asked Joseph Nourse to speak to the Commissioners of Public Buildings who were to select an architect, but Latrobe got the job.[1] In 1817, Latrobe alerted Mills that he was resigning, and Mills tried again. He sought a letter of recommendation from Jefferson to Madison, but this time the job went to Bulfinch.[2] Mill's first job at the Capitol—remodeling the House of Representatives to improve the acoustics—reflects his persistence. He wrote that "passing through Washington in 1821, I was requested by the architect of the Capitol [Bulfinch], and subsequently (1827) by the Secretary of State to give an opinion on the causes of the difficulty of hearing in the Hall."[3] He submitted a report with drawings, but Bulfinch did not forward Mills' ideas to the House. Applying Latrobe's theory, Mills felt there were several problems; the dome was too high, the back wall was broken into angular planes and the Speaker's podium was in the wrong place. Bulfinch tried to solve the problem by stretching a flat, fabric ceiling below the dome, but it made the House dark and was soon removed.

When Mills returned to Washington in 1830 nothing had been done to improve acoustics in the House; moreover, Bulfinch was gone, and now influential Carolinians in Congress were willing to help. South Carolina Represent-

1 RM to JM, March 5, 1814, PRM 0438. See also John Smith to RM, February 25, 1815, PRM 0504; RM to Joseph Nourse, March 13, 1815, PRM 0506.

2 RM to TJ, January 28, 1814; PRM 0429. Hamlin, *Latrobe*, 478–479, suggests that "however he might have been irked by Mills's almost stodgy rectitude, however much he might have deplored certain elements in the other's taste, Latrobe knew that, taken all in all, Mills was a real architect, thoroughly dependable, and that in suggesting to Mills that he should become his successor he was expressing a hope that the work would fall to the one he considered most worthy to carry it on." Latrobe wrote Mills: "Sir, I have an intention about the middle of Decr. To resign my

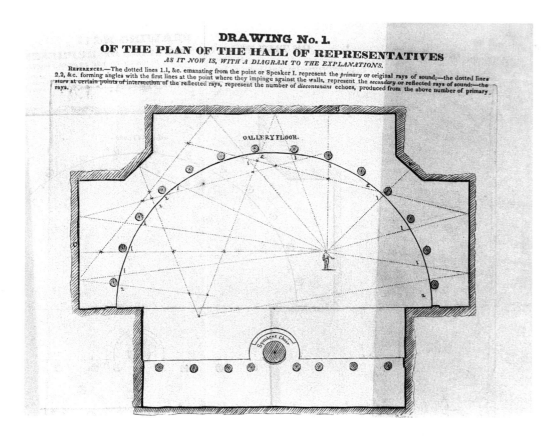

"Drawing No. 1 of the Plan of the Hall of Representatives." Robert Mills, architect, 1830–1832.

office. I cannot agree with the Commissioner. I give you this private notice, as a former friend & pupil in confidence, that you may use it as you please. The Salary is $2500 per annum. Respectfully yrs BH Latrobe Your portico of the Baptist Church is a beautiful thing." BHL to RM, November 20, 1817. 139/A8.

3 "Alteration of Hall House of Representatives," 22d Congress, 1st Sess., 1832, House Rep. 495, 2.

ative George McDuffie (1790–1851), who had written the inscription for the Maxcy Monument, presented Mills' proposal. McDuffie carried himself awkwardly as the result of a spinal injury suffered in a duel; nonetheless, he was an animated orator, an early advocate of states' rights and nullification, and an opponent of federally funded internal improvements. He helped Mills despite the fact that they disagreed on major political questions.

To test the effectiveness of the curved wall Mills proposed, a temporary partition was erected in 1830. It was well received, but after this initial success, he had to wait for the House to appropriate money for the renovation. Two years passed before an appropriation ($13,000) was approved, and then he spent eight months directing the work, for which he was paid $1,000 in 1834. This first job at the Capitol entailed raising the House floor approximately four feet, creating "a circular wall behind the colonnade in the galleries," adding a gallery for ladies on the south wall, opening windows behind the galleries, building a new, larger rostrum for the Speaker, and reversing the relationship between the Speaker and the members (so the members faced the circular wall). At the same time Mills installed a hot air furnace beneath the new raised floor, added two new entries with lobbies, and created a post office and a room for documents. He also ramped the aisles "instead of breaking them into steps, which occasioned frequent stumbling."[4]

Eliza and their daughters arrived early in the summer of 1830, and they moved into a house they rented on the south side of New York Avenue, between 13th and 14th Streets.[5] Their move to Washington coincided with a lull in major federal building projects, and for the next two years, while waiting for work to proceed in the House of Representatives, Mills undertook a variety of jobs, established contacts, and positioned himself as the most active local practitioner. On January 4, 1831, he advertised that he would prepare drawings and offer architectural lessons. Eliza advertised for boarders (December 3, 1830), and, as she had done in Abbeville, she opened the Washington Female Academy, a school for young women.[6]

From 1830 until July 6, 1836, when Andrew Jackson appointed him "architect to aid in forming plans, making proper changes therein . . . & seeing to the erection" of the Treasury Building (based on Mills' plan) and the Patent Office (based on a plan by Ithiel Town and William Parker Elliot), Mills sought various types of work, for he was initially unable to make a living as an architect.[7] He worked as a "Draftsman of Public surveys" in the General Land Office, a division of the Treasury Department, at a salary of $1150 per year, and later as a draftsman at the Patent Office for $1,000 per year, but he continued to seek architectural and engineering work.[8]

In addition to his alterations for the House, he made unsuccessful suggestions for sculptural ornament for the east pediment and alterations to the dome and offered plans, apparently never executed, for a reading and storage table for the Library of Congress. He designed and carried out alterations for the Supreme Court (then housed in the Capitol) to accommodate the trial of Judge Peck. He also introduced running water to the Capitol, and proposed a guidebook, a project he would bring to fruition in his *Guide to the Capitol of the United States* (1834).[9]

Among the early Washington projects, the unsuccessful plan for a tomb and monument for George Washington in the Capitol is especially memorable.

4 *National Intelligencer*, December 2, 1833; PRM 1376C.

5 Allen Clark, "Robert Mills, Architect and Engineer," *Records of the Columbia Historical Society* 40–41 (1940): 17; PRM 1420. In 1834 the Mills apparently moved to the corner of E and 13th Street. PRM 1177.

6 For Eliza's Female Academy, see PRM 1300A, 1318; for Mills' advertisement see Liscombe, 162.

7 PRM 1533.

8 *Register of all Officers and Agents . . . in the Service of the United States* (Philadelphia: Key & Biddle, 1834), 18; *Register of all Officers and Agents . . . in the Service of the United States* (Washington: Blair & Rives, 1835), 2. Mills is listed as a clerk, but is referred to as draftsman of surveys in his notification of employment, March 22, 1831, and he referred to himself as a draftsman in describing his work in a fragmentary manuscript autobiography; PRM 1214 and 2707. The work in the Patent Office was temporary, but probably congenial, for over the years he was interested in a wide range of applied technologies including a mechanical scythe (RM to TJ, June 16, 1808); a "hydrostatic and pneumatic machine for compressing air," which he patented with Henry B. Fernald, October 10, 1835; a forced air

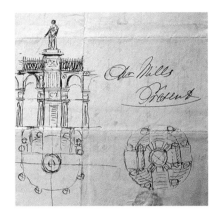

Proposed Washington Monument for the Rotunda of the Capitol. Robert Mills, architect, 1830.

central heating system, which he patented with Robert Mayo, October 24, 1836; improvements in steam engines to promote safety (RM to Editor, *Scientific American* 5 [August 21, 1852]: 387, PRM 3001); and the screw propeller as a replacement for paddlewheels (H.W. Herbert to RM, December 24, 1852). None of his tinkerings or collaborations proved to be profitable.

9 For paving Pennsylvania Avenue see PRM 1294.

10 PRM, 0033. See also Karal Ann Marling, "The United States Capitol as Mausoleum: Or, Who's Buried in Washington's Tomb?", 448–464, in Donald R. Kennon, ed., *A Republic for the Ages* (Charlottesville: University Press of Virginia, 1999). Correspondence with the Washington heirs is transcribed in George C. Hazelton, Jr., *The National Capitol, Its Architecture, Art and History* (New York: J.F. Taylor, 1914),. 287–295; also see Scott, "Robert Mills and American Monuments," in Bryan, ed., *Robert Mills, Architect*, 143–177.

A crypt had been approved beneath the rotunda in 1799, but it remained empty and undeveloped, for Washington's heirs never approved moving his remains from Mount Vernon. As the centennial of Washington's birth approached (1832), and because the nullification controversy was adding urgency to symbols of national unity, unionists hoped that John A. Washington would finally approve the relocation of Washington's remains. Mills promoted his proposal as a political symbol, writing the Committee on the Centennial Birthday that a tomb in the Capitol would make Washington's "warning voice . . . sound in our ears, and his sage advice would recur to our minds, to heal all our political bickerings, and make us like a band of brothers united in love, and determined to preserve the interests of the Union."[10]

This project was Mills' first suggestion for a monument to George Washington in the nation's capital. His proposal consisted of a circular hole in the rotunda floor above the crypt; this hole, surrounded by an iron fence, would provide light and a view of the crypt. There would be another hole in the floor of the crypt with a stair leading into the tomb itself. "In the center of this aperture a suitable cenotaph would be placed." Mills refined this plan in memos suggesting a statue on a column rising above the tomb through the holes in crypt and rotunda floors. He wrote that the statue should be colossal—eight to ten feet tall—in keeping with the scale of the rotunda and because "there is a moral dignity in a colossean figure (sic)." He said the statue should present Washington in modern dress resigning his commission. A stair spiraling around the column would give access to the tomb. A sketch on one of his drafts suggests—but does not clearly depict—what he had in mind. The major elements, however—a figure atop a column, a meaningful base (the crypt and tomb), spiral stairs, and dramatic lighting—evoke the Baltimore Washington Monument, a later unsuccessful suggestion for a National Mausoleum (1850–1853), and the base and shaft relationship of his first published (1848) design for the Washington National Monument.

The Washington heirs did not allow the remains to be moved, so nothing came of Mills' proposal. John Quincy Adams sadly noted in his diary: "Feb. 22, 1832.—Centennial birthday of Washington. The solemnities intended for this day at this place lost all their interest for me by the refusal of John A. Washington to permit the remains of George Washington to be transferred to be entombed under the Capitol... I did wish that this resolution might have been carried into execution, but this wish was connected with an imagination that this federal Union was to last for ages. I now disbelieve its duration for twenty years, and doubt its continuance for five. It is falling into the sear and yellow leaf."[11]

The resistance of Washington's heirs to re-interment in the Capitol contributed to the decision in 1832 to commission Horatio Greenough to create a statue for the rotunda. After working in Italy for the better part of a decade, Greenough presented Washington as Jupiter sitting on a throne, nude above the waist, resigning his commission by presenting his sword like Cincinnatus. Mills suggested using the statue to crown a monument rising from the crypt, complete with the hole in the rotunda floor and spiral stairs of his earlier proposal. Instead, he was directed to simply reinforce the floor and prepare a solid marble pedestal.[12] When the twenty-ton figure arrived in 1841, Mills arranged to transport it from the Naval Yard and directed the installation, exploring ways to improve the lighting, which, being largely from above, cast objectionable shadows.

The statue was ridiculed for its nudity and classical allusions and was moved to the east grounds of the Capitol. Mills unsuccessfully proposed gazebo-like shelters in several styles to protect it from the weather.[13] Beyond the Capitol, Mills did minor work on the drainage of the city streets and offered unsuccessful proposals for paving Pennsylvania Avenue, erecting a national clock tower, and creating a national mausoleum. He successfully directed the relocation of the Tripoli Naval Monument from the Navy Yard to the west terrace of the Capitol. (The monument was moved to Annapolis, circa 1861.) As part of this project, he designed a marble base or platform for the existing column—perhaps his first freestanding contribution to the cityscape.[14] He also found short-term employment as an engineer for the Washington Canal Company and designed an aqueduct to carry the canal over the Potomac to enable waterborne freight to reach Alexandria. The aqueduct he proposed consisted of a wooden flume flanked by towpaths supported by wooden trusses on masonry piers. A similar aqueduct was completed in 1843, but Mills apparently played no role in its final design or construction.[15]

11 Hazelton, 190.

12 "Foundation for Statue of Washington" 26th Cong., 1st Sess., House Doc. No. 124 (March 5, 1840): 2; "Annual Report, Commissioner of Public Buildings," 26th Cong., 2d Sess., House Doc. 58 (January 13, 1841): 8; "Statue of Washington," 27th Cong., 1st Sess., House Doc. No. 45 (August 4, 1841) 16.

13 Sylvia E. Crane, *White Silence, Greenough, Powers and Crawford, American Sculptors in Nineteenth-Century Italy* (Coral Gables: University of Miami Press, 1972), 69–85. Also see: Liscombe, *Altogether American*, 229; Hazelton, 74–79.

14 Pamela Scott, ed., *Guide*, 13–17. See also Liscombe, 156–169; Douglas Evelyn, *Patent Office*, 65–66; John M. Bryan, ed., *Robert Mills*, 182–183.

15 Donald Beekman Myer, *Bridges and the City of Washington* (Washington: U.S. Commission of Fine Arts, 1974), 7–9.

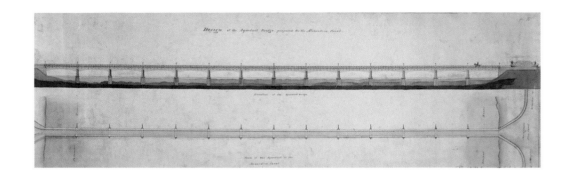

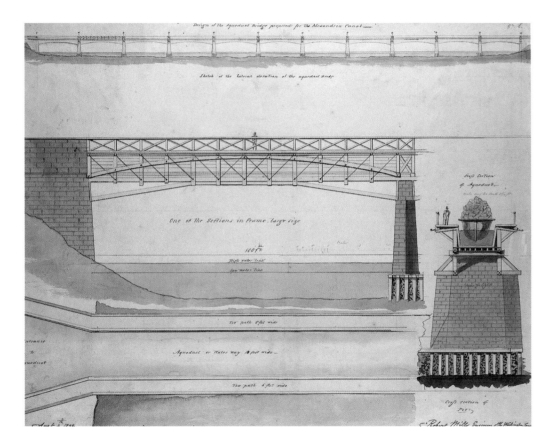

Potomac Aqueduct. Robert Mills, architect, 1832.

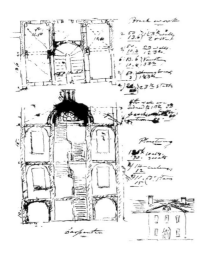

Fireproof Offices for the Treasury Department. Robert Mills, architect, 1831.

His most significant early architectural project in Washington was the creation of a suite of fireproof offices in the building occupied by the Treasury Department. Working within the existing brick building with its flammable floors (and presumably studded partition walls), he inserted a three-story stack of groin-vaulted offices on either side of a new stairwell. His sketches show three bays, two groins deep, with no openings on the end walls adjacent to the old building. The section depicts flues within the vaulted ceiling of the stairwell. The plan and section suggest a much simplified version of the interior of the Fireproof Building in Charleston, which also has a three-story stack of offices (only the ground floor being wholly fireproof) on either side of a central stairwell. At the Ainsley Hall House in Columbia, Mills had installed arched flues, as he did here, in the attic above a stairwell, in order to bring them symmetrically through the roof. The plan suggests that above the vaulted basement each room or vault was the same size as the one below it. This allowed the piers, which projected slightly in the corner of each room, to carry the weight of the vaulting to the foundation. Repeating the forms of the vaults permitted the centering to be re-used. Mills had not used hydraulic cement in his earlier vaulted buildings, and there is no mention of its use here. Structurally, he relied on the piers to carry the weight of the vaulting, for the walls (only one-and-a-half bricks thick) were economically, lightly built. The stairwell was not fireproof, for his notes indicate the carpenter was to re-use fifty-one risers from the old staircase. This modest, interior alteration introduced to Washington the modular fireproof system Mills had been refining since the construction of the Burlington County jail in 1808.[16]

The renovation was scarcely a year old when the Treasury was destroyed by fire on the night of March 31, 1833. Only Mills' section and an earlier fireproof vault by Latrobe were left unscathed. In a dramatic way, the fire simultaneously re-emphasized the need for fireproof facilities, proved the validity of Mills' technique, and focused officials' attention just as the executive departments were beginning to lobby for new buildings.

16 Evelyn, p. 66; PRM 1212, 1215, 1264.

17 Scott, *Guide and Index*, 14, 15.

18 Between 1833 and 1835 Mills designed custom houses at Mobile, Alabama, New London and Middletown, Connecticut, and New Bedford and Newburyport, Massachusetts. He also designed a warehouse for customs officials, the Appraiser's Stores, in Baltimore, Maryland (1833–1839), and was responsible for renovations to existing custom houses in St. Augustine, Florida (1833) and New York City (1833). In addition to the Charleston hospital, he designed Marine Hospitals in New Orleans (1837–1848) and Key West (1844–1845).

19 "Design No. 1 for a Marine Hospital on the Western Waters to accommodate 100 Patients" (Washington: P. Haas, 1837), and "Design No. 2 for a Marine Hospital on the Western Waters to accommodate 50 Patients" (Washington: P. Haas, 1837); *Document No. 3, Message from the President of the United State to the Two houses of Congress, Second Session, Twenty-fifth Congress* (Washington: Thomas Allen, 1837), 216–219. U.S. Congress, House, *First Annual Report of the Supervising Surgeon of the Marine Hospital Service for the Year 1872*, 10, quoted by Gale Shipman

The first buildings Mills designed for the federal government were located far from the capital. On September 9, 1830, he received $300 for "designs, estimates, specifications and drawings for the proposed custom house in Mobile, Alabama," and in 1831 he designed a marine hospital in Charleston, South Carolina.[17] In both cases, the primary client was the Secretary of the Treasury. Mills subsequently designed five more custom houses and directed interior alterations for two others; he also designed two more marine hospitals and influenced the design of at least seven others. It was these two building types that spread his work for the federal government across the eastern United States.[18]

For the marine hospitals and custom houses Mills developed basic plans that he modified or adapted, as he had done for courthouses and jails in South Carolina. His plans for marine hospitals were published (1837) as part of an appropriation, and as late as 1872 the Supervising Surgeon of the Marine Hospital Service wrote they had "been followed by the Government, without material change, down to the hospital...being constructed at Chicago."[19] In fact, however, with the exceptions of facilities at New Orleans and Key West, other architects modified Mills' plans and were responsible for the hospitals; consequently, the history of these projects entails the evolution of the administration of architectural projects by the federal government.

The importance of maritime trade and defense, the plight of seamen sick away from home, and public concern for infectious disease had prompted England to establish the Royal Hospital for Seamen in Greenwich in 1692. Initially developed for the Royal Navy, English marine hospitals soon accommodated merchant seamen. These hospitals were located in ports and funded by a tax collected by custom officials from the wages of seamen. The British hospital tax was collected in the American colonies, and shortly after the Revolution (1798) the federal government established the United States Marine Hospital Service—the cornerstone of later public health programs—and funded it through a tax of twenty cents per month on merchant seamen, naval personnel, and marines.

When Mills had visited Boston and Charlestown, Massachusetts, during his architectural tour in 1802, he probably saw the marine hospital then under construction in the Charlestown Navy Yard. It was designed by Asher Benjamin and based on Bulfinch's plan for the Leverett Street Almshouse. But it did not influence Mills, for its plan did not reflect current medical theories concerning ventilation, the segregation of patients by malady and class, or floor plans providing privacy for wards and sheltered exercise for ambulatory patients.[20] Medical theories had influenced Mills' plans for the South Carolina Asylum, and in addition to English literature on asylums, he must have known plans prepared circa 1808–1812 by Latrobe and Doctor William Barton of Philadelphia for a proposed (but never built) national marine hospital in Washington.[21] For his marine hospitals in the 1830s, Mills also had access to the naval hospitals in Philadelphia (1826–1829) by William Strickland and in Norfolk (1827–1832) attributed to John Haviland.

In 1831, Congress appropriated $12,500 to erect a marine hospital in Charleston, South Carolina. The City Council approved a plan submitted by Frederick Wesner (1788–1848), a local builder-architect who was active in civic affairs and who had served with Mills in 1824 as a Commissioner of Public Buildings in South Carolina. The Secretary of the Treasury, however, had authority to approve plans and award construction contracts, and he overruled the Charleston City Council and rejected Wesner's plan (which is unknown). On May 10, 1831, Mills received $300 for his plans, specifications, and estimates for the building. The bids he obtained from Charleston contractors averaged $20,000, and on his recommendation a contract for $12,100 was awarded to Daniel Homans, a builder based in Washington. The Charleston press, made sensitive to sectional interests by the nullification debate, criticized Mills and Homans as outsiders. The press portrayed the new Charleston Marine Hospital as a symbol of the federal "principal of extracting as much money as possible from the South, and of returning none that can possibly be avoided."[22] Mills' success, his first completed, freestanding federal building, was not celebrated in his hometown.

The Charleston Marine Hospital is a two-story building on an arcaded, partially raised basement. The most prominent exterior features are piazzas, or covered, open porches, on the principal and second stories on the front (west) and side (north and south) elevations. Strickland had used similar piazzas on the facade of his naval hospital in Philadelphia, but this feature also had long been a hallmark of residential architecture in Charleston, used precisely as Mills did here—to shield the facade from the sun and to catch the breeze. On the west facade, the piazzas are supported by clustered Gothic Revival columns, and at either end by piers spanned by pointed arches. The Charleston Marine Hospital was the first Gothic Revival building in the city.

Alder, "Robert Mills and United States Marine Hospitals," M.A. Thesis, University of Missouri, 1974, 42.

20 Harold Kirker, *The Architecture of Charles Bulfinch* (Cambridge: Harvard University Press, 1969), 316.

21 William P.C. Barton, *A Treatise Containing a Plan for the Internal Organization and Government of Marine Hospitals* (Philadelphia: by the author, 1817); also see Edward C. Carter, Jr., ed., *The Papers of Benjamin Henry Latrobe*, 92/B12.

22 *State Rights & Free Trade Evening Post*, Dec. 12, 1831; and *Mercury*, May 15, 1832, quoted by Kenneth Severens, *Charleston, Antebellum Architecture and Civic Destiny* (Knoxville: University of Tennessee Press, 1988), 70. For a brief biography of Wesner, see Beatrice St. Julien Ravenel, *Architects of Charleston* (Charleston: Carolina Art Association, 1945), 135–144.

Marine Hospital, Charleston, South Carolina. Robert Mills, architect, 1832–1833.

In 1836, Dr. William G. Ramsay described the interior as "commodious and airy" with accommodations for the steward and his family in the "front part of the building" and eight wards, three on the principal floor being used for surgical cases, one of the five wards on the second floor being set aside for venereal cases.[23] The wards were cross-ventilated. Each ward opened into a corridor on one side and onto a piazza on the other. Given Mills' tendency to re-use and adapt his designs, it is not surprising that major elements of the Charleston Marine Hospital reappear in the prototypical designs he published in 1837.

On March 23, 1837, Mills wrote Joel R. Poinsett (who had been chairman of the Board of Public Works when Mills returned to South Carolina in 1820), congratulating him for being appointed Secretary of War: "I see Congress has placed the location &c. of the Hospitals on the Western waters under your charge to report on the same with Plans Estimates &c. Please bear me in mind when you take up the subject."[24]

The immediate cause for the authorization of the western marine hospitals was a cholera epidemic along the Mississippi in 1832; by the spring of 1833, there were 1,000 deaths a week in New Orleans alone, and outbreaks of cholera continued up and down the Mississippi and its forty-four navigable tributaries through 1835.[25] Even before the epidemic, a dramatic growth in river traffic attracted the nation's attention. The value of cargo delivered by steamboat down river to New Orleans, for example, doubled every decade between 1820 ($12,637,000) and 1860 ($185,211,000). By 1840, New Orleans "was the largest exporting center in the United States."[26] The construction and launching of new steamboats doubled from 1835 to 1836, from fifty-one to 107, that is, as soon as the epidemic subsided.[27]

The marine hospitals on the western waters were designed to serve the river-based culture celebrated in the art of Currier and Ives, George Caleb Bingham, and Mark Twain. In *Life on the Mississippi*, Twain wrote of federal aids to navigation:

> ...now the national government has turned the Mississippi into a sort of two-thousand-mile torchlight procession. In the head of every crossing, and in the foot of every crossing, the government has set up a clear-burning lamp...But this thing has knocked the romance out of piloting, to a large extent. It, and some other things together, have knocked all the romance out of it. For instance, the peril from snags is not now what it once was. The government's snag-boats go patrolling up and down, in these matter-of-fact days, pulling the

23 Quoted by Mills Lane, *Architecture of the Old South, South Carolina* (Savannah: Beehive Press, 1984), 182–183.

24 RM to JRP, March 23 or 25, 1837, PRM 1590.

25 Walter Havighurst, *Voices on the River* (New York: Macmillan, 1964), 129–131; for the hospital service see Louis C. Hunter, *Steamboats on the Western Rivers* (New York: Octagon Books, 1969), 463–465.

26 Jack K. Bauer, *A Maritime History of the United States* (Columbia: University of South Carolina Press, 1988), p. 161. Charles H. Ambler, *A History of Transportation in the Ohio Valley* (Westport: Greenwood Press, 1970), 160.

27 Ambler, 161.

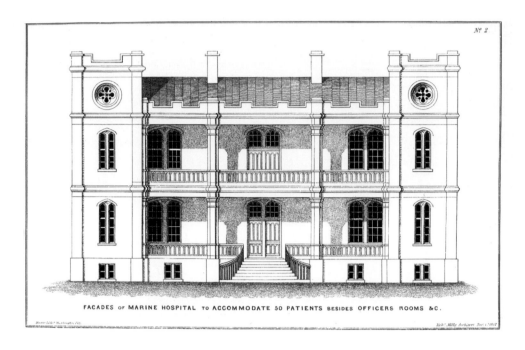

"Facades of Marine Hospital to Accommodate 50 Patients." Robert Mills, architect, 1837.

river's teeth...The military engineers...have taken upon their shoulders the job of making the Mississippi over again, a job transcended in size by only the original job of creating it. They are building wing-dams here and there, to deflect the current; and dikes to confine it in narrower bounds; and other dikes to make it stay there.[28]

The hospitals were one aspect of the federal response to the development of the Mississippi basin. On March 3, 1837, Congress authorized Poinsett, as Secretary of War, to acquire sites for marine hospitals. Army Surgeon General Thomas Lawson, who served under Poinsett, chaired a committee of army doctors; they selected St. Louis, Missouri, Natchez, Mississippi, and Napoleon, Arkansas, on the Mississippi River. On the Ohio River they recommended Wheeling, West Virginia (a recommendation later changed to Pittsburgh), and Louisville and Paducah, Kentucky. Based on the volume of traffic at these cities, they suggested hospitals accommodating fifty patients at Wheeling, Paducah, and Napoleon, and hospitals for 100 patients at Natchez, Louisville, St. Louis, and Cleveland.

28 Mark Twain (Samuel L. Clemens), *Life on the Mississippi* (London: Chatto & Windus, 1883), 261–263.

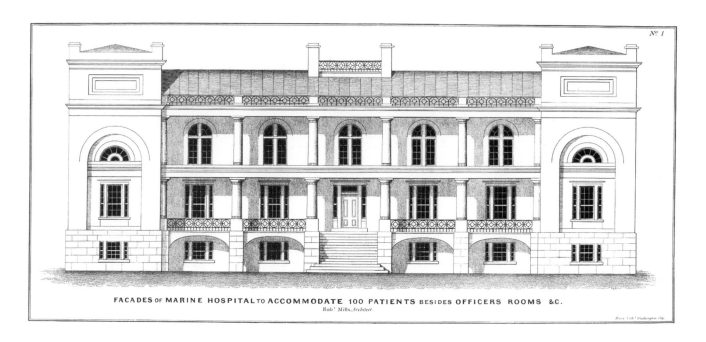

FACADES OF MARINE HOSPITAL TO ACCOMMODATE 100 PATIENTS BESIDES OFFICERS ROOMS &C.

Rob'. Mills, Architect.

ABOVE: *"Facades of Marine Hospital to Accommodate 100 Patients."*

BELOW, LEFT: *"Plan of the Basement or Office Story of the Marine Hospital."*

BELOW, RIGHT: *"Plan of the Principal Floor of the Marine Hospital"*

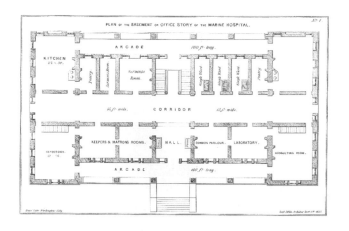

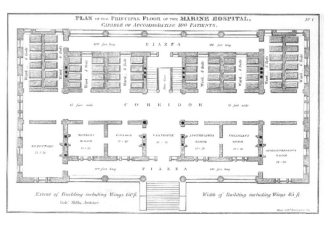

Following these recommendations, Mills developed two plans, which Poinsett sent to Congress at the end of the year.[29] Mills' description of the plans noted that they were intended to accommodate fifty and 100 patients and "so arranged as to admit of extension at any future time." He also said the plans met the medical criteria of "free ventilation, separation of patients by classes into distinct wards, and extensive galleries on the level of each floor, as well for shelter as exercise, that from the wards "passages lead, one way, into spacious corridors, and the other into wide piazzas." He clearly anticipated using heating systems similar to the furnace and underground ventilating tunnels used at the South Carolina Asylum, for his description notes that "provision is made . . . for diffusing a current of warm air in winter throughout the wards, and in summer a current of cool air."[30] Eight beds—the number recommended by Barton and Latrobe—are shown in most of the wards, and the description of the facade of the smaller prototypical design suggests an elaboration of the earlier Charleston Hospital. Mills described the fifty-bed prototype saying, "The façade of this building . . . is in the plain Gothic style, and presents a double piazza of two stories, supported by clustered columns, elevated upon a low basement, and flanked by two wings as towers. The piazzas as well as towers are surmounted with battlement enclosures."[31] Concluding his general description of the published plans, he said "when contracts are required to be made, more detailed drawings and descriptions will be furnished"—for he did not view the published plans as final and hoped to be retained to create plans, specifications, and contracts as each building was erected.

As events unfolded, however, he prepared drawings for only two of the nine hospitals erected prior to his death in 1855. The marine hospital law was changed in 1845 to permit alterations to Mills' prototypes. Using Mills' 1837 plans as guide, Rudolph Coyle was paid $120 for "services in the preparation of Drawings of the Hospitals at Louisville, Pittsburgh & Cleveland."[32] Similarly, James Kerr was paid $60 for "one months services as Architect, preparing drawings, estimates, &c. for Marine Hospital" in Pittsburgh.[33] A decade after Mills' plans were published, J. O. Sawyer was paid for architectural services associated with hospitals being begun in Louisville, Natchez, Napoleon, and Paducah.[34]

Mills did serve as architect for hospitals built in New Orleans (1837–1848) and Key West (1844–1845). For New Orleans he prepared drawings and specifications and negotiated with a contractor. His plans were approved in Washington, but regional collectors of customs were in charge of construction,

29 *Message from the President of the United State to the Two Houses of Congress, Second Session, Twenty-fifth Congress* (Washington: Thomas Allen, 1837), Doc. No. 3, 216–219.

30 *Message from the President of the United State to the Two Houses of Congress, Second Session, Twenty-fifth Congress*, Doc. No. 3, 216–219.

31 *Message from the President of the United State to the Two Houses of Congress, Second Session, Twenty-fifth Congress*, Doc. No. 3, 219.

32 Alder, "Robert Mills and United States Marine Hospitals." M.A. thesis, University of Missouri, 1974, 45–46.

33 Alder, 47.

34 Alder, 48.

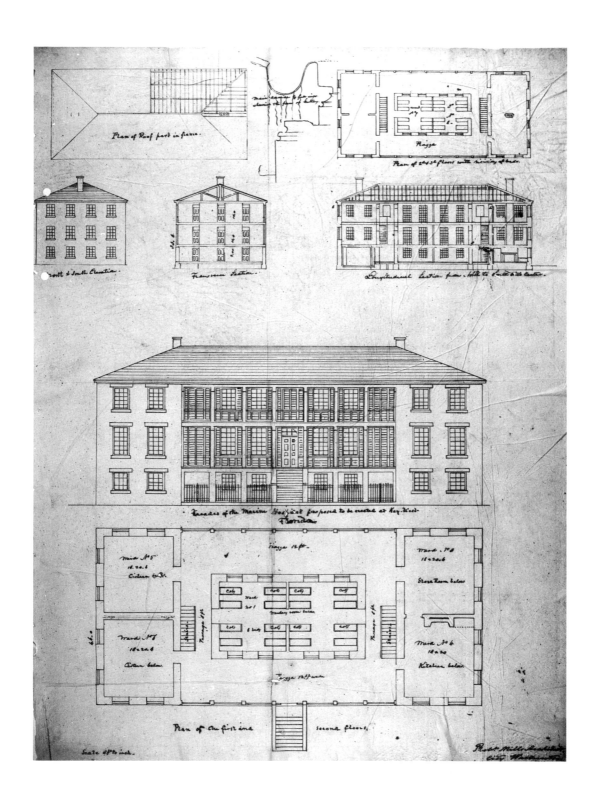

Plan of Roof put in frame.

Piazza

Plan of 2d & 3d floors with arrangement of beds.

Front & South Elevation.

Transverse Section.

Longitudinal Section from North to South Side Center.

Facade of the Marine Hospital proposed to be erected at Key West Florida

Piazza 12 ft.

Ward N.º 5
16.20.6
Cistern below

Ward N.º 7
16.2.6
Cistern below

Ward N.º 8
16.2.6
Store Room below

Ward N.º 6
16.20
Kitchen below

Piazza 12 ft.

Piazza 12 ft.

Plan of the first and second floors.

Scale of 16 to inch.

Robt Mills Architect
City Washington

231

ABOVE AND OPPOSITE: *Marine Hospital, Key West, Florida. Robert Mills, architect, 1844–1845.*

and when Mills' plan was sent to New Orleans, James W. Breedlove, the collector, rejected Mills' plan and hired two local architects, Anthony Mondelli and John Reynolds. They designed and erected the building, making minor changes to Mills' plan and claiming it as their own. As late as 1852 Mills requested compensation, and although he should be credited with the design, he was never paid.[35] Here he proposed an elongated version of his 1837 hospital for 100 patients, a building 200 by eighty feet, with piazzas 150 feet long. He added a cupola for ventilation and a third story and suggested "plain Gothic, or Anglo Saxon" detailing for the facade. Mondelli and Reynolds made the plan smaller, 160 feet by seventy-eight feet, more in keeping with Mills' 100-patient 1837 plan which was 150 by eighty feet. They retained Mills' third story and his disposition of the wards, corridors, and offices. They also included a cupola or belvedere and used Gothic fenestration and crenellations.

35 RM to George
Harrington, October 20,
1852.

Mills' final Marine Hospital was built in Key West (1844–1845). The local collector of customs, Adam Gordon, sent ideas and a roughly sketched ground plan to the Secretary of the Treasury. Mills' plan incorporated Gordon's suggestions. The most notable feature of the Key West plan is the division of the building into three units separated by open passageways, all three sections being covered by one, continuous hipped roof. The collector described this arrangement as "a centre building with wings all covered with one entire & uniform roof would give the most airy & comfortable quarters for the sick in that climate."[36]

Viewed from the exterior, the Key West hospital has much in common with the Charleston hospital and with the smaller 1837 plan—two stories on a raised basement with a piazza on each floor framed by the "wings" at either end. Mills' elevation shows louvered shutters mounted between the columns of the piazzas—a common way to shade the piazza in the southeast. The division of the building into three units beneath a single roof is based on a southern vernacular building type known as the "dog trot" house—typically a single-story dwelling with two units separated by an open passage way, all being covered by a single roof. The dog trot type was common in Georgia and South Carolina in the colonial period; it was used throughout the nineteenth century as far west as Texas.[37]

THE CUSTOM HOUSES

Mills' involvement with the marine hospitals began with the Charleston hospital in 1831, intensified in 1837, and essentially ended with the Key West hospital in 1844–1845. His engagement with a series of custom houses was more concentrated. On September 9, 1830, he received $300 for the designs, estimates, and specifications for a custom house for Mobile, Alabama (he did not visit the site or supervise construction), then during the summer of 1833 he received $200 apiece for plans and specifications for four customhouses to be located in Newburyport and New Bedford, Massachusetts, and Middletown and New London, Connecticut. At the same time (June 1, 1833), he was paid $150 for designing interior alterations for the New York Custom House, and several months later (September 18, 1833) he received $250 for plans for a custom facility, the Appraiser's Store—a warehouse—to be built in Baltimore. No architect had ever received such a spate of federal commissions. Heartened, Mills wrote Andrew Jackson requesting that the President suggest that he be retained as an architect

36 Quoted by Alder, 66.

37 John Linley, *The Georgia Catalog, Historic American Buildings Survey* (Athens: University of Georgia Press, 1982), 20–21, notes that when a rural family "outgrew its one-room house, a porch might be added, or another room...a mirror image of the first, but with a space between the two which could be roofed and floored, and thus serve as a pleasant out-door room in mild or hot weather. This room became the center of life for pets as well as people; it seems to have been a favorite haunt for the pack of dogs...and thus earned its name, the "dog trot." In southern Georgia the dog trot house was still being built in the late nineteenth century. Linley, 112, 187. See also William R. Ferris, Jr., "The Dog Trot: a Regional Home and Its Builder," *Perspecta: The Yale Architectural Journal* 17 (1980): 66–73; Al Larson, "From Dogtrot to High-Style: The County Courthouses of South-Central Texas," *PAST: Pioneer America Society Transactions* 20 (1997): 76–77; Arnold J. Aho, "Two Pens and a Passage: The Story of the Southern Dogtrot House," MA Thesis, Mississippi State University, 1990, and Linda Lavender, *Dog Trots and Mud Cats: The Texas Log House* (Denton, Texas: North Texas State University, 1979).

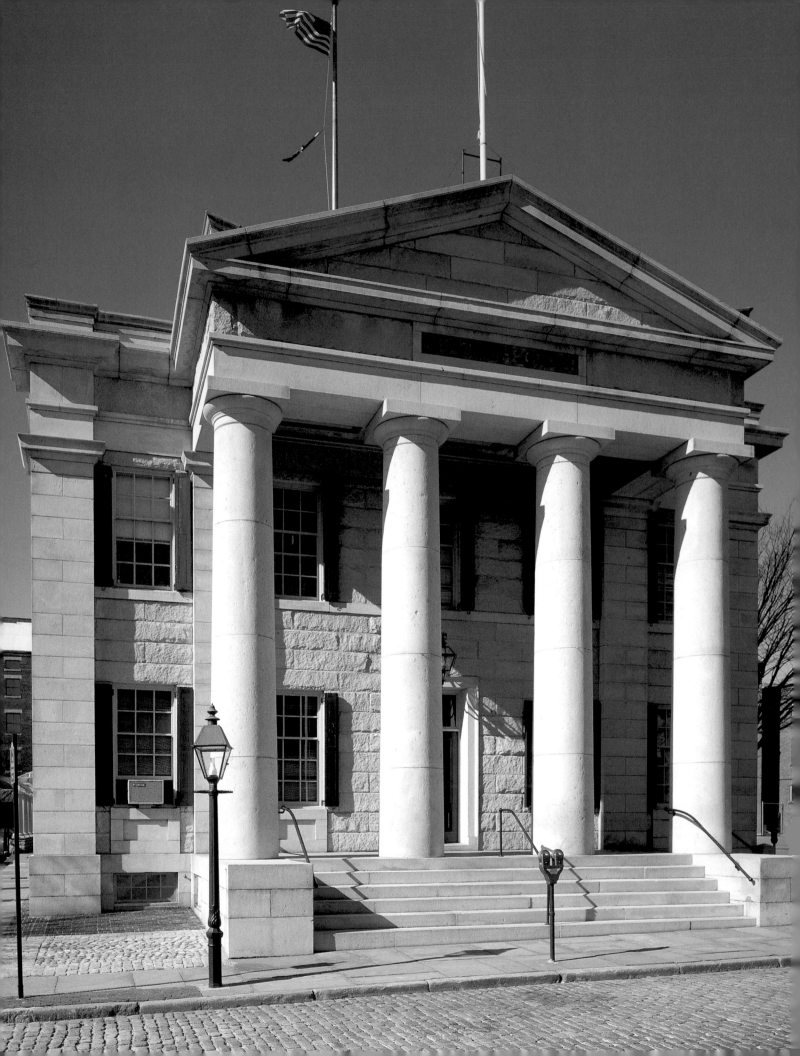

ABOVE, LEFT AND OPPOSITE: *Custom House, New Bedford, Massachusetts. Robert Mills, architect, 1834–1835.*

ABOVE, RIGHT: *Granite, underside portico floor, Custom House, New Bedford.*

by the Secretary of the Treasury. Confident in his prospects, the next day Mills resigned his position as a clerk-draftsman in the Land Office, July 9, 1834.[38]

The marine hospital and customhouse commissions reflected a growing federal budget surplus during the 1830s. From 1810 until 1830 the annual sale of western lands ranged between one and two million dollars. But between 1830 and 1834 sales rose to almost five million dollars per year, and then receipts soared to $14,757,600 in 1835. In addition to money from the land sales, during the period 1830–1835, protective tariffs yielded receipts that exceeded land sales every year.[39] The income from land sales and customs allowed Andrew Jackson to inform Congress in 1835 that the national debt had been entirely paid, funds had been set aside for all unredeemed outstanding debts, and that after this was done a surplus of $19,000,000 remained on deposit at the Treasury. For the first time the federal government was debt-free.[40]

38 RM to AJ, July 8, 1834, PRM 1425, see also PRM 1425, Liscombe, Altogether American, 176.

39 Davis Rich Dewey, *Financial History of the United States* (New York: Longmans, Green and Co., 1918), 216–219, 246. See also Edward G. Bourne, The History of the Surplus Revenue of 1837 (New York: Burt Franklin, 1968), 16.

40 John Watts Kearny, *Sketch of American Finances, 1789–1835* (New York: Greenwood Press, 1968), 152.

The following year revenue from land sales rose to $24,877,179, and 1836 was the first year in which land sales exceeded customs revenue ($23,409,000). After 1835, the allocation of the growing surplus became a major political issue. The proposed development of hospitals on the western waters and customhouses at Atlantic ports served regional interests and paralleled the two principal sources of revenue.[41] (Federal income in 1836 from sources other than land sales and customs totaled only $2,450,000.) Mills' marine hospitals and customhouses should be viewed as an architectural residuum, or legacy, of the Jacksonian surplus.

We know the Mobile customhouse through the description in Mills' draft advertisement for bids.[42] He called for it to be two stories high, sixty-six feet square, and built of brick, with its exterior stuccoed and scored to imitate stone. He specified cut stone for a water table, entry steps, and window and door sills and a belt course beneath the second-story windows. The roof was to be covered with slate or lead. The interior partition walls were to be built of brick, and the floors were presumably carried on traditional wooden joists, for Mills said nothing about masonry vaulting. A courtroom with a coved ceiling and adjacent offices—all reminiscent of the South Carolina courthouses—is specified on the second floor. In the paragraph describing stone, he specified that at the main entrance there was to be "a small Portico of two columns, of plain Doric proportions"—meant, no doubt, to resemble the porticos he later designed for the Newburyport and New London customhouses.

Having sent plans, specifications, and text for the advertisement to the collector of customs in Mobile, Mills apparently had nothing else to do with the project. He was more actively involved in the four customhouses in New England and the Appraiser's Store in Baltimore. In these projects, in addition to preparing plans and specifications, he visited the sites to refine the plans, lobbied within the Treasury Department for fireproof construction, and in the case of the New England buildings, he showed contractors and masons how to erect the essential, masonry groined vaults.

The plans for the New England buildings were prepared during the summer of 1833 and sent to collectors, who solicited bids. The original appropriation did not provide for fireproof construction, and Mills convinced Levi Woodbury, Secretary of the Treasury, they should explore the possibility of making the buildings fireproof. In the fall (circa September 20–October 30, 1833) he visited each site to help execute contracts for the foundations and prepare two esti-

41 Dewey, 216–234.

42 PRM 1179.

Appraiser's Store [warehouse], Baltimore, Maryland. Robert Mills, architect, 1833–1839.

mates for the completion of each building—one using traditional wooden joists and the other wholly fireproof.[43] In his report urging fireproof construction, Mills noted he had not seen or learned of a single fireproof warehouse in a major American city. His proposal to make the buildings fireproof was both unusual and expensive; nonetheless, it was approved for all five buildings. He also suggested using stone for the exterior walls of the customhouses—granite for New Bedford, Newburyport, and New London (he said it would be durable in salt air), and sandstone for Middletown—and this too was approved.

The customhouses and the Appraiser's Store were the first federal buildings Mills designed which were wholly fireproof: stone exterior walls and interiors of brick or stone partition walls carrying groin-vaulted masonry floors and ceilings. Mills later cited the customhouses in New England as a precedent when the stability of his groined vaults for the U.S. Treasury and the Patent Office

43 PRM, 1377.

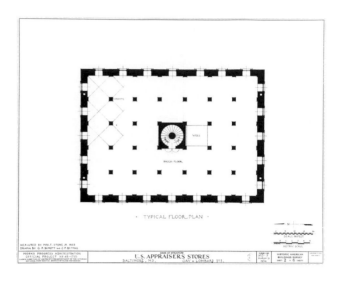

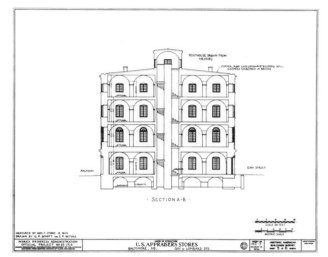

LEFT: *"Typical Floor Plan," Appraiser's Store [warehouse].*
RIGHT: *"Section A-B," Appraiser's Store [warehouse].*

came under attack in 1838. And as a precedent for these customhouses he pointed to the earlier South Carolina Asylum, the Records Office in Charleston, and "half a dozen of courthouses also, and jails . . . all of which were made fireproof in the office story . . . none of these have failed after a lapse of sixteen or eighteen years."[44] He described the vaulting system of the customhouses in detail to the House Committee on Public Buildings in 1838, and closed noting that the customhouses had introduced groin-vaulted masonry to New England.

When Mills set out to visit the customhouses in 1834, Levi Woodbury notified the collectors that they must try to reduce ornament in order to maximize money available for fireproof construction. This may partially explain the severity of the Baltimore Appraiser's Store, where the absence of a portico or traditional ornament emphasizes the geometry of the elevations. The repetition of like parts on the exterior and the undeviating pattern of groined bays on the interior suggest the influence of J.N.L. Durand, and given Mills' reading habits (he later cited Jean Baptiste Rondelet as an authority on masonry vaulting), this is plausible, but there is an additional possible precedent closer to home.[45]

While working on the Appraiser's Store, Mills worked in Massachusetts and Connecticut, refreshing his familiarity with building practices in New

44 House Report no. 737 (22d Congress, 2d Session), 22–23, PRM 7013.

45 For Mills' reference to Rondelet and Hutton, see House Report no. 737 (22d Congress, 2d Session), 27–28; also see Liscombe, *Altogether American*, 209; for an instance of his possible reference to Durand, see Evelyn, "The Washington Years, the U.S. Patent Office," in Bryan, ed., *Robert Mills, Architect*, 116.

Interior, granite pillars and groin vaulting, Appraiser's Store [warehouse].

England. The regional Boston Granite Style was then in vogue, and the Appraiser's Store bears all of the hallmarks of the early Granite Style. The Old Boston Customs House, built by Uriah Cotting, a real estate developer, had introduced monolithic granite posts and lintels to commercial architecture in Boston in 1810. Large building blocks of granite had only recently become economically feasible, due to the introduction of a new stone-splitting technique and the completion of canals providing waterborne freight access to quarries in Chelmsford, Tyngsboro, and Concord. In 1816, Cotting also developed Cornhill Street, which demonstrated the visual impact of the extended repetition of mass produced like parts. (Cornhill had facades of monolithic granite posts and lintels at grade and traditional brick walls above; it consisted of standardized facades lining both sides of a crescent-shaped street circa 440 feet long). By 1820 a new granite quarrying industry using the "wedges and feathers" stone-splitting technique was established along the New England coastline wherever granite was found adjacent to navigable water, and Cotting's formula was quickly adopted from Maine to South Carolina. By 1825 Mills' architect-peers—Alexander Parris, Ithiel Town, Isaiah Rogers, and Solomon Willard—were using and contributing to the evolution of the Granite Style.[46]

The Appraiser's Store (demolished 1936) had smooth hammered planar granite piers and lintels at grade, window sills and belt courses of the same material, and brick walls on the upper three stories. It embodied Cotting's early version of the Granite Style. On the interior of the Appraiser's Store monolithic granite piers, the critical component of the Granite Style, carried the groined arches on each level. Here—as with the Key West hospital and the dog trot house type—Mills blended a vernacular practice with functional requirements, including the need for fireproof construction—for which the Granite Style seemed ideally suited. The Appraiser's Store—four stories high, 100 feet by 82 feet six inches and containing 340,000 cubic feet of heated, fireproof space—was Mills' largest building prior to his major buildings in Washington.[47]

The Newburyport, New Bedford, and New London customhouses reflect the second phase (circa 1825–1840) of the Granite Style, which was characterized by the use of granite for entire facades. All three buildings have rough hammered granite exterior walls that contrast with the smooth, or fine hammered, surfaces of window sills, lintels, belt courses, and entablatures. The visual density of the stone, the stolid Doric porticos, slightly projecting corner piers and the absence of a raised basement combine to express stability and permanence. The Palladian raised basement and elevated entry, so typical of Mills' South Carolina courthouses, is notably absent, and the New England customhouses ay reflect a less formal, more pragmatic, literally and figuratively more "down to earth" view of government.

Mills' sensitivity to regional values and his responsiveness to local architectural traditions give substance to his claim to being "altogether American in his views."[48] The minimal ornament and the emphasis on functional planning in the marine hospitals and customhouses demonstrate what he meant by writing "Utility and economy will be found to have entered into most of the studies of the author, and little sacrificed to display; at the same time his endeavors were to produce as much harmony and beauty of arrangement as practicable. The principle assumed and acted upon was that beauty is founded upon order, and that convenience and utility were constituent parts."[49]

46 John M. Bryan, "Boston's Granite Architecture, circa 1810–1860," Ph.D. Dissertation, Boston University, 1972. For the evolution of the Granite Style see Bryan, "Boston's Granite Architecture," 48–109.

47 Anon., *A History of Public Buildings under the Control of the Treasury Department* (Washington: Government Printing Office, 1901), 255.

48 Gallagher, 168, quoting Mills' fragmentary manuscript "Architectural Works of Robert Mills."

49 Gallagher, 170.

Custom House, New Bedford, Massachusetts. Robert Mills, architect, 1833–1835.

Principal Front

see working drawing. RM

Robt Mills
Arch.t

Custom House, New London.

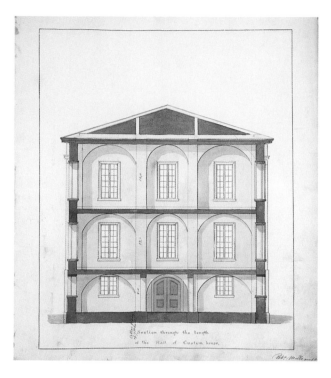

Section through the length of the Hall of Custom house.

Robt. Mills arct.

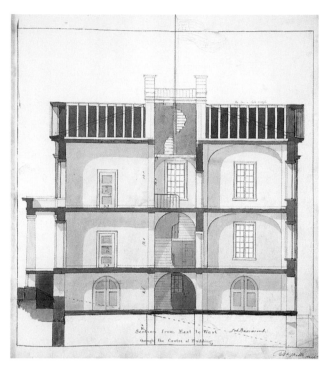

Section from East to West — Sub Basement through the Centre of Building.

Robt. Mills arct.

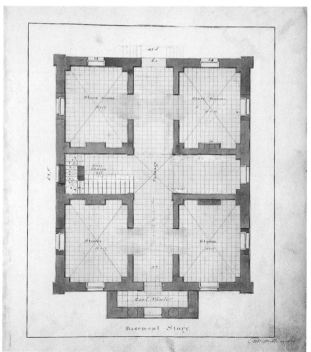

Store Rooms

Store Rooms

Stores

Stores

Coal Vaults

Basement Story.

Robt. Mills arct.

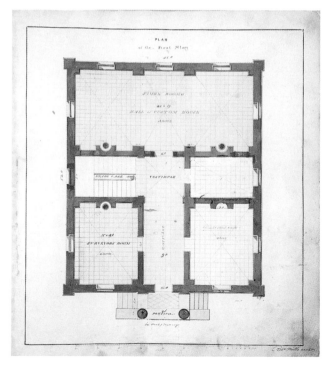

PLAN
of the First Story

STORE ROOMS
and
HALL of CUSTOM HOUSE
above

VESTIBULE

SURVEYORS ROOM

243

Custom House, New London, Connecticut. Robert Mills, architect, 1833–1835.

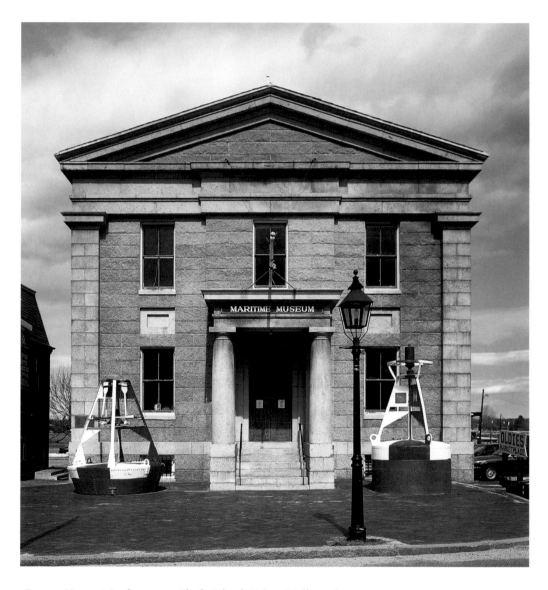

Custom House, Newburyport, Rhode Island. Robert Mills, architect, circa 1835.

The Appraiser's Store, the customhouses, and the marine hospitals are examples of Mills' ongoing involvement in designs directly related to transportation and trade—two prominent, recurring themes in his writing. When he was not fully occupied with architectural work, he often turned to writing, and he did so during his early years in Washington. In 1832 he published *The American Pharos, or Guide to American Lighthouses* (184 pages). It was the first comprehensive guide to American navigational aids written for mariners.[50] Mills undertook the project at the suggestion of Stephen Pleasanton, Fifth Auditor of the Treasury Department, who was responsible for the lighthouse accounts. The Treasury Department had received a query about American lighthouses from David Stevenson, a civil engineer in Edinburgh, Scotland, and Pleasanton circulated a questionnaire to lighthouse keepers. Mills borrowed their responses from August to October 1830, and acknowledged these reports as the source of his information.[51] The federal government had taken responsibility for navigational aids in 1791, and there were approximately 600 spindles, buoys, lightships, and lighthouses by Pleasanton's inventory (1835–1836). The publication of Mills' *Pharos* coincided with systematic efforts to regulate this far-flung system.

Historians usually dismiss the *Pharos* as a writing job to make money. It undoubtedly was a "pot boiler," but it also illuminates central characteristics of Mills' work. In compiling the *Pharos* he presented himself as a guide or pathfinder, the role he played in most of his publications. Moreover, he was drawn to buildings and monuments that expressed physical permanence and social purpose, and it takes little imagination to see why navigational aids were alluring to him. From childhood he was aware of the special significance of buoys and lighthouses. His repeated adaptation of Latrobe's design for the Frank's Island lighthouse creatively transforms beacon into a monument. On several occasions he blended the two functions. He described one of his proposals for the Bunker Hill competition as a beacon, and wrote in a proposal for a monument "to the Soldiers of the Revolution" in South Carolina:

> Monuments have always served as beacons of safety to public virtue and beacons of warning to the vicious. They display the gratitude and wisdom of a country and save the best public records of history. Whatever may be the lights of science, however learned in literary love we may become the brief inscription on a monument speaks more than Volumes written on the page of history.[52]

50 Robert Mills, *The American Pharos, or Lighthouse Guide* (Washington: Thompson & Homans, 1832) was republished as *The American Light-house Guide: with Sailing Directions for the Use of the Mariner* (Washington: Wm. M. Morrison, 1845).

51 Dated receipts signed by RM and HW Ball, PRM 1186, 1187, 1190. David Stevenson, *Sketch of the Civil Engineering of North America* (London: J. Weale, 1838), 307–308, transcribes a letter from Pleasanton to "David Stevenson, Civil Engineer, Edinburgh," so Stevenson, whose work includes a chapter on aids to navigation and describes American civil engineering in general, may have prompted Mills' *Pharos*.

52 PRM 0656, n.d.

Civic monuments draw significance from their historical context—beacons from their physical context. Both serve as guideposts, fixed, unchanging, and of real consequence. It is easy to see why they blended in Mills' mind.

The *Pharos* is straightforward. The title alludes to the famous beacon that marked the harbor at Alexandria, Egypt, and the title is one of the few literary flourishes in a book that was written for sailors, just as some of his early church proposals were framed for craftsmen. The text begins with a description of the coastline from Mexico to Canada based on the recently published *View of America* (1829) by William Darby. There are no charts, maps, or visual presentations. Navigational aids are presented verbally and organized by state. Describing the Charleston, South Carolina lighthouse, for example, Mills says: "This lighthouse is erected on Light House Island, at the entrance of Charleston harbor in latitude 32 40' longitude 79 40'. The elevation of the lantern is 125 $\frac{1}{2}$ feet above the sea, and contains a revolving light which may be seen 8 or 9 leagues, at which distance the time of darkness will be twice that of light; as you approach it the time of darkness decreases, and light increases, until you get within 3 leagues, when the light will not totally disappear. The intensity of the light is as 24 to 1. To enter over Charleston bar bring the light to bear W.N. W."[53] Taking into account the limited information available at the time, the *Pharos* anticipates the nine-volume *Coast Pilot* published today for the same purpose by the federal government.

In addition to the *Pharos*, Mills produced two other noteworthy publications while the customhouses were underway. In 1834, he prepared a series of newspaper articles, which he had printed as a pamphlet entitled *Substitute for Railroads and Canals embracing a New Plan of Roadway Combining with the Operation of Steam Carriages, Great Economy, in Carrying into Effect a System of Internal Improvement.* Here he argued for paving "the common road, and putting steam carriages to work on the same" instead of "constructing either Railways or Canals."

Two years earlier he had lobbied unsuccessfully to pave Pennsylvania Avenue between the Capitol and the White House. In a letter to the Committee of the District of Columbia he cited the twenty-nine military highways of Rome as "an object of *state policy*" noting that "all the chief cities of their vast Empire were connected by roads far superior to any that have been constructed in later times." He advocated paved roads, because he foresaw they were crucial to the use of engine-powered carriages, which he felt would prove superior to canal boats and trains. He presented accounts of experiments (circa 1829–1831)

53 PRM 0656, n.d., 83.

in England and Belgium with steam-powered carriages, then pointed out that paved roads would be cheaper to build than canals or railroads and that steam-powered carriages would be faster, more economical to operate and would offer more flexible routes and destinations. As it turned out, nineteenth-century steam engines proved too cumbersome for general ground transportation, and years would elapse before the network of paved, inter-city highways Mills envisioned became a reality. But in 1834, he glimpsed the future of transportation and offered, "Companies engaged in projecting works of internal improvement, and desirous of further information on the subject...by addressing the subscriber, (post paid) will have their inquires answered."[54]

No records indicate that anyone asked Mills to develop a paved highway. Nonetheless, he continued to promote the idea. He had exerpts from his pamphlet published in the *American Railroad Journal* in 1834.[55] And when Texas was admitted to the Union in 1845, he sent a twenty-seven-page memorial to Congress suggesting a paved highway as part of the fastest, most economical link to the far west. He emphasized the democratic nature of a "public highway for our people, whether through the medium of public vehicles, or by their own private conveyances." Highways, unlike railroads and canals, offered a means of "avoiding a monopoly...free...to all our citizens."[56] He estimated the cost of railroads and paved roads for four potential transcontinental routes and recommended the southernmost one: using steam navigation up the Rio Grande to the Rio del Norte, then a 300-mile paved road to the river Hiagui, then steam navigation to the Pacific. He said this route had three advantages: its overland section was by far the shortest of the alternatives; it lay wholly within "the temperate zone" (not subject to disruption by winter weather), and both ends terminated at the ocean—"the common highway of all the States, so that every city on our seaboard, as well as those in the interior, would be equally benefited by it."[57]

As he had done a quarter century earlier in the proposals for the Maryland and South Carolina canals, he put the transcontinental route and road in the broadest possible context: "With relation to our commercial interests, a speedy communication across to the Pacific would bring the Sandwich islands [Hawaii] within 2,000 miles of our territory; Canton could be reached in less than thirty days by steam, being distant only 6,000 miles from the terminus of our road." Or again, "A direct route to India has agitated the commercial world since the discovery of the continent; we now happily can accomplish this by

54 RM to House Committee on the District of Columbia, 1832, PRM 1294; Robert Mills, *Substitute for Railroads and Canals* (Washington: James C. Dunn, 1834), 11–12. In presenting the construction cost of railroads, Mills said "The Charleston (South Carolina) and Hamburg railroad, with two tracks, will cost per mile about $10,000.*" And in his footnote he claimed it was "being constructed upon a new and more economical plan...This plan of road was designed by Mr. Mills." Mills, *Substitue for Railroads and Canals,* 7.

55 *American Railroad Journal* (September 27, October 4, 11, 18, 1834): iii, 39–42, 594, 610–11, 626–627, 642–643.

56 "Memorial of Robert Mills, Submitting a New Plan of Roadway," *House of Representatives, 29th Congress, 1st Session, Doc. No. 173*, part 2, 1.

57 Memorial of Robert Mills, Submitting a New Plan of Roadway," *Doc. No. 173*, part 2, 20.

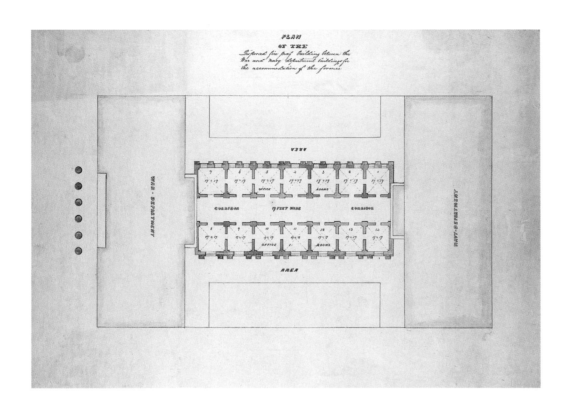

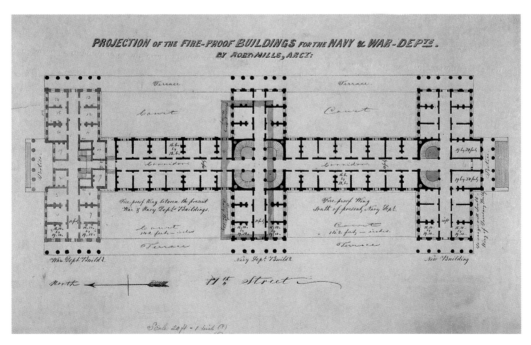

TOP:

"Plan of the proposed fire-proof building between the War and Navy Buildings." Robert Mills, architect, 1842.

BOTTOM:

"Projection of the fire-proof Buildings for the Navy & War Depts." Robert Mills, architect, 1844.

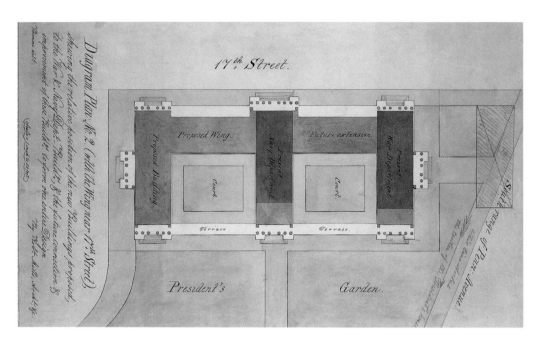

"Diagram Plan No. 2 . . . showing the relative position of the new Buildings proposed." Robert Mills, architect, 1843.

means of our roadway. The commerce of the east, in every age, has been the source of the wealth and power of every nation which has engrossed it. Commerce has been the handmaid to the moral, religious, and physical improvement of mankind."[58]

In 1834 Mills also published *A Guide to the Capitol* (64 pages), which offers a descriptive tour of the building and its major works of art. When Mills' *Guide* came out, William Elliot's *Washington Guide* (1822) was in its third printing, so Mills' book was not wholly innovative, but it was among the earliest American publications devoted to a single site. Here he dwells at length on stories evoked by the art, and his enthusiasm for allegorical sculpture is evident. Describing the Tripoli Naval Monument, for example, he says:

It is a white marble column, elevated upon a marble pedestal, base and zocle, and surmounted by an eagle, holding in her talons the symbols of the Union. The top of the zocle, or lower base, rises by steps towards the second base, and is ornamented with statues representing the Genius of America, History,

58 Memorial of Robert Mills, Submitting a New Plan of Roadway," *Doc. No. 173*, part 2, 21–22.

250

Commerce, and Fame. The latter is a winged figure, with a wreath in its hand, standing close to the column, and preparing to crown it....The Genius of America, the most interesting of the group, is represented as an Indian, leading two youths by the hand, one of which bears the fasces, and pointing their attention to the monument. The shaft of the column is decorated with the beaks of vessels and anchors; the pedestal with scrolls; the fretted cap of the base with Turks' heads, swords, &c.

Or again, following a thorough description and interpretation of the "emblematical character" of the figures in the pediment of the east portico, which he criticizes as too complex, he recalls an alternative he had offered "at the time a selection was to be made; it embraced simply this idea: Washington, in a chariot drawn by six horses abreast, coming out of the Capitol, crowned by Liberty and Wisdom; the whole encircled by a glory-studded with the thirteen stars, representing the Federal Union."[59] He had proposed a similar group for the Baltimore Washington Monument, and such an idea would appear again on the temple base of his published plan for the Washington National Monument.

The *Guide to the Capitol*, like his *Substitute for Railroads and Canals*, presents its author as an authority. Two years before his *Guide* was published, Mills had suggested a book of drawings of the Capitol both for reference and the convenience of visitors. He informed Verplanck that the only existing drawings were inaccessible and "much mutilated and imperfect." Neither Mills nor anyone else was hired to produce a definitive set of drawings, but his *Guide* may represent another tack toward the same goal—to fulfill a need, make a little money, and demonstrate authoritative knowledge of the Capitol.[60]

By 1834 Mills' far-flung federal commissions, his work around Washington, and his acquaintance with officials put him in a promising position just as the Jacksonian surplus came to fruition. For the past fifteen years he had rarely encountered serious professional competition, but now the increasing probability of significant federal construction attracted the attention of Ithiel Town and Alexander Jackson Davis from New York and William Parker Elliot of Washington.

William Parker Elliot's father, William Elliot, was an anti-Jacksonian Whig who had been turned out of his job at the Patent Office; his *Washington Guide* was in its third edition when Mills' *Guide to the Capitol* appeared in competition. The elder Elliot was a friend and associate of Ithiel Town (they owned land together in New York State), and when Town's partner, A.J. Davis,

59 Robert Mills, *Guide to the Capitol of the United States Embracing Every Information Useful to the Visitor* (Washington, privately printed, 1834), 5, 12. "Turk's heads" refers to a decorative knot traditionally used by sailors. William Elliot, *Washington Guide* (Washington, J.A. Brereton, 1822), subsequently reprinted in 1826, 1830, and 1837. Mills submitted a drawing of the east front of the Capitol and a proposed alteration of the dome to Gulian C. Verplanck, March 15, 1830. See PRM 1157.

60 RM to GCV, May 27, 1832, PRM 1305.

visited Washington, the elder Elliot accompanied him, making introductions. William Parker Elliot, the son, had a private business making drawings for patent applicants. He worked as a lobbyist for Town and Davis and advertised that he had "associated himself with Messrs. Town & Davis" and had "opened an office in the City Hall…where plans of Buildings, public and private, Bridges, &c. will be promptly executed, and furnished with the estimates to applicants in any part of the United States."[61] William Parker Elliot kept Town and Davis informed of possible projects and displayed their drawings in Washington. For example, on May 12, 1834, he wrote Davis that "all the talk is about the proposed new Patent Office &…I was much disappointed at not receiving a plan from you. The bill making the appropriation has passed two readings in the House of Representatives & will undoubtedly pass a third. Mills has submitted two or three plans; Lieut. Hood one—and Mr.—I forget his name also one: I think if I had one from you that I could have it adopted. At this moment it should be here that I might exhibit it to the Committee and also display it in the Library or Rotunda."[62]

Following the Treasury fire, two years passed before Congress agreed to appropriate money for fireproof buildings for the Treasury Department and the Patent Office. Each year after the fire, Jackson urged Congress to authorize fireproof offices, and Mills and Town and Davis and Elliot submitted proposals as discussion continued in committees. Initially there was interest in developing a cluster of new executive office buildings on Lafayette Square, or extending and re-modeling the existing buildings flanking the President's House. Mills presented several alternatives, all of which were fireproof and must have been based on the use of groined vaults carried on interior piers or columns like the Appraiser's Store in Baltimore, for he said "the system in the disposition of rooms admits of the enlargement or throwing of any number of them into one."[63]

In the end, no coordinated complex of office was built; nonetheless, Mills was surprised to see what he took to be "the most reduced" version of his plan published in the *National Intelligencer* and attributed to William Parker Elliot. Writing to the editor, Mills said: "Mr. E. under some requisition, undertook to make some modifications of my plan by substituting the Ionic for the Doric order, in the facades, (and in this he had before him one or more of my designs projected also on this order) so that his modification possesses no originality; the great features of my design being prominent in the drawing which he has exhibited and described." And Mills concluded: "Mr. E. is no architect. He never has

61 Jane B. Davies, "A.J. Davis' Projects for a Patent Office Buildings, 1832–1834," *JSAH* 24 (October 1965): 247.

62 Davies, "Six Letters by William P. Elliot to Alexander J. Davis, 1834–1838," *JSAH* 26 (March 1967): 71.

63 RM to Leonard Jarvis, n.d., PRM 1290.

erected a building to my knowledge, and can know nothing of design, practically, as the modification of my plan, which he exhibits, clearly manifests."[64]

The following week, the *National Intelligencer* published William Parker Elliot's acerbic response:

> ON THE PLAN OF THE NEW EXECUTIVE BUILDINGS
> Nothing can exceed my astonishment at reading a communication in your paper of this morning, signed "Robert Mills, Engineer and Architect," claiming to be the Author of the Plan for the New Executive Buildings adopted by the Select Committee of the House of Representatives which I designed and submitted.... He must be laboring under some strange mental delusion; for I can assure the public that there is not one idea in my design taken from his. Indeed, if I had wished to borrow from any Architect, I should hardly have chosen Mr. Mills as my Master, whose wild and visionary schemes have so often proved abortive. I should not certainly copy from his plan—his colonnades, without use or meaning, his bare and naked factory—like walls; his pigeon boxes placed over the pediments; his narrow and mean entrances, and still meaner stairs; his low obscure basement; and his disproportions in the whole building. How can it be supposed that I would copy from a man who has turned the House of Representatives upside down—who has made the seats to radiate from the circumference instead of the center of the diameter!—who has bedecked the Speaker's chair with such fantastic trumpery; and who has suggested the idea of dividing horizontally this magnificent Hall into two apartments.... Hereafter, but not now, I shall probably say something about his Engineering in South Carolina; and also about his Architecture in Philadelphia and Baltimore.[65]

Mills' response—the final shot in this exchange—merely reiterated that Elliot was not an architect: "The *study* of an art does not make an *artist*, but a *practical* knowledge of the art. While I appreciate Mr. E.'s talents as a *draughtsman*, he

64 RM to Editor, *National Intelligencer*, February 16, 1835; PRM 1478.

65 WPE to Editor, *National Intelligencer*, February 20, 1835; PRM 1479.

must excuse me from considering him as an *architect* until he proves himself such, by exhibiting his practical knowledge in the construction of an intricate building. When he does this I shall cheerfully award him the title of *Architect*."[66]

The momentum sensed by William Parker Elliot for a new Patent Office was based on three factors: first, the Patent Office had its own funds, the accrued balance of fees paid by patent applicants, and there was a sentiment that this fund should be used for construction that would benefit the patent process; secondly, it was widely recognized that patent records and models were a treasury of American ingenuity and must be made secure; and finally, the patent models were popular as an educational exhibition, a stimulus to further invention, and required suitable space for display. In 1834 the Patent Office shared Blodgets Hotel with the Post Office. The processing of applications and the storage and display of records and models were all hindered by inadequate quarters, and Samuel F. Vinton, Chairman of the House of Representatives Committee on Patents (without an approved appropriation for construction) sought plans for a new building.[67]

Robert Mills proposed a "parallelogram 150 feet long by 60 feet wide exclusive of the wing projection on each front, one of which is filled up by a Colonnade."[68] No elevations of Mills' proposal survive, but he must have intended a long Doric colonnade, for he wrote, "the order of the architecture adopted is massy, simple and substantial." The colonnade was to be framed by projecting end bays similar to the east facade of the Louvre, or not unlike Mills' later design for the Treasury Department building. He specified a full raised basement twelve feet high to accommodate "sub offices, lumber rooms, repairing shops, heavy, or cumbrous models &c." Offices of the Superintendent and clerks were on the principal floor on the south side "opening on the Colonnade." The remainder of the principal floor was designated for models. Staircases at either end of the longitudinal central hall led to "the grand Model Saloon above, covering the entire area of the second story 146 feet by 52 ft besides the wings." He said a similar exhibition hall could be developed by finishing an additional, third floor lighted by "lanterns" or monitors in the roof. The whole building was to be fireproof with a facade of cut free stone. Taken together, the raised basement, the colonnade, and the use of stone were intended to elevate the architectural status of the Patent Office. Mills made his intention clear by suggesting that if a new building was to be erected, perhaps it should be sited on the knoll reserved by L'Enfant for a national church, a prominent public square known as "the F Street

66 RM to Editor, *National Intelligencer*, February 21, 1835; PRM 1480.

67 Evelyn, dissertation, 85.

68 RM to William Noland, April 9, 1834; PRM 1402.

Ridge," bordered by 7th, 9th, F, and G Streets. When the time came, Mills was not selected as architect of the Patent Office. Nonetheless, the building was placed where he suggested; he devised the interior plan and structure.

John D. Craig, Patent Superintendent, also prepared a design in 1834. He suggested a plain, brick three-story building with a fireproof interior "supported by iron pillars...and constructed with iron joists & stays, as in the large fire proof factories now in England."[69] William Noland, the Commissioner of Public Buildings, directed a clerk to check the estimates and compare the probable cost of Mills' and Craig's plans. In commenting on the result, Mills argued for the first time that his system of masonry groined vaults was more economical and more "secure from fire" than cast iron.[70] Ironically, Mills, with a reputation for being visionary, would henceforward find himself arguing for an ancient technique and against a new technology.

William Parker Elliot alerted Town and Davis, informed them of the nature of Mills' and Craig's plans and soon received at least two and possibly three designs, which appear to have been developed primarily by Davis. Elliot arranged for these drawings to be displayed in the House and Senate chambers. Two years elapsed before Congress approved new construction. But from 1834 onwards, architectural standards promoted by Mills for many years—fireproof, monumental government offices—became a widely accepted goal and a formative influence in Washington.

69 Evelyn, dissertation, 88.

70 RM to William Noland, April 15, 1834; PRM 1406.

Washington National Monument, Washington, D.C. Robert Mills, architect, 1845–1854. Completed 1876–1884 by Thomas L. Casey, U.S. Army Corps of Engineers.

CHAPTER SEVEN

"Architect of Public Buildings"

Washington, D.C., 1836–1842, and Subsequent Practice

O N DECEMBER 16, 1835, a severe frontal system swept over Manhattan with high winds and temperatures plunging to seventeen below zero. About 9PM, at the corner of Exchange and Pearl Streets, a fire was discovered in a warehouse. Frozen hydrants, hoses, and cisterns hobbled the firemen, and wind swept flames from rooftop to rooftop. For two days and two nights, the fire raged unchecked; it was finally stopped at Wall Street by dynamiting buildings to create a firebreak. Six-hundred-seventy-four buildings were destroyed; losses were estimated between eighteen and twenty-six million dollars, and twenty-three of the twenty-six insurance companies in the city went bankrupt.[1] The disaster underscored the need for fireproof construction, and the next congress approved new fireproof buildings for the Treasury Department and the Patent Office.

Congress authorized the president to select the plans and designate the architect(s). Mills immediately wrote Jackson to "renew his application" for "the appointment of architect of the public buildings." He noted that over a period of thirty years he had erected numerous fireproof buildings and saved money for the government through the negotiation and management of contracts. He succinctly restated the controversy with William Parker Elliot: "The general designs, recommended by the committee of the house, for the public offices are originally and essentially mine, as the chairman of the committee, Mr. Jarvis knows, although another claims the authorship of the plan.... Undue

1 Edwin G. Burrows and Mike Wallace, *Gotham, A History of New York City to 1898* (New York: Oxford University Press, 1999), 596–598.

advantage was taken of my public exhibition of the designs; and simply by making a trivial modification in the plans, the whole of my labor for years was transferred to the benefit of another."[2]

Chairman Leonard Jarvis wrote Mills a strong letter of recommendation, saying Mills was "the only person to whom the committee on public buildings is indebted for any information."[3] The selection process demonstrated Mills' relationship with the Jacksonians, and a disgruntled William Parker Elliot wrote in his diary that William Noland, Commissioner of Public Buildings, arranged for Mills to wait in an adjacent office while Jackson considered the matter. Mills was then allowed to modify his design for the Treasury Building to incorporate suggestions made by Amos Kendall, Postmaster General, one of Jackson's Kitchen Cabinet; Elliot was not consulted.[4]

Jackson approved Mills' design for the Treasury Building and the Ithiel Town-William Parker Elliot design for the Patent Office (A. J. Davis had dissolved his partnership with Town in 1835). Jackson also appointed Mills as "Architect to aid in forming the plans, making proper changes therein from time to time and seeing to the erection of said buildings substantially in conformity to the plans hereby adopted—which are in their general outlines to be as to the Treasury Building that plan annexed by said Mills, and as to the Patent Office that annexed by Mr. Elliott [sic], the former building to be erected on the old site and the latter one on the square, north of the present office."[5] When Jackson made his decision, there were no working drawings or realistic appropriations for either building, so the discretion granted Mills was necessary. Nobody seems to have worried about the lack of definition at the outset.

The construction directed by Mills in the late 1830s established a new scale for federal offices. Earlier offices in Washington had been built of brick, visually closer to the domestic cityscape than to the larger public scale of the stone-clad Capitol and President's House. Mills' Treasury Building, Patent Office, and the new General Post Office set a new standard, and on these three buildings, like the pin of a hinge, turned the development of a monumental capital city. These buildings represent the culmination of Mills' commitment to permanent fireproof construction and his expression of the dignity of public works. They also reflect the final efflorescence of the Jacksonian surplus.

Like most of Mills' federal work, the new executive branch buildings were made possible by the prosperity of the early years of Jackson's presidency, a unique period when the economy was fueled by westward migration and the

2 RM to AJ, July 4, 1836; PRM 1529.

3 LJ to AJ, July 4, 1836; PRM 1527.

4 William Parker Elliot, Diary, July 5 and 7, 1836; PRM, 1531 and 1534.

5 AJ to William Noland, July 6, 1836; PRM, 1593.

Treasury Building, Washington, D.C. Robert Mills, architect, 1836–1842. Fifteenth Street façade and central wing. Completed 1855–1871, by Thomas U. Walter, Ammi B. Young, Isaiah Rogers and Alfred B. Mullett.

resulting land sales for settlement and speculation. Fortuitously, this coincided with a period of international stability and expanding trade following the Napoleonic Wars. Easy credit offered by proliferating, unregulated local and state banks buoyed up economic activity everywhere. Nobody in Jackson's circle realized the prosperity was, despite appearances, as fragile as a house of cards.

The week after Mills was authorized to proceed with the Treasury Building and Patent Office, Levi Woodbury, Secretary of the Treasury, issued the specie circular (July 11, 1836), directing banks and collecting agents to accept only gold or silver in payment for public land. The directive was intended to curtail the circulation of worthless commercial paper, and especially to stop speculators from using unsecured credit to acquire western land. By itself, the specie circular would have radically contracted credit, but its effect was unexpectedly compounded by Jackson's earlier decision to distribute the federal surplus to the states.

As commerce struggled to adjust to the species circular, on January 1, 1837, the first of four scheduled transfers of federal funds took place, with $9,000,000 being collected from banks where it was on deposit. The funds were distributed and redeposited based on representation in Congress. The transfer precipitated a sudden contraction of credit in metropolitan areas, often leaving established businesses gasping. Funds transferred to rural states often remained for a time unproductive, out of circulation. The second distribution was scheduled for April 1, 1837. The federal government began calling in the funds, and banks, unable to meet both local and federal demands, began collapsing. By May 10, 1837, New York banks suspended specie payments, and banking in Northern cities shuddered to a halt.[6] The ensuing hardship created a climate of retrenchment in Washington, and the Treasury Building and Patent Office, which had seemed a grand expression of prosperity, suddenly appeared indefensibly grandiose.

When Mills broke ground for the Patent Office and the Treasury in the summer of 1836, the financial panic of 1837 was just out of sight over the horizon. The part of the Treasury Building designed and built (1836–1838) by Mills was shaped like a T, with its long top bar running north-south along 15th street, and the vertical bar of the T a central wing projecting westward into the President's Square. Mills' plan provided for two additional wings extending west, paralleling the central wing, from each end of the top bar of the T. The original portion of the building contained 135 offices. Above its raised basement there were three stories, each having an unbroken barrel-vaulted central corri-

6 Davis Rich Dewey, *Financial History of the United States* (New York: Longmans, Green, 1918), 227–231; William MacDonald, *Jacksonian Democracy, 1829–1837* (New York: Harper & Brothers, 1906), 276–291.

Treasury Building,
Fifteenth Street façade
completed by architect
Thomas U. Walter,
1855–1864.

dor with uniform groin-vaulted offices on either side. At the intersection of the bars of the T, a pair of dramatically open staircases, their treads cantilevered from the wall, provided the principal vertical circulation. Secondary stairs were located halfway down either arm of the 15th street portion of the building. On the interior there was virtually no applied ornament. Everything, including the Delian Doric columns adjacent to the main staircase, was a direct reflection of the structural system.

As work got underway on the Treasury Building, Mills prepared a construction estimate for Town and Elliot's plan for the Patent Office. He quickly informed Jackson that the appropriation ($105,000) had been based on a traditional brick building and was not increased when the act was amended to require a fireproof building. He estimated that the Town and Elliot plan, made fireproof, would require $150,000. Rather than reduce the size of the building to stay within the appropriation, Mills and the Commissioner of Patents sought Jackson's approval to begin work on full-size foundations for a granite building on the assumption that a supplemental appropriation could be obtained. While they waited for authorization to proceed, work on the Patent Office was delayed.

When Mills submitted his first annual report as Architect of the Public Buildings (December 7, 1836), he reported that the foundations of both buildings had been laid; the interior brick walls of the Treasury Building had reached "the springing line of the groin arches, several of which are turned and laid in hydraulic cement; and the cut granite, facing on the west front, made up as high as the window seats."[7] The following week, on December 15, 1836 (only one day short of the anniversary of the Manhattan fire), Blodgets Hotel, where the Patent Office, the General (federal) and City Post Offices were housed was gutted by fire. Ten thousand patent records and some 3,000 models were lost.

Following the fire, and with the financial situation deteriorating, the House committee on Public Buildings became increasingly critical. They asked President Martin Van Buren, who had succeeded Jackson, to determine how much space was currently used or would be needed by each executive department. They also questioned the siting of the Treasury building, its implications for the adjacent Department of State building and the vista along Pennsylvania Avenue. They wanted to know why work on the Patent Office had fallen behind and were troubled "that the work had been carried forward with little understanding of the entire plan…that mistakes had been committed, and defects existed, not foreseen or apprehended in the commencement or prosecu-

7 "Report from the Commissioner of the Public Buildings," 24th Cong., 2d Sess., House Doc. 10, (December 7, 1836): 3.

tion. Indeed, little more of preparation appeared to have been made, at the time of entering upon the work, than the adoption of profile views and plans of elevation and dimensions of the buildings, and their... locations."[8] In 1838 the committee, led by its chairman Levi Lincoln, embarked on a full investigation.

Called before the committee, Mills testified that Jackson had designated the site of the Treasury Building "to preserve the present office of the State Department." The committee did not believe him, for the new building was closer to the street; floors and corridors were on different levels, and "it was obvious upon inspection, that the position of this edifice was such as to imply a decision on the part of the architect, to destroy the building at present occupied by the State Department.... In their judgment, the architect either never did entertain the design to preserve the old building, and bring it into harmony of appearance and use with the new, or he was destitute of the requisite ability to accomplish these ends." They observed that siting the new building against the sidewalk precluded the use of landscaping to ameliorate the disadvantages of the sloping site. Having expressed dissatisfaction with the siting, they criticized the interior plan. They found the corridors too narrow and dark; they felt the attic and basement would be too dark for offices, and the basement too damp for archival storage. Dissatisfied on every point and having been advised that both the Treasury Building and the Patent Office were "insecurely constructed," they arranged for Philadelphia architect Thomas Ustick Walter to undertake "a careful examination of the whole work."[9]

Walter's report was damning. His opening observation forecast the thrust of his critique: "... should the building be completed according to the present design, the plan of the city will be materially interfered with, its beauty will be marred, and the objects of its founders thwarted." In his opinion, both buildings were fatally flawed structurally. He declared their exterior walls too thin to counter the lateral thrust of the vaults; the interior brick walls and arches not sufficiently tied to the stone facing; iron tie rods and cramps had been omitted; and antae, or pilasters, were not an integral part of the exterior walls and therefore provided no counter-thrust or lateral support. He claimed the vaulting system of the Treasury Building's vestibule and open areas above it adjacent to the main stairs "can never be executed with safety to the building."

Walter found the open interior spaces in the Patent Office especially alarming. Mills was responsible for the interior plan and structural system of the Patent Office, for he never received detailed drawings or sections of any

8 RM to William Noland, September 21, 1837; PRM 1643; "New Treasury and Post Office Buildings," 25th Congress, 2d Session, Ho. Rep. No. 737 (March 29, 1838); PRM 7013.

9 RM to William Noland, September 21, 1837; PRM 1643; "New Treasury and Post Office Buildings," 25th Congress, 2d Session, Ho. Rep. No. 737 (March 29, 1838); PRM 7013. Thomas Ustick Walter (1804–1887) trained under John Haviland and William Strickland. Establishing his own practice in 1831 Walter quickly became one of the most prominent architects in the generation that followed Mills. Girard College for Orphans, Philadelphia (1833–48) established Walter's reputation as a Greek Revivalist and cemented his relationship with Nicholas Biddle who subsequently promoted Walter's career. For Walter's contact with Mills, see James Moore Goode, "Architecture, Politics, and Conflict: Thomas Ustick Walter and the Enlargement of the United States Capitol, 1850–1865" (Ph.D. dissertation, George Washington University, 1995), 5–39.

kind from Town and Elliot. Mills planned for the west end of the basement to be one room, sixty-five by seventy-five feet, spanned by nine groin arches carried by piers. Above this was to be the open model room, also sixty-five by seventy-five feet, and above that, on the top floor, Mills called for an Exhibition Hall, sixty-five by 260 feet. Walter foresaw catastrophe: "All the arches are to spring from columns to the exterior walls, suspending over this vast room more than 300,000 bricks, without any possibility of preventing the lateral thrust from acting on the outside walls; and that, too, almost at the very top of the building. Had the exhibition-room been vaulted on this plan, the building must have spread with the keying, and the arches have come down."[10]

Thus far, and for his critique of the interior accommodations of the Treasury, Walter could visit the construction sites, but his evaluation of the "architectural appearance" of the Treasury Building, was based on Mills' drawing of the approved 15th Street facade—an unbroken, 336 foot long Ionic colonnade of thirty columns three stories high, elevated on a raised basement above the sloping street. Walter condemned it "as by no means creditable to the nation...without any break or projection to relieve the monotony.... It will always present an unfinished appearance, and the building will look as if it had once been surrounded with columns, which (by the way) would have given a much better architectural effect...the building unquestionably wants beauty as well as grandeur." He concluded that the Treasury Building was "beyond the reach of any remedy; and that the course dictated alike by prudence and economy, is, to take down the whole building."[11]

He held out only slightly more hope for the Patent Office, noting that the disastrous outward thrust of the groined arches could be stabilized if "every piece of ashlar in the building...[was] cramped to the brickwork" and partition walls built between the exterior walls and the pillars carrying the groin vaults. Iron tie rods would be concealed in the partitions.[12]

Mills wrote a clear, convincing rebuttal. Concerning the Treasury Building site, he pointed out that in 1835 and again in 1836 Congress specified the executive offices should not be relocated. Congress, Mills suggested, "no doubt influenced the late Executive in his selection of the spot." He said that only a corner of the new building intruded into the vista and argued that this would "affect the vision but little." Most of his response confronted the structural issues raised by Walter. Mills said his vaulting system was based on thirty years of experience. "It has been my endeavor," he wrote, "and I have proved its prac-

10 RM to William Noland, September 21, 1837; PRM 1643; "New Treasury and Post Office Buildings," 25th Congress, 2d Session, Ho. Rep. No. 737 (March 29, 1838); PRM 7013.

11 RM to William Noland, September 21, 1837; "New Treasury and Post Office Buildings" (March 29, 1838); PRM 7013.

12 RM to William Noland, September 21, 1837; "New Treasury and Post Office Buildings" (March 29, 1838). Walter made a number of other suggestions and concluded by observing, as Mills and others had several years earlier, that the best solution for the executive offices would be to develop a coordinated complex for them all on Lafayette Square.

ticability, to give to vaulted or fire-proof buildings the lightness of walls little exceeding that of good common buildings…as much on the ground of economy, as of safety and comfort." He offered examples of buildings "now standing as intact as on the day they were finished"—the state fireproof office in Charleston, the Asylum in Columbia, the New England customhouses, and the Appraisers Store in Baltimore. He juxtaposed his practical experience to Walter's theories:

> He must yield his theory to facts, after repeated trials. If he has constructed his arches according to the rules laid down in the books, he has secured a superfluous degree of strength, but at great and unnecessary cost, and certainly at the expense of comfort to the inmates of the house.
>
> If…I know my business, all that he alleges to the contrary must amount to naught; and if the fact has been proved, that I have constructed permanent arches of equal span, sustained by walls of half the thickness laid down by Mr. Walter, who deduces his results from theory; then, either the theory is erroneous, or does not embrace all the circumstances of the case, or my system of construction has some merit in it, and I have gained for the profession an important advantage, namely, to economize in the construction of fire-proof structures, and remedy the evil of very thick walls in such buildings.[13]

Defending his proposed colonnade, Mills mentioned the "admired and often celebrated" unbroken colonnades of the Louvre and the Bourse, and noted that an earlier drawing showing the potential north and south wings with "the colonnade…proposed to be carried round." He also stated that the Treasury's narrow corridors were an inevitable consequence of the site and number of offices required; like Walter, he would have preferred a more durable stone, and he reminded the committee he had proposed a coordinated office complex on Lafayette square in 1834.

Faced with the irreconcilable reports by Walter and Mills, the committee retained another architect, Alexander Parris of Boston. Parris concurred with Walter in almost every respect. If, however, the Treasury Building were to be continued, he suggested "that cast-iron beams, with brick arches, be substituted for the groined arches." He noted he had recently used this English system at the Charlestown Navy Yard. For the Patent Office, in addition to the iron tie rods and cramps suggested by Walter, Parris recommended that vaulting above the second

13 After turning in his report, Mills consulted two "writers on the subject, J. Rondelet and Professor Hutton, who corroborated his calculation of the stability of arches, and he sent the committee an addendum; "New Treasury and Post Office Buildings" (March 29, 1838): 27–28; PRM 7013.

story "should be of a spheroidal form"—circular domes with their bases belted or hooped with iron. He also suggested that furnaces be used in lieu of fireplaces.

After taking additional testimony, the committee recommended that the Treasury building be demolished, that the structure of the Patent Office be modified to incorporate suggestions made by Walter and Parris and that Mills be removed from office and replaced by Parris. The final debate on the bill took place in the House on June 8, 1838, and lasted for three hours. John Quincy Adams, then a representative from Massachusetts, noted in his journal that the bill would have been successful if Levi Lincoln had not droned on too long. Adams wrote that Mills was defended by George H. Keim of Pennsylvania who "looks at this object, and all others, through the smokey lens of party politics, and stands by the wretched bungler in architecture, Mills, because he was recommended by Mr. Jefferson."[14]

Keim told his colleagues to visit the Treasury Building and see for themselves that the centering had been removed and "the walls stand firm and unmoved, without showing either settlement or crack." The ringing conclusion of Keim's speech suggests he had talked to Mills: "Some effort should be made on our part to be inventors, instead of followers.... If science is progressive, so should the polite arts keep pace with them, and American architecture become a new school, in which might predominate...the principles of economy, simplicity, and convenience.... Let us compare our government to a plain, unadorned column, whose base is the people; the shaft the constitution; and the capital the laws."[15]

For Mills and the Treasury Building it was a narrow escape. The bill was tabled by a vote of ninety-four to ninety-one. The commissioners of public buildings then directed Mills to resume work, and as an aside in a letter to Robert Gilmore, Mills reflected that "the only error I committed in this business was in not getting the President [Jackson] to endorse the paper on which the Plan was drawn, as the one adopted."[16]

Although the Treasury Building and Patent Office occupied much of his time in 1837–1838, Mills continued to seek other projects, and two of these—the Alexandria Court House (1838–1839) and the South Carolina College Library (1836–1840)—reflect thematic continuities in his career. He received $300 for designing and superintending construction of the courthouse for the Commissioners of Public Buildings. It was his last courthouse and is the only one for which contemporaneous plans and an elevation exist. In some respects it was a distillation of earlier work. Once again, he elevated the court above

14 Charles Francis Adams, ed., *Memoirs of John Quincy Adams* (Philadelphia: J. B. Lippincott, 1876), X, 13–15; PRM 1752A.

15 *Appendix to the Congressional Globe, 25th Congress, Second Session,* 420; quoted by Pierson, 416.

16 Commissioners of Public Buildings to RM, June 11, 1838; PRM 1753; RM to RG, June 29, 1838; PRM 1759.

Alexandria County Courthouse, Alexandria, Virginia, circa 1890.

offices on the ground floor. The plan of the courtroom included a raised dais for the judge with flanking curved walls and a public gallery reminiscent of the auditorium churches. The Alexandria plan is also a refined, truncated version of a preliminary diary sketch (1830) for a proposed, but unrealized, courthouse in Savannah, Georgia. The clear geometry of the Alexandria facade was established by a raised Doric portico with lateral stairs, and made emphatic by the vertical alignment of the portico pediment and ventilating cupola on the peak of the hipped roof.

The South Carolina College library was Mills' last public building in South Carolina. The college began discussing the need to build a freestanding library in 1836. A local builder, Charles Beck, contracted to build it on October 10, 1838, for $20,000. The contract refers to seven drawings, none of which survive. Mills'

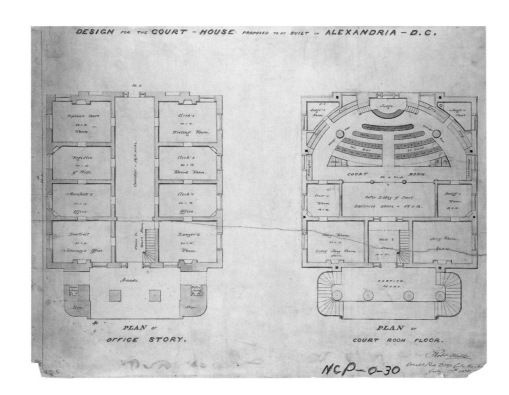

TOP:
Plans of the "Office Story" and "Court Room Floor," Courthouse, Alexandria, Virginia. Robert Mills, architect, 1838–1839.

BOTTOM:
"Façade" of the Courthouse, Alexandria, Virginia. Robert Mills, architect, 1838–1839. National Archives

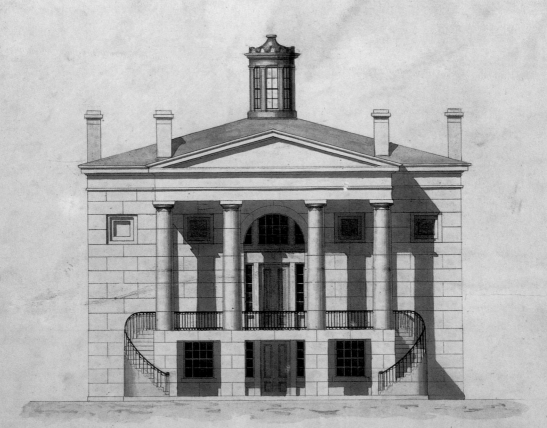

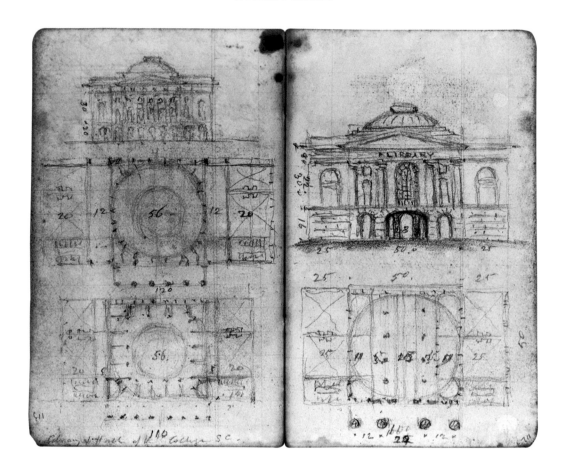

Sketches for the South Carolina College Library, Columbia, South Carolina.
Robert Mills, architect, 1837.

diary contains sketches, six elevations and six plans, measurements, and estimates for "Library and Hall of the College SC" and "West Façade of Library &
Hall." The diary entries date from January 27, 1837, at the outset of efforts by the
college to obtain funding for the library. In addition to the diary sketches, two
finished plans signed by Mills survive among college records, and these show
the ground floor and principal floor of the diary elevations.[17]

The difference between Mills' diary estimates, "$38,800 Est—not fireproof"
and $64,000 "Est—Fire proof," and the initial budget of $15,000 probably explains
why the dramatic raised basement with its arched carriage way entrance to the
campus was deleted. The domed rotunda reading room on the principal story was

17 RM, *Journal*, 1836–1840;
PRM 4006.

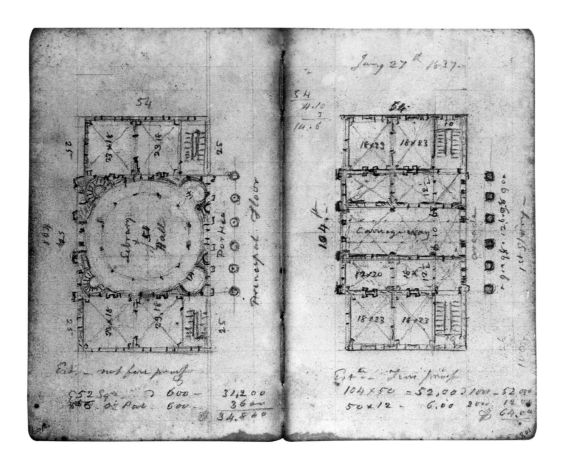

Sketches for the South Carolina College Library.

no doubt rejected for the same reason. The construction contract notes that drawing "No 4 represents the alcoves and galleries, which are to be finished precisely in the same manner as the congressional library at Washington of which [illegible] is a drawing" and drawing "No 6 represents the ceiling overhead, which is to be done in plaster in the very best stile [sic], equal to that of the congressional library, with the exception that instead of its being coved, it is to be straight."[18]

Today the reading room of the South Carolina College library, perhaps the best Greek Revival public room in the state, resembles the Bulfinch Library of Congress in plan and detail—right down to shelving arranged in alcoves reflecting "Mr. Jefferson's arrangement, corresponding 'to the faculties of the mind

18 Bryan, *An Architectural History of the South Carolina College,* 86.

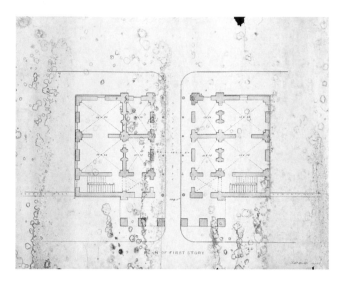 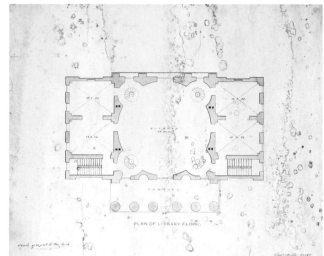

LEFT: *"Plan of First Story," South Carolina College Library.*
RIGHT: *"Plan of Library Floor," South Carolina College Library.*

19 RM, *Guide to the Capitol*, p. 47; Bryan, "Current Research Concerning Robert Mills and the South Caroliniana Library," *University of South Caroliniana Society 55th Annual Meeting* (Columbia: Caroliniana Society, 1991), 3–10; Liscombe, *Altogether American*, 85–87; PRM 6021.

employed on them.'" Mills described the Library of Congress at length in his 1834 *Guide to the Capitol*, and when his rotunda was rejected, he probably provided the drawings mentioned in the contract as a rectangular alternative.

This was his second unrealized rotunda library. He had proposed a circular library for the Baltimore Library Company in 1817, but the Company was unable to raise the money to proceed. Mills' Baltimore plan called for a rectangular building with a round library as its core on the principal floor above offices on the ground floor. The Baltimore plan, like the South Carolina proposal, was tall enough to accommodate a balcony beneath its dome; both plans were based on Jefferson's University of Virginia library, and like Jefferson, Mills wanted to give dignity to the library as a building type, just as he had done with his courthouses.[19]

In attributing the final design of the South Carolina College library to Mills, it is worth noting that the semi-circular projection from the rear facade that houses the stair was rarely used in South Carolina. Mills, however, had used a similar stair tower on the Asylum and would use another one at the Patent Office. At the library and the Patent Office, the external stair allowed the principal room to extend without interruption along the length of the building.

South Caroliniana Library. Robert Mills, 1836–1838.

The months following the congressional inquiry were marked by rapid progress on the Treasury Building, the Patent Office, and a new project, the General Post Office. Mills' 1839 annual report notes the roof of the Treasury Building was complete; interior stairs were nearing completion; running water was piped into the building; ninety offices were occupied and 125 rooms were finished. Work remained to be done on the cornice, colonnade, and retaining walls, but much of the stone required was already on site. The Patent Office exterior walls were complete, and its roof was sheathed over half the building. Inside the groined and vaulted masonry was largely finished; interior plastering had begun in the basement. The granite for the portico and stone flagging for the corridors and exhibition halls was ready to be set. Laconically and without irony, Mills reported "The centers of the grand model room arches will be all struck this winter—most of them are already removed; the great arch in the centre is complete."[20]

The Patent Office interior accommodated shops, storage, and processing at grade in the raised basement, office space and display space on the principal floor; and the "grand model hall" occupied the whole top floor. The patent process was widely viewed as a cornerstone of American prosperity, and the display of patent models was recognized as an educational celebration of American ingenuity. The Patent Office was called "a temple of invention." The model hall—its nave and sanctuary—was the first large fireproof exhibition facility in the United States. Mills described it in his 1842 *Guide to the Executive Offices and Capitol*:

> This room is the largest in the United States, taken as a whole, being two hundred and sixty-four feet in length, sixty-three feet in width, and thirty feet high. It is ornamented with a quadruple row of massive stone columns, rising with their entablature twenty feet; above which spring a series of arches, which, covering the whole area, form a highly ornamental ceiling. In the centre a grand barrel arch, of forty feet span, towers above the rest, pierced with an aperture thirteen feet in diameter, to admit light from above.[21]

He took pleasure in the Patent Office interior despite having been forced to add pillars, columns, and partitions recommended by Walter and Parris, but he later wrote of "the unwarrantable interference of others" and the

> ...unnecessary and injurious encroachment which they made upon the interior harmony.... Had the interior been constructed as...originally designed,

20 26th Cong., 1st Sess., 1839. House Doc. No. 32 (December 30, 1839).

21 RM, *Guide to the National Executive Offices and the Capitol* (Washington: Peter Force, 1842), 37.

Patent Office, Washington, D.C. Ithiel Town and William Parker Elliot, architects; Robert Mills, supervising architect, 1836–1840, 1849–1852. Completed by Thomas U. Walter and Edward Clark, architects, 1852–1857.

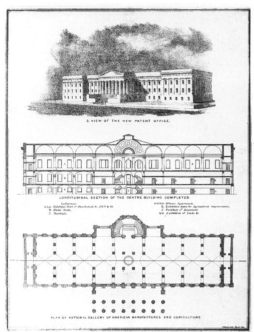

Patent Office, Washington, D.C.

the great rooms in the building would be much more beautiful and harmoniously light than they now are. Lofty and airy groins, springing from single columns, would have supplied the dull and monotonous barrel arch which now sits upon a heavy entablature and cluster of columns. It is a sorrowful and grieving sight to view this monument of the inroads of ignorance upon the truths of science—this testifier of the injustice of subjecting the conceptions of the artist to the rough hands and distorting touch of officious persons.[22]

The General Post Office got underway as he was finishing the first phase of construction on the Treasury Building and the Patent Office. In several respects the Post Office was his most successful major federal project. On December 24, 1838, the Commissioner of Public Buildings, without holding a public competition, asked Mills to design the Post Office. Coming on the heels of the Congressional inquiry, the commission certified the commissioner's confidence in Mills. The building was to be erected on the site of the old Blodget's Hotel.

22 27th Cong., 2d Sess. 1842. House Rep. No. 460 (May 10, 1842): 4.

Mills' first proposal, a three-story granite building topped by a 140 foot high clock tower, was replaced by his design for a marble clad, two story Italianate building on a raised basement. The design evolved harmoniously over several months in consultation with the commissioner and the Commission of Public Buildings. Public reaction, even before the building was occupied, was consistently favorable. Louise C. Tuthill said, "It is unfinished, but when completed will be one of the most splendid buildings in the United States." Robert Dale Owen called it "the most chaste and best proportioned of the public buildings in the metropolis." *Harper's New Monthly Magazine* agreed: "We doubt if there is a building in the world more chaste and architecturally perfect than the General Post-Office as now completed.... It is so symmetrical, and the details so faithfully executed, that it carries us back to the palmy days of Italian art." The architect, Charles B. Cluskey, affirmed the popular reaction: "the Treasury, General Post Office, and Patent Office buildings are comparatively of recent construction. They are fire-proof, and the only buildings of their class having any pretensions to architectural taste and proportion; and of these the Post Office is justly regarded as the most chaste and uniform in its construction, and is the only one of all the public buildings of indestructible materials."[23]

The Post Office was the first marble building in Washington. The porous Aquia sandstone—Mills called it "free-stone"—used on the Capitol and President's House was already weathering, spalling, and discoloring, and Mills suggested the possibility of using marble "according to ancient practice." The commissioners of public buildings advertised for bids before settling on a final design or materials. They sought bids for masonry vaulted construction with a six-inch facing of free stone, granite, or marble. Only after advertisements had been published did they agree to use marble on the public facades and granite on the rear, courtyard elevation. After awarding contracts, they adopted additional changes in the design, including increasing the thickness of the stone cladding from six to nine inches, altering windows and modifying the pilaster capitals. Mills recognized that the use of marble was a precedent in Washington, and he based the design for the pilasters on the Temple of Jupiter Stator, which Palladio said was the first marble building in Rome.[24]

The design was still evolving when the cornerstone was laid on May 24, 1839. Construction proceeded smoothly during the first building season, and at the end of the year Mills reported the foundations had been laid, the first tier of arches turned, and that the marble and granite facing was rising with the inte-

23 Denys Peter Myers, "Historic Report of the General Post Office Building (Now International Trade Commission Building)" (Washington: General Services Administration, n.d.), 6, 7.

24 Scott and Lee, *Buildings of the District of Columbia*, p. 192; Myers, 7, 10.

General Post Office, Washington, D.C. Robert Mills, architect, 1839–1842. Completed by Thomas U. Walter, 1855.

rior walls and arches. Mills and William Noland, the commissioner of public buildings, praised the craftsmen and contractors—who were led by a team of supervisors, most of whom had worked with Mills on the Treasury Building and Patent Office. Robert Brown was the superintendent of all stone work; he inspected and accepted or rejected stone as it arrived on site. Jeremiah Sullivan supervised the stone cutters; Charles L. Coltman directed the bricklayers, and Joel B. Downer was superintent of carpenters, in charge of the all-important wooden centering on which the vaults were laid.

Despite public approval of the design and gratifying progress on site, administrative problems arose. Each superintendent had authority to hire, fire, and pay laborers, and this, coupled with the seasonal nature of the work, led to resentment and charges of favoritism. The design changes angered unsuccessful bidders, who understandably felt Masterson & Smith, who won the initial marble contract, privately were re-negotiating the advertised specifications to their advantage. Masterson & Smith were also aggrieved; they believed Robert Brown was unreasonably rejecting marble after comparing it with the sample they submitted when they won the contract. Another problem was rooted in the federal system of funding multi-year projects with annual appropriations. Having exhausted the 1840 appropriation, Mills, Noland, and their superiors—the commissioners of public buildings—kept construction on schedule by giving contractors and laborers notes—with the employees "taking the risk of a further appropriation by Congress for their compensation."[25] Every note issued exceeded the authorized budget and presented the next Congress with a moral obligation, but deficit financing seemed justified to Mills and his colleagues because the labor force wanted to continue working, and Amos Kendall, Postmaster General, was anxious to move the post office into a fireproof building.

Mills and Noland were able to sustain the pace and quality of construction until they confronted the implacable hostility of the Whigs, who, led by William Henry Harrison, won the presidency and control of Congress in 1840. Harrison died after a month in office, and on March 27, 1841, his successor, President John Tyler, appointed a Commission of Examination and Inquiry to review federal construction initiated by the Jackson administration. Recapitulating the administration of construction, the commission noted that from July 6, 1836, until March 3, 1838, when the law authorizing construction of the Post Office provided for the appointment of an architect, Mills' position was based on an executive order without a specific foundation in law.[26]

25 "Expenditures—Public Buildings," 26th Cong., 1st Sess., Rep. No. 649 (July 10, 1840): 4.

26 "Reports of the Commissioners appointed to inquire into the condition of the Public Buildings, and the conduct of the Superintendents thereto," 27th Cong., 1st Sess., Senate Doc. 123 (August 25, 1841–September 11, 1841): 5.

The commissioners took written and verbal testimony from superintendents, laborers, and contractors, and they inspected the buildings. They criticized the "location and arrangement" of the Treasury Building, specifically citing the adverse effect of the sloping site and proximity to the President's House. They claimed the basement was too damp for storage and too dark for offices; the attic was "one invariable mass of confusion, disorder, and dirt, totally irreconcilable with the idea of a public office got up at great expense." On the remaining floors "the rooms themselves may be fire-proof, yet the crowded desks, cases, and lumbering papers form sufficient fuel to consume all within their walls." These "defects...have perfectly convinced us that no substratum of a plan could ever have been furnished to the architect, looking to the attainment of the purposes of Congress in the erection of the building; and that the skill of the architect and others in authority was exhausted on the composite of the exterior, utterly regardless of its interior fitness for use." They pointed out that in June 1838, Mills had estimated the total cost of the initial phase of construction (the T without the north and south wings) as being $500,000, yet by January 1841, $597,470.03 had been spent, and they estimated that finishing the colonnade, terraces, railings, and privies would bring the total to $677,470.03. Assuming the north and south wings would cost the same per foot as what had already been done, they predicted a total cost of $1,208,470.03. Finally, they objected to the use of sandstone on the exterior and expressed dissatisfaction with "unworkmanlike defects" in the granite work.[27]

The commission praised the plan of the Patent Office, but they attributed it to Town and Elliot without qualification. As with the Treasury Building, they criticized the management of construction and condemned cost overruns on the Patent Office. They offered one sentence of praise for the Post Office—"The material of which this building is constructed is of good quality, the work is well done, the superintendents are intelligent and attentive"—but avoided complimenting Mills. They condemned the Post Office bidding process, stating Mills "inserted bids which were never made" and that he suppressed an explanatory note from one of the unsuccessful bidders. They were incensed by design changes made after bids had been submitted, changes they felt were "calculated to deceive the public, and trifle with the industrious and enterprising mechanic. The propositions [bids] were asked for apparently in good faith, and were made in truth. What officer under this Government has a right to treat them as speculative, and, especially, to do it covertly?"[28]

27 "Reports of the Commissioners appointed to inquire into the condition of the Public Buildings, and the conduct of the Superintendents thereto," 9, 10, 18.

28 "Reports of the Commissioners appointed to inquire into the condition of the Public Buildings, and the conduct of the Superintendents thereto," 47.

THE GENERAL POST-OFFICE, NORTH AND EAST FRONTS.

"North and East Fronts," General Post Office, Washington, D.C. Robert Mills, architect, 1839–1842. Completed by Thomas U. Walter, 1855.

LEFT AND
OPPOSITE:
*Interiors, General
Post Office*

The inquiry report focused on two of Mills' minor projects as exemplifying everything reprehensible about the management of federal construction. They concluded that as salaried "architect of public buildings" Mills should not have been paid extra ($300) to design the Alexandria Court House. Mills' superiors, the commissioners of public buildings, had appointed Samuel Butts, a resident of Alexandria, superintendent of construction, and the inquiry found he exceeded his authority by amending the initial construction contract to allow James Dixon, the contractor, to seal the raised basement with rough cast in lieu of using hard fired "stock bricks." As a direct result, "this well-defined and unambiguous contract proved incompetent to protect the public interests from official misrule, or honest competitors for the public service from palpable injustice—because, unless we have entirely mistaken the force and effect of subsequent results, they were better calculated to favor the contractor than benefit the public—in the probable relief afforded the contractor against the consequences of an injudicious undertaking, by the readjustment of plans and fixing of prices, without the impediment of an opposing competitor, whereby he obtained a decided advantage over the original competitors he had underbid." Or again: "permitting public officers and disbursing agents to alter and modify contracts for the public service at their own discretion...render(s) the matter of competition a mockery."[29]

The commissioners of inquiry were equally harsh in their assessment of the Washington Jail. Here Mills served as designer and superintendent of construction, and although the building was unfinished, the $31,000 appropriation had been spent, and they estimated that $5,000 worth of work remained to be done. Despite this extra expense, they argued that "the workmanship is by no means creditable either to the contractors or the architect. The roof has proved to be ruinously defective" and the walls "run up, as it might be, with bad brick, thick joints, and careless masonry, to be forthwith covered up" with rough cast. The commissioners felt the jail bore no resemblance to descriptions submitted to Congress by Mills and Noland, and "whatever may have been the intention of the commissioner and the architect, these reports were well calculated to deceive and mislead Congress in its action on this subject."[30]

Throughout the late summer and fall of 1841 while the inquiry report was working its way through the House of Representatives, Mills and Noland directed work on the buildings. In January 1842, Mills reported that "the progress made...has been commensurate with the means provided" by

29 "Reports of the Commissioners appointed to inquire into the condition of the Public Buildings, and the conduct of the Superintendents thereto," 29, 33.

30 "Reports of the Commissioners appointed to inquire into the condition of the Public Buildings, and the conduct of the Superintendents thereto," 40, 42.

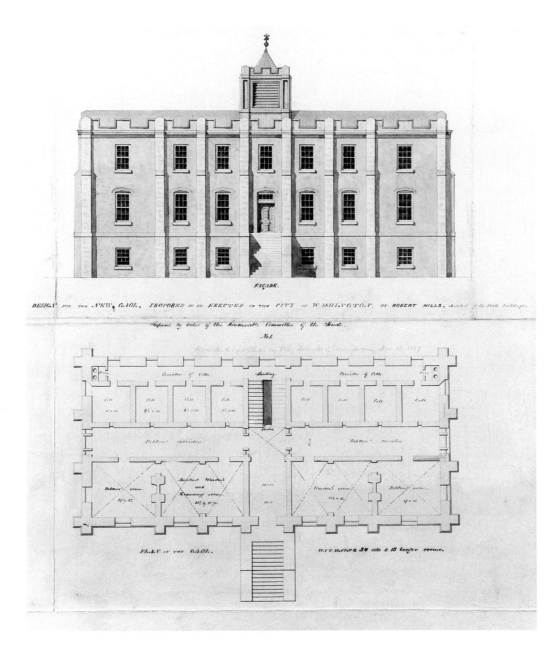

Jail, Washington, D.C. Robert Mills, architect, 1839–1841.

Congress.[31] He urged completion of the Treasury Building's north and south wings to relieve its already over-crowded offices. And he fueled the ire of critically inclined Congressmen by enthusiastically describing his vision of the colonnade—"the most extensive of modern times"—and the projected enclosed courtyards and fountains. The portico of the Patent Office was complete, but work remained on its grounds and privies, and its annual appropriation was exhausted. The government collections of the South Seas Exploring Expedition managed by the National Institution for the Promotion of Science had been installed in the grand exhibition hall; the Patent Office was filling up, and Mills recommended that work on its wings should begin. He tersely noted that the jail (excepting its privies) was finished, but his description of the state of the Post Office conveys satisfaction:

> The progress made in the erection of this building, during the past season, has been very rapid. Not only has one entire story been carried up, and the whole roofed in, but the plastering throughout completed; all the windows and doors hung; the corridors, passages, and staircases paved; and a double flight of marble circular steps carried up three stories, so as to render the building fit for occupancy at the present time. Little more that two years have elapsed since the foundations were laid; and the erection of a building of such magnitude, materials, and workmanship, in so short a time, is altogether new in the annals of architecture. Great praise is due to the superintendents and contractors, for their zeal and faithfulness…few contract jobs can be found to have been executed with equal fidelity. The work throughout will compete with similar works in any country.[32]

Mills wrote as if he anticipated appropriations to finish what he had begun. Instead, the House Committee on Public Expenditures adopted the report of the inquiry commission. They concluded that "one of the great causes of extravagance in our Government is the unnecessary multiplication of offices," and since the Treasury Building, Patent Office, and Post Office were nearing completion, they proposed a bill abolishing the office of architect.[33]

Mills' response was published by the House, and it adds to our understanding of his working conditions. For example, he said the approved plans for the Treasury Building were prepared "from 9 o'clock on the 5th of July to 10 o'clock on the 6th of July, when they were laid before the President. It was

31 "Letter from the Commissioner of Public Buildings," 27th Cong., 2d Sess., Doc. 40 (January 13, 1842): 5.

32 "Letter from the Commissioner of Public Buildings," 27th Cong., 2d Sess., Doc. 40 (January 13, 1842): 8.

33 "Committee on Public Expenditures," 27th Cong., 2d Sess., Rep. No. 460 (March 29, 1842): 3.

owing to this circumstance (the insufficiency of the time to mature the plans) that the President was induced to remark, in his letter of appointment of the architect, 'in forming the plans, making proper changes therein from time to time.'" Construction was slow at first, for he had to train masons to construct the groined arches; initially "the turning of an arch took six days, whereas now it takes but three." At the Treasury Building laborers were paid by the day, and as the architect "has no direct control over the operatives" he had no control over the costs. Cost overruns were minimized at the Post Office by using contracts or basing payment on a measurement of work completed. Having observed that the architect cannot logically be held responsible for a budget unless he controls the work, Mills pointed out that many costs assigned to his projects ("grading streets, providing grates, conducting water into the buildings," or paying laborers while work was halted by Congressional order during the Walter/Parris inspection of the vaulting) should not be computed as part of the cost of the buildings. He admitted an error in addition in a table comparing the Post Office bids, but on reviewing the figures, he found it did not affect the outcome; in any case, he argued, "a discretion should be allowed to the architect to select first-rate mechanics, and he should not be compelled to take any one to do the work who happens to make the lowest offer." He concluded by appending correspondence with Noland and M. St. Clair Clarke, the President of the Board of [Inquiry] Commissioners, for all the world to see.[34]

Although forceful, his defense was futile. On July 2, 1842, he was directed to vacate his office in the basement of the Treasury Building, and his tenure as "architect of the federal buildings" was over.[35]

For the next decade he sought work and published articles, as he had in South Carolina under similar circumstances. But now he bore the stigma of the Congressional inquiry and was competing with ambitious, younger professionals, most of whom advocated new, cast-iron systems for fireproof construction. His long-standing association with southern politicians, formerly an asset, became a liability as the shadow of secession lengthened, and for the remainder of his career he received few major federal commissions.

In his search for work for the next several years Mills was rebuffed at almost every turn. To make matters worse, after forty years of architectural practice he was financially insecure. Casting about he unsuccessfully submitted a standard plan for fortified barracks to be used in the West.[36] He offered to design fireproof storage for naval charts, saying he would accept "small com-

34 Ibid., appended "Memorial of Robert Mills of injustice done him in the report of the Commissioners on Public Buildings" (May 10, 1842): 8, 12, 2, 9.

35 Evelyn, 121, in Bryan, ed., Robert Mills, Architect; also see Liscombe, *Altogether American*, 236.

36 PRM 6089; Liscombe, 240–241.

Washington National
Monument,
Washington, D.C.
Robert Mills, architect,
1845–1854. Completed
1876–1884 by Thomas
L. Casey, U.S. Army
Corps of Engineers.

pensation for any services rendered, as I am at present out of employment...
destitute of means to support my family."[37] He wrote he would direct the construction of marine hospitals "at half what was formerly paid me...I am suffer-
ing for want of employment."[38] His government commissions, in the period
between 1842 and 1845, were all small—up-grading heating and plumbing and
minor re-modeling at the President's House and Capitol. Even these jobs were
only sporadically available and paid poorly. He protested on being offered $25
for work for the House Naval Affairs Committee when Walter had been paid
$1,000 for "his opinion of the stability of certain Public Buildings...not a weeks
labors." And Parris had received $300 "for a day or twos work on the same busi-
ness." His letter to Henry A. Wise, chairman of the committee, sadly reiterates
points made to Benjamin Chew at the outset of his career—that "the regular
charge of the profession [should be] 2 $\frac{1}{2}$ per ct. on the estimate" and "the
expense of educating an architect, is equal to that of any other profession" and
"you, as a lawyer, would think yourself poorly paid by receiving such a fee."[39]
The Mobile (1842–1849) and Key West (1844) marine hospitals were his major
federal commissions during this period. Throughout the decade, along with
William Strickland and William Parker Elliot, he pursued the possibility of a
fireproof building for the War and Navy departments, but it was never funded.

Prospects brightened in 1845 when the Washington National Monument
Society adopted Mills' design. The society was formed in 1833 by citizens dissatisfied with Greenough's statue and chagrined that earlier resolutions by
Congress for a monument had produced nothing. They hoped to raise a million
dollars—with contributions limited to one dollar per donor—and create a truly
national monument, "whose dimensions and magnificence shall be commensurate with the greatness and gratitude of the nation." Predictably, the money came
in slowly. After five years, they had received circa $31,000 and advertised for
designs. On June 6, 1837, they passed a resolution thanking John McClelland and
E. Barame from Baltimore, S.M. Stone and Benne and Platte from New Haven,
and William Parker Elliot and Robert Mills from Washington, but they did not
approve any of the proposals.[40] In 1844, a subcommittee consisting of George
Watterston, William Seaton, and Peter Force was delegated to obtain a design,
and on April 26, 1845, they recommended "the plan furnished by Mr. Mills &
estimated by him to cost, when completed $200,000; with a shaft to cost $50,000
be adopted as the plan of the projected monument."[41] Their phrasing suggests
they viewed the major part of Mills' plan as the Pantheon temple base, for they

37 Liscombe, 243.

38 Liscombe, 243.

39 RM to Henry A. Wise, August 13, 1842; PRM 2384.

40 Mills left sketches and descriptions of various possible Washington Monuments, and it is probable that his initial submission bore little or no resemblance to the design approved in 1845. See PRM 1610; also see Scott, "Robert Mills and American Monuments," in Bryan, ed., *Robert Mills, Architect*, 176 n43.

41 Scott, 158.

mentioned the shaft as a secondary, separate (and more economical) element of the design. Mills' proposal was adopted by the society on November 18, 1845, and he was paid $100. Construction did not begin until the summer of 1848, but Mills must have felt his luck had changed, for although the monument did not promise a salary, now he could anticipate, rather than seek, an important project.

The society distributed detailed descriptions of the plan. The perimeter of the foundations and raised base provided accommodations for the "keepers of the Monument, or those having charge of . . . attending on visitors" and galleries and artists' studios. The interior of the foundations "may be appropriated to catacombs for the reception of the remains of such distinguished men as the nation may honor" with the center being reserved for Washington's remains "should they be removed thither." Above the raised base was "a grand circular colonnade building, 250 feet in diameter, and 100 [feet] high". It had thirty Doric columns, each twelve feet in diameter and forty-five feet high. The coat of arms of each state ornamented the frieze above the columns. A statue of Washington in a "triumphal car" flanked by "appropriate figures and trophies" surmounted the portico. Statues of the signers of the Declaration of Independence were to stand behind the columns against the outside wall of the circular temple. Inside the temple, the circular gallery was forty feet high and was broken into alcoves by projecting pilasters. These alcoves provided areas for the display of paintings, sculpture, and inscriptions. The roof of the Pantheon temple served as a "grand terrace" 700 feet in circumference. This terrace was elevated seventy-five feet above the ground and offered vistas of the city and the Potomac. (For the adventurous, there was also an outer walkway along the top of the cornice.) The obelisk was to rise through the center of the grand terrace; it was to be fifty feet square at terrace level and taper to 40 feet square with a total height of 500 feet. Bas-relief ornament and tripods embellished the base of the obelisk, but "above this the shaft is perfectly plain to within fifty feet of its summit, where a simple star is placed, emblematic of the glory which the name of Washington has attained."[42]

42 George Watterson and the Board of Managers of the Washington National Monument Society to the American People. National Archives. RG 42, Records of the Office of Public Buildings and Grounds; PRM 2455A.

Unable to raise the money to build the adopted plan, the society determined to shorten the shaft to 300 feet. And in 1848—the year the cornerstone was laid—they circulated engravings of the obelisk based on terraced steps in lieu of the Pantheon. When the federal government finished the project (1879–1884) alternative designs were discussed, but the Pantheon was not among them.

Deleting Mills' temple base changed the meaning of the monument. The round temple was intended to be a repository of patriotic icons; it was designed to literally surround Washington with his national historical context. Today the unadorned obelisk is popularly known as the Washington Monument—not the Washington *National* Monument—and the modern name accurately, if inadvertently, captures the consequence of the loss of Mills' Pantheon.

There are a number of possible prototypes for Mills' design. The raised base supporting a classical peripteral temple surmounted by an Egyptian obelisk appeared in Comte de Caylus' reconstruction of the mausoleum of Halicarnassus and in the "Monument to be Raised on the Ruins of the Bastille" by Jean Molinos and Jacques Le Grand.[43] Comte de Caylus shows a "triumphal car" or chariot on top of the mausoleum's obelisk (as Mills had suggested for the Baltimore Washington Monument and the pediment of the Capitol, as well as for the entrance of the National Monument) and depicts figural sculpture behind the colonnade. European sources apparently provided details, but the massing, the juxtaposition of an horizontal architectural base and a soaring vertical monument, resembles Latrobe's design for the lighthouse for Frank's Island, Mississippi.

Whatever the sources, Mills and the managers of the society meant for the monument to be unique in size. They wanted it to "surpass every other in the world in elevation and the grandeur of its proportions." They associated height with emotional impact and said the monument would be a "massive and sublime pile, as it rises to the clouds," like Washington himself "who stands alone in the annals of the world 'without a model and without a shadow.'" The evocative link between height, mass and meaning was reiterated by R.C. Winthrop in his address at the cornerstone-laying ceremony: "Build it to the skies; you cannot outreach the loftiness of his principles! Found it upon the massive and eternal rock: you cannot make it more enduring than his fame!" Winthrop also emphasized the *national* implications of the whole undertaking:

> Let the column which we are about to construct, be at once a pledge and an emblem of perpetual union! Let the foundations be laid, let the superstructure be built up and cemented, let each stone be raised and riveted, in a spirit of national brotherhood! And may the earliest ray of the rising sun—till that sun shall set no more—draw forth from it daily...a strain of national harmony, which shall strike a responsive chord in every heart throughout the Republic![44]

43 Scott, 161–162, figs. 5.13 and 5.14.

44 George Watterson to the People of the United States. National Archives, RG 42, Records of the Office of Public Buildings and Grounds, 1845–1848; PRM 2454.

45 Rippy, 177–178. The description is quoted in James F. O'Gorman, et. al., *Drawing Toward Building, Philadelphia Architectural Graphics, 1732–1986* (University of Pennsylvania Press, 1986), 84–85, entry 30 by Jeffery A. Cohen. For details on the dome see RM to Joel R. Poinsett, June, 1839, PRM 1890, and Joseph G. Totten to Richard Delafield, June 15, 1839, PRM 1897.

46 Poinsett was also largely responsible for the formation of the Topographical Engineers, the civil engineers, largely trained at West Point, who came to dominate federal construction in the 1850s. Colonel Joseph G. Totten of the Army Corps of Engineers, and Col. J.J. Abert, of the Topographical Engineers, joined Poinsett as founders of the National Institute. Dupree, 70–71; also see Albert E. Cowdrey, *A City for the Nation, The Army Engineers and the Building of Washington, D.C., 1790–1967* (Washington: U.S. Government Printing Office, 1978), 20. James Smithson, an English scientist and the illegitimate son of the Duke of Northumberland, died in Italy in 1829. He left his estate in trust to a nephew, who died without issue in 1835. Anticipating this possibility, Smithson's will provided that if the nephew had no heirs the balance of the estate (which proved to be

While Mills waited for the society to raise sufficient funds to begin construction, he obtained two additional, notable private commissions. He typically played an early, formative design role in the major construction in Washington, circa 1836–1850, and his major projects were usually finished by others. This happened with the Treasury Building, the Patent Office, the General Post Office, and the Washington National Monument, and the pattern held true for the Smithsonian Institution as well.

The earliest plans for the Smithsonian stemmed from a Library and Observatory building Mills designed for the U.S. Military Academy at West Point in 1839. Joel R. Poinsett, who directed the Internal Improvements program when Mills returned to South Carolina in 1820, was Secretary of War (1836–1841) in the Van Buren administration. To improve facilities at West Point, he obtained plans from the superintendent of the academy, Major Richard Delafield, and others—including Mills. Poinsett apparently asked Mills to revise Delafield's plans. The resulting plan called for "a stone structure, 160 feet front and 78 feet in depth, castellated and corniced with red sandstone, in the Elizabethan style....The east wing contains the Library....The offices of the Superintendent, Adjutant, Quartermaster, and Treasurer of the Academy occupy the first floor of the west wing, while above them are the Lecture Hall and apparatus of the Philosophical Department [laboratories]. The Equatorial Telescope, in a circular dome twenty-seven feet in diameter, surmounts the whole, while the Mural Circle occupies a similar tower in the northwest angle." The ogival dome was to be framed in iron, sheathed with copper or zinc, and would rotate on ball bearings to accommodate the telescope.[45]

While the West Point building was under construction, Poinsett was lobbying for Congressional designation of the new National Institute for the Promotion of Science, a private, Washington-based learned society, as the agent and beneficiary of the Smithson bequest.[46] Poinsett was a creator of the National Institute and served as its first director. Mills was a founding member. Addressing their first annual meeting in 1841, Poinsett advocated combining the institute with the still-to-be defined Smithsonian Institution. National Institute members, Senators Lewis F. Linn of Missouri and William C. Preston of South Carolina, then introduced bills to establish the Smithsonian, incorporate the National Institute and authorize the Institute to manage Smithsonian funds and use a portion of the bequest to erect one building for both organizations. The building was to be a repository for all federally owned collections,

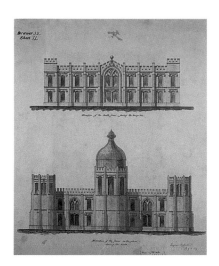

Library and Science Building, U.S. Military Academy, West Point, New York. "Elevation of the South Front" and "Elevation of the front . . . facing the North." Robert Mills, architect, 1839.

works of art, books, and "curiosities" not germane to the duties of other agencies or departments.[47]

Poinsett asked Mills for a design to use in the deliberations, and Mills turned to the new West Point building, which—besides being recent—was his largest educational building. Its dome contained an observatory, and John Quincy Adams was pressing the idea of creating a national observatory with the Smithson bequest.[48] The towers at West Point contained staircases, which left the interior library and classrooms uninterrupted (Mills had earlier employed projecting stairs adjacent to the Caroliniana Library reading room and the grand model hall in the Patent Office). This also seemed desirable for the proposed Smithsonian. The Smithsonian, like West Point, needed laboratories, lecture halls, and offices. Finally, the Elizabethan or Norman Style was associated with institutions of higher learning—Oxford and Cambridge—and this seemed doubly appropriate given James Smithson's background.

Mills added several features specifically designed for the Smithsonian. There were greenhouses along the facade for botanical collections, and he pointed out that the buttresses on the exterior wall, which countered the thrust of the fireproof groined vaults, extended into the interior where they formed thirty-six alcoves, "one allotted to each state in the union, for the reception of subjects of natural history &c."[49]

He sent four drawings and an essay to Poinsett. He said the building should be located between 7th and 12th streets where there was ample open ground for a botanical garden and an agricultural area devoted to "the propagation of useful and ornamental trees, native and foreign." He laid out the garden in "serpentine and in picturesque divisions" with fountains and irrigation fed by the adjacent canal ". . . within this space a continual variation of the scene

$508,318.46) was to be given to the United States government to create an institution for "the increase and diffusion of knowledge among men." The English probate process took two years, and then Congress weighed what to do with the money for eight more years. Webster P. True, *The First Hundred Years of the Smithsonian Institution, 1846–1946* (Washington, 1946), 1–4.

47 George Brown Goode, ed., *The Smithsonian Institution, 1846–1896, The History of its First Half Century* (Washington, 1897), 41.

48 Hafertepe, 15.

49 RM to JRP, February 23, 1841, PRM 2179. Had they been developed, the state-based "natural history" alcoves at the Smithsonian would have been matched down the Mall by "history" alcoves in the Washington National Monument. Designing libraries, Mills had used Jefferson's idea of housing different types of subject matter in separate alcoves.

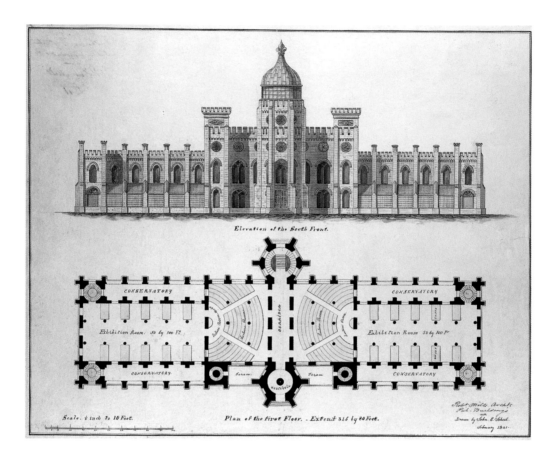

"Elevation of the South Front" and "Plan of the First Floor," proposal for the Smithsonian Institution. Robert Mills, 1841.

might be preserved for several miles. By means of groups and vistas of trees picturesque views may be obtained of the various buildings and such other objects as may be of a monumental character and thus there would be an attraction introduced which would draw many of our citizens and strangers to part take of the pleasure of promenading here." The landscape plan incorporated Poinsett's interest in botany, a desire expressed in Congress to use the Smithson bequest to support agriculture and horticulture, the growing popularity of Picturesque landscape design, and the possibility of realizing L'Enfant's hope of placing major public monuments on the Mall. The plan also anticipated Andrew Jackson Downing's Picturesque design for the Mall (1851), and may have reflected an awareness that George Washington, among others, had suggested the creation of a botanical garden in the capital.[50]

But Congress moved slowly, and before anything was done Poinsett resigned and returned to South Carolina. Without his guidance the National Institute languished. Desultory debate about the Smithson bequest dragged on in Congress, and Mills watched from the sidelines for an opportunity.

The act establishing the Smithsonian Institution was finally signed by President James K. Polk on August 10, 1846.[51] Robert Dale Owen of Indiana, who worked to pass the legislation, served on the initial Board of Regents, and without delay he sought Mills' advice about an appropriate plan. Mills wrote to him at length about the Norman or Saxon Style and sent some of the drawings prepared earlier for Poinsett. Robert Dale Owen forwarded Mills' material to his brother, David Dale Owen, a scientist. Robert Dale Owen praised parts of Mills' plans—"Tower staircases, permitting, on the second floor, a museum or exhibition room…without interruption, the entire length of the building." He also endorsed the choice of architectural style, viewing "the Anglo-Saxon style, a selection which seem[s] to me judicious, as being solid, imposing, & probably the most economical among ornamental styles." But he also told his brother, whom he asked to provide preliminary plans for the Smithsonian based on Mills' ideas: "My chief inducement to apply to you in preference to a regular bred architect, is that I know you will consult utility first, in the various internal arrangements, and let architectural elegance follow as a secondary, though not unimportant, consideration."[52]

David Dale Owen's design projected a building much larger than Mills', and although he altered many of the details, he retained major features, including the tower stairs and uninterrupted exhibition hall and library, and greenhouses. He endorsed the Norman Style (and like Mills, showed his research by citing books and buildings and making distinctions) and felt "that the exterior, when completed, will present an appearance at once picturesque, imposing and substantial."[53] Robert Dale Owen then had Mills review and comment on David Dale Owen's plan, and Mills prepared a closely reasoned response. He had reason to anticipate the commission.[54]

In September 1846, the Board of Regents formed a subcommittee to select an architect. Using the plans and criteria drafted by Mills and David Dale Owen as a design program, the subcommittee sought proposals from other architects. Plans were solicited from or submitted by Isaiah Rogers, John

50 Scott, "Robert Mills Design for the Mall, Washington, D.C.", in O'Gorman, 87–88.

51 Congressmen from the Deep South voted against creating the Smithsonian by a margin of forty-two to six. Those from the North voted in favor by a margin of forty-eight to thirteen. The western and border states were more evenly divided, voting in favor by a margin of thirty-one to twenty-six. Congressmen from the South were increasingly resistant to anything which added luster to the federal government. Poinsett, who helped Mills over a period of twenty-five years, was one of the last influential southern politicians to rise above sectional interests. He applauded Mills' association with federal projects, and with his departure in 1841 Mills lost his last powerful advocate. See: Hafertepe, 16–17, and JRP to RM, February 14, 1849, PRM 2597.

52 RDO to DDO, August 15, 1845, PRM 2472.

53 DDO to RDO, October 10, 1845, PRM 2475B.

54 RM to RDO, n.d. [1845], PRM 2455B.

Picturesque View of the Building,
and Grounds in front.

TOP:

"Picturesque View of
the Building," proposal
for the Smithsonian
Institution. Robert
Mills, 1841. National
Archives

BOTTOM:

Plan "No. 2." For
the Mall adjacent the
proposed Smithsonian
Institution. Robert
Mills, 1841.

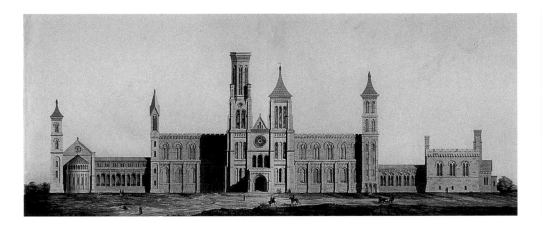

Smithsonian Institution, Washington, D.C. James Renwick, architect, 1846–1851. Robert Mills, supervising architect, 1847–1849.

Notman, Thomas U. Walter, William Strickland, John Haviland, Richard Upjohn, Owen G. Warren, Joseph Wells and David Arnot, James Renwick, Jr., Ammi B. Young, Henry Walters, and Howard Daniels. The choices available to the subcommittee demonstrated the growth of the architectural profession; their decision to award the commission to James Renwick, Jr., however, may have been based on an appeal by James Renwick, Sr., to two of the Regents, Alexander Dallas Bache and Joseph G. Totten.[55] Mills worked from February 1847 through March 1848, at a salary of $83.33 per month, as supervising architect overseeing the initial construction of Renwick's Smithsonian.[56]

In hindsight, the Smithsonian competition showed that Mills' draftsmanship was outmoded. His drawings, although often meticulous, were rarely evocative. He had always drawn primarily to convey information, and as the profession became more competitive, compelling presentation drawings became more and more important. Mills typically presented subjects at right angles to the picture plane; he rarely used raking light to throw forms into relief; he almost never put figures in the foreground to establish scale and give a sense of animation. Unlike Latrobe, Mills rarely sketched or painted for pleasure. He knew his limitations and seldom attempted perspective; indeed, in 1853, Montgomery C. Meigs, engineer of the U.S. Capitol, advised Jefferson Davis not to hire Mills, for "as a draftsman Mr. Mills was tried in the Engineers office & not found qualified."[57]

55 Hafertepe, 28–29.

56 Liscombe, *Altogether American*, 256–257.

57 An annotation signed "MC Meigs, Capit Engr." On the back of RM to JD, September 12, 1853, Office of the Architect of the U.S. Capitol.

58 Anon., *A History of the Public Buildings under the Control of the Treasury Department* (Washington: Government Printing Office, 1901), 87. Also see William Winder to Robert J. Walker, July, 1848 (?), PRM 2650B. Winder leased the building for $175 per room per year; tenants included the Navy and War departments, the Bureau of Topographical Engineers and other offices. Winder notified the government he was going to increase the rent by almost thirty percent in 1854 when the initial lease expired. This convinced the government to purchase the building for $200,000.

59 "The Winder Building," 33rd Cong., 1st Sess., House of Representatives Rep. No 193 (June 13, 1854): 19; PRM 7065. For Mills' certification of construction see RM and U Ward, February 17, 1849, PRM 2599.

60 "The Winder Building," 33rd Cong., 1st Sess., House of Representatives Rep. No 193 (June 13, 1854): 11. Willian Archer, a Washington builder and self-proclaimed architect, writing to accuse Mills of fraud (see the discussion of the Patent Office wings below), singles out the Winder building along with the Treasury building and Patent Office: William Archer to Alexander H.H. Stuart, February 21, 1851; PRM 2824.

Circumstantial evidence suggests that the Winder Building (1848) was Mills' third major private commission after the Congressional inquiry. The four-story office building is in the form of an L with a 209 foot facade facing G Street and an 101 foot facade fronting 17th Street; both wings are fifty-three feet deep. Above the basement it contains 130 rooms, exactly the number of offices in the Treasury building. The Winder Building is wholly fireproof, "the floors being carried on brick arches sprung from iron beams about 8 feet apart. The corridors have barrel arches sprung from partition walls."[58] It is reputed to be the first complete building in Washington to use cast iron beams to carry masonry arches, and this was the system of fireproof construction that would replace masonry vaulting during the second half of the nineteenth century. The new system was introduced to Washington by James Renwick, Jr., at the Smithsonian, but the Regents balked at the cost and initially limited fireproofing to the central portion of the building. At the Winder Building "in addition to the very great number of girders visible, exceeding a ton each, there are great numbers buried in the walls over the windows. At the corners of the building, and at all the cross-walls of the rooms, at every few rows of bricks are wrought-iron ties, bracing the building strongly together."[59]

William H. Winder erected the building to lease to the government when it became clear that appropriations for fireproof offices were unlikely. It was a utilitarian, speculative project with brick exterior walls covered with mastic cement and just enough detailing to echo the tripartite, Italianate style of Mills' General Post Office. When construction was complete, Mills certified the quality of the work for Winder, and several years later when Winder began negotiations to sell the building, Mills appraised it by comparing the cost per room ($2,000) with the per room cost of the more lavish Treasury building ($4,923) and the General Post Office ($5,844). Nobody received public credit as the architect of the Winder Building. Perhaps the developer and Mills, who was still controversial, agreed Mills should keep a low profile, for it was clear from the outset that the War and Navy departments would be the primary tenants. Thomas U. Walter, who had reviewed Mills' work during the Congressional inquiry, was asked to inspect the Winder Building prior to the sale. Finding nothing amiss, he offered a terse compliment: "I have examined the building.... I have only to say, that I believe it to be a substantial, well-built house."[60] Walter was already at odds with Mills, and his brevity is suggestive.

Winder Building, Washington, D.C. Attributed to Robert Mills, architect, 1848.

With the Winder Building and Smithsonian under construction, Mills met with the Board of Managers of the Washington National Monument to participate in plans for a cornerstone-laying ceremony scheduled for July 4, 1848. Confronted with breaking ground, the enormity of the design and the difficulty of raising money, the Board decided to scale back the proposal rather than leave it "unfinished, and in a few years, fall into ruin, a monument of indescretion [sic] of those who undertook to rear it." They asked Mills and Renwick, to prepare estimates for a "Monument, 300 feet high, with the Temple or Pantheon, according to the present design." Mills and Renwick reported the probable cost of six obelisks ranging in height from 330 to 500 feet all with Pantheon bases of various diameters; they also suggested an alternative might be to "raise the base of the obelisk on a flight of massive steps (as shown in plan No 2)" and build the Pantheon later when funds were available. But they did not intend to abandon the base, for they suggested making its symbolic ornament more emphatically American. They also proposed sharpening the apex of the obelisk.[61] July 4th arrived before any final decision was made on the design, and the monument—like all of Mills' big federal projects—began without an agreed upon budget or detailed plan.

By all accounts the corner-stone ceremony was a grand affair. "Great multitudes" came on special trains. The Mall, Pennsylvania Avenue, the Patent Office, and the President's House were crowded with people waiting for the great work to begin. Bleachers and grandstands framed the excavation. Vendors set up tents and awnings on the Mall. Down Pennsylvania Avenue came dignitaries in carriages: the President and his cabinet, then prancing cavalry units, infantry in ranks and military bands, volunteer militia companies from Washington and Baltimore and Boston, twenty odd fire companies with gleaming engines, benevolent and fraternal orders—the Independent Order of Odd Fellows, the Freemen's Vigilant Total Abstinence Society, the Sons of Temperance, the Junior Brothers of Temperance, Knights of Temperance, the German Benevolent Society, the Young Men's Baltimore Delegation—more bands and members of Congress. The procession was said to stretch a mile and a half. Near the end in a carriage by himself was the architect with the box of memorabilia for the recess in the cornerstone.[62]

In the box were several images in various mediums of Mills' design for the Monument-lithographs, a medallion, and an electrotype. His *Guide to the Capitol* was among the many publications, and he was listed as Architect on the

61 Minutes of Meetings, Washington National Monument Society, February 22, 1848; PRM 2515; see also PRM 2523, 2525, and 2527.

62 *National Intelligencer*, July 6, 1848; PRM 2545.

copperplate that sealed the box in place. Given the recent past, he must have basked in the ceremony and put aside concerns about funding for the project and his own financial problems. But even in this bright scene the specter of sectionalism must have crossed Mills' mind like a cloud-shadow, for the box contained newspapers from across the nation, with "articles relative to General Washington or the erection of the proposed National Monument." There were thirteen newspapers from New York, thirteen from Ohio, twelve from Pennsylvania, five each from Massachusetts and Maryland, four each from Virginia, the District of Columbia, and Alabama, three from Mississippi, two each from Kentucky, North Carolina and Georgia. There was one from Connecticut and another one from Florida. But there were no newspapers from South Carolina. And the principal speech of the day, by Robert C. Winthrop of Massachusetts, articulated the Unionist sentiments Mills' Pantheon was meant to convey:

> The heart of Washington was the union of the States; and no opportunity was ever omitted by him, to impress upon his fellow citizens the profound sense which he entertained of its vital importance at once to their prosperity and their liberty....The Union, the Union in any event, was thus the sentiment of Washington. The Union, the Union in any event, let it be our sentiment this day![63]

The Winder Building, the Smithsonian, and the Washington National Monument signaled a renewal of construction in the capital, and Mills' participation must have been helpful as he tried to re-establish himself as "architect of the public buildings." Throughout the 1840s, he had never stopped trying to obtain federal work. On the contrary, he remained pro-active, never waiting for projects to be advertised. Instead, he offered suggestions and sketches to individuals and committees whenever he sensed a need or learned construction was being considered. To Poinsett, for example, in 1841 he had proposed the addition of short wings to the Patent Office to house the National Institute for the Promotion of Science before the Smithsonian was established. Mills' proposal to add short wings (seventy by ninety feet) to the Patent Office was forwarded to Congress by the patent commissioner in 1845, and for the next several years appropriations were requested. Congressional authorization was triggered in 1849 by the need to provide accommodations for the newly created Department

63 Frederick L. Harvey, *History of the Washington National Monument and of the Washington National Monument Society* (Washington: Norman T. Elliott, 1902), 130–37.

of the Interior, but Congress only appropriated $50,000 to be used "towards the erection of wings...according to the original plan...to be done by contract, in the same manner as...the General Post Office."[64]

Thomas Ewing, the newly appointed head of the Department of the Interior, promptly hired Mills, and Mills advertised for bids, asking that proposals be returned to the "Office of Architect and Superintendent of Public Buildings." Mills' use of the title was unauthorized, for he was hired to direct construction; no provision had been made for defining the plan or acquiring drawings. Ewing's clerk pointed out that the law which had abolished the office of the architect in 1843 prohibited paying for architectural services without explicit legislative authorization. An administrative review resulted in withdrawing the advertisements and re-issuing them, directing applicants to contact the commissioner of public buildings, Ignatius W. Mudd. The review also produced a precise job description for Mills—he was the "Superintendent of the erection of the wings of the Patent Office building" and was to submit all documents to the Commissioner of Public Buildings or the Secretary of the Interior for approval.

Ewing and Mills were immediately faced with several interrelated problems. First, the legislation failed to specify which plan was to be used (the 1836 Town and Elliott plan, or the 1841–1845 alternative by Mills with truncated wings). Secondly, no matter which plan was adopted, the $50,000 appropriation was obviously inadequate; and finally, the competition for space between the Patent Office and the new Department of the Interior was complicated by the fact that the Patent Fund—fees collected from patent applicants—had subsidized construction of the Patent Office, so patent holders and the scientific community felt the building should not be diverted to other uses. Ewing decided the "original plan" cited in the legislation meant the 1836 proposal which occupied the full block, so he directed Mills to lay foundations for two wings, 290 feet long and seventy feet deep. When money ran out, they continued work by issuing notes to contractors and laborers who relied on Congress to provide compensation with a deficiency appropriation. Although risky, these administrative decisions got the project underway, but the competition for space proved to be more intractable.

Ewing decided the interior of the east wing should be divided into offices for the Department of the Interior. It would be three stories high above the basement, all groin-vaulted masonry and fireproof. The west wing, adjacent to

64 Evelyn, "the Washington Years: the U.S. Patent Office," in Bryan, ed., *Robert Mills, Architect,* 122.

existing Patent Office exhibition spaces, would consist of two large open halls for the display of models and works of art. Mills drafted plans accordingly, and foundations for both wings were laid during the first building season. In June it became clear that the appropriation would be exhausted before Congress convened again, and Ewing halted work on the west wing and focused on the east wing, for he thought fireproof offices took precedence over the immediate need for galleries and storage for models.

While debating the deficiency bill, senators criticized Ewing and Mills for initiating the larger, more expensive version of the plan and using deficit financing. Their debate aroused William Archer, a local builder who had criticized Mills during the inquiry of 1838. Archer wrote a flurry of letters to members of Congress and other officials, accusing Mills of deception, fraud, and embezzlement. William Parker Elliot joined in, criticizing Ewing and Mills in the nationally distributed *Scientific American*. Elliot presented himself as designer of the building and spokesman for patent applicants. He said the Patent Office should be reserved for its original purpose and called the intrusion of the Department of the Interior, "the greatest outrage ever perpetrated against the interests and feeling of the inventive community" and an act of "Gothic pillage." His criticism was illustrated with the interior plans he claimed had been approved in 1836.[65] Mills published a response noting that he had always credited the "outline and architectural order used" to "the original inventors, or designers," but said no interior plans ever "came into my possession even to this day (fifteen years). I was compelled, de novo, to form a plan of my own conception." He recounted the construction, but never mentioned the Congressional inquiry or the criticism put forward by Walter and Parris, and closed by observing that he "was gratified in finding the accommodations proved satisfactory to the government" and said he felt some credit was due to him as the "practical architect."[66]

Congress approved the deficiency appropriation, and work proceeded on the wings of the Patent Office. To an outsider, the controversy seemed to have passed without consequence. But Mills was troubled, for the adverse publicity coincided with the competition for the enlargement of the U.S. Capitol, and he knew how little it took to tip the scales when a big commission hung in the balance.

Mills' career in Washington had begun in the House of Representatives as he sat in the balcony watching George McDuffie deliver his proposals to the Speaker. His career would end with the competition for the extension of the Capitol. Mills' involvement with the Capitol spanned a longer period than his

65 William Archer and Alexander Rutherford to Daniel S. Dickinson, April 6, 1850; PRM 2732. See also WA to Alexander H.H. Stuart, January 14, 1851; PRM 2811; and WA to William Easby, March 26, 1851; PRM 2829; and WA to [Alexander H.H. Stuart], August 30, 1852; PRM 3002A. For articles attributed to W.P. Elliot, see *Scientific American* 6 (February 1, 1851): 156–157; PRM 2818, and (February 8, 1851): 165; PRM 2821.

66 RM to Editors, *Scientific American* 6 (August 23, 1851): 387; PRM 2919. See also RM to Editors, *Scientific American* 7 (October 1851): 30; PRM 2932B.

67 WS to J.J. Abert, April 22, 1844, transcribed in Gilchrist, 104–105; also see James M. Goode, 42–43, and Liscombe, *Altogether American*, 243.

68 RM to Senate Committee on Public Buildings and Ground, April 8, 1846; PRM 2489A, 5, 12.

69 J.M. Goode, 44–45. Also see: Homer T. Rosenberger, "Thomas Ustick Walter and the Completion of the United States Capitol," *Records of the Columbia Historical Society* 50 (1952): 279, for selected data from Daniel Webster's table of statistics on the growth of the nation which necessitated enlargement of the Capitol.

association with any other building. He had undertaken a series of remodeling and up-fitting projects at the Capitol during the 1830s and responded quickly when a proposal for an additional wing to provide a larger House of Representatives, archival storage, and office space, was made in 1844 by Col. John J. Abert, of the U.S. Army Topographical Engineers. Working with William Strickland, Abert explored the possibility of remodeling the existing Library of Congress to accommodate the House. Mills suggested lowering the ceiling of the House to improve the acoustics and proposed placing a library between the new ceiling and the dome.[67] He also developed several plans, submitted in 1846, predicated on extending the east wing to balance the west wing, and these plans showed a lower dome for the House (thirty-five feet instead of the existing sixty) to match the French Chamber of Deputies, which was reputed to have superb acoustics. He said his plan provided a new House, "with its Officers' and Committee rooms attached," a new Senate Chamber "also with its officers and committee rooms annexed," a new Library located in the existing House of Representatives, and a new Supreme Court room located in the existing Senate. The Rotunda was at the center of this plan, a hub or common lobby, a true "Hall of the People." The dome was to be altered to light the Rotunda, but other than saying it had "disfigured the building externally ever since its erection," he did not describe its altered profile.[68]

At mid-century, several factors prompted Congress to consider enlarging, rather than remodeling, the Capitol. In 1849, architect Charles B. Cluskey surveyed the Capitol and other federal buildings for the House Committee on Public Buildings. He pointed out the need for renovations, but to provide space for the growing numbers of Representatives, Senators, and staff personnel, he suggested adding wings on the north and south, or an extension to the east. The political climate breathed life into Cluskey's recommendations: the Nashville convention (where states' rights advocates from across the South convened for the first time to foment secession) ended peacefully on June 12, 1850. This was followed by passage (September 20, 1850) of the final element of the Compromise of 1850. Both events underscored the value of symbols of unity, and on September 25, 1850, the Senate Committee on Public Buildings, led by Jefferson Davis, was authorized to advertise a design competition for the enlargement of the Capitol. In addition to the Senate's decision to seek designs, Congress approved an initial $100,000 for the work and complicated the ensuing competition(s) by authorizing the President to select a design.[69]

"Proposed Improvements in the Hall of Representatives." Robert Mills, 1844.

There was little support for this plan, and Mills prepared other options. He suggested duplicating the Capitol 300 feet to the east and developing a square courtyard by erecting "buildings of communication," or offices, which would frame the courtyard on the north and south and link the new and old Capitols. Another alternative consisted of adding wings to the north and south of the existing Capitol. Here, to balance the extended facade, he suggested a more monumental dome (210 feet high instead of the existing seventy feet), based on "St. Peter's Church at Rome, St. Paul's, London, the Church of the Invalids, Paris." In presenting this latter plan to the Senate, Jefferson Davis' committee noted it was "originally suggested by the topographical bureau, but altered by Mr. Robert Mills."[70]

Instead of endorsing any of Mills' plans, the Senate authorized Davis to hold a competition. (The Senate competition is known as the competition of 1850; the President's subsequent competition is called the competition of 1851.) The 1850 competition attracted numerous applicants including Charles B. Cluskey (who had settled in Washington), Charles F. Anderson (New York), Ammi B. Young (Boston), Col. John J. Abert (Washington), John Billings (Hartford), James King (Washington), Thomas McClelland (Alexandria), Cyrus W. Warner (New York), Frank W. Vodges (St. Louis), T.J. Hilton (Washington), William Parker Elliot (Washington), Thomas U. Walter (Philadelphia), and Mills. The Senate committee divided the $500 prize unevenly among five of the competitors and directed Mills to prepare a new plan, a synthesis incorporating the features that must have appealed to the committee.[71] Mills' synthesis showed the House in a new wing to the north, the Senate in a new wing to the south, the Library in an extended east wing, and an elevated central dome (albeit not the profile Mills had suggested) flanked by prominent secondary domes over the House and Senate. Whatever the merits of the synthesis' interior plan, its elevations lack the unity of Mills' major buildings. The emphatic elements—domes, circular colonnades and the dramatic, repeated juxtaposition of recessed and projecting forms—are not characteristic of Mills' work and probably reflect the influence of the committee.

While the Senate competition was underway, in addition to the Patent Office wings, Mills was working on several projects. He had submitted (January 8, 1850) a design for a Washington Monument to be erected in Richmond, and although Thomas G. Crawford won the commission, Mills was retained to design the base. It was an unhappy collaboration, for Mills persisted in trying to erect a column or make the base large and elaborate. Crawford protested, and

70 Liscombe, 275–276.

71 J.M. Goode, 62 n8. The records of the Senate 1850 competition are incomplete, but the winners were: William Parker Elliot ($125), Philip Harry ($125), Charles F. Anderson ($100), Thomas McClelland ($50) and Robert Mills ($100). Goode, 46.

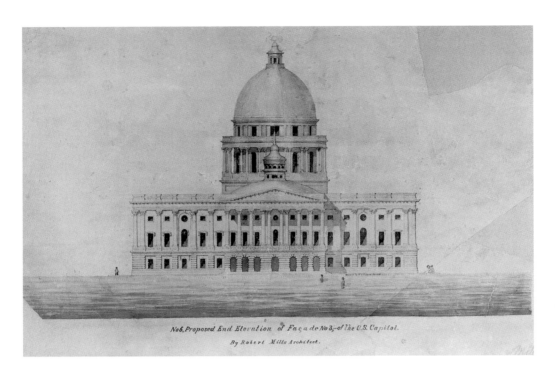

No.6. Proposed End Elevation of Façade No 3,- of the U.S. Capitol.

By Robert Mills Architect.

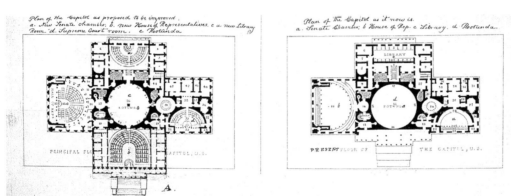

TOP: *"No. 6 Proposed End Elevation of Façade No. 3, of the U.S. Capitol." Robert Mills, architect, 1850.*

BOTTOM: *"Plan of the Capitol as proposed to be improved" and "Plan of the Capitol as it now is . . ." Robert Mills, 1846.*

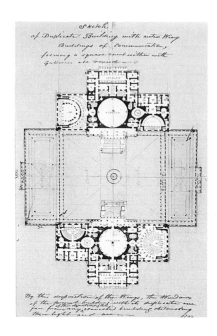

U.S. Capitol with "Duplicate Building with outer Wing Buildings of Communication forming a Square." Robert Mills, 1850.

Mills was terminated in October 1852.[72] He also tried unsuccessfully to obtain a commission for a customhouse to be built in San Francisco and wrote Thomas Corwin, Secretary of the Treasury, suggesting the use of rammed earth, *pise de terre*. Claiming the technique was suited to the climate, economical, and durable, Mills cited Rondelet and quoted Pliny. He must have known the technique first-hand, for it was used in South Carolina by William Wallace Anderson in the 1820s at the Borough House in Stateburg.[73] But the unusual technique did not interest the Secretary, and Thomas U. Walter won the commission.[74]

Mills' last major building, a multi-functional annex for Jefferson's Rotunda at the University of Virginia, was designed at this time. On January 3, 1851, he presented plans to the building committee of the University of Virginia for a four-story brick annex (105 feet by fifty-four feet) linked to the Rotunda by a portico-like colonnade. It contained lecture halls, laboratory classrooms, and exhibition space. The budget precluded fireproof construction and the monument to Jefferson which Mills wanted to place in the north portico; nonetheless, construction went smoothly, and the building was well received when it was put into use in 1852–1853.[75]

The act authorizing the President to select a design and designate an architect meant the Senate competition was only a prelude. President Millard Fillmore and his cabinet invited applicants to attend a meeting and explain their designs on February 20, 1851. Thirteen architects are known to have entered this second competition, but from the outset the front-runners were Mills and Thomas Ustick Walter. For the next four months the architects lobbied for and amended their designs. They sought out Congressmen and cabinet members, visited individually or wrote the President, obtained letters of recommendation, and met with the House and Senate Committees on Public Buildings.

72 Liscombe, Altogether American, 271–273. Also see Crane, 342, 350.

73 Lane, 153–155. Also see RM to TC, October 18, 1850; PRM 2790 and 2791.

74 J.M. Goode, 355–356.

75 Liscombe, 282–283. Mills' library annex burned and damaged the Rotunda in 1895.

Addition to the Library of the University of Virginia. Robert Mills, architect, 1851–1852.
Lithograph, Bohn, 1853.

Walter, the winner, submitted five variations of the two plans he had entered in the Senate competition, but he did not rely on the drawings alone. His diary records how he pursued the commission.

Walter visited Washington thirteen times—spending forty-three days there—between September 28, 1850, and June 10, 1851, when he learned he had won. Before the competition began, he met with the president twice (November 24 and December 3, 1850) and twice more during the spring (two and a half hours on March 20 and another two hours on May 1, 1851). Between visits to Washington, most of his time in Philadelphia was devoted to refining his proposal.[76]

While Walter was refining and promoting his plans, Mills' situation at the Patent Office was becoming increasingly contentious and tenuous. On March 2, 1851, Ignatius W. Mudd, the commissioner of public buildings, died and was replaced by William Easby, a local lime and stone supplier who had several reasons to dislike Mills. Easby had bid unsuccessfully on contracts for both the

76 J.M. Goode, 354–358, Appendix E, "Program to Win the Competitons of 1850–1851," an abstract from the Diary of T.U.W.

Washington National Monument and the Patent Office, and Mills had rejected stone Easby supplied for the monument. In addition, Easby was a Whig and left his job at the Navy Yard when the Jacksonians swept into office. Now the Whigs were in control, and Easby was in a position of influence, and apparently he set out to even the score. A. H. H. Stuart, Secretary of the Interior, authorized Easby to conduct an investigation of the construction and administration of the Patent Office wings. Without notifying Mills, Easby fired Mills' superintendents and watchmen, demanded the construction records, and established a review committee consisting of William Parker Elliot, John Harkness, a bricklayer, and William Birth, a builder. The committee found nothing structural to criticize; nonetheless, Easby said Mills had altered specifications without authority, and—citing the same concerns that had been raised and refuted during the Congressional inquiry of 1838—he created another committee to examine Mills' vaulting system.[77]

The second committee included Ammi B. Young and Thomas U. Walter, both active competitors for the extension of the Capitol, and Robert Brown, who had been a general superintendent for Mills at the General Post Office. The second committee recommended filling in flues that ran vertically in some of the pilasters and introducing iron tie rods to minimize the lateral thrust of the arches on the third floor. While their investigation was underway, Mills learned Walter would be the architect of the Capitol extensions. Meanwhile, construction halted at the Patent Office as Mills appealed to the Secretary of the Interior, who sought an outside opinion from Army engineers. The report of General J. G. Totten (June 27, 1851) vindicated Mills by endorsing his use of iron tie rods only at the cornice line and as temporary braces at the spring of the arches while the mortar cured. But Easby persisted and, using what Mills claimed were "malevolent misrepresentations," charged that the construction documents contained troubling discrepancies. A month after the Army engineers confirmed the structural integrity of the work, Mills was fired and learned he would be replaced by Thomas U. Walter.[78]

For more than a year Mills tried to obtain a hearing. Like L'Enfant, he documented and recounted what had happened, but nobody in authority listened. With the election of Franklin Pierce in 1853, Mills rallied and tried to replace Walter. Writing directly to the President, Mills explained that former President Fillmore had approved his plan "in outline" and placed it "in the hands of another Architect to arrange the Details, who finally was appointed to carry out

77 Evelyn, 322–329.

78 A.H.H. Stuart to RM, July 29, 1851; PRM 2906. Also see: Evelyn, 320–329.

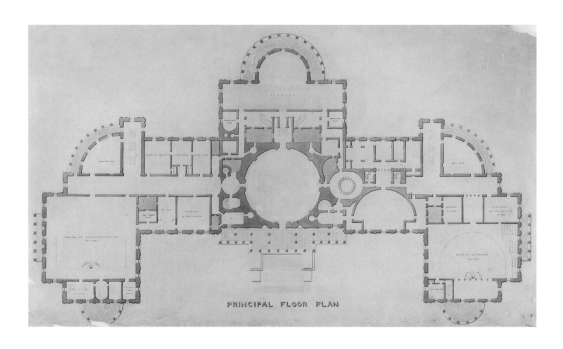

PRINCIPAL FLOOR PLAN

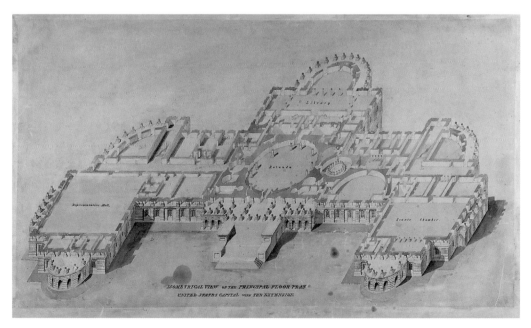

ISOMETRICAL VIEW OF THE PRINCIPAL FLOOR PLAN
UNITED STATES CAPITOL WITH THE EXTENSION.

TOP: *"Principal Floor Plan" proposed extension of the U.S. Capitol. Robert Mills, et. al., 1851.*
BOTTOM: *"Isometrical View of the Principal Floor Plan United States Capitol with Extension."*
Robert Mills, et. al., 1851.

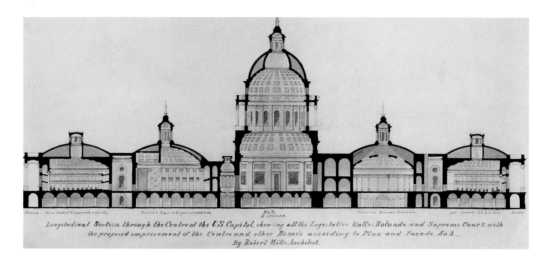

"*Longitudinal Section through the U.S. Capitol showing all the Legislative Halls, Rotunda and Supreme Court.*" *Robert Mills et al.*

79 RM to FP, March 1, 1853; PRM 3033. Also see: RM to Pendleton, March 3, 1853; PRM 3035.

80 RM to MM, April 8, 1853; PRM 3042.

81 Linn Boyd, et. al. to the President of the United States [Franklin Pierce], March 1, 1853; PRM 3032, and D.R. Atchison, et. al. to the President of the United States, March 1, 1853; PRM 3034.

82 JBF to the Secretary of the Interior, March 8, 1853; PRM 3036A.

the work."[79] Mills wrote Montgomery Meigs, the Army engineer in charge of construction at the Capitol, that his final plan for the extension was influenced by his annex for the University of Virginia Rotunda. Both projects entailed relating new construction to an historic structure, and Mills wrote that

> having just ... designed an addition or Wing to the Rotunda of the University of Virginia ... I made a new Plan [of the Capitol] by intervening an open colonnade between the Wings & the main building; this arrangement met the President's views.... It was during the period between the adoption of the Senate plan and the adoption of the Colonnade Plan by the President that I was subject to a violent persecution, the object of which, was apparent[ly] to defeat my appointment as Architect to carry out the adopted Plan for the extension of the Capitol & how well my persecutors succeeded is seen in my dismissal from the Public service.[80]

Twenty Senators and seventeen Representatives signed a letter endorsing his appointment as "Architect of the Capitol and other public buildings."[81] John B. Floyd, the governor of Virginia, wrote to the Secretary of the Interior on Mills' behalf.[82] R.W. Thompson of Indiana sent the President a long,

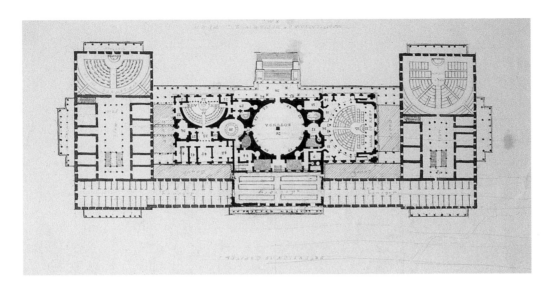

Proposed "Colonnade Plan" of the U.S. Capitol. Robert Mills, circa 1853.

closely reasoned recommendation. He began by noting Mills was "the first native born American citizen who has studied and pursued the science of architecture as a profession...that he has designed and constructed more public buildings than any man in America." And he pointed out that the Treasury building arches Walter condemned in 1838 "have not since then sprung or become dislodged to the width of a single hair." Thompson emphasized the economy of Mills' masonry vaulting by comparing the cost per square foot of nine major public buildings:

BUILDING	COST PER SQUARE FOOT
The Capitol by Latrobe	$45.15
The President's House by Hoban	$37.00
The Treasury Building by Mills	$16.00
The Patent Office (center) by Mills	$19.22
The Patent Office (east wing) by Mills	$24.50
The General Post Office by Mills	$24.18
The New York Custom House by Town	$94.07
Girard College by Walter	$118.98
The Boston Custom House by Young	$91.80

He stressed the wasteful thickness of walls designed by Walter and said that, prior to Easby's appointment, work at the Patent Office "was carried on, without murmuring or complaint from any quarter.... Mr. Mills had previously incurred the personal hatred of this officer," who "pursuant to what must have been a settled design...commenced a system of persecution against Mr. Mills, and all the workmen who had been employed under his superintendence." Thompson concluded by observing that although he was a Whig and Mills was a Democrat, "integrity and virtue are not the exclusive property of either party."[83] The new President ignored all appeals on Mills' behalf.

Mills wrote Jefferson Davis, who was then Secretary of War, asking, "if it be possible Sir to give me some professional employment at the Capitol I should be greatly obliged, for I am without the means of providing for the necessary wants of my family."[84] Davis passed the request on to Captain Montgomery Meigs, the Army engineer in charge of construction at the Capitol. Meigs reaction was the death knell of Mills' architectural career:

> There would be manifest impropriety in employing upon the Capitol...a rival of the architect who made the design & who claims the [credit] of them because there is...general likeness in the ground plan adopted by the late President to one of the many different plans submitted at various times by Mr. Mills.
>
> I have seen some of Mr. Mills working drawings of the Patent Office & I should not be willing to trust to his assistance in carrying on this work.
>
> As a draftsman Mr. Mills was tried in the Engineers office & not found qualified.
>
> MC Meigs
> Capit
> Engr[85]

83 RWT to FP, February 7, 1853; PRM 3030.

84 RM to JD, September 12, 1853, PRM 3069.

85 Meigs' comment appears on the cover of RM to Jefferson Davis, September 12, 1853; PRM 3069. See also RM to MM, April 7 and 8, 1853; PRM 3041 and 3042.

As he had done before in times of trouble, Mills turned to writing. His final spate of publications, circa 1848–1853, deal mainly with transcontinental transportation and communication. Often printed as memorials to Congress, they reflect the annexation of Texas (1845), the acquisition of Oregon (1846), the Mexican Cession (1848), the Texas Cession (1850), and the Gadsden Purchase (1853), which together expanded the size of the country by more than a third and sparked public interest in establishing overland routes to the far west.

During this period he also produced a carefully researched proposal for a municipal water system for Washington and short newspaper articles on potential applications of new technologies. With one exception (an article on architecture in Virginia) none of the late publications deal with architecture.

The "new route to the Pacific ocean, with a plan for the transportation of dispatches to Astoria in fifteen days" (1848) suggests placing a telegraph line from Laredo to the Pacific. Laredo was accessible by steamboat up the Rio Grande and "may be attained in about five days from New Orleans: the distance, then by telegraph to the California waters, would be as *naught* in mental travelling; and the steamer of the Pacific would convey the intelligence communicated by telegraph to Astoria in less than ten days."[86] He was enthusiastic about the telegraph and cited the experience of W.J. Brown, Second Assistant Postmaster General, who received a telegraph from Masillon, Ohio, dated "1 o'clock A.M., and received here long before 2 o'clock, transcription and messenger's time included." Masillon was 717 miles from Washington, and Mills observed, "This is indeed annihilation of space."[87]

The steamer-telegraph-steamer route refined ideas he had presented in his 1834 pamphlet "Substitute for Railroads and Canals...New Plan of Roadway," and he revisited the southern route again (1852) in a memorial for "a railroad and telegraphic communication with the Pacific ocean." Here he suggested a railroad route beginning in the east at Van Buren, Arkansas, crossing the mountains south of Santa Fe and terminating at San Diego. Combining potential benefits, he proposed laying a telegraph line inside hollow railroad tracks. He viewed the transcontinental railroad as a national project; therefore "no single state or people should have the control of its operations, it must be the joint stock of all the states expressed through the act of the general government." To finance construction he proposed the same idea he had offered for canals in South Carolina; after the work was done, the government would recoup its investment by selling abutting land made valuable by improved transportation.[88]

In 1826 he had proposed an elevated monorail for the delivery of the mail from Washington to New Orleans, and he returned to this idea in 1853 with a plan published in the *Scientific American* for a suspended, steam-driven train capable of speeds of 100 miles per hour. If "it is wished to combine architectural effect with this construction, the space between the posts or pillars, under the rail, may be arched, and while thereby strengthening the mass, will give them the effect of a continuous arcade." The elevated track would also "furnish the

86 "Memorial of Robert Mills Respecting a new route to the Pacific ocean, with a plan for the transportation of despatches to Astoria in fifteen days," February 15, 1848, 30th Cong., 1st Sess., Senate, No. 51, 5.

87 "Memorial of Robert Mills Respecting a new route to the Pacific ocean...," 7.

88 "Memorial of Robert Mills, proposing a plan for a railroad and telegraphic communication with the Pacific ocean," 32d Cong., 1st Sess., Senate, No, 344 (August 18, 1852), 1, 9.

means of providing a series of dwellings below, for the operatives and others on the roads, especially in the crossings of ravines and sinkings in the country."[89]

The railroad proposals show he studied maps and surveys of the far west, gathered reports by Army engineers and travelers and ferreted out obscure facts to bolster his ideas. For his other major publication, the thirty-six-page *Water-Works for the Metropolitan City of Washington*, he read widely and compiled a recapitulation of water-works world-wide. Approximately eighty percent of the essay is devoted to the historical review of tanks, pumps, aqueducts, and artesian wells in Asia, Africa, Turkey, Peru, Mexico, Europe, and England, as well as several American cities. He emphasized the need for fire protection for the federal records and reminded readers he had installed the first fire hydrants along Pennsylvania Avenue in 1831. To expand the system for the city as a whole, he recommended reservoirs, settling basins and pumps on Rock Creek which, he said, could provide twenty million gallons every twenty-four hours. This was comparable to Jones Falls, which supplied Baltimore, a city with a population then three times larger than Washington.[90]

The proposal for a municipal water system for the capital first appeared in the *National Intelligencer* in 1849. Montgomery Meigs was directed to develop a plan for a municipal waterworks in 1852—the nadir of Mills' career—and Mills may have republished his earlier essay the following year as a reminder, or evidence, of his own contribution to civic improvements. Mills' essay cites Roman precedents: "two of our Presidents recommended the bringing in of a supply of water to our city from the Great Falls of the Potomac. This would indeed be a work worthy of our Republic, and would place it on a footing with the proudest of the ancient Governments—even Rome herself, that surpassed all other people in the grandeur of her water-works."[91] Meigs thought in those terms too in describing the fourteen-mile aqueduct he designed to bring water from the Great Falls on the Potomac, saying it would be "great in the very contrast between its republican simplicity and its more than imperial beneficence; and great in the name it will bear of Washington, a fitter monument to that name than obelisk or statue."[92]

Most of Mills' writing promoted public works on a grand scale; he would have endorsed Meigs' aspirations for the aqueduct. In 1854, when Meigs compared the aqueduct to an obelisk or statue, Mills would also have agreed that the unfinished obelisk was not a fitting monument, for it stood 153 feet high (approximately half the height its creators intended), and having raised and

89 *Scientific American*, 8, no. 47 (August 6, 1853). *The Charleston Courier* (September 8, 1853) republished a review of Mills' plan which had appeared in the Baltimore American Times: "to us it appears better calculated to amuse the fancy, than for practical use." He also wrote the city council of New York suggesting an elevated monorail for Broadway. See RM to the City Council of New York, 1853; PRM 3024.

90 RM, *Water-Works for the Metropolitan City of Washington* (Washington: Lemuel Towers, 1853), 29–31.

91 RM, *Water-Works*, 31.

92 M. C. Meigs to John W. Maury, June 9, 1854, quoted by Harold Skramstad, "The Engineer as Architect in Washington: The contribution of Montgomery Meigs," *Records of the Columbia Historical Society* 69–70 (1969–1970): 268. For the Cabin John Bridge, Meigs aqueduct, see Myer, 80–81. President Pierce appointed Meigs superintendent of the Capitol extensions and designer and superintendent of the aqueduct on March 29, 1853. Cowdrey, 19.

Elevated Railroad. Robert Mills, 1853.

spent $230,000, the Washington National Monument Society had run out of money and energy. The monument became embroiled in controversy when a stone donated by the Pope was stolen and presumably destroyed by the anti-Catholic Know-Nothing party on March 5, 1854. The Know-Nothings subsequently (February 22, 1855) manipulated an election and took control of the board of the society. For the remainder of Mills' life there was no hope of finishing the obelisk—let alone the Pantheon temple base.[93]

Many of Mills' papers have not survived, but the almost total lack of documents from 1854, when he was seventy-three years old, suggests his energy was ebbing.[94] Recounting his final days, his daughter Sarah Zane Mills Evans recalled he "proposed republishing a new and improved edition" of the *Atlas of South Carolina*, for "he was talking of it but a few weeks before his death."[95] He died at home on March 3, 1855, and was buried in the Congressional Cemetery, site III, range 35.

Two obituaries went beyond a recitation of facts and platitudes:

...nor was it alone as an architect that Mr. Mills was distinguished. As a man of general science he had few superiors; as a civil engineer he planned and executed several important works, and foresaw and foreshadowed many of the greatest and most useful of our public improvements. In advance of the age in which he lived, he was looked upon as an enthusiast and visionary—as one

93 Harvey, 52–61.

94 One of his last ideas appears to have been for a Washington Monument in Charleston, South Carolina. A partial description (without drawings), tentatively dated 1854, indicates he was thinking of a bronze equestrian figure, in "Roman military costume" atop a twenty-two foot high round pedestal which was based on a cube eight feet high. Allegorical figures at the base of the pedestal were to spout water into a basin "circumscribing nearly the whole base." PRM 3077.

95 Sarah Zane Mills Evans to Charles T. Jackson, June 28, 1861; PRM 3121.

Eliza and Robert Mills, circa 1850.

Unfinished Washington National Monument with the Smithsonian Institution in background.
Montgomery Meigs, 1854.

who dreamed and foretold a magnificent net-work of internal communications which startled the slow conceptions and scoffing incredulity of less creative and sanguine minds. And yet, vast as were his predictions, how much has the reality outstripped some of his most prophetic imaginings! With the unerring instincts of true genius, his faith in the truth of his theories and the future glories of his country never wavered for a moment. He surrendered to incredulity no vision of his early manhood; in maturer age his ardor never cooled or faltered; and he lived long enough to see many of his suggestions adopted, acted upon, and fulfilled by those who originally derided and condemned them.

He lived long enough to add one more to the long and melancholy list...who have made others rich and brought no addition but honor to themselves. It is consoling, however, to know that the world will not willingly let die the fame of those who have helped to make it richer, and wiser, and better; of those who lived not for an age, but for all time.... From the window of his chamber, dying, he could look upon the last and greatest monument of his genius, the stupendous pile climbing towards the skies in honor of the Father of his Country.... From the future summit of...the cenotaph the patriot will behold the last resting place of him who conceived and designed it, and of him who, alone of all the world, was worthy of such a memorial.[96]

Or again:

DEATH OF AN ARCHITECT

In the *Washington Union*, of March 4th, we find the following announcement: Died, on Saturday morning, March 3d at 7 1/2

A letter to the *Courier & Enquirer* says of Mr. Mills:

He had superintended the erection of the post office, patent office and other public edifices in this place, and was architect of the national monument. Provision has just been made for completing two of the buildings begun upon his plans. He thought he had been promised the superintendency of them, but learned a few days since that they were to be placed under the supervision of Capt. Bowman and Cat. Meigs, of the engineer corps. The disappointment was too much for him. He became deranged and died.[97]

[96] *National Intelligencer*, March 7, 1855; PRM 3117. See also PRM 3114 and 3115.

[97] An unidentified clipping in the files of the Architect of the Capitol.

Selected Bibliography

Adams, Charles Francis, ed. *Memoirs of John Quincy Adams, Comprising Portions of His Diary From 1795 to 1848*. Philadelphia: J.B. Lippincott, 1875.

Adams, William Howard. *The Eye of Thomas Jefferson*. Washington: National Gallery of Art, 1976.

Alder, Helen Gale. "Robert Mills and United States Marine Hospitals." M.A. thesis, University of Missouri, 1974.

Alexander, Robert L. "Maximilian Godefroy in Virginia." *Virginia Magazine of History and Biography* 18 (1961), 420–431.

Alexander, Robert L. *The Architecture of Maximilian Godefroy*. Baltimore: Johns Hopkins University Press, 1974.

Ambler, Charles H. *A History of Transportation in the Ohio Valley*. Wesport: Greenwood Press, 1970.

Ames, Kenneth. "Robert Mills and the Philadelphia Row House." *Journal of the Society of Architectural Historians* 27 (1968), 140–146.

Bauer, Jack K. *A Maritime History of the United States*. Columbia: University of South Carolina Press, 1988.

Bourne, Edward G. *The History of the Surplus Revenue of 1837*. New York: Burt Franklin, 1885.

Brayley, A.W. *History of the Granite Industry of New England*. Boston: National Association of Granite Industries, 1913.

Brown, Glenn. *History of the United State Capitol*. New York: Da Capo Press, 1970.

Bryan, John M. *An Architectural History of the South Carolina College, 1801–1855*. Columbia: University of South Carolina Press, 1976.

——. *Creating the South Carolina State House*. Columbia: University of South Carolina Press, 1999.

Bryan, John M., ed. *Robert Mills, Architect*. Washington: American Institute of Architects Press, 1989.

Carrott, Richard G. *The Egyptian Revival: Its Sources, Monuments, and Meaning, 1808–1858*. Berkeley: University of California Press, 1978.

Clark, Allen C. "Robert Mills, Architect and Engineer." *Records of the Columbia Historical Society* 40–41 (1940), 1–32.

Clemens, Samuel L. (Mark Twain) *Life on the Mississippi*. London: Chatto & Windus, 1883.

Cohen, Hennig. "The Journal of Robert Mills, 1828–1830." *South Carolina Historical and Genealogical Magazine* 53 (1952), 133–200.

Cohen, Hennig. "An Unpublished Diary by Robert Mills, 1803." *South Carolina Historical and Genealogical Magazine* 51 (1950), 187–194.

Crane, Sylvia E. *White Silence, Greenough, Powers and Crawford, American Sculptors in Nineteenth-Century Italy*. Coral Gables: University of Miami Press, 1972.

Cowdrey, Albert E. *A City for the Nation, The Army Engineers and the Building of Washington, D.C., 1790–1967*. Washington: U.S. Government Printing Office, 1978.

Davies, Jane B. "A.J. Davis' Projects for a Patent Office Building." *Journal of the Society of Architectural Historians* 24 (1965), 229–251.

Davies, Jane B. "Six Letters by William P. Elliot to Alexander J. Davis, 1834–1838." *Journal of the Society of Architectural Historians* 26 (1967), 71–73.

Dewey, Davis Rich. *Financial History of the United States*. New York: Longmans, Green, 1918.

Evans, Richard X. "Daily Journal of Robert Mills, Baltimore, 1816." *Maryland Historical Magazine* 30 (1935), 257–271.

Evans, Richard X. "Letters from Robert Mills." *South Carolina Historical and Genealogical Magazine* 39 (1938), 110–124.

Evelyn, Douglas E. "The National Gallery at the Patent Office." *Magnificent Voyagers: The U.S. Exploring Expedition, 1838–1842*. Herman J. Viola and Carolyn Margolis, eds. Washington: Smithsonian Institution Press, 1985.

Evelyn, Douglas E. "A Public Building For a New Democracy: the Patent Office Building in the Nineteenth Century." George Washington University. PhD. Dissertation, 1997.

Fisher, George D. *History and Reminiscences of the Monumental Church, Richmond, Virginia, from 1814–1878*. Richmond: Whiltet and Shepperson, 1880.

Frary, Ihna T. *They Built the Capitol*. Freeport: Books for Libraries Press, 1969.

Gallagher, H.M. Pierce. *Robert Mills, Architect of the Washington Monument, 1781–1855*. New York: Columbia University Press, 1935.

Gebhard, David and Deborah Nevins. *200 Years of American Architectural Drawing*. New York: Whitney Library of Design, 1977.

Giger, George J. *A Model Jail of the Olden Time: Designs for "a Debtors' Gaol and Workhouse for Felons."* New York: Russell Sage Foundation, 1928.

Gilchrist, Agnes Addison. *William Strickland, Architect and Engineer, 1788–1854*. Philadelphia: University of Pennsylvania Press, 1950.

Goode, George Brown. *The Smithsonian Institution, 1846–1896*. Washington: Government Printing Office, 1897.

Goode, James Moore. "Architecture, Politics and Conflict: Thomas Ustick Walter and the Enlargement of the United States Capitol, 1850–1865." George Washington University. PhD. Dissertation, 1995.

Green, Constance McLaughlin. *Washington, Village and Capital, 1800–1878*. Princeton: Princeton University Press, 1962.

Hafertepe, Kenneth. *America's Castle, The Evolution of the Smithsonian Building and Its Institution, 1840–1878*. Washington: Smithsonian Institution Press, 1984.

Hamlin, Talbot. *Benjamin Henry Latrobe*. New York: Oxford University Press, 1955.

Hamlin, Talbot. *Greek Revival Architecture in America*. New York: Dover Publications, 1944.

Harnsberger, Douglas James. "In Delorme's Manner..." A Study of the Applications of Philibert Delorme's Dome Construction Method in Early 19th Century American Architecture." M.A. thesis, University of Virginia, 1981.

Harris, Neil. *The Artist in American Society*. New York: George Braziller, 1966.

Harvey, Frederick L. *History of the Washington National Monument and of the Washington National Monument Society*. Washington: Norman T. Elliott, 1902.

Havighurst, Walter. *Voices on the River*. New York: MacMillan, 1964.

Hazelton, George C. *The National Capitol, Its Architecture, Art and History*. New York: J.F. Taylor, 1914.

Hoyt, William D. "Robert Mills and the Washington Monument." *Maryland Historical Magazine* 34 (1939), 144–160.

Hunter, Louis C. *Steamboats on the Western Rivers*. New York: Octagon Books, 1969.

John Milner Associates. *Burlington County Courthouse and Burlington County Prison Museum*. Burlington County: Board of Chosen Freeholders, 1978.

Kearny, John Watts. *Sketch of American Finances, 1789–1835*. New York: Greenwood Press, 1968.

Kennon, Donald R., ed. *A Republic for the Ages, The United States Capitol and the Political Culture of the Early Republic*. Charlottesville: University of Virginia Press for the United States Capitol Historical Society, 1999.

Kirker, Harold and James Kirker. *Bulfinch's Boston: 1787–1817*. New York: Oxford University Press, 1964.

Kirker, Harold. *The Architecture of Charles Bulfinch*. Cambridge: Harvard University Press, 1969.

Kohn, David and Bess Glenn, eds. *Internal Improvement in South Carolina, 1817–1828*. Washington: Privately Printed, 1938.

Lane, Mills. *Architecture of the Old South, South Carolina*. Savannah: The Beehive Press, 1984.

Liscombe, Rhodri Windsor. *The Church Architecture of Robert Mills*. Easley: Southern Historical Press, 1985.

Liscombe, Rhodri Windsor. *Altogether American, Robert Mills, Architect and Engineer, 1781–1855*. New York: Oxford University Press, 1994.

Lowry, Bates. *Building a National Image: Architectural Drawings for the American Democracy, 1789–1912*. Washington: National Building Museum, 1985.

MacDonald, William. *The American Nation, vol. 15, Jacksonian Democracy, 1829–1837*. New York: Harper & Brothers, 1906.

Massey, James C. "Robert Mills Documents, 1823: A House for Ainsley Hall in Columbia, S.C." *Journal of the Society of Architectural Historians* 28 (1963), 228–232.

Mickler, Margaret Pearson. "The Monuimental Church." M.A. thesis, University of Virginia, 1980.

Miller, J. Jefferson. "Baltimore's Washington Monument." M.A. thesis, University of Delaware, 1962.

Miller, Lillian, ed. *The Collected Papers of Charles Willson Peale and His Family*. Millwood, N.Y.: Kraus Microfilm, 1980.

Mills, Robert. *Statistics of South Carolina*. Charleston: Hurlbut and Lloyd, 1826.

Mills, Robert. *Mills' Atlas, Atlas of the State of South Carolina, 1825*. Easley: Southern Historical Press, 1980.

Myer, Donald B. *Bridges and the City of Washington*. Washington: U.S. Commission of Fine Arts, 1974; revised edition, 1992.

Myers, Denys Peter. *Historic Report of the General Post Office Building (Now International Trade Commission Building)*. Washington: General Services Administration, 1980.

Nelson, Lee H. "The Colossus of Philadelphia." *Material Culture of the Wooden Age.* Brooke Hindle, ed. Tarrytown: Sleepy Hollow Press, 1981.

O'Gorman, James F., Jeffrey A. Cohen, George E. Thomas, G. Holmes Perkins. *Drawing Toward Building, Philadelphia Architectural Graphics, 1732–1986.* Philadelphia: University of Pennsylvania Press, 1986.

Owen, Robert Dale. *Hints on Public Architecture.* New York: George P. Putnam, 1849.

Pierson, William H., Jr. *American Buildings and Their Architects, The Colonial and Neoclassical Styles.* Garden City: Doubleday, 1970.

Pierson, William H., Jr. *American Buildings and Their Architects: The Colonial and Neo-Classical Styles.* Garden City: Doubleday, 1970.

Poore, Ben. Perley. *Perley's Reminiscences of Sixty Years in the National Metropolis.* Philadelphia: Hubbard Brothers, 1886.

Ravenel, Beatrice St. Julien. *Architects of Charleston.* Charleston: Carolina Art Association, 1945.

Reiff, Daniel. *Washington Architecture, 1791–1861.* Washington: Government Printing Office, 1971.

Reps, John W. *Monumental Washington: The Planning and Development of the Capitol Center.* Princeton: Princeton University Press, 1967.

Ristow, Walter. "Robert Mills' Atlas of South Carolina, 1825: The First American State Atlas." *Quarterly Journal of the Library of Congress* 34 (1977), 52–66.

Scott, Pamela and Antoinette J. Lee. *Buildings of the District of Columbia.* New York: Oxford University Press, 1993.

Scott, Pamela, ed. *Guide and Index to the . . . Microfilm Edition of the Papers of Robert Mills, 1781–1855.* Wilmington, Delaware: Scholarly Resources, 1990.

Scott, Pamela. "Robert Mills's Washington National Monument." M.A. thesis, University of Delaware, 1985.

———. *Temple of Liberty, Building the Capitol for a New Nation.* New York: Oxford University Press, 1995.

Severens, Kenneth. *Charleston, Antebellum Architecture and Civic Destiny.* Knoxville: University of Tennessee Press, 1988.

Smith, Darrell Hevenor. *The Office of the Supervising Architect of the Treasury, Its History, Activities, and Organization.* Baltimore: The Johns Hopkins Press, 1923.

U.S. Treasury Department. *A History of Public Buildings under the Control of the Treasury Department.* Washington: Government Printing Office, 1901.

Viola, Herman J. and Carolyn Margolis, eds. *Magnificent Voyagers, The U.S. Exploring Expedition, 1838–1842.* Washington: Smithsonian Institution Press, 1985.

Waddell, Gene and Rhodri Windsor Liscombe. *Robert Mills's Courthouses & Jails.* Easley: Southern Historical Press, 1981.

Waddell, Gene. "Robert Mills' Fireproof Building." *South Carolina Historical Magazine* 80 (1979), 105–135.

Wallace, David Duncan. *South Carolina, A Short History, 1520–1948.* Columbia: University of South Carolina Press, 1969.

Wheildon, W.W. *Memoir of Solomon Willard.* Boston: Bunker Hill Monument Association, 1865.

Whitehill, Walter Muir. *Boston, A Topographical History.* Cambridge: Harvard University Press, 1968.

Woodman, Betsy H. "A Customhouse for Newburyport (1834–1835) by Architect Robert Mills (1781–1855)." *Essex Institute Historical Collections* (July 1985).

Illustration Credits

Index